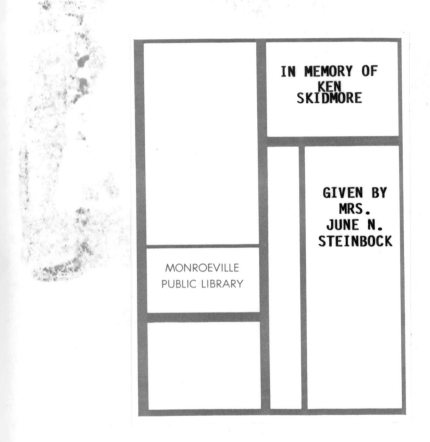

THE LAST MISSION

THE LAST MISSION

THE SECRET STORY OF
WORLD WAR II'S FINAL BATTLE

Jim B. Smith

and

Malcolm McConnell

BROADWAY BOOKS / NEW YORK

PHOTO CREDITS: pp. 1–2 Courtesy of Jim Smith; p. 3 Courtesy of Jim Smith (top), Courtesy U.S. Army (bottom); p. 7 Official U.S. Navy photograph, #80-G-350027 (top), Official U.S. Navy photograph, #80-G-379158 (middle), Official U.S. Navy photograph, #80-G-490487 (bottom); p. 8 Courtesy of U.S. Army Signal Corps, #USA C-2719 (top), Official U.S. Navy photograph, #80-G-332701 (middle), Courtesy The MacArthur Memorial Archives (bottom).

Broadway Books titles may be purchased for business or promotional use or for special sales. For information, please write to: Special Markets Department, Random House, Inc., 280 Park Avenue, New York, NY 10017.

PRINTED IN THE UNITED STATES OF AMERICA

BROADWAY

BROADWAY BOOKS and its logo, a letter B bisected on the diagonal, are trademarks of Broadway Books, a division of Random House, Inc.

Visit our website at www.broadwaybooks.com.

First edition published 2002

Designed by Richard Oriolo
Maps and illustration by Jeff Ward

LIBRARY OF CONGRESS CATALOGING-IN-PUBLICATION DATA

McConnell, Malcolm.
The last mission : the secret story of World War II's final battle /
Jim B. Smith and Malcolm McConnell.—1st ed.
p.   cm.
Expanded and rev. version of Jim B. Smith's 1st person account: The last mission. 1995.
Includes bibliographical references and index.
ISBN 0-7679-0778-7
1. World War, 1939–1945—Aerial operations, American. 2. United States. Army Air Forces. Bombardment Wing (VH), 315th. 3. B-29-bomber. 4. Hiroshima-shi (Japan)—History— Bombardment, 1945. 5. World War—Japan—Armistices. 6. Japan—Politics and government—1926–1945. 7. Nagasaki-shi (Japan)—History—Bombardment, 1945. 8. World War, 1939–1945—Personal narratives, American. 9. World War, 1939–1945— Japan. I. Smith, Jim B. II. Title.

D790 .M29 2002
940.54'4973—dc21
2002022336

10 9 8 7 6 5 4 3 2 1

The story is dedicated first to my dad, who told me years ago that I had a "tiger by the tail" and advised me to never let go. I also want to thank Darin C. Maurer, an airline pilot, who is like my son. He encouraged me in the face of seemingly impossible odds to write the original account of *The Last Mission*. Without his prodding, I'm convinced the story never would have come to light.

This book is dedicated especially to the crew of *The Boomerang*, on which I served. Without the teamwork of Carl Schahrer, Dick Marshall, John Waltershausen, Hank Gorder, Tony Cosola, Rich Ginster, Henry Carlson, Hank Leffler, and Sid Seigel, I wouldn't have been able to relate my story.

I salute my 315th Bomb Wing and every B-29er for giving their best in the face of the enemy. I thank Sally Ann Wagoner and her B-29 Internet group for the collective recall of some details that had faded.

And lastly, this book is in honor of every American, both military and civilian, who delivered a team effort in World War II and preserved the freedom that has given us the greatest country in history.

JIM B. SMITH

I dedicate this book to my brother, Sergeant Bartley F. McConnell, 852nd Bomb Squadron, 8th Air Force, Killed in Action, January 5, 1945.

MALCOLM MCCONNELL

CONTENTS

THE PACIFIC THEATER 1945

SIBERIA

MONGOLIA

SAKHALIN
ISLAND

Vladivostok

HOKKAIDO

Peking

Sea
of Japan

KOREA

JAPAN

HONSHU

Tokyo

Yellow
Sea

CHINA

Nanking

Area of detail

East
China Sea

SHIKOKU
KYUSHU

INDIA

OKINAWA

CHICHI JIMA

Taipei

Ryukyu Islands

IWO JIMA

Bonin Islands

BURMA

Hanoi

Hong Kong

FORMOSA
(TAIWAN)

*Philippine
Sea*

Rangoon

HAINAN
ISLAND

Philippine Islands

LUZON

Mariana Islands

SAIPAN

THAILAND

Manila

TINIAN

FRENCH
INDOCHINA

*South
China Sea*

GUAM

LEYTE

Saigon

MINDANAO

MALAYA

*Celebes
Sea*

Singapore

BORNEO

EQUATOR

Dutch East Indies

SUMATRA

CELEBES

WESTERN
NEW GUINEA

Java Sea

Batavia

JAVA

INDIAN OCEAN

© 2002 Jeffrey L. Ward

AUSTRALIA

95°   100°   105°   110°   115°   120°   125°   130°   135°   140°   145°

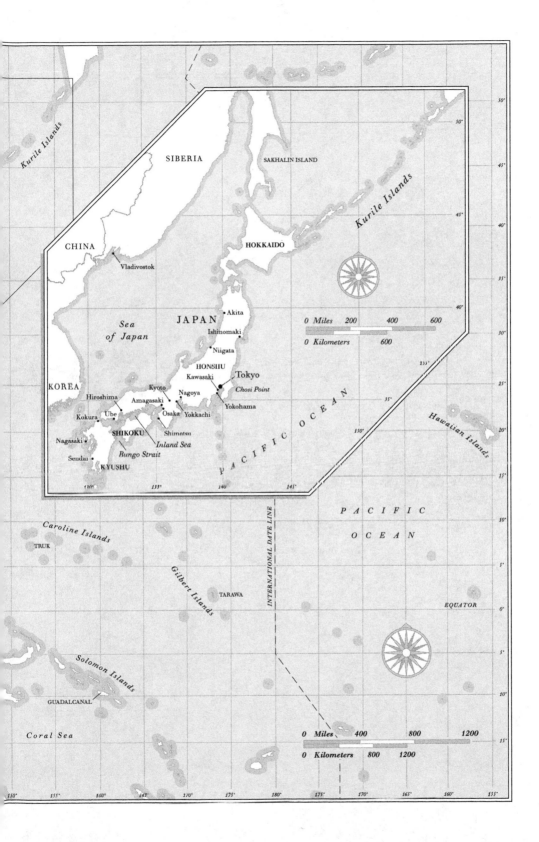

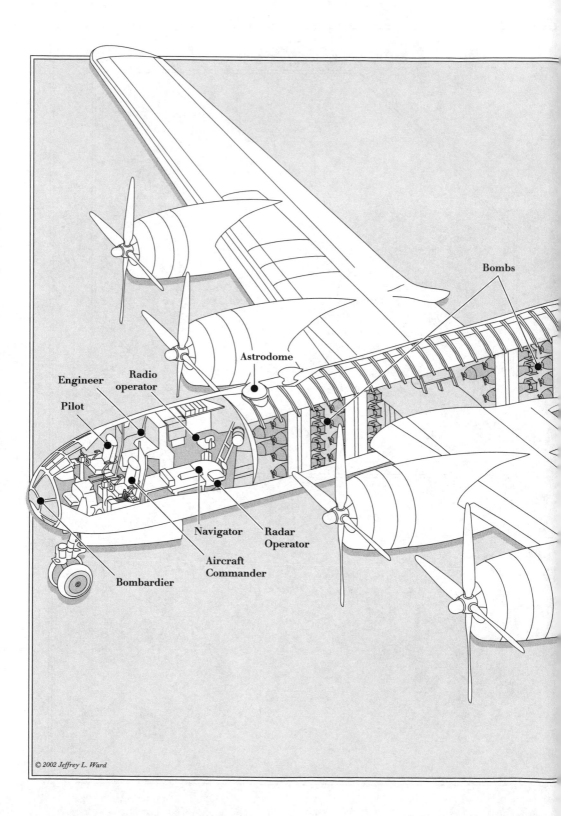

Bombs

Astrodome

Engineer

Radio operator

Pilot

Navigator

Radar Operator

Aircraft Commander

Bombardier

© 2002 Jeffrey L. Ward

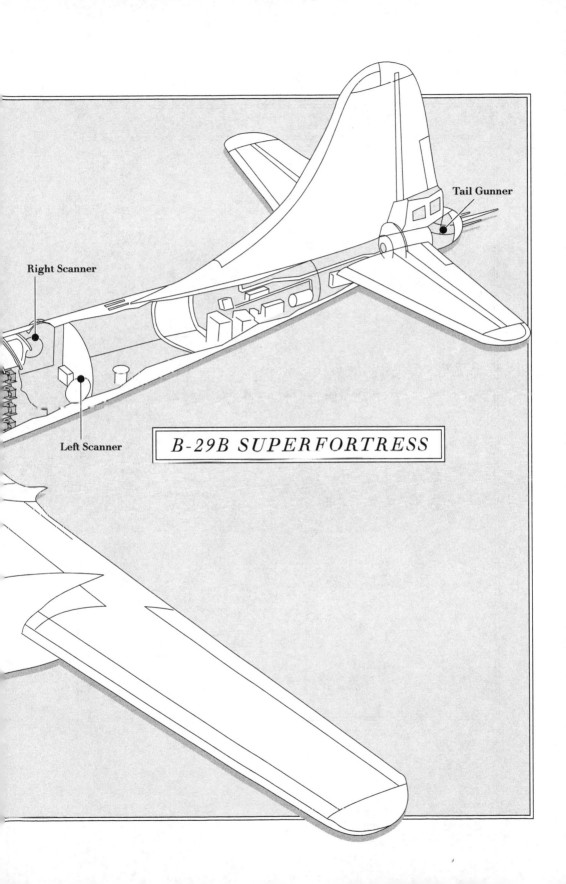

Right Scanner

Tail Gunner

Left Scanner

B-29B SUPERFORTRESS

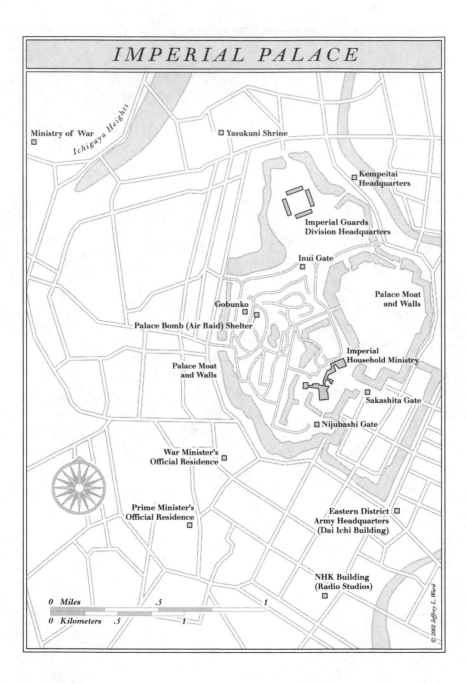

IMPERIAL PALACE

Ministry of War

Ichigaya Heights

Yasukuni Shrine

Kempeitai
Headquarters

Imperial Guards
Division Headquarters

Inui Gate

Palace Moat
and Walls

Gobunko

Palace Bomb (Air Raid) Shelter

Imperial
Household Ministry

Palace Moat
and Walls

Sakashita Gate

Nijubashi Gate

War Minister's
Official Residence

Prime Minister's
Official Residence

Eastern District
Army Headquarters
(Dai Ichi Building)

NHK Building
(Radio Studios)

0 Miles   .5   1

0 Kilometers   .5   1

© 2002 Jeffrey L. Ward

PARTIAL LIST OF INDIVIDUALS
APPEARING IN THE BOOK

I. THE TRUMAN ADMINISTRATION

Harry S. Truman, President

Admiral William D. Leahy, Chief of Staff to the President

Henry L. Stimson, Secretary of War

James F. Byrnes, Secretary of State

James V. Forrestal, Secretary of the Navy

General George C. Marshall, Chief of Staff, U.S. Army

General Douglas MacArthur, Commander, Allied Forces Southwest
Pacific
Later, Supreme Commander, Allied Forces

General Henry H. "Hap" Arnold, Commanding General, U.S. Army
Air Forces

General Carl Spaatz, Commander, U.S. Strategic Air Forces

Major General Curtis E. LeMay, Commander, XXI Bomber Command

Major General Leslie Groves, Commander, Manhattan Project
Dr. J. Robert Oppenheimer, Chief Scientist, Manhattan Project
W. Averell Harriman, U.S. Ambassador to the Soviet Union
General George C. Kenney, Commander, Allied Air Forces
Lt. General Ennis C. Whitehead, Deputy Commander, Allied Air Forces
Admiral Chester W. Nimitz, Commander, U.S. Pacific Fleet

II. THE IMPERIAL PALACE, TOKYO

Hirohito, Emperor of Japan, 124th Descendant of the Imperial Line
General Shigeru Hasunuma, Chief Aide-de-Camp to the Emperor
Kiichiro Hiranuma, President of the Privy Council
Chamberlain Sukemasa Irie
Marquis Koichi Kido, Lord Keeper of the Privy Seal
Sotaro Ishiwatari, Minister of the Imperial Household
Motohiko Kakei, Chief of General Affairs Section, Imperial Household Ministry
Susumu Kato, Director of General Affairs Bureau, Imperial Household Ministry
Prince Fumimaro Konoye, Ex-Premier and Adviser to the Emperor
Imperial Chamberlain Yasuya Mitsui
Chamberlain Yasuhide Toda
Chamberlain Yoshihiro Tokugawa

III. THE SUPREME COUNCIL FOR THE DIRECTION OF THE WAR ("THE BIG SIX")

General Korechika Anami, Minister of War
Baron Admiral Kantaro Suzuki, Prime Minister
Shigenori Togo, Minister of Foreign Affairs
Admiral Soemu Toyoda, Imperial Navy Chief of Staff
General Yoshijiro Umezu, Imperial Army Chief of Staff
Admiral Mitsumasa Yonai, Minister of the Navy

IV. SENIOR JAPANESE GOVERNMENT OFFICIALS

Genki Abe, Home Minister
Naoto Kobiyama, Minister of Transportation
Shunichi Matsumoto, Vice Minister of Foreign Affairs
Hiromasa Matsuzaka, Minister of Justice

Hisatsune Sakomizu, Chief Cabinet Secretary

Hiroshi Shimomura, Director of the Cabinet's Information Bureau

General Hideki Tojo, former Prime Minister

V. IMPERIAL JAPANESE ARMED FORCES OFFICERS

Field Marshal Shunroku Hata, Commander, 2nd General Army

Major Saburo Hayashi, War Minister Anami's Adjutant

Lt. Colonel Michinori Shiraishi, Staff Officer of 2nd General Army

Lt. General Masao Yoshizumi, Director of Military Affairs Bureau, Ministry of War

VI. MINISTRY OF WAR, IMPERIAL GUARDS DIVISION, AND OTHER UNIT OFFICERS INVOLVED IN COUP ATTEMPT

Colonel Okikatsu Arao, Chief of the Military Affairs Section, War Ministry

Major Kenji Hatanaka, Military Affairs Section, War Ministry

Lt. Colonel Masataka Ida, Military Affairs Section, War Ministry

Lt. Colonel Masao Inaba, Military Affairs Section, War Ministry

Major Sadakichi Ishihara, Staff Officer of the Imperial Guards Division

Major Hidemasa Koga, 1st Imperial Guards Division

Captain Yasuna Kozono, Commander, 302nd Air Corps, Imperial Navy

Captain Takeo Sasaki, Commander of the Yokohama Guards

Lt. Colonel Jiro Shiizaki, Military Affairs Section, War Ministry

Lt. Colonel Masahiko Takeshita, Military Affairs Section, War Ministry

Captain Shigetaro Uehara, Imperial Air Academy

VII. 1ST IMPERIAL GUARDS DIVISION

Colonel Toyojiro Haga, Commander, 2nd Regiment, 1st Imperial Guards Division

Colonel Teisaku Minami, Commander, 7th Infantry Regiment, Imperial Guards Division

Colonel Kazuo Mizutani, Chief of Staff, Imperial Guards Division

Lt. General Takeshi Mori, Commander, Commander, 1st Imperial Guards Division

VIII. EASTERN DISTRICT ARMY

Major General Tatsuhiko Takashima, Chief of Staff of the Eastern
District Army

Lt. General Shizuichi Tanaka, Commander, Eastern District Army

IX. JAPAN BROADCASTING CORPORATION (NHK) OFFICIALS

Hachiro Ohashi, Chairman, Japan Broadcasting Corporation (NHK)

Morio Tateno, Japan Broadcasting Corporation Broadcaster

Nobukata Wada, Japan Broadcasting Corporation Announcer

X. OTHER

Professor Kiyoshi Hiraizumi, Tokyo Imperial University

XI. ALLIED OFFICIALS

Joseph Stalin, Secretary General, Soviet Communist Party

Vycheslav Molotov, Soviet Foreign Minister

Chiang Kai-shek, Chinese Nationalist Leader

Winston Churchill, British Conservative Party Prime Minister

Anthony Eden, British Conservative Party Foreign Secretary

Clement Attlee, British Labour Party Prime Minister

Ernest Bevin, British Labour Party Foreign Secretary

XII. CREW OF *THE BOOMERANG*

1st Lieutenant Carl Schahrer, Aircraft Commander

1st Lieutenant John Waltershausen, Pilot

1st Lieutenant Dick Marshall, Bombardier

Technical Sergeant Hank Gorder, Flight Engineer

1st Lieutenant Rich Ginster, Radar Operator

1st Lieutenant Tony Cosola, Navigator

Sergeant Jim Smith, Radio Operator

Sergeant Hank Leffler, Left Scanner

Sergeant Henry Carlson, Right Scanner

Sergeant Sid Siegel, Tail Gunner

MOST WORKS OF HISTORY ARE written either as first-person memoirs or third-person chronicles. The narrative of this book is written in the third person, with the action experienced by the crew of the B-29B Superfortress *The Boomerang* revealed through the perspective of coauthor Sergeant Jim B. Smith, who was then the bomber's radio operator.

The 315th Bomb Wing's B-29Bs were specially modified aircraft, equipped with the APQ-7 Eagle radar, which permitted all-weather precision bombing, and stripped of all defensive armor and gun turrets—except for radar-controlled tail guns. It was the unique, highly sensitive Eagle radar that permitted the Wing to conduct the demanding assignment it received from Major General Curtis LeMay in June 1945: methodically destroy the Empire of Japan's ability to refine oil or produce gasoline and lubricants—especially the aviation gasoline needed for warplanes. The

Wing performed brilliantly, always flying at night from Northwest Field in Guam on exhausting over-water missions to Japan that usually averaged more than 3,000 miles and fifteen hours.

The 315th Bomb Wing began combat operations in June 1945 and flew its last strike—the longest continuous mission of the war—against the Nippon Oil Company refinery near Akita in northern Honshu on the night of August 14–15, 1945.

The nature of these B-29B operations was kept secret from both the enemy and the American public during the war. Following VJ-Day, most in the West came to believe that the Japanese surrender followed almost automatically after atomic bombs struck Hiroshima on August 6 and Nagasaki on August 9, 1945. In fact, there were approximately 1,000 individual B-29 missions (combat sorties) between the bombing at Nagasaki and Japan's final surrender on August 15.

The Boomerang flew on two of these missions, August 9–10 to Amagasaki and August 14–15 to Akita. Although Smith had no way of knowing it at the time, on August 14, the Wing's long bomber stream, passing through the moonless sky near Tokyo, was detected by Japanese radar, triggering a night-long blackout in the capital.

In turn, this blackout disrupted a coup d'état under way at the Imperial Palace. The rebels' original objectives were to prevent the Emperor from recording his Imperial Rescript announcing Japan's surrender, seize the Palace, and hold him incommunicado. The recorded Imperial Rescript was scheduled to be broadcast the next day, August 15, 1945, at noon. But the blackout caused the rebels to fail in their attempt to prevent the recording, so they sought in vain to find and destroy the records. Had the blackout not derailed the rebels' plans, they would have proclaimed a revolt throughout the Imperial armed forces.

But the coup did fail. After the war, both Japanese and Western historians investigated these events with varying degrees of scrutiny. None, however, directly connected the nightlong blackout caused by the northbound and southbound flow of the 315th Bomb Wing with the failure of the attempted coup.

However, in the 1970s Jim Smith began investigating the connection between his Wing's mission and the coup. During the course of decades of research, he discovered startling facts that no historian had previously uncovered. For example, the blackout was effected at 11:05 P.M., exactly as the Emperor was leaving his quarters to drive across the Palace grounds to the Imperial Household Ministry to record his surrender rescript. In the darkness, he was able to slip by the hidden rebel troops, who failed to seize him and prevent him from recording the vital surrender message.

Intrigued by the connection between his last combat mission and the failed coup, Smith continued his research, unearthing declassified military reports in the 1980s that revealed that the decision to bomb Akita on the last, longest mission of the war was at least as much concerned with depriving America's wartime ally the Soviet Union of the refinery and its surrounding oil fields, should the Russians gain a zone of occupation in northern Japan, as it was with strategic considerations of World War II.

Smith assembled all this and much more into a book, *The Last Mission: An Eyewitness Account*, that he self-published in 1995. All who read the book, especially former B-29 aviators, were impressed by his diligent research, insights, and attention to detail.

But Smith wanted to reach the widest audience possible and also to expand the historical perspective of his original story. To do so, he needed to have a widely distributed book. Through the William Morris Agency, he and experienced military historian Malcolm McConnell collaborated on this expanded project.

Given the narrative structure of the work, Jim Smith's first-person eyewitness voice had to be adapted. Thus he became a third-person character in the book of which he is the coauthor.

This perhaps is a unique feature in a military history. But the authors believe their book provides unique insights into major historical events.

TOTAL WAR

Rescript: A written message of the Japanese Emperor carrying both temporal and religious authority and defining the position of the state.

—Webster's Third New International Dictionary

THE SUPERFORTS

1630 HOURS, 5 AUGUST 1945

The long rows of four-engined bombers sat on the asphalt taxi ramps to the two parallel runways at Northwest Field, Guam, shimmering in the tropic afternoon. They were B-29Bs of the 315th Bomb Wing (Very Heavy), U.S. Strategic Air Forces XXI Bomber Command. This base in the Marianas was 1,500 miles south of the "Empire," the name American airmen had given the Japanese Home Islands. Today, loaded with nine tons of 500-pound bombs and almost 6,500 gallons of aviation gasoline, the Superforts were pushing their 140,000-pound maximum takeoff weight. But that was an increasingly normal risk their crews faced at this stage in the air campaign against Japan.

Halfway down the line of Superforts, waiting for the order to start engines, *The Boomerang* sat on its hardstand, the sun glare flooding the multipane Plexiglas greenhouse cockpit. A jeep approached, and a full colonel from headquarters climbed a ladder to the nosewheel hatch.

He would be "observing" tonight's mission, aircraft commander First Lieutenant Carl Schahrer announced to his crew over the intercom. This intrusion could be either an unnecessary occasion for a staff officer to rack up some combat hours or the legitimate desire for an experienced leader to watch one of the Wing's smoothly functioning crews in action. In any event, he didn't feel he had to explain himself. The Colonel sat on the deck beside Schahrer's central control console but did not offer to shake hands with anyone, making it clear that he wasn't interested in friendly relations with the plane's crew of junior officers and NCOs.

Tonight's target was the sprawling Ube Coal Liquefaction Company synthetic oil facility near the extreme southwest tip of Honshu. Round-trip mission time had been briefed for just over fifteen hours, thirty minutes. As always, the Superforts carried a marginal fuel reserve, so that they could accommodate a maximum bomb load for the distance flown and predicted winds aloft. This reserve was certainly not the comfortable safety margin peacetime aviators would have expected or indeed demanded on such a long over-water flight.

This was not peacetime, however. It was the fourth year of relentless war that had begun for America with the Imperial Japanese Navy's bombing of Pearl Harbor. During the forty-four months since Pearl Harbor, sixteen million Americans had put on uniforms and scores of millions more had gone to work in war industries. The three-year campaign against Nazi Germany and its Italian Fascist ally, which had cost America more than 200,000 killed or missing, had finally ended with victory in May 1945.

In the Pacific, the Japanese had been invincible for the first six months of the war, defeating weaker American, British, and Dutch forces in the Philippines, Malaya, Burma, and the Netherlands East Indies—and capturing hundreds of thousands of Allied prisoners as well as seizing a trove of natural resources that Japan desperately needed to maintain its huge fleet and support its armies, which had been engaged in Manchuria and China for years.[1]

The American counteroffensive in the Pacific had gathered momentum slowly because President Franklin D. Roosevelt and British Prime Minister Winston Churchill had agreed on a "Germany first" strategy in which the major Allied effort would be focused on the European Theater of Operations (ETO) until Hitler was defeated; only then would the Allies' full might shift to Japan.[2] The protracted and bloody island-hopping campaign resulting from this policy that began at Guadalcanal in the Solomon

Islands in 1942 had involved savage sea and naval-air battles, costly amphibious assaults, and bypassing strong Japanese garrisons on belea-guered fortresses such as Rabaul and Truk. American strategy had been to drive a line of air bases north from the Solomons across the vast blue void of the Pacific, so that the Japanese Home Islands could be brought within range of the B-29 Superfort as soon as that revolutionary new bomber was available in "sufficient numbers."[3] More than 100,000 Americans had been killed, seriously wounded, or were missing in action in the Pacific up to this point in the war.

But the strategy had eventually proved sound. With the retaking of Guam, a prewar American territory, and the capture of Saipan and Tinian farther north in the Marianas, the United States finally had its B-29 bases. And the airmen aboard *The Boomerang* this stifling afternoon of August 5, 1945, were just one of more than a thousand Superfort crews flying from airfields that had transformed these islands into the world's largest air base.

The Boomerang's ten crewmen greeted the coolly distant Colonel as they accepted so many other minor irritants of life in a combat wing. Schahrer glanced around to verify that, despite the heat, everyone within sight of the Colonel had his parachute harness clipped correctly over his yellow rubber Mae West and nylon mesh survival vest and that the sleeves of his tan nylon summer flying suit were rolled down as regulations required. Carl Schahrer, 26, a short, slight, and soft-spoken aviator devoted to his crew, now ignored the senior officer and worked through the Pre-Start checklist with his flight engineer, Technical Sergeant Hank Gorder, who sat facing aft behind the pilot, First Lieutenant John Waltershausen, seated at the controls on the right of the flight deck.

Gorder, at 28, was the oldest man on the crew. A big, rawboned Nor-wegian from the small town of Grafton, North Dakota, he hunched at his complex panel of multiple instruments, switches, and engine controls. Among many other tasks, Gorder faced the challenge of establishing the optimal "cruise control" that would balance the variables of altitude, air temperatures, winds, and aircraft weight to conserve fuel during the long mission. He also had to continually adjust the cowl flaps to keep the tem-peratures of the four powerful but notoriously trouble-prone Wright-Cyclone R3350 engines within safe limits.

Bombardier First Lieutenant Dick Marshall's "office" was forward of the flight deck, in the exposed Plexiglas nose of *The Boomerang*. He came from a well-off California family with interests in the furniture business. At 27, he was the second-oldest man in the crew, but he seemed even more mature.

An open bulkhead separated the flight deck from the so-called navigator's compartment aft of the pilots. In reality, navigator First Lieutenant Tony Cosola, a handsome, coolly competent Italian-American from San Francisco, shared the compartment with First Lieutenant Rich Ginster, the radar operator, and Sergeant Jim Smith, the radio operator. Ginster, Waltershausen, and Cosola were all just 23, the youngest officers on the crew. Studious and unobtrusive, Ginster did his job with quiet efficiency.

Radio operator Sergeant Jim Smith, who would be 21 in fifteen days, sat on the starboard side of the compartment, his cramped, windowless station jammed with boxy transmitters, receivers, antenna tuners, and his small Morse code transmission key table. Hoping to become a pilot, Smith had enlisted in the Army Air Corps in 1943 after graduating from high school in Des Moines, Iowa. After Basic Training at Sheppard Field, Texas, Smith was sent to the College Training Detachment at Creighton University, Nebraska, for academics and flight instruction. Smith graduated near the top of his class, and it looked as if his dream of becoming a pilot was about to be realized. But when he reached the next base in Santa Ana, California, he learned that further training for potential flying officers had been closed because of an overabundance: Pilots, navigators, and bombardiers from Europe were being transferred to the Pacific Theater.

Qualified men like Smith had two options: radio operator or gunnery. He chose the radio operator's course because he'd learned that the students who graduated in the top 10 percent would be sent to officers' candidate school. But even when Smith made this grade, the regulation was changed again. Now the top radio school graduates were to be rewarded with assignments to B-29s. Because the new Superforts were suffering so many mechanical problems—with related fatal training accidents—Smith and his classmates did not know if this distinction was much of a reward. But the saga he'd undergone since enlisting was typical of countless other patriotic young Americans caught up in the faceless machinery of the war.

Finally, after training for several months with one B-29B crew, Smith was sent to join *The Boomerang*'s as a last-minute replacement in May 1945, just before the bomber departed for the Pacific.

Behind this compartment, a narrow twenty-six-foot cylindrical tunnel ran above the twin bomb bays, connecting the forward and aft pressurized sections. In the compartment aft of the wings, Sergeants Henry Carlson and Hank Leffler, the right and left scanners, both 21, knelt at their flat circular view ports on either side of the fuselage, prepared to observe the dangerous ritual of engine start, during which volatile high-octane aviation gasoline surged through the fuel systems into the double rings of cylinders, driven by whining turbochargers.

Henry Carlson came close to matching the image of the All-American Boy. Open-faced and good-looking, Carlson always seemed serene and impressed his fellow crew members as a guy who sincerely cared for their welfare. Leffler was tough and stocky, an outdoorsman from Colorado with a ready smile, who usually responded an upbeat "You bet" to questions. The tail gunner, Sergeant Sid Siegel, also 21, came from Connecticut and delivered his stream of good-natured wisecracks with an eastern accent. His combat position was another thirty feet aft of the scanners, in a small, separate pressurized compartment beneath the bomber's towering vertical stabilizer. Sid provided *The Boomerang*'s sole defensive firepower, and the crew knew they could trust him.

Now the afternoon sun beat down on the bomber's aluminum fuselage and the crews' flying suits became sodden with sweat. This was their eighth mission over the Empire, and, as they waited for engine start, each young man had time to quietly reflect on the nature of the war they were fighting.

The Boeing B-29 was a quantum step beyond the B-17 Flying Fortress and B-24 Liberator, America's premier heavy bombers at the start of World War II. The standard Superfort was twice as heavy and had a fuselage almost a third longer than the 'Fort and the Liberator and could carry a heavier bomb load twice as far.

And the modified B-29Bs of the 315th at Northwest Field had also been assigned a special mission to match the aircraft's unique characteristics. The Wing was the most specialized unit in the Army Air Forces (AAF) and flew Superforts equipped with the APQ-7 Eagle radar and stripped of all defensive armor and gun turrets—except for three radar-controlled tail guns (twin .50-caliber machine guns and a slow-firing, ineffective 20mm cannon)—which reduced drag and eliminated 7,500 pounds. This modification allowed the 315th's Superforts to carry a bomb of over ten tons to more distant targets than could the other B-29s in the Marianas. Without the turrets, the B-29B did retain two scanners in the waist compartment who spotted fighters for the tail gunner and visually monitored the sensitive engines, watching for oil leaks, smoke, or flames.

But the precision radar bombing system was the plane's most distinguishing feature. The Eagle radar had been designed by legendary Massachusetts Institute of Technology professor Luis W. Alvarez and Bell Telephone Laboratories. It operated at a much higher frequency than did earlier radars. Originally developed under a Top Secret project code-named EHIB ("Every House In Berlin"), the Eagle almost lived up to its promise of precision. Although it never saw full combat deployment in the European Theater of Operations, the new radar was perfectly suited for the big B-29Bs flying from the Marianas. The radar employed electronic scanning from an eighteen-foot-long, forty-inch-wide vane fixed parallel to the wings between the Superfort's twin bomb bays. This gave the Eagle-equipped bombers a bizarre appearance, as if engineers had somehow grafted a smaller aircraft to the Superforts' bellies. But the awkward-looking Eagle antenna produced a ground image of unprecedented sharpness, allowing crisp resolution of structures as small as 1,500 feet from high altitude in total darkness or overcast.[4]

In training, the 315th's crews had to perfect the demanding technique of "synchronous radar bombing." The radar operator identified the target in the Eagle's radar beam, which swept a pie-shaped, sixty-degree wedge ahead of the aircraft. Once the distinctive shape of a particular target had been verified, the radar operator tracked it using a reticle on his scope, the Eagle automatically feeding this information to the Norden bombsight in the nose compartment. Meanwhile, if cloud cover permitted, the bombardier was checking his optical sightings against the radar data. A simplified version of this tracking appeared on an indicator in the cockpit, which allowed the aircraft commander and pilot to stabilize the bomber's speed and altitude, working with both the radar operator and the bombardier. When the precise radar data matched the briefed target aiming point, bombsight indices converged, a red light flashed, and the huge load of bombs was released through the open double bomb bays in a preset "shotgun" pattern, which an electromechanical intervalometer automatically controlled to maintain the aircraft's center of gravity while sequencing the bombs to inflict maximum damage.[5]

Over western test ranges in the United States, this technique had worked well, even though the aircrews averaged only 125 flying hours in

B-29s, which, by ordinary standards, would have made them grossly unprepared for this sophisticated aircraft. But this was a vastly complex war far too enormous for the airmen to grasp. Nobody—even most of their senior officers, they correctly surmised—understood "the big picture." The demands of that war forced the young men who flew the B-29Bs from Guam—and some were indeed very young—to be ingenious and adaptive. They were eager and proud to be flying the Superforts, wanted to be courageous, and were determined not to fail. In night combat missions over the Japanese Empire, synchronous radar bombing was to prove just as effective as it had on bombing ranges in America.

The order came to start engines. When the four big Wright-Cyclones were throbbing loudly and flight engineer Hank Gorder announced his instruments looked good, Schahrer waited for the ground crew below to wave him forward and *The Boomerang* taxied ahead with the other bombers toward Northwest Field's thinly asphalted crushed-coral runways. Planes were alternating takeoffs every thirty seconds, first one runway, then the other.

The Boomerang rolled to position, and Dick Waltershausen set the brakes while Carl Schahrer ran up the engines to check RPM, magnetos, and manifold pressure. Bombardier Dick Marshall sat in the nose watching the plane ahead of them gather speed on its takeoff run. The heavily laden Superfort passed the concave dip in the asphalt at the midpoint on the 8,500-foot runway but did not seem to be gathering sufficient speed.

"He's not going to make it," Marshall grimly said over the intercom.

In the distance, the tail and fuselage of the bomber disappeared in the rippling heat mirage. The aircraft seemed to have run out of paved runway, crossed the coral overrun, and disappeared down the sheer 500-foot limestone cliff at the far end. *The Boomerang*'s crew realized that ten men had just been killed. And now they were about to attempt taking off in a similarly laden bomber in this hot afternoon air. They all hated the war that forced them to do this. But no one spoke.

In reality, that Superfort's aircraft commander, Captain Horatio W. Turner, III, and his pilot, Second Lieutenant John T. Newburg, had managed to brake the bomber just before reaching the cliff. Turner groundlooped around on the coral overrun with the plane's brakes on fire. Emergency crews extinguished the fires; maintenance men cooled and checked the brakes, pronounced the plane fit for combat, and topped off the fuel load. Turner's aircraft was the last of the 315th's Superforts to take off that afternoon.[6]

A flare arced up from the wooden-stilt control tower. Carl Schahrer advanced the throttles slightly and turned onto the runway.

"Everything in the green," flight engineer Hank Gorder reported after anxiously scanning his banks of engine dials.

Schahrer clamped his left hand on the four throttle knobs and steadily advanced them full forward. The engines rose to a rumbling howl and the four RPM needles swung to maximum. He released the brakes, and the bomber surged ahead. As the plane gathered speed, Schahrer felt the rudder pedals come alive beneath his boots as the tall control surface in the tail bit the slipstream.

"Forty . . . sixty . . ." John Waltershausen was calling out the airspeed. ". . . eighty . . ." With this nine-ton load of bombs and 6,480 gallons of fuel, *The Boomerang* would need an airspeed of at least 135 miles per hour for takeoff.

The control tower flashed by, halfway down the runway.

"One ten . . . one twenty . . ."

Ahead, the darker end of the runway stood out clearly against the dirty beige of the coral overrun. If Schahrer did not lift off soon, *The Boomerang* would suffer the same fate as the bomber that had preceded them.

"One thirty-five . . ."

Schahrer pulled back on his control yoke, and the bomber's nose lifted ponderously over the crushed coral.

"Gear up," Schahrer called. Waltershausen was already reaching for the lever.

The big landing gear came grinding up and seated with a comforting thump.

The Boomerang flashed past the edge of the sheer cliff, and Schahrer eased the yoke gently forward so that the bomber descended to just above the soft blue waves. They were past the cliff; no one saw smoke or wreckage below. That Superfort had probably just plowed beneath the surface, engines still screaming. No one spoke of the incident.

Schahrer slid the throttles back from their maximum power settings as Hank Gorder opened the cowl flaps. They would fly at this altitude for fifteen minutes to cool the engines sufficiently before the slow climb to the cn-route altitude of 8,000 feet. Once near the Home Islands, with the plane's fuel load several tons lighter, they would climb again to their bombing altitude of 10,600 feet.

Seated beside Carl Schahrer, the headquarters colonel stared straight ahead, betraying no emotion, making no comment. After a while, he leaned back against the bulkhead, adjusted his parachute for a pillow, and fell asleep.

When *The Boomerang* had reached cruising altitude and Hank Gorder had synchronized the engines for the best cruise control to optimize fuel consumption, Schahrer and Waltershausen set "George," the Honeywell autopilot. Now most of the crew could relax, saving their energy for the long night and morning ahead. But navigator Tony Cosola still took regular sextant sights on the low afternoon sun from the Plexiglas astrodome protruding above the pressurized tunnel leading to the aft compartment in order to update his dead reckoning before darkness swallowed the plane.

And Sergeant Jim Smith had to stay at his station, monitoring the base and distress frequencies for calls of any American bomber in trouble. Only in an emergency would he be allowed to break radio silence, because there was mounting evidence that the Japanese were intercepting American radio traffic to plot B-29 flights en route north from the Marianas. As professor Ronald H. Spector has noted, the confirmation of this Japanese capability was itself derived from the Pentagon's Top Secret "Ultra" program in which the Americans intercepted and decoded Japanese Imperial Army and Navy messages.[7]

Like other crew members, Smith sat on his one-man dinghy pack and his chair had an adjustable backrest, but nothing could ease the sheer pain of hunching at his station for long hours. Further, the radio operator's distress was intensified by having to listen to the Japanese jamming signal, an incessant *dah dit dah dit, dah dit dit dit* that rose and fell, growing steadily louder, hour by hour, as the bombers droned north. Although this signal could be interpreted either as an endless "BC," or a "CB" in international code, in fact it was a mechanically generated nonsense message meant to disrupt American communications and break the concentration of B-29 radio operators. But it was more a nuisance than a tactical success.

During these endless hours of tense monotony, Smith mentally rehearsed survival procedures to be used if the crew had to bail out over enemy territory or *The Boomerang* was forced to ditch at sea. But the uneven record for rescuing the crews of ditched B-29s in the yawning emptiness of the Pacific—especially in bad weather—did not inspire confidence. And the prospect of bailing out over the Empire was not pleasant. He knew mistreatment, probably severe torture, and possibly execution faced him if he was captured. He also wondered when the Japanese would discover the secret that the 315th Wing's Superforts had been stripped of most guns and had practically no defenses against fighters.

So Smith tried to divert himself by thinking about what the cooks had prepared for the crews' meals on the mission. The advance elements of the 315th Bomb Wing had arrived on Guam in mid-April 1945 to find very primitive conditions. The last of the big air bases constructed on the Marianas, Northwest Field had been literally bulldozed from the surrounding jungle. At first, both ground personnel and aircrew lived in tents that flooded in the tropical downpours. They ate C rations until the mess halls were constructed. But the "fresh" food now provided was a dubious exchange for Spam or canned beans. The Merchant Marine transported the 315th's provisions all the way from Australia by slow refrigerator ship, and the food included goat, mutton, butter, and cheese so moldy that a rotten essence permeated everything the mess halls served. At least the aircrew was given more appetizing food in their flight rations, hot meals stowed in insulated containers that often included ham, roast beef, or chicken. But when they returned to Guam, they ate in the same mess halls as everyone else.

The worst aspect of chow hall food was that the water barrels outside the doors meant to sterilize mess kits were never kept at a boil, so most men developed chronic diarrhea. This was an annoyance on the ground. But on long missions, the problem became acute. There was a portable commode in the scanner's compartment, but getting to it meant crawling through the narrow tunnel, something no one with a cramping case of the "G.I.s" wanted to do. So most of the airmen were obliged to keep cardboard boxes at their stations in the Superforts. After use, they dumped the leaky portable box toilets into the bomb bays to be dropped over the target. This was like adding an insulting dash of salt to the wounds of the hated enemy.

Earlier in 1945, as the Engineer Aviation Battalions—assisted by Wing ground crew and airmen tired of sleeping in leaky tents—had slapped together squadron headquarters, operations rooms, and plywood barracks huts at Northwest Field, Major General Curtis E. LeMay, commander of the XXI Bomber Command, was formulating an important specialized mission for the 315th Bomb Wing. The unit would be his principal weapon against the Japanese oil industry, which as yet had been spared because it had not been "specified as a top priority objective."[8] But the oil industry, particularly refineries, had been an important target in the ETO, and intelligence indicated that its destruction had caused critical damage to the German war effort. There was another reason for assigning the 315th oil targets. Every important refinery was located on a coast for off-loading crude oil or delivering finished product to tankers, a geographic pattern that would provide the best possible land–water radar contrast for the Eagle synchronous bombing system.

But the most important factor was that Japan was critically short of oil. Small deposits in the Home Islands had produced fewer than two million barrels a year at the beginning of World War II. To compensate, Japan's militarist government in the 1930s had built up a strategic reserve of fifty-five million barrels. Naval expansion, the long war in China, and the U.S. embargo had reduced this reserve by the time of the Pearl Harbor attack in 1941. It was hunger for oil that had driven the Japanese far south into the Pacific to capture the Netherlands East Indies, which provided their wartime oil requirements until the increasingly effective U.S. submarine and air offensive virtually strangled the Home Islands of imported crude oil by April 1945.

When the 315th Bomb Wing began combat operations against the Japanese oil industry in June, the enemy was reduced to refining its last strategic reserves, speeding up synthetic oil production from coal, refining an improvised low-grade oil from pine roots (which destroyed aircraft engines after a few hours' use), and exploiting its sole native oil field near Akita in northern Honshu. But the Japanese were still short of the monthly production of 30,000 tons of aviation gasoline they needed to defend the Home Islands against the steadily expanding American air campaign and the Allied invasion of Kyushu that the Japanese military intelligence anticipated would begin that autumn.[9]

The Japanese had valid reason for deep concern. Their homeland had tasted the unrestrained wrath of American airpower for almost nine months. It was an air campaign unlike any that had come before.

Decades after World War II, most people have retained a conception of heavy bomber raids based on the daylight missions B-17 Flying Fortresses and B-24 Liberators flew in the European Theater of Operations.

By the later years of the war in Europe, most of these missions entailed dense formations of several hundred bombers, with lead navigators and bombardiers guiding entire groups. Once the lead navigator had taken the formation to the target, the lead bombardier would drop his plane's load, signaling the following aircraft in the formation to "toggle" their bombs (for the act of flipping, or toggling, a switch on the Norden bombsight). The other crucial role of the formations, of course, was defense, with each plane's .50-caliber heavy machine guns providing overlapping protection against German fighters.

And the bomber crews fighting above Europe usually encountered savage enemy resistance, in the form of both vicious fighter attack and radar-directed flak. If there was any compensation to combat flying in that theater, it was that the aircraft and their engines were incredibly robust. The round-trip distances to most targets in Germany averaged about 1,500 miles. Navigation over Europe during clear daylight weather also did not present a major obstacle, because there were enough distinctive landmarks on the terrain below.

But the situation was almost exactly reversed for B-29 crews flying against the Japanese Empire from bases in the Marianas. Although these Superforts never encountered the extreme heavy flak concentrations or enemy fighter resistance that bomber crews in Europe faced, American airmen bombing the Empire were confronted with other challenges. The trip to and from their targets was usually at least 3,000 miles flown over fourteen to fifteen hours, almost all of it above the featureless Pacific. Sheer fatigue became a major factor for the Superfort aircrews, especially those flying the B-29Bs of the 315th Bomb Wing that always bombed at night.

After leaving home base, these Superforts flew in an extended stream. The individual planes usually disappeared into darkness about two hours after takeoff. The bombers showed no navigation lights and observed strict radio silence except for Mayday emergency calls and the brief poststrike report. To preserve night vision, the crews kept their instrument lights dimmed. The navigator used a shielded lamp to work at his small chart table. From the perspective of the crews, for the next seven or more hours en route to the Empire, each bomber might as well have been the sole airplane on the planet.

Although the airmen felt isolated, the seemingly fluid hundred-mile train of aircraft actually contained a flexible structure. The 315th Wing's lead navigator, Captain William C. Leasure, had devised the demanding "compression" technique by which the bombers were stacked in precise altitude steps, their horizontal separation already assured by the thirty-second takeoff sequence. Under this procedure, the bombers could fly safely through the often-stormy darkness toward Japan in a loose trail formation. Once near the Empire, the pilots had to carefully control their altitude and airspeed, so that the long column of bombers that had left Guam would squeeze into a tight vertical line and horizontal stack to minimize exposure to flak and fighters over the target.

All but a few minutes of most missions was over water, with only a few short-range VHF radio beacon navigational aids. The long-distance LORAN introduced to the northern Pacific in 1945 was often of questionable reliability, because there were no land receiving stations in American hands to aid in calibrating the signals.

During training, the B-29B crews had flown practice missions from Borinquen Field, Puerto Rico, to Venezuela meant to simulate the 3,000-mile round trip from the Marianas to Japan. No one complained about this training, which took the crews away from the frigid conditions in Fairmont, Nebraska.

But Superforts from other wings returning from similar training missions got lost in storms over the Caribbean, ran short of fuel, and were forced to land at bases spread across the U.S. Gulf states.[10]

This was a taste of what lay ahead in the Pacific between the Marianas and Japan, an area that was tormented by typhoons and other violent storm fronts during much of the year. Weather during combat missions was a continual problem, accounting for a large number of losses. And when Superforts went down at sea during this savage weather, there were rarely survivors.

Conventionally equipped Superforts had begun the Very Heavy bomber campaign against Japan in June 1944, flying sporadic and ineffective raids on southern Honshu from advanced bases in China. Five months later, in November 1944, larger numbers of B-29s were operating out of the Marianas, flying high-altitude daylight precision missions that depended on optical sighting with the Norden bombsight. But, in spite of the new bomber's immense potential, the results of those early missions had been disappointing. Weather over the Empire frequently disrupted accurate bombing of industrial targets—mainly aircraft factories—selected for their strategic value. Bombing at altitudes from 27,000 to 33,000 feet, the pressurized B-29s encountered jet-stream winds of more than 150 knots, an unexpected phenomenon. These high-altitude winds often gave the already fast bombers ground speeds above 440 miles per hour, rendering the bombardier's task of placing an individual plane's load of 500-pound bombs within the confines of a single factory complex virtually impossible.

The B-29s on these early daylight raids also usually encountered enemy fighters. Even though the Superfort with its turbocharged R3350 engines could outperform most Japanese (and many American) fighters at high altitude, the Japanese pilots dogged the American bomber formations. But, defensively, the B-29 was indeed a *super* fortress, much more effectively armed than the B-17. The standard B-29 Superfort bristled with turret-mounted .50-caliber machine guns, which three gunners in the separate pressurized compartment aft of the wing operated by remote control, manning electro-optical central fire-control sights that permitted the two upper and two lower turrets to track and fire on enemy fighters with amazing speed and accuracy. After Japanese fighter resistance to the Superforts increased, the forward top turrets were modified to carry four machine guns. The tail gunner in his own pressurized compartment manually fired two .50-caliber machine guns sighting visually. (On the B-29B, which always bombed in darkness, the tail gunner used the AN/APQ-15 fire-control radar.) Thanks to the Superfort's tremendous lift capability, the bomber could carry 8,000 to 12,000 rounds of ammunition, which allowed gunners to fire almost nonstop on attacking enemy fighters reckless enough to venture into range.

But, undeterred, Japanese fighter pilots continued to defend their homeland with brave determination, increasingly resorting to the ruthless expedient of ramming the B-29s. Cumulative B-29 aircrew losses by August 1945 were nowhere near as costly as the appalling carnage of the ETO, where almost 20,000 British and American bombers had been shot down and 80,000 aircrew killed. But there were far fewer Superforts available in the Pacific Theater. This meant that B-29 crews' casualty rates due to enemy action and "operational" emergencies such as engine failure and navigational error inherent in such long over-water missions—casualties that reached as high as 34 percent in the early strategic bombing campaign—wore on the morale of the American airmen.

When Major General Curtis LeMay took over the XXI Bomber Command on January 20, 1945, he found himself under intense pressure from

General Henry H. "Hap" Arnold, Chief of Staff of the AAF, and from the Joint Chiefs of Staff to increase the effectiveness of B-29 operations. Historians of the American air war in the Pacific Wesley F. Craven and James Lea Cate have documented that high-altitude precision bombing of Japanese industries was not accomplishing the results envisioned by the overall strategic timetable for the defeat of the enemy in the Pacific. Beyond the problems of weather and the extreme distances involved in these missions was the factor that much of Japanese industry was widely dispersed in home workshops and tiny "shadow factories" that assembled the products of these workshops. So huge, densely populated residential areas of cities such as Tokyo, Kobe, Kawasaki, and Nagoya were in effect honeycombed with small-scale but highly productive armament and aircraft plants.[11] And there was no way B-29s could bomb these targets using traditional precision techniques. Even before LeMay took charge, American tactical planners had considered switching to lower-altitude night incendiary attacks on Japanese cities.

Now, with LeMay, a relentless, combat-tested leader, in command of the B-29s in the Marianas, the stage was set for decisive action. He was one of the most experienced American bomber tacticians, having led the first group of 8th Air Force B-17 Flying Fortresses bombing Europe from bases in England between 1942 and 1944. On August 17, 1943, he flew the lead B-17 of 146 bombers on a mission against the ball-bearing plant at Regensburg, deep inside Germany, a raid that lost twenty-four aircraft and 240 airmen to flak and fighters. The cigar chomping LeMay acquired the moniker "Iron Pants" in the patriotic wartime press, but he was known as "Iron Ass" to many of the aircrews who had to follow him into combat. After leading the isolated XX Bomber Command flying out of bases in China, LeMay was ordered by General Arnold to relieve Major General Haywood S. Hansell, Jr., who had organized the XXI Bomber Command in the Marianas.

The Joint Chiefs of Staff wanted Japan's war industry—particularly aircraft construction—destroyed before making the hard final decisions on when or whether to proceed with an invasion of the Home Islands. Japanese garrisons on islands like Tarawa and Palau in the south and central Pacific had either been captured in hard-fought battles or been bypassed. General Douglas MacArthur's huge combined land and air command was engaged in protracted combat to retake the sprawling Philippine archipelago in the face of stubborn and well-commanded Japanese resistance. But entire enemy divisions and corps had been left intact in the Netherlands East Indies, Malaya, French Indochina, and on Formosa and the vast Chinese mainland.

As LeMay took command, the main American strategic thrust was still almost due north through the Pacific, with the small volcanic island of Iwo Jima invaded on February 19, 1945, and the much larger Ryukyu island of Okinawa due for invasion in April. Iwo Jima, midway between the Marianas and the Japanese Home Islands, would be an emergency base for B-29s in distress and also provide airstrips for long-range American P-51 Mustang fighters to escort Superforts over Japan. Once captured, Okinawa was meant to make available multiple air bases for B-24s and shorter-range American bombers of the Far Eastern Air Forces (later to be supplemented by B-29s and the new B-32). These would join with carrier planes to continue softening up the Home Island of Kyushu for the Allied invasion, which was tentatively scheduled for November 1, 1945, under the code name Operation Olympic, part of the larger Downfall plan that included the Operation Coronet invasion of the Kanto Plain near Tokyo in March 1946.[12]

But the leadership of the AAF had strongly advocated reducing Japan through airpower alone. When daylight precision attacks failed to produce desired results, however, the chain of command leaned heavily on LeMay to find a solution. He revived earlier plans to use the B-29 on night incendiary missions, meant to exploit the fact that structures in most Japanese cities were built of highly flammable wood or bamboo, but he added risky refinements to these plans. If the bombers flew at dangerously low altitudes—well below 10,000 feet—their fuel loads could be reduced by the several tons of gasoline needed to climb to a high-altitude bomb run. Further, LeMay decided to remove three of the gunners and most of the 8,000 rounds of machine-gun ammunition the Superforts normally carried on daylight raids, leaving only the tail guns armed.[13] These steps would allow the B-29s to carry much heavier loads of M69 500-pound incendiary cluster bombs. But deprived of their defenses and flying well within the range of even light-caliber Japanese antiaircraft guns, the B-29 losses might be prohibitive. Indeed, the flak experts on LeMay's intelligence staff advised him that it would be "suicidal" to send B-29s over Tokyo or Osaka as low as 5,000 feet. But LeMay gambled his career—and the lives of hundreds of American airmen—that these experts were wrong.[14]

LeMay's theory was tested on the night of March 9–10, 1945. He ordered three wings of B-29s, totaling 334 bombers, to attack the Japanese capital, Tokyo, concentrating on the city's most densely populated districts bordering important industrial targets. The mission was led by a squadron of Superfort pathfinders, each plane carrying 180 70-pound M47 napalm bombs meant to start highly visible fires to mark aiming points. The bombers following in a long stream behind them each carried six-ton loads of M69 incendiary clusters, small firebombs dropped in patterns to saturate more than "8,000 separate munitions per square mile."[15]

Flying between 4,900 and 9,200 feet, the B-29s began dumping their incendiaries soon after midnight. The initial Japanese resistance, mainly from light-caliber flak, was eventually dampened as the stiff wind blew the fires into a raging conflagration, but not before the guns shot down or severely damaged fourteen Superforts (four of which were able to ditch at sea). Fighters were less effective. Forty attacked the bomber force and scored hits when B-29s were caught in searchlights. But none of the bombers were lost to fighters, probably because the Japanese pilots prudently avoided pressing home their attacks in view of the proven defensive firepower of the *Bi-ni-ju-ku,* or *bikko,* as they called the B-29s.[16] The Japanese airmen, of course, had no way of knowing that only the tail guns of the B-29s were armed.

Kenneth P. Werrell has graphically described the Tokyo fire-bombing in *Blankets of Fire:* In city wards such as Asakusa, with a population density of 135,000 per square mile, the overlapping wooden structures were quickly consumed in an uncontrollable firestorm. The American planes dropped a total of 1,665 tons of incendiary bombs over three hours. Tokyo civil defense and fire-fighting teams were powerless to contain the flames, which leapt over the firebreaks that the hundreds of *tonarigumi* neighborhood fire associations had prepared in anticipation of air raids. Seen from the bombers, central Tokyo was a roiling sea of fire. The thermals created by the firestorm grew so intense that several of the lowest-flying B-29s were inverted by these fierce updrafts and crashed into the flaming city below. The bomber crews attacking when the fires were well developed flew blindly through clouds of acrid smoke, and the stench of burning bodies permeated many of the planes.

Almost half of the city's fire and emergency medical stations were destroyed. Hundreds of firefighters and civil-defense workers died as more than fifteen square miles of Tokyo containing almost 270,000 individual buildings was burnt to the ground. Approximately a million people were made homeless. The civilian casualty toll was unprecedented in the history of warfare: 83,793 dead and 40,918 wounded, many with terrible burns. In the spreading panic caused by the firestorm, some people had found refuge in sewers and canals, but the heat was so intense that the water in shallower canals boiled, killing those who had fled there.[17]

This was total war at its most brutal. But LeMay (and the American military leadership to which he reported) viewed the attack as highly successful. Not only had the losses among the attack force been within acceptable levels, the degree of destruction had surpassed expectations. With the Joint Chiefs of Staff's approval, LeMay ordered the XXI Bomber Command to step up low-altitude night incendiary raids on Japanese urban centers. The B-29s struck Nagoya, the third-largest Japanese city and the center of aircraft production, after midnight on March 12. In the coming weeks, forces averaging more than 300 Superforts repeatedly attacked Japan's largest cities. The industrial and residential centers of Osaka, Kobe, and Kawasaki were hit hard. When rain or calm winds dampened the desired firestorm effect, some cities were struck again. LeMay kept the Japanese air defenses guessing about the B-29s' armaments by issuing the low wing on some missions ammunition for their turret guns, which the crews used to knock out searchlights. The streams of .50-caliber tracers looping down from the bombers seemed to confirm that the Superforts remained invincibly well defended.

LeMay received a free hand to intensify the relentless firebombing blitz. By now his forces had burned out the hearts of the largest urban areas, so he turned the XXI Bomber Command on secondary cities. But LeMay also mixed daylight formation missions into his tactics to make certain the large surviving aircraft factories were destroyed or disabled. These raids were costly, however: A May 14 mission against the Mitsubishi bearing plant in Nagoya cost the Americans ten B-29s, with sixty-four damaged when swarms of Japanese fighters and intense flak greeted the attacking force.

Despite the intense American bombing campaign, the Japanese *zaibatsu* corporate cartels such as Mitsubishi, Kawasaki, and Nakajima somehow managed to produce more than 11,000 military airplanes—including almost 5,500 fighters—in the first seven months of 1945.[18] Regardless of the American air strategists' plans, the Japanese were clearly not being bombed into defenseless submission by the night incendiary raids.

Daylight attacks such as the May 14 mission, however, with fully gunned B-29s fiercely defending their formations—American crews claimed eighteen Japanese fighters destroyed—served to remind the enemy that the Superfort was a formidable opponent.

But the B-29s on night incendiary missions mostly flew without their central fire-control gunners and only 200 rounds for their tail guns. Should the Japanese ever learn this secret, fighter attacks against low-flying B-29s would become much more vigorous. And maintaining this secret was critical to the survival of the 315th Wing's virtually unarmed B-29Bs. To do so, the Wing's planes never approached Japan in daylight, and Northwest Field was isolated from scattered enemy holdout troops who might radio the secret to Imperial forces.

Through May and into June, LeMay's bombers attacked the Home Islands almost nightly. Smaller groups of specially equipped bombers mined the Inland Sea between the southern Home Islands and the approaches to Japan's principal Pacific harbors.

While this relentless air offensive continued, American forces finally secured their costly victory on Iwo Jima. It had taken the U.S. Marines two months to annihilate the Japanese defenders of the tiny island. American losses were horrendous, with more than 5,500 killed and 17,000 wounded. The Marines estimated that almost 21,000 Japanese troops had been killed, while only 216 had surrendered. But after a U.S. Army regiment took over from the departing Marines, the GIs encountered pockets of hidden Japanese in caves, of whom more than 1,600 were killed.[19]

On March 4, even while Japanese resistance was fierce, a battle-damaged B-29 returning short of fuel from Japan made an emergency landing on Iwo Jima's former Japanese Central Airfield, which U.S. Navy Seabees (Construction Battalions) were desperately working to extend and pave to accommodate Superforts safely. That B-29 eventually was repaired and flew back to its home base in the Marianas.

But, as military historians Thomas B. Allen and Norman Polmar detail in their book, *Code-Name Downfall, The Secret Plan to Invade Japan—And Why Truman Dropped the Bomb,* no sooner was Iwo Jima captured than the long, even bloodier battle for Okinawa began. A multi-division Marine and Army force invaded the largest island in the Ryukyus, just 350 miles from the Home Island of Kyushu, on April 1, 1945. The landings themselves were only lightly opposed. Within a few days, the true savagery began. While U.S. Marines secured the northern end of the long, narrow island, Army forces encountered fierce Japanese resistance from dense bands of cave and bunker complexes south of Okinawa's narrow waist. The Japanese had expertly sited their defensive positions with interlocking fields of fire from machine guns, mortars, and light and heavy artillery. They had ample reserves of ammunition, and their determination to make the Americans pay for every meter of sacred soil they captured was both courageous and fanatical. The battle cry of the 32nd Imperial Army defending the island was chilling:

One Plane for One Warship
One Boat for One Ship
One Man for Ten of the Enemy or One Tank

The Japanese commander, Lieutenant General Mitsuru Ushijima, had more than 70,000 regular army and naval troops and had organized a hastily trained home guard militia, the *Boeitia*, of about 18,000 students as young as fourteen. They were formed into *Tekketsu* (Blood and Iron for the Emperor Duty Groups), which served as front-line communications units. Girls received a few hours of basic medical training to care for the wounded, while other civilians worked on defensive positions. In all, about 100,000 Japanese defenders faced an equal number of American invaders on the island, a bad ratio under standard military doctrine, which usually requires at least a "three-to-one" numerical advantage in the offensive force.[20]

And this was not a conventional land offensive, but instead an amphibious operation almost on a par with the earlier landings in Normandy and in the Philippines in 1944. Nearly 1,500 U.S. and British warships ranging from flat-bottom landing craft to sleek destroyers and hulking battleships, to immense fast fleet carriers capable of launching more than 100 combat aircraft, churned the waters around Okinawa. Given the relatively short distance between this flotilla and Japanese air bases in Kyushu and Formosa, it was inevitable that the enemy would launch a vicious air attack against the Allied fleet.

What made this attack particularly shocking and effective was the number of kamikaze suicide planes involved. These were the "one-plane" human missiles to which the 32nd Army's war cry referred.

Kamikaze attacks, in which Japanese pilots intentionally crashed their aircraft into American ships, had begun in October 1944 during the Battle of the Leyte Gulf in the Philippines.[21] Short of aircraft and experienced combat pilots after the devastating losses in the Battle of the Philippine Sea, and increasingly stymied by the bristling antiaircraft defenses on American warships and fighters from U.S. aircraft carriers, the Japanese Imperial Navy organized the Kamikaze Corps, named for the "Divine Wind," a typhoon that destroyed a Mongol invasion fleet threatening Japan in 1281. Kamikaze planes were loaded with at least one bomb and a full tank of gasoline. In *The Last Kamikaze*, Edwin P. Hoyt has shown that Japanese tactics involved simultaneous diving attacks by several aircraft in an attempt to render less effective enemy antiaircraft fire. The degree of damage from a kamikaze hit depended on the size and armor of the vessel suffering the strike. Small escort carriers—converted tankers with short plank flight decks—were especially vulnerable, as were destroyers. But larger fleet carriers also suffered heavy damage.[22]

During World War II, kamikaze planes were often regarded as primitive—indeed barbaric—weapons born of desperation. In fact, the aircraft represented the first truly operational and effective "smart" bomb. And kamikazes appeared in the Pacific more than half a century before the global television audience was dazzled by the performance of American smart bombs during the Persian Gulf War. What made kamikazes such a devastating weapon was the unparalleled sophistication of their guidance system: the human brain. Kamikaze pilots were brave and determined to strike enemy ships, and to do so often attacked "from every quadrant of the compass" in order to overpower the defending vessel's defenses.[23]

The kamikaze campaign at Okinawa began the week of the invasion and continued in periodic waves throughout the entire campaign, not ending until mid-August 1945. In all, 1,465 kamikaze planes attacked, sinking twenty-one American ships and so heavily damaging another forty-three that they had to be scrapped. The Allied fleet suffered more than 4,000 killed—and thousands more critically wounded, often with terrible burns—in these kamikaze attacks. This battle was the bloodiest single engagement in U.S. Navy history.

Assault by kamikaze planes, however, was not the only suicide tactic that Imperial Japanese Headquarters employed to break up the Allies' Okinawa landings. Historians Dan van der Vat and William Craig have described a huge naval kamikaze force. On April 6, 1945, a powerful Imperial Navy task force centered on *Yamato*, the world's largest battleship, named for the mythical race of ancestral warriors' homeland, steamed south from the Inland Sea toward Okinawa. This "Surface Special Attack Force," composed of *Yamato*, a cruiser, and eight destroyers, carried only enough fuel for a one-way trip to Okinawa. But the ships' magazines were "crammed to bursting" with loads of ammunition and torpedoes. Their mission was to destroy the massed American transports and savagely pound the beachhead with *Yamato*'s 18.1-inch guns, and then, inevitably, be destroyed by Allied planes in the process. American submarines spotted the task force leaving the Home Islands and alerted Vice Admiral Raymond A. Spruance's carrier group. More than 300 American planes attacked "out of low clouds and rain" on April 7 before the ships reached

Okinawa, sinking the *Yamato*, her cruiser consort the *Yahagi*, and four of the destroyers. More than 3,500 Japanese seamen were killed.[24]

Despite this naval victory, the battle for Okinawa augured very badly for the Allies' planned November Olympic invasion of Kyushu, in which massed U.S. Navy forces would have to operate much closer to kamikaze bases. Further, on Okinawa, combat had degenerated into a war of attrition reminiscent of the vicious trench warfare of World War I. As the Marines and Army regiments fought their way south toward the island's capital, Naha, they encountered one zone of cave and bunker defenses after another. But the enemy defense was not merely static; in some hotly contested sectors, Japanese troops launched savage counterattacks almost nightly to dislodge American forces from the ground they had captured at such great cost.[25]

By the end of the bitter Okinawa campaign in late June, American ground and naval forces had suffered 12,520 men killed or missing, the highest casualty rate to date in the Pacific war, a level of carnage proportionate to the Battle of the Bulge six months earlier in Europe. Japanese casualties had been horrendous, with almost the entire combined regular and paramilitary force of 110,000 either fighting to annihilation or choosing suicide rather than surrender.

After the brutal punishment the kamikazes had inflicted on the Allied fleet at Okinawa, the destruction of Japanese oil targets became even more crucial for obvious reasons: Suicide planes needed gasoline and lubricants to operate. If the Allies were going to unleash their Downfall plan's Operation Olympic invasion of Kyushu—with "X-Day" projected for November 1945, and the even larger Operation Coronet invasion of Honshu scheduled for spring 1946—it was essential that the Japanese be deprived of fuel to operate the armada of kamikaze planes that intelligence reports now estimated they were hoarding to repel these invasions.[26] The Chairman of the Joint Chiefs of Staff, General of the Army George C. Marshall, was particularly anxious about the buildup of "suicide planes" in anticipation of the American invasion of the Home Islands. His concerns were warranted: American intelligence estimated that by midsummer 1945, the Japanese had dedicated as many as 8,000 aircraft as kamikazes and had dispersed them widely to small, camouflaged grass airstrips, caves, and underground hangars in Honshu and Kyushu, and were feverishly training young pilots to fly them. The intelligence on aircraft dispersal was correct; Japan was feverishly building "fortress" airfields across the country.[27]

But by August 1945, the number of suicide aircraft was actually far higher than Allied estimates: The Japanese Imperial Army and Navy *each* had about 5,000 kamikaze planes prepared to repel the invasion.[28] One way to gauge the destructive potential of that force to the Allied fleet operating close to the Home Islands is to recall that only a few hundred conventional Japanese combat planes had virtually crippled America's Pacific fleet at Pearl Harbor in less than two hours.

And American planners realized that Japanese resistance to Operation Olympic on the ground and sea would be even more savage than the fanatical defense of Okinawa. Indeed, as Japan entered the final summer of the war facing the prospect of foreign invasion of the sacred Home Islands in the autumn, the somber slogan "Hundred Million Die Together" had increasingly become a rallying cry.

1840 HOURS, 5 AUGUST 1945

Sergeant Jim Smith finished the last of his sliced ham and candied sweet potatoes and wiped off his fork and spoon. Ahead through the cockpit greenhouse he watched the red afterglow of the Pacific sunset. They had just passed east of Iwo Jima and Tony Cosola had called in a slight course correction to the northwest, which Carl had dialed into the autopilot. With night once more enveloping the bomber, Smith fought down the emptiness he always felt on leaving this last safe base behind. Ahead lay only enemy territory. Like other B-29 crewmen, he was beginning to feel the exhaustion of the unique nature of the missions they flew. And, like them, he just had to stay on the ball and do his job.

But tonight, for some reason, Smith found himself thinking unpleasant thoughts about the plane's engines. *The Boomerang* had taken off with a gross weight of almost 140,000 pounds, just on the edge of the aircraft manufacturer's recommended maximum. Even new R3350 engines, each producing 2,200 horsepower, could not take that kind of abuse very long. But none of the engines were new. When the Wing arrived on Guam in June, XXI Bomber Command had authorized maintenance crews to change a maximum of three of each engine's eighteen cylinders before junking the entire power plant itself. But a strike of union workers at the Cincinnati Wright-Cyclone factory had choked off the flow of replacement engines to the Pacific Theater.[29] So mechanics were often obliged to replace all eighteen cylinders with "reconditioned" parts, a dubious practice that undoubtedly contributed to engine failures both on takeoff and during the long cruise to and from the target.

Tonight, the "Beasts," as the R3350s were known, seemed to be firing smoothly, perfectly synchronized, thanks to Hank Gorder's expert care. With a reputation for failing under the terrible stress of takeoff, the engines were also known to "swallow" valves unexpectedly at cruising altitude, often resulting in catastrophic failure in which the lightweight magnesium shafts exploded in a shower of fiery debris, slicing off the bomber's wing.

There was nothing Smith could do about the engines, so he simply accepted combat for what it was, a hell of a tough job. But, as always, he hoped *The Boomerang* would remain true to the talismanic name the crew had chosen for the bomber, flying far out into the unknown and returning safely. On leave at home in Oakland, California, after finishing navigator's school the previous January, Tony Cosola had been given an authentic Aborigine boomerang from a family friend, John Frazer, who had served in the Australian Army during World War I. The crew considered it an appropriate lucky charm, and, on arrival at Northwest Field on Guam after the long flight across the Pacific, they had the name painted on the plane's nose. Bombardier Dick Marshall made the design, the curving sweep of the aboriginal weapon with the name printed inside. He then cut a wide stencil and had the name spray-painted beneath the pilot's window. The artwork was nowhere near as brazen as many of the provocative nudes decorating the noses of other bombers. But once they had named the plane, *The Boomerang*'s crew felt deeply attached to the symbol and insisted Cosola carry the real polished wood weapon on each mission, beginning with their first.

Now Jim Smith thought back to that first Empire mission on June 26, 1945.

The 315th Wing's combat operations over Japan had begun on the night of June 26 with an attack on the Utsube Oil Refinery near Yokkaichi on southern Honshu's deeply indented Ise Wan Bay, which the Strategic Air Forces considered a critical target because the plant was one of Japan's largest hydrogenation facilities for aviation gasoline.[30] The Wing was ordered to mount a maximum effort, with all thirty-eight Superforts of the 16th and 501st Groups then ready for combat to bomb the target from an average altitude of only 11,000 feet—well within range of Japanese night fighters and flak—and much lower than the altitudes of between 30,000 and 40,000 feet that the crews had trained to fly back in the States.

But the airmen had to accept orders.

Smith had awoken on Guam in the humid dawn on June 26 to confront the grim knowledge that they would be bombing Japan that night. Lying in his bunk in the stuffy barracks, he had feigned sleep so that he wouldn't have to talk to his buddies who were beginning to roll out of their sweaty cots. The detailed mission briefing would come later in the day; he knew, however, that his plane would no doubt be toward the head of the bomber stream because his group commander, Colonel Boyd Hubbard, Jr., was scheduled to fly up front on the first mission in order to measure winds and to gain as accurate an appraisal as possible of the synchronous radar bombing technique in combat. Maybe that was not a bad place to be. The fact was, few of the members of the Wing had ever seen combat, so they had no way of estimating their chances.

But everyone had great confidence in their wing commander, Brigadier General Frank A. Armstrong, Jr., who would be flying lead. He was a combat leader as strong as Curtis LeMay. Armstrong had flown some of the early daylight precision-bombing missions over Europe with the 8th Air Force and helped restore the shattered morale of several groups that had suffered horrendous casualties. At the controls of the lead B-17 of the 306th Bomb Group, Armstrong had led the first American daylight raid over Germany. He was the true-life model for Colonel Frank Savage, immortalized in the novel and film *Twelve O'Clock High*. Jim Smith and the other young airmen knew they could trust leaders such as Armstrong and Hubbard. But they had yet to test their own courage and skills in the harsh and unforgiving arena of combat over the Empire.

As Smith furtively watched the tropical sunlight work across the peaked ceiling of the hut, he found himself beginning to think about Japanese flak. During the Wing's intelligence orientation, the crews had learned that before surrendering in May, Germany had managed to ship Japan by submarine an unknown number of Wuerzburg-type flak radars.[31] This was an advanced antiaircraft fire-control radar, which when linked to 88mm cannons could guide Japanese searchlights, enabling non-radar-controlled guns to hit their targets more easily. The only defense the Wing's crews had against Wuerzburg radar was to dump bundles of aluminum foil strips, which the British who developed the technique had code-named "Window" and the Americans in the Pacific called "rope." These bundles burst in the plane's slipstream and drifted down like clouds of tinsel, disrupting the radar search beam.

Smith's crew had tested rope during the first practice mission against

Moen Airstrip on the bypassed Japanese garrison island of Truk. That training raid had been a nightmare introduction to combat from the beginning. On the late-night takeoff, First Lieutenant Floyd W. Wilkes's bomber had rolled down the runway but stalled after rising above the cliff at the end. The bomber pitched down, crashed into the sea, and exploded, killing all ten men on board. And the rest of that mission had proved to be a terrifying, confused melee of near collisions among B-29Bs lost in the turbulent clouds while dodging the chalky white pillars of the searchlights.

Now, on this June morning, remembering Truk, Smith's thoughts had shifted briefly to the morality of war. Intelligence had reported that there were few if any civilians on Truk, and for every bomb placed into that airfield, the threat against U.S. forces in the Pacific nearby was reduced. But Japanese civilian workers operated the oil refinery they were going to strike this first night over the Empire. Before sunrise tomorrow, Jim Smith would share the responsibility of killing some of those noncombatants. That was the way it had to be. Smith's two years of training were over. This was what war meant: killing the enemy before they killed you. Suddenly his mind lurched yet again to the relatively defenseless nature of the B-29B. If the other shoe ever dropped and the Japanese realized that these planes had been stripped of all their guns except the two .50 calibers and the slow-firing 20mm cannon in the tail, the fighters would close to short range and attack with their own devastating, faster-firing cannons.

That image helped Smith dispel the questions about the morality of the war. This was not a movie with Spencer Tracy in a sheepskin flying jacket, but—despite the sophistication of the weapons involved—an atavistic, no-quarter-given struggle. Now he thought of the Japanese sneak attack on Pearl Harbor that had killed more than 2,000 Americans on one Sunday morning in 1941. He thought of the tens of thousands of other young Americans who had been killed fighting the Japanese across the Pacific in the past three and a half years. He remembered the Bataan Death March after the fall of the Philippines when the Japanese drove the starving GI prisoners ruthlessly, bayoneting those who fell behind in the tropical heat, forcing others to bury their wounded comrades alive. He remembered the newsreel footage of Japanese captors beheading downed Allied airmen in the East Indies.

He hated the Japanese, and he wanted to destroy them. At age twenty, he had learned to be merciless. His world, and that of his buddies, had narrowed to the primitive emotions of revenge and survival.

When he finally rose that morning, any vestigial compassion remaining from the normal civilian world he'd known as a high school kid in Iowa was completely gone. The short years of his young adulthood had been consumed by this war, by the lonely knowledge that he would be tested in combat and that there was a very good chance he would not live to return home. But his job now was not to think about dead enemy civilians or dwell on his own odds, but rather to help his crew survive and to destroy the Japanese oil industry as quickly as possible.

Just before midnight on June 26, *The Boomerang* was nearing the bomb run. Smith reached his combat station by bending backward, grabbing a pair of handholds, and sliding into the entrance of the narrow pressurized tunnel. With his chest facing forward, he sat, head thrust beneath the navigator's astrodome, legs hanging over the circular lip of the tunnel. He had donned his heavy armored flak vest and steel helmet and made sure that his chest-pack parachute lay on the deck within easy reach before squeezing into his cramped position. Then he checked that the mike of his intercom was not snagged.

Smith's job was to spot fighters and warn the pilots if other Superforts flew too close. Swiveling his head, he scanned for nearby aircraft. There were none immediately visible; it was as if the bomber were still the only airplane that had flown the long leg from Guam. But as Smith's eyes adjusted to the starlight, he recognized the unmistakable gleaming length of the B-29B flying ahead. That bomber was within half a mile and only 100 feet lower than *The Boomerang*. Looking aft, Smith caught a glint of the trailing bomber, holding its altitude 100 feet higher than his plane.

Luckily on that first mission, the now-compressed stream of bombers had not yet encountered clouds, which would have rendered this tight bombing formation extremely hazardous. This would not be the case on later missions, when scores of bombers that had taken off from Guam at thirty-second intervals and flown most of the 1,500 miles to the Empire out of sight of each other in darkness suddenly converged over the Initial Point, supposedly at exact altitude and horizontal separation maintained by altitude and airspeed. As the 315th Wing's oil campaign continued, there would be catastrophic mishaps in which B-29Bs broke proper interval and the higher plane accidentally dropped its bombs on an aircraft below. For some of the aircrews, this specter was more threatening than Japanese defenses.

Suddenly, bombardier Dick Marshall called over the intercom: "Fighters at ten o'clock high." His voice was precise. Smith swung his gaze high in time to see two single-engine Japanese fighters diving at their nose. The enemy planes fired tracers, orange balls that seemed to hang in the sky and then suddenly blaze past with incredible speed. Smith watched powerlessly as the fighters continued their dive straight toward the bomber. *They're kamikazes*, Smith thought, certain the fighter pilots intended to ram *The Boomerang*. His concern was well founded. That afternoon near Nagoya, a B-29 of the 19th Bomb Group went down in flames after a Japanese pilot intentionally rammed the Superfort.

The fighters flashed by within a hundred yards of the bomber's wings. "Keep tracking them, Sid," Carl Schahrer told tail gunner Siegel. "But don't fire unless they make a run on us from behind." Schahrer did not want to give the enemy pilots a good aiming point by revealing gun flashes and tracers from the tail turret.

Then two more fighters appeared.

"I've got one flying alongside my wing, just out of range," Hank Leffler called from the left-scanner window.

"Same here," Henry Carlson, the right scanner, reported. "My guy's just keeping formation with us."

"They think we've got guns," Schahrer said to reassure his crew. "But they're staying away and pacing us into the target to give our altitude, speed, and heading to the flak units."

Now *The Boomerang* entered bumpy layers of altostratus clouds, and Smith felt confident the fighters would have to break away with this poor visibility. But when the bomber reached clearer air, the two fighters were still out there, flying parallel, just beyond .50-caliber-machine-gun range. Even if this target did not have radar-controlled flak guns, these pacing fighters had simplified the calculations of the gunners protecting the refinery ahead at the mouth of the Utsube River.

Marshall called, "Clutch in," signaling that he had linked his Norden bombsight to Ginster's radar through the circuits of the synchronous system and was now controlling the aircraft. Simplified data appeared on Carl Schahrer's cockpit display.

Smith saw glaring searchlights sweep through the undercast ahead. Just when they needed solid clouds below, that protection seemed to be thinning. The fighters banked and climbed steeply away. "There go our escorts," Smith reported.

"Rope," Schahrer ordered Leffler and Carlson. "Keep dumping it."

The two young scanners pushed bundle after bundle through the flare tubes.

Smith gazed into the sky around the bomber. No flak. The rope was working. Then a flak shell burst incandescent red-and-white, like fireworks on the Fourth of July, 200 yards off the port-side wing. His body was flooded with adrenaline. Flak exploded even closer to the starboard side, and he heard the solid crack of the shell over the engine roar. Just as he'd always been told, images of his life cascaded through his mind. He saw in stark detail both the good and the stupid things he had done as a kid. Flak blasted sporadically on either side and ahead of the bomber.

"Ready . . . mark," Dick Marshall called with amazing calm, aligning his aiming reticle.

Watching his cockpit indicator, Schahrer almost stood on the right rudder pedal to crab *The Boomerang* starboard and hold course in the suddenly fierce wind. Marshall's bombsight and radar indices converged. Schahrer's red light blinked on. A keening rose from below as the double set of wide bomb-bay doors whistled in the turbulent slipstream.

"Bombs away," Marshall called.

The Boomerang lurched upward, her nine-ton load of 500-pound bombs dropping free. The clouds below had closed again, shrouding the target from view.

Schahrer banked left but was careful to maintain their air speed. Even so, he had to throw *The Boomerang* through several sharp turns to avoid Superforts converging from other directions. When they had finally broken free of the clouds and the compressed bomber stream began to extend again, Schahrer called his crew: "Good job, everybody."

Smith climbed out of the tunnel and shucked off his flak jacket. His rubber Mae West and nylon-mesh survival vest were clammy with sweat. The men in the compartment began to unwind. Tony Cosola smiled broadly in the glow of the instruments. Smith breathed deeply to steady his hands and gave Cosola and Ginster a confident double thumbs-up. Now radio silence was no longer required, and Smith sat at his table to transmit the coded strike message:

BOMBING ALTITUDE 15,400 FEET. 10/10TH CLOUD UNDERCAST. FLAK MEAGER. SEARCHLIGHTS. 4 OUT-OF-RANGE FIGHTERS. BOMBS AWAY AT 1241 ZULU. NO DAMAGE TO AIRCRAFT. RETURNING TO NORTHWEST. OUT.

While Smith tapped out the Morse code message on his radio key, Cosola and radar operator Ginster coordinated navigational fixes to calculate wind drift and note the exact time of reaching land's end at Kumano on a steep peninsula along Honshu's Pacific coast. This chart work was essential if *The Boomerang* was to survive the long return flight to Guam on the remaining fuel and not have to risk landing on the still-unfinished B-29 runway on Iwo Jima.[32] Cosola completed his task and passed on the compass course for Carl Schahrer and John Waltershausen to carefully set on the autopilot. Now flight engineer Hank Gorder went to work with his slide rule and engine-efficiency tables, calculating the throttle setting, prop pitch, and fuel mixture needed for optimal gas-conserving cruise control back to Northwest Field.

As that endless June night wore toward dawn on *The Boomerang*'s first Empire mission, the excitement, spent adrenaline, and strong black Army coffee that had sustained the crew so far drained away. They felt dragged down by a bone-aching fatigue that none had ever experienced. Smith clamped his earphones tight on his head and rubbed his eyes hard. Now the endless *dah dit dah dit, dah dit dit dit* of the Japanese jamming oscillating across the frequency from high to low, low to high, was grating enough to keep him awake. He grinned. The Japs' intention of disturbing American radio operators was paying off. Smith knew he could stay awake for the next seven hours—

Suddenly he woke with a stab of panic. How long had he been asleep? The clock on his radio panel read almost 0400 local time. His forehead was sore and there was a bump just below the hairline. He could picture what had happened: He'd collapsed facedown onto the radio table from sheer exhaustion into a deep sleep. Cosola and Ginster were also sleeping at their stations. Peering around the flight-deck bulkhead, Smith saw Schahrer fighting to stay awake in his seat. But Waltershausen's head was slumped on his chest and Dick Marshall was curled up sleeping in the glass cage of the nose. About every fifteen minutes, Schahrer roused Waltershausen to monitor the autopilot so that he could nap. If both of them simply could not stay awake, Marshall assumed the responsibility. Smith did not worry about Hank Gorder, knowing from the long flight from California across the Pacific to Guam, in which *The Boomerang* had touched down at Hawaii and Kwajalein, that he would be resolutely busy at his station, scanning engine gauges, transferring fuel among the tanks to even aircraft trim, and adjusting cowl flap settings to keep the engines from overheating.

This was a solid crew, Smith realized. If he had to fly such brutally taxing combat missions, these were the guys he wanted to fly with.

2150 Hours, 5 August 1945

By August, that first night in June seemed to Smith to have happened decades earlier in the life of an impossibly younger man. Tonight was *The Boomerang*'s seventh mission over the Empire. And on each mission, the enemy reaction had become more intense. Although the Japanese fighters were still not pressing home their attacks, they had perfected the tactic of pacing the Wing's compressed stream of aircraft—just out of .50-caliber-machine-gun range—from the Initial Point to the bomb run, and radioing information to the flak gunners below.

And the flak had become deadly. On the night of July 26, multiple searchlights had locked onto a B-29B of the Wing's 502nd Group as the bombers neared a huge, heavily defended oil refinery complex on the Kawasaki waterfront. The plane, commanded by Captain Henry G. Dillingham, took a direct hit from heavy flak, rolled over, in flames and out of control, and spun to the sea below. There were no survivors. That night, thirteen other Superfronts were hit by flak but managed to return to Guam. (Fortunately for *The Boomerang*, the plane had not flown that mission because of a mechanical abort before takeoff.)

Now, on the night of August 5, as Jim Smith sat uncomfortably at his station, head clamped in the heavy earphones, he managed to relax and concentrate on his job. It did not do a bit of good to dwell on what lay ahead below that dark Pacific horizon. All he and the others aboard *The Boomerang* could do was complete this mission, and the next, and the one after that, until the enemy was defeated and this long war ended.

KOKUTAI AND KETSU-GO

T HE ISLAND EMPIRE OF JAPAN toward which the 315th
Wing's bombers flew on the night of August 5, 1945, was insular in
both the literal and figurative sense. Lying off the Asian mainland, Japan
had been isolated for long periods during two millennia. Its culture had
been influenced by, but had evolved largely separately from, the region's
dominant civilization, dynastic China. By World War II, Japan had developed a society unique among the world's industrialized countries: a
mélange of twentieth-century capitalism and militarism grounded on a
docile population devoted to the living deity of Emperor Hirohito, the
arahitogami, who could trace his lineage back "through a line of succession unbroken for ages eternal" to the Sun Goddess, Amaterasu.[1]

Japan had not had sustained contact with the West until the mid-
nineteenth century, after which its leaders chose to emulate the other
emerging power across the Pacific, the United States. But much of Japan's

subsequent exposure to the outside world had come during wars of imperial expansion in Asia. In theory, life in modern Japan was governed by
a written constitution promulgated by Hirohito's grandfather, the Meiji
("Great") Emperor, in 1889, which provided for a two-chamber parlia-
ment, the Diet, and an appointed cabinet. But by the 1930s, virulently
nationalistic military leaders had become the dominant figures in Japanese society.[2] They launched the Japanese Empire into increasingly vicious
aggression in Manchuria and China, resulting in widespread atrocities,
including the wanton massacre of Chinese prisoners of war and civilians
in Nanking.[3] Although these campaigns greatly expanded Japan's conquests, they led to its withdrawal under pressure from the League of
Nations, which further deepened the Empire's isolation on the world stage.

The Meiji Emperor had overthrown the last medieval shogun war-
lord less than a century before and launched the modernization reforms of
Japanese society. But his grandson Hirohito was no reformer, and he certainly was not the pro-Western liberal he has often been portrayed in
post–World War II (i.e., Cold War) propaganda. In fact, since the war,
scholars have revealed convincing evidence that—far from being an aloof
Imperial figurehead—Hirohito took an active role in Japan's preparation
for entry into World War II, including the attack on Pearl Harbor.[4]

Emperor Hirohito, whose birth name was Michinomiya Hirohito,
was born at the Imperial Palace in Tokyo on April 29, 1901. According to
traditional myths greatly augmented and formalized during his grandfather's reign, he was the 124th direct descendant of Jimmu, Japan's legendary first emperor. A thin, short-statured boy with poor eyesight, he was
conspicuously shy among his classmates at the Peers' School and the
Crown Prince's Institute. His great interest was marine biology. His 1921
tour of Europe made him the first Japanese crown prince to travel beyond
the Home Islands. It was while Hirohito was abroad that his father,
Emperor Taisho, retired from the throne due to mental illness, and his son
was named Prince Regent on his return. In 1926, Hirohito became
emperor on the death of his father. When the young emperor assumed the
throne in Tokyo's Imperial Palace, his reign was proclaimed Showa (Bright
or Enlightened Peace).

Less than five years later, Japan embarked on its policy of aggression
in Asia, precipitating fifteen years of war.

The single most important factor underlying this aggression was the
structure of Japan's government and societal self-identity, the *kokutai*,

which is generally translated as "the national polity." This unique cultural artifact was a relatively modern phenomenon that sprang from the Meiji Emperor's consolidation of Imperial power in the nineteenth century and reached its final distinctive form during the rise of the militarists in the 1930s. The national polity, which has been described as a highly structured paternalistic state, had at its apex the benign, infallible authority figure of the emperor, who was both the father of his people and the Imperial family's living link to its divine roots in the mythical past.[5]

To say that the fully developed *kokutai* system of the late 1930s and 1940s was a cult of emperor worship is at once accurate and misleading. Certainly the average Japanese peasant or urban worker had been inculcated with the belief that their emperor was a living god. Until the Meiji Emperor took the throne in the 1860s, it had been a capital offense for commoners to actually view the face of the emperor. During Hirohito's reign, state-authorized photographs of His Majesty's "holy likeness"— which many conservative Japanese draped to avoid lèse-majesté—were venerated in most Japanese households. At dawn each day, millions bowed to these framed portraits as they did to their Shinto household shrines. When Hirohito's motorcades passed through the streets, people were cleared from upper floors and drapes were pulled tight so that "none might look down on the sacred personage." [6] The only images of the Emperor the vast majority of his subjects ever enjoyed were elaborately choreographed newsreels of Hirohito performing obscure court rituals, periodically addressing the Diet, posing in the Imperial Palace grounds or at the seaside with his family, and, increasingly by the late 1930s, reviewing military parades astride a white stallion.

It had in fact been the violent factionalism within Japan's military, which triggered assaults by radicals on civilian authority and culminated in the bloody Army revolt of February 1936, that had solidified the *kokutai* in its ultimate wartime form, with the Emperor and a body of trusted military leaders providing each other mutual support. This alliance was necessary because an ultranationalist and irrational mysticism still simmered beneath the restive surface of the military. Many radical officers yearned for abandonment of Western values and a rebuilding of the modern samurai warrior state based on the carefully reconstructed Imperial myth. Cultural and racial superiority were definitely part of their beliefs, as was the deep-felt conviction to purge Japan of all "externally derived isms, such as Western democracy, liberalism, individualism, and communism."[7] As the commander-in-chief of Imperial forces, Hirohito had to ride the military tiger with great caution.

But for the Emperor, the advantage of this increasingly spiritualized national polity was that he could expect the devoutly loyal military to protect the Imperial throne, provided he acquiesced to their demands for stepped-up armament and an expanded war in China. This loyalty was a major consideration following earlier violent upheavals that had almost caused him to abdicate. For the military, the new *kokutai* provided the cachet of the Emperor's authority, solidifying their powerful new role in the nation. Every rifle, machine gun, artillery piece, and naval cannon was stamped with the sixteen-petal Imperial chrysanthemum, a symbol that the modern samurai of the Imperial Army and Navy made divinely sanctioned war.

This belief was instilled in the Japanese people and fighting man through a rigorous process of internal propaganda that drew on the taproots of their indigenous Shinto religion's urge to sweep Asia clean of the cultural pollution spread by the Western colonial powers. Even as Japanese troops were conducting bestial massacres in China, the people at home docilely watched staged propaganda newsreels of Chinese peasants welcoming their Imperial Japanese Army liberators. But, as historian Herbert P. Bix has shown in his exhaustive study of the Japanese Empire, *Hirohito and the Making of Modern Japan*, in the Home Islands, the military tightened their grip on Japanese society. The phrase the "Emperor's benevolent heart" was now commonly used in the Domei News Agency, the heavily censored press, and on the Japan Broadcasting Corporation (NHK), to bolster civilian morale and deliver a not-so-subtle warning to those who might resist his Imperial "compassion" that they faced the wrath of the notorious antisubversive agents of the *kempeitai* secret police.[8]

But the larger war the Japanese had entered so enthusiastically in the 1930s had not gone well. After a surge of victories following the December 1941 attack on Pearl Harbor that had expanded Japanese conquests across Asia and deep into the Pacific, Imperial forces began to suffer a mounting series of defeats. By summer 1945, Emperor Hirohito and his closest advisers were desperate to find a way to end the long years of strife that had begun in 1931 in Manchuria in a manner that would satisfy their particular requirements, especially maintaining the Emperor-centered *kokutai*, the sovereignty of the Home Islands, as well as the retention of traditional

Japanese overseas territories such as Korea, Formosa, and their Manchurian puppet state of Manchukuo. But with the American capture of Saipan and all the Marianas in 1944, followed by General Douglas MacArthur's invasion of Leyte in the Philippines, most rational Japanese military leaders realized they could no longer win the war.

Japan had gone to war with the West in 1941 to seize natural resources, particularly the petroleum from the rich oil fields of the Netherlands East Indies and rubber in British Malaya. Many Japanese militarists, especially those in the Army favoring the expansionist policies of Prime Minister General Hideki Tojo—one of the architects of Japanese aggression on mainland Asia—had been convinced that the Empire had no recourse but to launch a wider war after the United States had embargoed oil and other crucial exports in 1941 following Japanese occupation of French Indochina. For three years, oil, rubber, bauxite, tin, and other vital resources had flowed to the Empire from their southern conquests. Now American sea and air power had choked that flow.

And with the American transformation of the Marianas, Iwo Jima, and Okinawa into major air bases and the arrival off the Home Islands of strong Allied aircraft carrier task forces, the Japanese leaders feared they only could expect more devastating aerial assaults. Their fears were valid. Japan was besieged. Her once-great Combined Fleet and merchant marine had been sunk, her harbors mined. Even the most optimistic senior officers had to face the reality that Japan no longer had the means to counterattack into Southeast Asia.

To deal with this unfolding crisis, the Imperial government had undertaken a series of radical changes. An inner cabinet, the Supreme Council for the Direction of the War, known informally as the "Big Six," had been created in August 1944 after the fall of Saipan, to better coordinate the bolstering of Japan's defenses against the approaching Allied juggernaut.[9] Hirohito withdrew his support of General Hideki Tojo's wartime cabinet and it crumbled. And, in May 1945, with the military situation drastically worsening, the Jushin, Japan's body of elder statesmen, invited retired Admiral Baron Kantaro Suzuki to become Prime Minister.

Suzuki, 78, who had served heroically as a naval officer in the Russo-Japanese War forty years earlier and had gone on to become a grand chamberlain to the Emperor, despised the fanatically ultranationalist young officer factions that had risen to prominence in the 1930s during the chaos of the Great Depression. In the abortive military revolt of February 1936, those young fanatics had tried to assassinate Suzuki but succeeded only in wounding him severely.[10]

Now Suzuki was the senior civilian official in the Supreme Council for the Direction of the War, whose other members included Japan's foreign minister and the highest military leaders. During a series of cloistered meetings and secret Imperial conferences in the spring and summer of 1945, the Big Six would become divided over the most critical question before them: whether Japan should quickly seek the most advantageous peace conditions the Allies might still be willing to offer, or press on with the heroic defense of the shrinking Empire while simultaneously preparing for the Ketsu-go operation, the Decisive Battle for the Homeland, which the Japanese expected would begin on the beaches and bays of Kyushu when the enemy invaded later that year.[11]

These deliberations acquired a tone of renewed urgency in June and July, as American B-29s began a devastating incendiary campaign against Japan's secondary cities. By the end of July 1945, smaller cities such as Hachioji, Toyama, and Fukui had virtually been reduced to heaps of blackened ash.

Prime Minister Suzuki, who had served on diplomatic assignments in the West and spent much of his later life occupied with other than purely naval affairs, vacillated between advocating a compromise peace with the Allies and seeing the war through to the cataclysm of the Ketsu-go. Soon after assuming office, the elderly Suzuki stunned the Japanese public by issuing a press statement expressing deep sympathy to the Americans on the death of President Roosevelt, noting, "I must admit that Roosevelt's leadership has been very effective, and has been responsible for the Americans' advantageous position today."[12] His words came just five weeks after General Curtis LeMay's firebombing of Tokyo and at the height of the crucial battle for Okinawa. These sentiments indicated that Suzuki, who had long been close to the throne, might be staking out his own position as the leader of the pro-peace faction on the Supreme Council for the Direction of the War. But several weeks later Suzuki seemed to reverse course, endorsing a bellicose "Fundamental Policy" that called for mobilization of all military forces and civilians in preparation of the Decisive Battle for the Homeland, while simultaneously seeking a diplomatic démarche to the Soviet Union, toward which Japan had been neutral since 1941, a move that might help Japan "to facilitate the prosecution of the war."

In a June 8 Imperial conference, the Council presented the Fundamental Policy to the Emperor. He tacitly approved its unflinching stance toward the final defense of the homeland. Hirohito even assented to the decision of the Council not to move Japan's capital and court to a subterranean fortress in the mountains above Nagano. In his authoritative book, *Behind Japan's Surrender*, historian Lester Brooks has revealed that, should Fate decree, the Emperor and his government would fight their own Ketsu-go in the flaming ruins of Tokyo.[13]

The vague description of the diplomatic approach toward the Soviet Union epitomized several Council members' (and the Emperor's) unrealistic hope to negotiate with Joseph Stalin's war-battered Soviet Union to reach a secret quid pro quo by which the Soviets might agree, in exchange for small postwar territorial concessions in Asia (including the southern half of Sakhalin and the Kuril Islands), to offer their "benevolent neutrality" toward the Japanese—and perhaps even to provide Japan desperately needed oil and aircraft. (This proposed Japanese diplomacy came weeks *after* the Soviet Union had announced to the world on April 5, 1945, that it would not extend its Neutrality Pact with Japan, which had been signed in 1941.) Nevertheless, the Japanese placed inordinate hopes in the secret démarche. If successful, the initiative would allow Japan to continue transferring military forces from Manchuria to the Home Islands, secure from Red Army pressure on the Manchurian–Siberian border. The complete success of this diplomacy could see the Soviets acting as peace mediators between Japan and Russia's wartime allies, the United States, Great Britain, and China, with terms acceptable to the Japanese being reached before the Allies were prepared to invade the homeland.

When the Emperor and the Council approved the secret initiative, Foreign Minister Shigenori Togo asked former prime minister and veteran diplomat Koki Hirota and the Soviet Ambassador to Japan, Jacob Malik, to begin negotiations in Tokyo in June. These talks sputtered inconclusively for most of the summer.

The Lord Keeper of the Privy Seal, Marquis Koichi Kido, 55, a politically astute, right-leaning aristocrat, had followed the deliberations of the Supreme Council for the Direction of the War closely, casting himself in the role of Hirohito's private observer. Kido had been one of the young Emperor Hirohito's "Big Brothers" (close advisers) at court in the 1920s, and could be expected to watch out for the throne's interests at this critical juncture of the war. Marquis Kido had favored Japan's attack on the West in 1941 (with the acquiescence of Hirohito).[14] But in 1945 the Lord Keeper of the Privy Seal advocated ending the war on terms most favorable to Japan. To accomplish this, Kido had joined an unofficial peace faction comprising civilian officials and certain senior military officers to work toward this goal.[15] In this regard, Kido reflected Hirohito's growing but closely held opinion that Japan had to find a means to extract itself from the war in the most timely and advantageous manner.

The other civilian member of the Council was Foreign Minister Togo, 63. A career diplomat, fluent in English and German—he had married a German woman—Togo had been first secretary at the Japanese embassy in Washington and served as ambassador to both Nazi Germany and Soviet Russia. Foreign Minister Togo probably understood the dynamics of geopolitics better than any other member of the group. He was an austere, hard-driving man whose few vanities included expensive tailored suits and handmade striped shirts with French cuffs. Togo had deftly managed the diplomatic spadework of the prewar Soviet-Japanese Non-Aggression Pact, which had allowed both countries to pursue their respective territorial ambitions, at least temporarily, without fear of each other's formidable military power on the Asian mainland. Togo had envisioned Japan becoming the dominant power in Asia, which it would sweep clear of decadent Western colonial control, but he had not favored close alliances with the European Fascists. This view had put Togo in conflict with the right wingers coalescing around Prime Minister Hideki Tojo at the start of World War II. Togo resigned as foreign minister in the first year of the Pacific war, reportedly disillusioned and guilt-ridden that his earlier policies had spurred Japanese military aggression deep into Southeast Asia and the Pacific.

Now, after almost four years of that wider war, with either ignoble defeat or the catastrophe of Ketsu-go in the offing, Shigenori Togo accepted Suzuki's invitation to become Japan's foreign minister once more. But Togo saw the Empire as a shattered hulk of its former self, reminiscent of the Imperial Germany that had tottered on the edge of defeat in 1918 at the end of World War I. He believed it was imperative that peace with the Allies somehow be hammered out at the earliest possible moment, so that Japan as a nation and its unique *kokutai* could remain intact.[16]

The third member of the Council inclined toward peace was Admiral Mitsumasa Yonai, 65, the Navy Minister. Yonai, who had never served in combat during major naval engagements, had spent much of his later career as a government official and Imperial councilor. During the upheavals of the

1930s, he had proven himself loyal to the throne. His brief tenure as prime minister in 1940 ended when he ran afoul of pro-Axis militarists. But before the Pearl Harbor attack, Yonai had made it known that he opposed an expanded war in the Pacific.[17] After the sweeping Japanese victories of 1941 and 1942, Yonai had voiced the unpopular opinion in government and military circles that Japan should take the opportunity to negotiate peace with the shattered Allies. Following the loss of Saipan and the Marianas in 1944, he argued that Japan should now make vigorous peace overtures.

But the other three members of the Council were certainly not inclined to seek peace.

Navy Chief of Staff Admiral Soemu Toyoda, 60, an able, forceful, and extremely nationalistic officer with lifelong antiforeign views, accepted the reality that Japan's Combined Fleet virtually no longer existed, but saw no honorable means to cease hostilities. This was because the Allies had done nothing to modify the terms of their Cairo Declaration of 1943, by which Japan would be stripped of its empire and see its sovereignty restricted to the Home Islands. Naturally distrustful of the two civilian members of the Council, Toyoda was swayed by the arguments of his military colleagues on the body.

Army Chief of Staff General Yoshijiro Umezu, 63, had been a devoted young officer decorated for gallantry during the Russo-Japanese War. After the antigovernment Army unrest in the 1930s, Umezu prospered by helping purge the officer corps of its most dangerous fanatics. As a senior officer, he had been repulsed by Japanese Army atrocities—especially the Rape of Nanking—and again exercised his new authority to regain control of renegade elements and restore discipline. He spent over four years commanding Japan's Kwantung Army in occupied Manchuria, during which he modernized the force. Umezu had reportedly dabbled in the ultranationalist right-wing Amur (Black Dragon) Society as a young man, which left him with his deep-seated xenophobic perspective. Like Toyoda, Umezu considered any discussion of outright surrender anathema.

The most vigorous anti-peace member of the Council was Umezu's onetime protégé, War Minister General Korechika Anami, 58, the vigorous and popular leader of Japan's Imperial Army, which still numbered in the millions and was spread throughout Asia and the Pacific. A pragmatist who had eschewed politics and intrigue, Anami had advanced by dint of dogged determination rather than intellect after graduation from the Imperial Military Academy in 1907. Just before Japan's entry into World

War II, he had served as Vice Minister of War, and then gone on to command an Army corps in China. In 1943, Anami had led a stubborn retrograde defense of the New Guinea jungles, a campaign that had reaffirmed his faith in the tenacity of the well-commanded Japanese soldier, who could make the Allies pay dearly for every meter of territory they attacked. An officer who had never taken extremist political positions, Anami was renowned for being affable to his close military colleagues.

War Minister Anami saw himself as a modern samurai, a member of Japan's traditional warrior class who now commanded forces armed with machine guns, tanks, and aircraft instead of wielding curved swords. But he could trace his ancestry to the samurai of the thirteenth century who had used forged steel to defend Nippon's sacred soil from the invading Mongols. He was devoted to the samurai's code of Bushido, "the way of the warrior," which had been influenced by Zen Buddhism and Shintoism and encompassed bravery, loyalty, self-discipline, and stoicism, among other virtues. To maintain his discipline, General Anami tried to practice with the samurai long bow at dawn each day and was devoted to kendo, a traditional martial art using bamboo staves, in which he had attained the highest rank. Also in the samurai tradition, he read and wrote classical poetry.

Late in 1944, Anami assumed responsibility for military aviation, a daunting challenge. Although aircraft production had greatly diminished by the standards of the first war years, Anami's strong-willed leadership resulted in Japan's building an impressive reserve of planes, which were stockpiled for use as kamikazes in the Ketsu-go battle.

For War Minister Anami, the concept of Japan surrendering the still-formidable Imperial Army to which he had devoted his life was virtually unthinkable.

During a meeting of the Council in mid-May 1945, General Anami reassured his colleagues, "While Japan is still occupying large areas of enemy territory, the enemy has invaded only a small area of Japanese-owned territory. Thus we must keep this fact in our view in discussing the peace conditions to be sent to the United States and Great Britain. We must not base our discussions on the assumption that we are proposing peace because we are being defeated."[18]

There would come a time, War Minister Anami argued to his colleagues at another Council meeting, when Japan would have to face the inevitable Allied invasion. But that would be the moment of the Army's greatest glory. In the Ketsu-go operation, the Japanese military could inflict such devastating casualties on the Allies that they would be forced to withdraw and end the war on terms favorable to Japan.

General Anami delivered these defiant words at the Foreign Ministry, a Western-style office complex that had so far escaped the devastation of the B-29s. Less than two weeks later, on May 25, the building was severely damaged in yet another incendiary bomb attack that laid waste to previously unbombed sections of central and northern Tokyo. Although the U.S. Army Air Forces had specific orders to avoid hitting Hirohito's palace, that same air raid had burned twelve Imperial pavilions on the Palace grounds that had been built for the Meiji Emperor's family and court in the nineteenth century. Hirohito was forced to move to the Gobunko, the Imperial Library, which, being built of reinforced concrete, offered much greater protection from bomb damage. The adjacent air raid shelter now became his de facto Imperial conference room.[19]

General Anami's confidence about defending the Empire was not irrational. Japanese Imperial General Headquarters had assigned many of its most skilled staff officers to the detailed planning of the Ketsu-go operation. The Home Islands had been divided into seven Ketsu defensive zones, with the heaviest concentrations of ground forces and aircraft in Ketsu No. 3, the Kanto coastline of Honshu around Tokyo-Yokohama, and Ketsu No. 6, Kyushu. The military hoped that the linkage of the *kokutai*'s religious patriotic fervor with the traditional xenophobic sentiment of the Japanese people would convince both fighting men and civilians that it was preferable to die in the Decisive Battle for the Homeland than to surrender the sacred soil of Japan to the hated enemy. In a decree issued by the Imperial Japanese Army in April, soldiers were exhorted to die to the last man defending the "eternally existing Imperial land . . . where our eternal race will live." Civilians were also expected to join enthusiastically in the Ketsu-go, with every man, woman, and child fighting until death. Soldiers were ordered to abandon their wounded comrades to fight on as best they could, then to die honorably. Indeed, the entire nation was expected either to repulse the invasion force or to perish in the effort. The words and music of a chilling song titled "One Hundred Million Souls for the Emperor" were widely circulated in military units and among civilians.[20]

As Lt. General Ija Kawabe, the former Deputy Chief of Staff, Imperial Japanese Army, stated to American intelligence officers after the war,

"The Japanese, to the very end, believed that by spiritual means they could fight on equal terms with you, yet by any other comparison it [the battle] would not appear equal."[21]

Japan was by no means a militarily defeated power as it prepared for the Ketsu-go. The Imperial General Staff had correctly estimated that Kyushu and its small outlying islands would be the first objective in the anticipated Allied invasion of the Home Islands. This assumption was only logical. Allied strategy from the Mediterranean campaigns to the advances north from the Solomons had rested on pushing air bases closer to the enemy's homeland in order to achieve air superiority over the battlefield. As with Okinawa, the Allied lodgment on Kyushu would be transformed into a vast warren of air bases to prepare Honshu for the ultimate invasion of the Kanto Plain.

Not only did Japanese military intelligence officers accurately foresee Kyushu as the major American objective of Operation Olympic, they specifically plotted the major Olympic invasion beach sites on Ariake Bay, the Miyazaki Plain, and the coast at Kushikino.[22] One particularly astute intelligence officer, Major Eizo Hori, whose estimates of enemy intentions had proven so accurate that his colleagues had dubbed him "MacArthur's staff officer," displayed almost preternatural insight into Allied plans. By walking Kyushu's beaches and carefully examining the inland topography, Hori confidently predicted landing sites that coincided with other intelligence estimates. But Major Hori went further. He knew it was unlikely that the Allies would put a massive invasion armada to sea during the summer typhoon season, so he wrote a well-reasoned analysis of Allied intentions predicting that their invasion would come in late October. In fact, in its June 29 meeting, the U.S. Joint Chiefs of Staff had firmly set November 1, 1945, as Operation Olympic's "X-Day," the start of the landings.[23]

This skillful intelligence work allowed the Japanese military ample time to concentrate its Ketsu No. 6 forces in the most advantageous positions in Kyushu. The defense of the island had originally centered on the 57th Army, then, by July 1945, had shifted to the larger 16th Area Army, heavily augmented with independent brigades as well as armored and artillery regiments and battalions. Relying on Ultra radio intercepts, the American Military Intelligence Service estimated the island's defensive force in early July to be approximately 350,000 troops organized around six well-equipped divisions.[24] These figures proved to be a gross underestimate of actual Japanese preparations for the Ketsu-go battle in Kyushu. By the end of July, American Ultra code breakers had received stark evidence from radio intercepts that Japanese troop strength on Kyushu was almost *double* the original estimate and now totaled at least 574,000 men in eleven divisions and independent formations. Moreover, there were two more combat divisions en route to Kyushu, which would bring enemy forces to 600,000.[25]

But regular Imperial Army troops were not the only Ketsu-go defensive forces. As the military situation worsened, the Japanese staff officers planning the Decisive Battle for the Homeland ordered the mobilization of all fit men and women into home-defense units similar to those that had fought so tenaciously on Okinawa. Classes were canceled at schools and universities throughout the country, which freed several million young people for the Ketsu-go manpower pool. Three types of units totaling more than 13,000,000 men were undergoing training by the summer of 1945. Older men with previous military service were assigned to Special Guard Forces attached to regular units to build fortifications and transport supplies. They would take part in combat under the control of the regular units. The Independent Companies were mobilized reservists who worked feverishly, joining virtually all able-bodied persons in Japan building small camouflaged kamikaze airstrips.[26] And these reservists also trained relentlessly for combat. The Civilian Volunteer Corps, formed in June 1945, was an omnibus body that absorbed all remaining boys and men between ages fifteen and sixty and all girls and women seventeen to forty. They were assigned to intensive munitions and food production, which included preparing subsistence rations and manufacturing crude but functional infantry weapons in vast quantities.

As military historians Thomas Allen and Norman Polmar have found in their research, all these civilian auxiliaries received some form of combat training, which often required heroic self-sacrifice. The instruction centered on the training manual *People's Handbook of Resistance Combat*. There were illustrations on how to disable an American tank with a gasoline-filled "flame bottle" (Molotov cocktail). A tank could also be stopped by attacking it with a satchel charge strapped to the volunteer's back. For those who were not issued the hastily built infantry weapons, the handbook provided detailed instructions on how to kill enemy soldiers with bamboo spears, farm implements, kitchen knives and cleavers, or sharp tools. The short-statured Japanese were instructed to "always thrust tall Yankees in their belly."[27]

Exhorting the people to form a single national Tokko, or "Special Attack Force," one hundred million strong, the booklet urged all Japanese to exterminate Allied invaders "to protect our native soil and to maintain our everlasting Empire."[28]

Was this simply empty rhetoric born of last-ditch desperation? Post-war intelligence analysis suggests not. Although Japanese civilians were growing steadily war-weary, they had not lost the will to resist: Residents of coastal areas welcomed newly deployed Ketsu-go Army units and, despite Allied bombing, readily joined in the building of fortifications and training for what would be irregular and clearly suicidal combat. In fact, when Japan surrendered later that summer, the people of the Miyakonojo region of Kyushu, who had been prepared to die in the defense of the homeland, rioted in protest.[29]

Many westerners often apply the term "blind fanaticism" to describe such self-sacrifice. But, while Japanese forces definitely were fanatical in battle—the banzai charge being one of their hallmarks—they were hardly blind about the nature of the sacrifice they undertook. Their culture valued the survival of the family and the nation over the individual. In Shinto tradition, a child had incurred a debt to both the family and the society that had nurtured him. That debt had to be repaid by the symbolic age of forty-one. The spirits of younger men who died of natural causes would never advance in rank in the afterlife. But the spirits of warriors killed in battle defending the Empire would receive that greatest of Imperial blessings, admission to Tokyo's Yasukuni Shrine, an honored, eternal resting place for "national deities."[30] Given this prevalent belief, it is probable that the vast majority of Japanese military forces—and most civilians—would have fought to extinction had the Decisive Battle for the Homeland occurred.

But conventional and auxiliary Japanese ground forces were certainly not the only threat the Olympic planners had to consider. Massive air and naval Special Attack units were also being prepared to defend both Kyushu and Honshu.

The Allies had come to dread the swarms of kamikaze aircraft that had attacked their fleets during the invasions of the Philippines and Okinawa. Now the Japanese had built or converted thousands more airplanes for use as kamikazes in the crucial first days of the anticipated

Allied landings. And these planes were widely dispersed either in underground hangars or small camouflaged airstrips that had largely escaped the destruction that both B-29s from the Marianas and the increasing numbers of Allied ground- and carrier-based tactical bombers had inflicted. This effort allowed the Japanese to abandon many of their larger air bases, which continued to be the focus of Allied air attack, while the new dispersed and concealed airstrips remained as sanctuaries for the thousands of kamikaze planes that had been kept in reserve for Ketsu-go.[31]

For the first time, the Imperial Army and Navy, which had previously jealously guarded their independence, cooperated closely in planning a large and complicated combined operation.[32] Ironically, had the two branches of the Imperial armed forces done so during the first days of the Okinawa invasion, their coordinated waves of kamikazes flying from Formosa and Kyushu might have inflicted much heavier damage on the American landing force. Now the Imperial Air Army and naval Air Fleet were dedicated to accomplishing this mission in the waters off the sacred Home Islands.

As noted, the tactics of the kamikaze aerial attacks were far more sophisticated than the mindless and uncoordinated fanaticism that has permeated many Western accounts of the War. Before the Ketsu-go began, Japanese forces would conduct far-ranging surveillance of the sea-lanes and potential Allied invasion staging bases in the Philippines and Marianas using submarines and reconnaissance flights flown from the Home Islands, Formosa, and the Netherlands East Indies. Once it was clear that the unmistakably massive Allied invasion task forces had assembled and were en route for Kyushu, the kamikaze forces would be put on a state of high readiness. They would launch their first strike during the initial phases of the invasion, with Allied troop transports to be attacked on the open sea by more than 600 kamikaze planes concentrated in two dense waves.[33] Next, a force of at least 5,000 Army and Navy planes—many trainers and hastily built fighters lacking guns, which had been converted into kamikazes—would continue the attack on the invasion fleet as the transport convoys reached their anchorages close inshore. The ferocity of these kamikaze attacks would be far more intense than the savage assaults at Okinawa. By launching waves of 300 to 400 kamikaze an hour during daylight, the Japanese intended to decimate the invasion convoys in the first few days, even if fewer than one in four aircraft managed to reach their targets.[34]

According to military historians Allen and Polmar, Olympic would deploy "a total of 1,371 transport, cargo, landing and evacuation ships with a capacity to carry 539,290 and 61,190 tanks and vehicles."[35] But the Japanese military estimated that the Allies would employ around 2,000 transport vessels and hoped to sink approximately 470 in the first days of the invasion by devoting up to 7,500 kamikazes to the mission, including more than 2,000 drawn from reserves hidden on Honshu.

This Japanese projection reflected an effectiveness ratio of one ship sunk for every three kamikazes launched. That was probably overly optimistic. As historian Richard B. Frank discovered, at Okinawa only 18.6 percent of the suicide planes to reach the fleet actually struck or damaged Allied ships with near misses, and just 1.8 percent of the kamikazes dispatched to Okinawa "actually sank ships."[36]

But, at Okinawa, the kamikazes had concentrated on armored naval vessels bristling with antiaircraft guns. And radar identified the attacking planes at a great distance. However, if the Ketsu-go defenders focused their overwhelming kamikaze attacks on the more vulnerable transports and used the mountainous terrain of Kyushu to mask the waves of attacking aircraft from radar detection, the results could have been catastrophic for the Allies. Certainly, the U.S. Navy had learned the danger of operating increasingly closer to the Japanese Home Islands earlier in 1945. In just two days in mid-May, Task Force 58 Commander Vice Admiral Marc A. Mitscher had two fast-attack aircraft carriers, the USS *Bunker Hill* and the veteran USS *Enterprise,* crippled in kamikaze attacks northwest of Okinawa. If a relative handful of kamikazes could wreak that kind of carnage on fleet carriers, the threat of suicide attacks on transports on the shores of Japan was especially grave.

This was one of the reasons that the Ketsu-go planners rigorously hoarded their vital reserves of kamikaze aircraft. But there were more practical considerations as well. Many of the most experienced Navy and Army pilots had been killed in conventional aerial combat or had already been lost in the kamikaze campaigns during the Philippines and Okinawa operations. And the fuel shortage remained an insurmountable problem, which drastically reduced training hours for new kamikaze volunteers. However, those assigned to suicide missions close to the coast were not expected to perform skilled maneuvers, but simply to crash their bomb-laden planes into the Allied transports.

Morale in most kamikaze units remained generally high despite the grim nature of their mission and the toll Allied tactical bombing of their bases had taken before the dispersal and concealment campaign succeeded. Imperial Japanese Navy Ensign Ichizo Hayashi, 23—a Christian from Nagasaki—epitomized the dedication of these pilots. He flew his suicide mission against the Allied fleet off Okinawa in early April 1945. In a letter to his mother, he summarized the feelings he shared with so many of his comrades. "Please do not grieve for me, mother. It will be glorious to die in action. I am grateful to be able to die in a battle to determine the destiny of our country."[37] Like other kamikaze pilots, Ichizo spoke proudly of the distinctive Rising Sun headband he would wear over his helmet and the snow-white muffler embroidered with Shinto prayers that would show at the neck of his flight suit. Kamikaze pilots were treated with ritual respect on the day of their missions, receiving special rations of luxuries such as delicately spiced tofu almost impossible to find in the war-torn country.

Further, the Ketsu-go planning staff did not intend to passively submit to the scourge of Allied tactical bombing once the Decisive Battle had begun. To help reduce the threat that American fighter-bombers, B-25 Mitchells, and B-24 Liberators based in Okinawa posed to the Ketsu-go kamikaze campaign, the Japanese had prepared a bold counterattack. The Imperial Army had trained an elite airborne raiding brigade of 1,200 men, who would fly aboard one hundred transport planes, in the night and at wave-top level to avoid enemy radar, then conduct assault landings at all the American air bases on Okinawa. Using rocket launchers, grenades, and satchel charges, this suicide brigade would destroy as many aircraft as possible before they themselves were inevitably wiped out. To avoid American air attacks on the transport planes prepared for this attack, which had disrupted a similar operation planned against B-29 bases in the Marianas, the Japanese dispersed and hid the planes.

Japanese military leaders drew on the cultural trait of self-sacrifice when they devised new weapons that would be deployed in large numbers during Ketsu-go. The Ohka (Cherry Blossom) suicide aircraft, which had first appeared in 1944, and which the Allies derided with the Japanese term Baka, "Fool," was a unique weapon. Basically a piloted glider-bomb with a solid rocket motor for the final dive to the target, the Ohka was designed to be carried to high altitude by a "mother" bomber, usually a G4M Betty, then dropped to glide at a speed of 230 miles per hour toward a target up to fifty miles distant. In the final 50-degree suicide dive, the pilot would ignite his rocket motor, boosting speed to 570 mph, which made these flying bombs extremely difficult to shoot down. The combination of this speed and the 2,645-pound high-explosive warhead in the nose gave the Ohka the potential to deliver a "sure-hit, sure-death" blow to the ship it struck.[38] By March 1945, 755 Ohkas had been built; in mid-summer 1945, underground factories were mass-producing the piloted rocket bombs.

The Kaiten was an Imperial Navy suicide weapon with equally devastating potential. It was a manned version of the widely manufactured 24-inch-diameter Type 93 "Long Lance" torpedo that the Japanese Combined Fleet had used with such effectiveness during Pacific sea battles. But a human pilot rather than a gyroscope guided the Kaiten and its powerful warhead toward enemy ships at a maximum speed of 40 knots and a mission duration of up to an hour. With this capability, the Kaiten could outrun any American destroyers protecting the inshore invasion transport force. The Kaiten pilot's cockpit was installed midway down the length of the torpedo, which he controlled, shallowly submerged, clad in a light diving suit, breathing through a stored oxygen apparatus. Kaitens could be launched either from the deck of a submerged submarine or from secret concrete pens that the Japanese were building in small bays and inlets on Kyushu and Honshu.[39] The Japanese had only 120 operational Kaitens in June 1945 but were rapidly adding to their force, which U.S. intelligence analysts discovered with alarm late that month.

Longtime proponents of midget submarines for close-in attack on enemy vessels, the Japanese prepared large numbers of this weapon for homeland defense. It was a Japanese miniature sub that had been the first casualty of World War II in the Pacific, sunk by an American destroyer's guns as it headed toward Pearl Harbor one hour before the air attack. Now, almost four years later, the Japanese were building hundreds of similar Koryu and Kairyu midget submarines to be launched against the Allied fleet during Ketsu-go. Although small, these subs had impressive potential as close-range weapons. With a five-man crew, the Koryu Type D could cruise submerged at 16 knots for forty minutes or creep along at 2.5 knots for fifty hours. Koryus were normally armed with two Long Lance torpedoes, but many were being fitted with contact warheads for use as suicide weapons. Working in dispersed, hidden factories, the Japanese were confident of having 540 Koryus operational by the end of the summer and planned to produce more at a rate of 180 per month.

Two-man Kairyu midget subs were a more advanced version of the Koryu. Because Allied bombing had cut into torpedo production, many of the 360 submarines that had been completed by early August 1945 had been fitted with suicide warheads, which would have been as effective as torpedoes in the crowded anchorages of the invasion task force transport convoys.[40]

But the Imperial Army had also developed a surface suicide weapon, the Shinyo, a boat powered by a truck engine, carrying two 120-kilogram depth charges as contact explosives. Although nowhere near as fast as standard torpedo boats, the one-man Shinyos would have torn through the American transport anchorages because the Army had produced the small suicide vessels in vast numbers. By the end of the war, there were 6,200 ready for service in Ketsu-go.

Among the greatest menaces to small American landing craft infantry (LCI) and amphibious tractors were the Japanese Fukuryu ("hiders") of the Water's Edge Surprise Attack Force. The human-mine volunteers were equipped with bubble-free oxygen rebreather systems, which would not betray their presence as they lurked beneath the surface among beach-landing obstacles. When American landing craft approached, the Fukuryu would swarm out, thrusting mines with contact fuses mounted on sticks. Each man was expected to sink one enemy landing craft or amphibious tractor, trading his life for up to forty invaders.[41] The Imperial Navy planned to have 4,000 men trained to serve in Ketsu-go. Some would have been killed in the prelanding bombardment, but many would have survived to take their toll of the American landing craft.

But the Japanese did not plan on relying solely on suicide missions to repel the Allied invasion. Beyond the thousands of planes that had been converted as kamikazes and hoarded at hidden airstrips, the Imperial Japanese Navy retained about 2,500 combat aircraft for use during Ketsu-go. They were meant to guide flights of inexperienced kamikaze pilots through the terrain-shielding mountains and toward their targets and provide them air cover, to conduct night torpedo attacks on Allied transports, and to strafe landing craft.[42]

In the bloody battle of Okinawa, which many Allied planners feared was a rehearsal for Operation Olympic, the Japanese defenders had allowed American forces to land relatively unopposed, then conducted a suicidal defense, retreating slowly from one line of fortifications to the next toward the south of the island. But the basic Japanese plan for Ketsu-go was exactly the reverse. The Decisive Battle operations order was to challenge the main landing forces in their anchorages and at water's edge, "before the enemy can successfully secure beachheads."[43] This would be accomplished by rapidly massing all the main Japanese ground, air, and naval forces within the first two days, as the enemy struggled to secure and reinforce the beachheads. The Japanese would concentrate their armor and artillery on these constricted beachheads, followed up by concerted infantry assaults, hoping to inflict crippling losses on the enemy.

There is also evidence that the Japanese were prepared to use poison gas or possibly even germ warfare on the invading forces, a tactic the Imperial Army had employed in China.[44]

Given preparations on both the Japanese and Allied sides, the Ketsu-go opposition to Operation Olympic would undoubtedly have rendered the Kyushu landings one of the bloodiest battles of World War II, rivaling the great slaughters of the Eastern front such as the siege of Stalingrad or the Red Army's capture of Berlin.

But would the Japanese defenders have succeeded in stopping the nine U.S. Army and Marine Corps divisions scheduled to land on thirty-four separate beaches on Olympic's X-Day, November 1, 1945? That question is impossible to answer. The only amphibious operation of comparable size was the D-Day invasion of Normandy on June 6, 1944. Then, the Allies had only secured their beachhead at great cost. But it is important to remember that neither the German Air Force nor the Kriegsmarine had opposed the D-Day flotilla with more than token resistance.[45] And the German Panzer divisions massed north of the Normandy beaches on the other side of the Seine had been held in reserve, because the German General Staff (and Adolf Hitler) were convinced that the main Allied invasion thrust would come across the shortest width of the English Channel at the Pas de Calais. This misconception had been augmented by a massive and skillful Allied deception plan that had created an entirely bogus invasion army replete with dummy tanks and trucks spread across the countryside in bivouacs and villages northeast of London.

But the situation in Kyushu would have been radically different. Japanese intelligence had pinpointed the Olympic invasion beaches. The Ketsu-go operations plan called for a furious concentration of all available forces—including impressive reserves of tanks—on the American beachheads. Many of the surviving Japanese combat aircraft would also have attacked the invasion fleet, targeting transports and landing craft. And the swarming waves of kamikaze planes would have posed a threat far beyond anything the Normandy D-Day fleet had faced. Nor, of course, had the

Third Reich's defenders of the Normandy coast employed suicide weapons such as the Kaiten manned torpedo, the Koryu or Kairyu midget submarines, the hordes of Shinyo, or the Fukuryu human mines.

Certainly the battle would have been a bitterly contested melee. Chaos would have undoubtedly prevailed among both defenders and attackers, with inexperienced young kamikaze pilots flying converted training planes overladen with bombs into the dense ranks of the American transports discharging landing craft while the close-in fire-support ships struck the beaches with rocket salvos and shellfire. Midair collisions would have been inevitable as the Japanese pilots dodged Allied fighters and clouds of antiaircraft fire. The carnage among kamikaze pilots would have been great, because the American Air Force would have been able to maintain combat air patrols over the beachheads day and night using long-range P-51s, P-47Ns, and P-61 Black Widow night fighters. But the mountainous terrain favored the Japanese, while the vast numbers of kamikaze reserves would have guaranteed that many would have reached their targets. And the suicide vessels and human mines would have exploited this wild confusion to its optimum potential. Farther offshore, the American battleships and cruisers laying down heavy supporting fire for the landing would have presented ripe targets for the approximately forty large fleet submarines the Imperial Navy had reserved for Ketsu-go to act both as Kaiten carriers and in conventional roles.[46]

We can only speculate as to whether such determined Japanese resistance would have crippled the Olympic landings by inflicting unacceptable casualties and rendering the American invasion forces combat ineffective. In June 1945, Japanese Navy Chief of Staff Admiral Soemu Toyoda privately estimated that Allied casualties would not have exceeded 25 percent had the invasion come in September, but he arbitrarily doubled that estimate during a June meeting of the Supreme Council for the Direction of the War in June to join in the then-bellicose spirit. However, Operation Olympic was scheduled for November 1945, not September. These additional two months would have allowed the Japanese to continue strengthening their forces in Kyushu.

The recent declassification of American analyses of sensitive Ultra signals intelligence radio intercepts has made it clear that American war planners viewed the Japanese buildup for Ketsu-go on Kyushu with deep and growing concern, particularly over the deployment of kamikazes to concealed bases and the relentless augmentation of conventional ground forces. Alarmed by the new projections of Japanese forces on Kyushu,

General Douglas MacArthur's chief intelligence officer, Major General Charles A. Willoughby, noted somberly on July 29, 1945, "This threatening development, if not checked, may grow to the point where we attack on a ratio of one to one, which is not the recipe for victory."[47]

Indeed, once the Allies recognized that the Japanese would have in place 600,000 troops to oppose the Olympic landings, there was definite cause for deep concern. By standard military doctrine, an invading amphibious force needed to enjoy a three-to-one numerical advantage over the defenders, as well as air superiority and naval domination of the inshore waters, a situation that clearly would not exist on the coast of Kyushu in November 1945. In this regard, mounting American pessimism about Operation Olympic paralleled Japanese War Minister Korechika Anami's optimism toward Ketsu-go.

Anami stubbornly maintained this position into the hot, desperate summer of 1945. And the rift widened between the prowar military leaders and those in the civilian and military leadership actively seeking peace.

Lord Keeper of the Privy Seal Marquis Kido had quickly rejected the Council's Fundamental Plan leading Japan toward Ketsu go as tantamount to national suicide. He drew up his own counterproposal, the "Tentative Plan to Cope with the Situation." Discussing the proposal in his diary, Kido raised for the first time the previously unthinkable prospect of Japan's outright capitulation to the Allies. He further stated that the nation's "proper course" was to start peace negotiations after waiting "until the opportunity matures." The purpose of this bold approach was to avoid the fate of Nazi Germany and in so doing to safeguard the Imperial Household and preserve the national polity.

When Kido conferred with Hirohito on this grave issue, he found a sympathetic ally. The Emperor confided that he had grown heartily sick of the war and personally favored direct peace overtures to the Allies. But the members of the Big Six were deeply divided over the question of peace negotiations. Navy Minister Yonai concurred with Kido that surrender was an "urgent" matter. And on June 15, Foreign Minister Togo met Kido and agreed to work diligently toward "an early peace."[48]

Three days later, however, War Minister Anami met Kido. The General carried a samurai sword and wore a dress uniform resplendent with multiple rows of decorations. His already strong resolve had been visibly stiffened by the authority to mobilize the entire nation for the Ketsu-go he had received under the Fundamental Policy. He rejected out of hand any question of seeking an early peace. Army Chief of Staff Yoshijiro Umezu and Navy Chief of Staff Admiral Soemu Toyoda also remained vehemently opposed to the thought of peace negotiations.

But on June 22 the Emperor called the Supreme Council for the Direction of the War to a conference at the Palace and spoke openly and directly to the members for the first time about the necessity of both preparing for the Decisive Battle and simultaneously doing their "utmost to end the war as quickly as possible."[49]

For several weeks, the Japanese peace faction's hope rested with the secret negotiations between senior diplomat Koki Hirota and Soviet Ambassador Jacob Malik. Impatient for progress, Hirohito wanted to send a special envoy to Moscow to negotiate directly with the Kremlin. The Emperor ordered Foreign Minister Togo to secretly instruct the Japanese ambassador in Moscow, Naotake Sato, to explore whether the Soviet Union would accept longtime Imperial adviser Prince Fumimaro Konoye as this envoy. But as the stagnant humidity of July took hold and the B-29s returned almost nightly to rain fire across Japan, it became increasingly clear that the Soviets were only stalling and had no intention of extending their neutrality toward Japan or of intervening as peace mediators.

None in the Imperial court or on the Supreme Council for the Direction of the War could have guessed that Marshal Joseph Stalin had secretly implied to President Franklin Roosevelt and Prime Minister Winston Churchill during the Allies' Tehran Conference in late 1943 that the Soviet Union could be prepared to join the war against Japan after Nazi Germany's defeat.[50] During subsequent discussions with Churchill the next year in Moscow, Stalin promised his Western Allies that the Soviet Union would enter the war in Asia no later than three months after the Germans surrendered, a pledge he reconfirmed at the Yalta Conference of February 1945, with the proviso that the Soviet Union be granted much more territory in Asia than the Japanese were later prepared to offer in their own secret negotiations. The Soviet claims made at Yalta included regaining all the Asian possessions lost during the Russo-Japanese War of 1904–1905 as well as other concessions in Manchuria. In order to guarantee Soviet participation in the Pacific war, Roosevelt and Churchill acquiesced.[51]

Germany had surrendered on May 8, 1945. Japan's ultimate fate had already been determined. Now it was a question of how much blood would be shed on all sides before that point in history was reached.

CHAPTER THREE

POTSDAM AND TRINITY

Late on the night of july 6, 1945, a small motorcade left the White House for Washington's Union Station. There, President Harry S. Truman joined a group of fifty-three staff members, personal assistants, and a select pool of news correspondents aboard a special train. That train reached the U.S. Navy base at Newport News, Virginia, just before dawn the next day. Truman and his entourage went aboard the heavy cruiser USS *Augusta*, which cast off almost immediately. While stewards were unpacking his bags in the Admiral's suite, the President watched as the cruiser's consort, USS *Philadelphia*, preceded them through the doglegged mine-free channel of Hampton Roads. These two warships, comprising Task Force 68, were bound from the Chesapeake Bay to the war-ravaged port of Antwerp, Belgium.

Harry Truman, who had suddenly assumed the presidency upon the unexpected death of Franklin D. Roosevelt in Warm Springs, Georgia, on

April 12, 1945, seemed to many Washington insiders an unfit and unlikely replacement for the venerated FDR. Born in rural Missouri in 1884, Truman had been raised on a farm, where his father bred and traded mules. Although he was among the minority of boys in his county to graduate from high school, his family could not afford to send him to college; his strong desire to attend West Point was blocked because of his poor eyesight. After clerking in a bank and working in minor civil service posts, he tried business (a partnership in a lead mine and oil wildcatting); both enterprises failed.

But in World War I, Captain Harry Truman, commander of a Missouri National Guard artillery battery serving in the U.S. Army 35th Infantry Division, showed his true mettle. During fierce combat in the Argonne offensive in 1918, Truman displayed unusual qualities of bravery, initiative, and leadership.

After the war, he and his new wife, Bess, moved to Kansas City, where Harry became a partner in a haberdashery, yet another failed business. But his popularity among Missouri World War I veterans attracted the interest of Tom Pendergast, the local Democratic Party boss. For the next twelve years Pendergast was Truman's political patron in good times and bad. During most of this period, Harry Truman served in relatively minor county positions, earning a reputation for fairness and honesty, despite Pendergast's blatant corruption. In 1934, Truman was elected to the U.S. Senate as the Pendergast candidate. Although he arrived trailing the suspicious aura of crooked ward-heeling politics, Truman soon proved himself to be diligent in his duties and free of corruption.

After reelection in 1940, Truman devoted his full energies to the Special Committee Investigating National Defense, an effort that exposed waste, corruption, and dangerously shoddy war matériel. This gave the previously obscure senator from Missouri national prominence and persuaded FDR to choose Truman as his vice presidential candidate for the 1944 campaign. Truman's rather cloistered vice presidency lasted less than three months. Now, as President, he was en route to the tranquil, wooded lakeside resort of Potsdam, southeast of Berlin, where he would confer with British Prime Minister Winston Churchill and Soviet dictator Marshal Joseph Stalin on ending World War II and on the future of the postwar world.

Truman had opted for the seven-day Atlantic crossing in lieu of a much faster but more tiring flight aboard the presidential C-54 transport

Sacred Cow because he wanted more time to prepare for the Potsdam Tripartite Conference and to confer with his chief of staff, Fleet Admiral William D. Leahy, and Secretary of State James F. Byrnes. The tentative Potsdam agenda was thick with vexing issues, particularly the need to reach agreement among the wartime Allies concerning the postwar governments in the countries of east and central Europe that Stalin's Red Army had overrun on its advance toward Berlin.[1] Another major question facing the American delegation at Potsdam was whether Stalin would abide by his promise to enter the war in Asia against Japan in time for that intervention to prove militarily significant before the Olympic invasion of Kyushu in November—*or* whether Japan would capitulate before the huge Red Army spread out of Siberia and engulfed Manchuria as it already had so much of eastern Europe.[2] A further troubling problem facing Truman was whether America was prepared to allow victorious Russian forces to share in the actual occupation of the Japanese Home Islands, with each Allied power allotted its own sector as it now was in defeated Germany.

This challenge was not made any easier by the Western Allies' long-stated strategic goal: the "unconditional surrender" of the Axis powers. Nazi Germany and Fascist Italy had surrendered without condition. After assuming office, Harry Truman seemed determined to force Imperial Japan to do the same. In a speech on May 8, 1945, commemorating Victory in Europe Day, Truman directly addressed the Japanese government and people in a translated version of his remarks beamed by Office of War Information shortwave radio.

> Our blows will not cease until the Japanese military and naval forces lay down their arms in *unconditional surrender.*
>
> Just what does the unconditional surrender of the armed forces of Japan mean for the Japanese people?
>
> It means the end of the war.
>
> It means the termination of the influence of the military leaders who brought Japan to the present brink of disaster.
>
> It means provisions for the return of soldiers and sailors to their families, their farms, and their jobs.
>
> And it means not prolonging the present agony and suffering of the Japanese in the vain hope of victory.
>
> Unconditional surrender does not mean the extermination or enslavement of the Japanese people.[3]

Significantly, Truman's warning and appeal to the Japanese to end the war made no mention of the Emperor's future status or the national polity. In fact, the address was no more specific than the intentionally vague unconditional-surrender rhetoric that Franklin Roosevelt had unexpectedly announced while speaking to the press during his January 1943 conference in Casablanca with Winston Churchill. On returning from Casablanca, Roosevelt had solidified unconditional surrender as the "only terms" on which the Allies would deal with the "barbaric leaders" of the Axis nations.[4] The Allies continued to reiterate the unconditional-surrender policy at further strategic and political conferences, including the December 1943 Cairo Conference at which Roosevelt and Churchill met with Chinese Nationalist leader Chiang Kai-shek to discuss the fate of a defeated Japan's postwar future.

This staunch unconditional-surrender position had been appropriate when the Soviet Union was fighting alone on the Eastern Front, when the Western Allies had not yet invaded Sicily and Italy, when Chiang's armies were on the retreat, and when the plans for the D-Day landings in France were still vague—and there was a real possibility that the Allied coalition could disintegrate and lose the war. But in May 1945, with Mussolini's Italy and Hitler's Germany reduced to scorched rubble and Stalin's Red Army occupying Europe from the Balkans to the Elbe River, an inflexible position toward Japan did not make as much strategic sense.

However, Harry Truman, who understood domestic politics quite well, could gauge the temperament of the American people. On June 1, 1945—a day on which he gave yet another uncompromising demand for Japan's unconditional surrender—a Gallup poll was released in which nine out of ten Americans called for taking the Pacific war directly into the Japanese homelands, no matter how costly the invasion might prove. Another poll revealed that an overwhelming majority of Americans saw Hirohito as "personally responsible" for the war. As Richard B. Frank has noted, "When asked to pass on his fate, 33 percent favored execution, 17 percent trial, 11 percent imprisonment, and 9 percent exile. Only 4 percent viewed him as a figurehead, and an almost imperceptible 3 percent viewed him as a potential asset in managing Japan after the war."[5] Clearly the political climate this soon after the dreadful losses at Iwo Jima and during the ongoing bloodbath on Okinawa was not conducive to offering generous (or any) concessions to the Japanese.

And even though Truman found himself faced with a level of geopolitical complexity in the European discussions far above anything he had previously encountered, his principal focus remained bringing the war in the Pacific to a rapid and successful conclusion without further massive American casualties—while somehow also satisfying the American people's desire to crush the Japanese militarily. When he assumed the presidency, Harry Truman also became commander-in-chief of the world's most powerful armed forces, part of which was involved in uniquely vicious combat to capture Okinawa. Not only did the daily casualty figures and ship losses to kamikazes reach Truman each morning at his White House Map Room headquarters, but also the President was now given access for the first time to the Top Secret Ultra radio intercepts revealing that the Japanese Imperial Army intended to fight to the last. The Ultra messages further revealed the growing Japanese buildup on Kyushu. As American casualties mounted, Truman became "very much disturbed over losses on Okinawa," the Army's Director of Operations, Major General J. E. Hull, would later report.

In mid-June, the President called a conference of his principal military advisers to discuss projected casualties during the Operations Olympic and Coronet invasions of Japan. The planning officers of the Joint Chiefs of Staff and General Douglas MacArthur's headquarters in the Philippines scrambled to prepare a casualty estimate for the President. But these staff officers based their estimates about Olympic on the badly out-of-date intelligence that the Japanese Imperial Army had garrisoned Kyushu with only six combat divisions and two depot divisions, totaling 350,000 troops. This assessment dated from mid-1944. Now, however, Ultra intercepts revealed that the Japanese were steadily reinforcing the island. Therefore, the Joint War Plans Committee at the Pentagon responsible for assembling various estimates admitted that their projections could be only an "educated guess."[6]

If the American Sixth Army landing force, divided into three corps, assaulted southern Kyushu in November 1945 and the even larger U.S. First, Eighth, and Tenth Armies went ashore near Tokyo and advanced across the Kanto Plain in March 1946, the Pentagon projection foresaw 43,500 Americans killed and missing and 150,000 wounded, for a total of 193,500 casualties out of an overall combat troop strength of more than a million. The planners envisioned much lower casualties if southern and northwestern Kyushu were invaded simultaneously and Japan then surrendered. But if combined Kyushu invasions did not bring about the Japanese surrender and Operation Coronet was required, American casualties could total as many as 220,000 for the entire campaign.[7]

But there were clearly reservations among the senior officers of the Joint Chiefs and their supporting Joint Planning Staff to take these figures to the President, because the estimates were hopelessly vague and based on "scenarios" that could not be reliably determined at that stage. Instead of providing the detailed estimates for Olympic and Coronet that the President's Chief of Staff Admiral Leahy had requested, the Pentagon planners constructed a table of previous Pacific campaigns that showed a ratio between American and Japanese losses. For example, on Luzon in the Philippines, U.S. forces had suffered 31,000 total casualties, while the Japanese had lost 156,000 (mainly killed), a ratio of 1:5. But on Iwo Jima, the ratio of American to Japanese casualties had been 1:1.25, while on Okinawa, where the battle still continued, the ratio to date had been 1:2.[8]

Beyond these dry figures lay a bloody reality: Even if the defeat of the Japanese was inevitable, Downfall's two invasions of the Home Islands would entail tens of thousands of American dead and missing, and hundreds of thousands of wounded. Further, the Downfall plan, which called for the building of multiple Allied air bases after the Olympic forces seized suitable flatland on Kyushu and isolated the mountainous interior in order to soften up Honshu, would drag the war well into 1946. As Harry Truman would later note, "It had been estimated that it [Downfall] would require until the late fall of 1946 to bring Japan to her knees."[9]

This was another political factor Truman had to consider. Despite the bellicose tone of the opinion polls, however, America was truly sick of the war, especially of the mounting casualties in the Pacific. Men who had already seen combat in Europe were back in the United States being reequipped for the Downfall invasions. They were not happy with the prospect of facing the Japanese, and they complained to their congressmen. Political professional that he was, Harry Truman fully understood that 1946 was a midterm congressional election year, when the party in power traditionally did badly. If his administration were still bogged down on the bloody soil of Japan, those elections might break the back of the Democratic Party.

At the meeting with his military advisers, which took place at the White House on Monday, June 18, 1945, Truman made it clear that he had to decide among three competing strategies to defeat Japan: the Downfall invasion plan, an intensified bombing campaign, and a tightening sea blockade to augment the already devastating campaign of submarine interdiction and aerial mining of the shipping lanes connecting the Home Islands with the ports on the Asian mainland through which passed so much of Japan's food and resources.

Army Chief of Staff General George C. Marshall—known to be adamantly opposed to the Air Forces' and Navy's arguments that they could subdue the Japanese by either bombing or naval blockade—presented the case for the two-phase Downfall invasion plan. Concerning Olympic casualties, he confidently said, "There is reason to believe that the first thirty days in Kyushu should not exceed the price we have paid for Luzon"—in other words, a total of 31,000.[10]

Truman listened, then questioned these senior officers about the possibility that the Japanese could reinforce Kyushu from garrisons elsewhere in the Home Islands (which was exactly what was happening at that time) rather than from Imperial Army forces blockaded on mainland Asia. General Marshall assured the President that the Home Islands sea channels to Kyushu had been effectively mined and were being continually interdicted by Allied airpower (which was in fact not accurate).

Now Admiral Ernest J. King, Chief of Naval Operations and Commander-in-Chief of the U.S. fleet, stated that a more realistic figure would be closer to 50,000 casualties, 7,000 more than were suffered during the first thirty days of the Normandy operation. The group discussed the previous Pentagon estimates that had maximum casualty progressions of 200,000 killed, missing, and wounded during the entire Downfall operation. And Admiral Leahy would not accept Marshall's casualty comparison between the battle for Luzon and the projected invasion of Kyushu, which, Leahy argued, would prove just as bitter as the struggle to capture Okinawa. Further, the Office of Strategic Services (OSS) had provided the Joint Chiefs of Staff a detailed assessment of the specific risk from suicide swimmers and boats that the Japanese were preparing to throw against the Olympic landings in much greater numbers than had been employed in the Philippine or Okinawa invasions.

But General Marshall and Admiral King, the two service chiefs of staff, and the senior Army Air Force's representative, Lt. General Ira C. Eaker, voiced their strong support for Downfall. King had previously been in favor of an invasion of the much less heavily defended Chinese coast to establish an invulnerable American lodgment on which to create multiple air bases, almost as close to Honshu as Kyushu. But now King favored Downfall. The only senior military leader to adamantly oppose the invasion of the Home Islands was Admiral Leahy, who remained in favor of a tightened naval blockade.[11]

Truman weighed these arguments and made it known that he was still deeply troubled by the projected casualties. Nevertheless, he approved plans for Operation Olympic and tersely announced that he would decide on Coronet later.

There was a reason President Harry Truman was not more forthcoming concerning his decision. Only a few of the men at the White House conference had been "read in" on the greatest secret of World War II: that the United States was on the verge of testing and deploying nuclear weapons.

On Wednesday, August 2, 1939, German-born physicist Albert Einstein interrupted his vacation at a small summer house on Long Island's Nassau Point to sign a letter to President Franklin Roosevelt that several other prominent European émigré scientists exiled in the United States had urged him to write. Gordon Thomas and Max Morgan Witts, authors of the classic *Enola Gay*, have indicated just how alarmed Einstein was. He warned the President that Nazi Germany was conducting secret research to release the tremendous potential energy of radioactive uranium, the heaviest naturally occurring element. This research might result in "extremely powerful bombs of a new type."[12] His admonition was particularly relevant: He was inarguably the most original thinker of the millennium; his famous e=mc² formula had revealed the previously unknown relationship between matter (mass) and energy in his special relativity theory. He understood the devastation that could be caused by a weapon that would convert just a few grams of uranium into pure energy. However, he also grasped the tremendous technical difficulties of developing a uranium bomb and added the caveat in his letter that "such bombs might very well prove too heavy for transport by air . . . ," as airpower historians Wesley F. Craven and James Lea Cate have noted.[13]

Einstein's letter did not reach the President until October 11, 1939, six weeks after Hitler's Wehrmacht rolled across the Polish frontier, igniting World War II. But with the urgency of this new global conflict and Roosevelt's certainty that the United States would be drawn into it, the President told the American emissary who had delivered Einstein's letter, Alexander Sachs, that the great physicist's warning was well taken.

"What you are after is to see that the Nazis don't blow us up," Roosevelt told Sachs.

"Precisely," Sachs replied.

"This requires action," the President told his aide, General Edwin M. Watson.

From that presidential decision, limited funds were allocated in 1940 to conduct research with uranium to determine whether a sustained "chain reaction," in which neutrons from the radioactive element cascaded among the atoms and broke free ever-increasing numbers of other neutrons until a portion of the uranium was annihilated in a searing blast of energy, was both possible and practical.[14] But with America's entry into the war after the attack on Pearl Harbor, the uranium experiments acquired even higher priority because the War Department now believed that Nazi Germany had a two-year lead in uranium-bomb research over the Allies.[15]

This pressure led to the creation in 1942 of the "Manhattan Engineer District," code name for the supersecret American effort to create a bomb before the Germans did. Soon the program became known simply as the Manhattan Project among the growing body of scientists and engineers drawn behind its curtain of absolute secrecy. In December 1942, émigré Italian physicist Enrico Fermi led the Manhattan Project research team that successfully created the first sustained chain reaction, working with a graphite-block "pile" that separated metallic uranium pellets at a distance safe enough to demonstrate the energy release from the experiment without the reaction's bursting beyond control.

Scientists had determined that naturally occurring uranium, U-238, would never be practical for bombs in which a violent, uncontrollable chain reaction was required to liberate vast amounts of energy in thousandths of a second. A much more exotic isotope of uranium, U-235, however, would meet this requirement, as would another, man-made uranium isotope—plutonium, Pu-239. The basic theory of the atomic explosion was straightforward: If sections of metallic U-235 or Pu-239 could be precisely slammed together at sufficient speed, they would form a "critical mass," during which nuclear fission would occur.[16] That fission had the potential of producing a blast of unprecedented power.

Working with pitchblende uranium ore shipped from the Belgian Congo, the Manhattan Project set about the monumental task of separating these rare isotopes. The program's new commander, a hefty U.S. Army Corps of Engineers brigadier general named Leslie R. Groves, ordered the construction of a huge secret industrial facility along the Clinch River in the Appalachian backcountry of eastern Tennessee. The Oak Ridge facility, which grew to several hundred buildings, eventually used a unique gaseous diffusion technique by which the lighter molecules of U-235 were slowly separated from their heavier parent element. Even though this technique was functioning by autumn 1943, the yield of precious U-235 was so slow that scientists worried the method would take years to produce the estimated total of 60 kilograms of weapons-grade material needed for one bomb. To produce plutonium, Groves selected the semidesert banks of the Columbia River at a site named Hanford, in open country of south-central Washington State. At this remote location, the Manhattan Project constructed several uranium-fuel piles in which uranium in sealed aluminum cylinders would be bombarded by neutrons from the pile long enough to "transmute" the original element into Pu-239, which would then be separated by chemical processes.

With work progressing slowly on the two major production facilities, the Manhattan Project's civilian scientific director, University of California and California Institute of Technology physicist J. Robert Oppenheimer, one of America's most towering intellects, brought his leading scientists together at a remote former boys' school at Los Alamos atop a mesa northwest of Santa Fe, New Mexico. The group assembled there was as exotic as the isotopes they had been charged to work with. In addition to the European émigrés such as Hungarian physicists Leo Szilard and Edward Teller, there were brilliant young American scientists drawn from the country's leading academic and industrial laboratories. The Los Alamos facility was the single most secret U.S. military installation in the world. Not only was the entire mesa top fenced and patrolled by military police, but an inner fenced and guarded perimeter isolated the laboratories from the living quarters and dining facilities.

In April 1943, the scientific team assembled on "the Hill" had begun to seriously focus their attention on producing practical nuclear bombs from the fissionable material they hoped would soon be available at Oak Ridge and Hanford. One of the first hurdles the Los Alamos scientists had to surmount was the size and weight of the eventual bomb. Their efforts would be in vain unless they could design a weapon small and light enough for an existing Allied bomber to carry to a distant target. Although the proven British Avro Lancaster and the experimental American B-32 could carry very large bombs, the most suitable bomber was the Boeing B-29 Superfort, which would come into production in fall 1943. Therefore, "the atom bomb was tailored to fit the plane rather than the reverse."[17] This meant the bomb would have to fit the dimensions of a B-29 bomb bay, no greater than 12 by 6 by 6 feet (depending on loading points and sway braces), and not exceed five tons.

By fall 1944, more than 100,000 scientists, engineers, and workers were secretly employed in the Manhattan Project, all contained within "compartmentalized" security buffers, so that only a few leaders understood the true nature of the gigantic, expensive effort. Such an endeavor required unprecedented organizational abilities and discipline not normally available in the civilian world—or, for that matter, in the peacetime military.

The process advanced ponderously, slowly producing U-235 and Pu-239. At Los Alamos, the scientists and design engineers struggled at their tasks. The original brute-force theory of violently slamming two subcritical masses of fissionable material together to form one explosive supercritical mass was determined through bench-top laboratory experiments to be practical for a uranium bomb. From this work evolved the "gun barrel" concept in which a smaller lump of U-235 would be fired at a velocity of at least 2,000 feet per second into a larger subcritical mass to spark the nuclear blast. It was discovered relatively early in the engineering work at Los Alamos that an actual artillery tube would in fact be the ideal firing mechanism in the core of the U-235 bomb.

But exhaustive calculations revealed that this method would not prove practical for a plutonium bomb, which would need a faster collision velocity and thus required a more complex method of reaching critical mass. Then Hungarian-born American John von Neumann, a mathematician from Princeton's Institute for Advanced Study, presented a novel solution. Rather than blast one subcritical mass of plutonium into another, why not use conventional explosives to squeeze a hollow shell of plutonium into a tiny ball that would reach critical mass as the shock waves from the external explosive sphere drove relentlessly inward?[18]

In December 1944, Manhattan Project scientists estimated the explosive potential of the uranium bomb to be at least 10,000 tons (or 10 kilotons) of TNT high explosives, while estimates on the plutonium weapon varied anywhere from 500 tons to 2.5 kilotons of TNT. The designs for the two different nuclear weapons were basically completed in spring 1945. "Little Boy," the simpler U-235 bomb, would be a relatively straightforward gun-barrel device in which one heavy cylindrical plug of weapons-grade uranium would be fired down a six-foot section of modified naval cannon into a heavier nest of stacked target rings at the barrel's opposite end. Oppenheimer and his staff considered this method so inherently reliable that it was not deemed necessary to test the weapon before use in combat. All Little Boy needed for final assembly was enough U-235 from Oak Ridge to shape into the core components.

But because the implosion technique, which involved an intricate layering of explosive "lenses" stacked around the Pu-239 core, was anything but straightforward, this spherical "Fat Man"–design plutonium bomb would have to be tested before dropping.[19] And there would not be enough U-235 or Pu-239 available from Oak Ridge and Hanford until summer 1945. By that time, it was clear the enemy against whom the atomic bomb would be used would not be the Nazis, whose threat had engendered the Manhattan Project, but the Japanese.

As Gordon Thomas and Max Morgan Witts describe in *Enola Gay*, on September 1, 1944, a husky Army Air Force lieutenant colonel named Paul Tibbets met with the commanding general of the U.S. Second Air Force, Uzal G. Ent, Navy Captain William Parsons, and the youthful Harvard physicist Norman Ramsey at Ent's Colorado Springs headquarters office. Parsons, who had been introduced as an "explosives expert," and Ramsey quizzed Tibbets briefly about his knowledge of atomic energy. Tibbets was a veteran pilot with extensive combat time in the ETO who had returned to the States to test-fly the new, accident-prone B-29. He was not a scientist, but he answered the questions as best he could, noting that the Germans had been trying to "split the atom" before the war.

Ramsey was impressed. Then the young professor added, "The United States has now split an atom. We are making a bomb based on that. The bomb will be so powerful it will explode with the force of twenty thousand tons of conventional high explosives." (That was the then-current Manhattan Project estimate for the U-235 bomb.)

General Ent then turned to Tibbets. "Colonel, you have been selected to drop that bomb."[20]

That December, Tibbets officially organized the 509th Composite Group, a hybrid unit built on a squadron of specially modified Superforts similar in appearance to the B-29Bs of the 315th, a squadron of transports, and extensive ground support. The 509th was meant to operate independently as a self-contained unit. For both security and practical considerations, Tibbets's group was attached to the 315th Wing, in which *The Boomerang* also flew. Although the 509th's bombers lacked the distinctive winglike Eagle radar antenna, they had no protruding top or belly gun turrets and could be mistaken for the 315th's B-29Bs or photoreconnaissance planes if observed from a distance by an Axis agent. The new unit's thirty-six modified Superforts also had more powerful fuel-injection engines with reversible-pitch propellers, which allowed the planes to take off with unusually heavy loads and land on shorter fields in the event of an emergency.

Flying out of Wendover Field, Utah, during the winter and spring of 1945, the 509th's crews repeatedly practiced dropping large single bombs—filled with concrete ballast—on test ranges in the desert southwest. Some of these bombs were cylindrical, others spherical or pumpkin-shaped. Soon, the 509th's bombardiers could consistently hit a small circular target from an altitude of 30,000 feet.

In March 1945, with Nazi Germany collapsing, it was obvious that the 509th would not be deployed to drop an atomic bomb in the ETO. Instead, the unit's air and ground elements were sent to North Field on Tinian in the Marianas, the island that American engineers had transformed into the largest single military air base complex in the world. Tibbets's airmen would be ready for their mission when they had live bombs to drop on the Empire of Japan.

Secretary of War Henry L. Stimson, who had overseen the development of the atomic bomb from its inception, had not briefed President Truman on the Manhattan Project until April 25, 1945, ten days after Truman had assumed office. Like Truman, Stimson had been a Field Artillery officer in France during World War I. Now they spoke of inconceivably more powerful explosives. Truman grasped immediately that nuclear weapons might hold the potential of overwhelming the stubborn resistance of the Japanese before an invasion of the Home Islands proved necessary. Beyond his preoccupation with American casualties in Okinawa, Truman was deeply troubled by memorandums that former president Herbert Hoover sent Stimson and him in late May concerning probable American losses during the Downfall invasions. Relying on unspecified sources, Hoover, who was normally very well versed on international matters, predicted "500,000 to 1,000,000" American combat deaths. This haunting estimate undoubtedly caused Truman to order the formal White House review of Downfall casualty estimates that took place on June 18.

.   .   .

Pioneering nuclear weapons historian Richard Rhodes has vividly described the frantic atmosphere at Los Alamos during the last months of the war in *The Making of the Atomic Bomb*. The Manhattan Project's scientific and engineering teams had finally perfected their implosion detonation technique by May 1945. Now they had to wait for the fissionable plutonium core material to arrive for processing from Hanford. General Groves and Robert Oppenheimer hoped to conduct the first test at a bleak site of empty New Mexico desert—the Jornada del Muerto, "The Trail of Death"—northwest of Alamogordo on July 4, 1945. But the bomb was not yet ready. President Truman wanted to have a proven, practical bomb in the U.S. arsenal before he left for Potsdam, so that America would not have to accede to unreasonable Soviet political and territorial demands in postwar Europe in order to assure Stalin's participation in the Pacific war before the Downfall invasions.[21] Had the bomb been successfully tested by July 4, it would have given President Harry Truman, who was an old Kansas City poker player, a valued high card on the eve of his departure for Potsdam on July 7. But Groves sent word that the bomb could be ready before mid-July.

On July 15, 1945, the USS *Augusta* with the presidential party aboard made its way slowly up the Schelde Estuary, carefully avoiding buoys marking unexploded mines and sunken ships, and tied up to a hastily repaired bomb-damaged dock in Antwerp at 10:00 A.M. As the President flew toward Gatow Airfield near Berlin that afternoon, passing over wargutted German cities en route, he had heard no news on the success or failure of the first bomb test.

Last-minute difficulties assembling the cast pieces of the bomb's spherical high-explosive outer casing had caused the test firing—codenamed "Trinity"—to be delayed. The new date was July 16, 1945, at 0530 hours mountain war time.

By the hot morning of July 15, the final assembled Fat Man plutonium bomb had been mounted at the top of an oil rig–type tower at the Trinity site's Ground Zero. Hundreds of technicians and scientists took their places at scattered control and observation bunkers, one less than five miles from the bomb tower.

The main body of visitors from the Los Alamos laboratories arrived at their observation site on Compania Hill, twenty miles northwest of

Ground Zero, at 2:00 A.M. Thunderstorms swept across the desert, bringing rain and gusty wind, with lightning illuminating the lines of jagged mountains to the east. But the severe weather had passed to the northwest well before firing time. In S-10000, the control bunker housing the bomb's electrical firing circuits connected to the tower by a long electrical umbilical cord, the countdown began at 5:25 A.M. A green flare arched up in the darkness, signaling observers to begin taking cover. Sirens and more warning rockets continued as firing time approached. Some observers had rubbed their faces with suntan lotion in anticipation of the bomb's flash. Many had pieces of dark welder's glass through which to observe the explosion.

As the final moments ticked off the firing clock in S-10000, Robert Oppenheimer, looking gaunt and exhausted, muttered, "Lord, these affairs are hard on the heart."

In *The Making of the Atomic Bomb,* Richard Rhodes describes in stark detail the first nuclear explosion. Just before 05:30 hours, a web of detonators, evenly spaced on the surface of the high-explosive sphere, fired simultaneously, igniting a complex, converging shock wave that drove relentlessly inward toward the nickel-plated plutonium core. As the core softened and collapsed, the beryllium and polonium initiator released a minuscule shower of sub-atomic particles sufficient to jolt neutrons free from the super-dense "eyeball" of liquefied plutonium. The uncontrolled chain reaction had been triggered. The fission multiplied "its prodigious energy release through eighty generations in millionths of a second, tens of millions of degrees, millions of pounds of pressure. Before the radiation leaked away, conditions within the eyeball briefly resembled the state of the universe moments after its primordial explosion."[22]

To the observers waiting in the predawn desert chill, the first indication that the bomb had fired was an enormous flash of light, so intense it seemed to engulf and invade their bodies. Physicist Edward Teller, watching from Compania Hill twenty miles distant, saw the bomb's initial glare "like opening the curtains of a darkened room to a flood of sunlight." Others felt it was like a giant magnesium flare that seemed to burn a long time, but that actually lasted only moments. A few seconds after the initial flash, a ghastly, churning fireball like a distended "half-risen sun" appeared, surrounded by great swirls of flame. Now the closest observers felt the searing blast of the bomb's thermal pulse, which was painful to the skin, "like opening a hot oven" even to those at Base Camp ten miles from Ground Zero.

The Manhattan Project scientific director, Robert Oppenheimer, was stunned by the enormity of the destructive spectacle. A man with a far-ranging intellect, well read in the world's literature, he suddenly recalled a line from Hindu scripture, the Bhagavad-Gita. In the text, Lord Vishnu slips off the cloak of his human identity and assumes his fearsome multiarmed form to proclaim, "Now I am become Death, the destroyer of worlds."

General Leslie Groves, the hard-driving, practical engineer who had supervised the single most complex scientific and industrial effort in history, was more prosaic. As a mushroom cloud of churning purple and green flames rose high above Ground Zero, Groves turned to his deputy, Brigadier General Thomas Farrell. "The war's over," Groves proclaimed. "One or two of these things and Japan will be finished."[23]

President Harry Truman had arrived at the pleasant village of Babelsberg about twelve miles southeast of Berlin between the shattered German capital and the town of Potsdam. Spread along the thickly wooded shore of the Tetlow Canal and the grassy-banked Griebnitzsee, Babelsberg had been a summer resort popular with Berlin's upper classes and the site of the prewar German movie industry. The President's quarters were in the "Little White House," a yellow stucco three-story structure surrounded by trees on the edge of the lake. Prime Minister Churchill's residence for the conference was in another large house about two blocks away, while Marshal Stalin had taken quarters farther up the road toward the Cecilienhof Palace, where the formal conference sessions would be held.

Because Stalin's armored train had not yet arrived from Moscow, Truman took the opportunity to tour the ruins of Berlin on July 16. That evening a brief, cryptic message arrived through War Department channels from General Groves concerning the Trinity test firing: "Operated on this morning. Diagnosis not yet complete, but results seem satisfactory and already exceed expectations."[24] Further messages arrived in the coming hours revealing the scope of the explosion—a blast of fifteen to twenty kilotons—and making it clear to Truman that "the United States had in its possession an explosive force of unparalleled power," as he later wrote in his memoir.[25]

The next day, Truman conferred in Babelsberg with Secretary of War Stimson, Secretary of State Byrnes, Admiral Leahy, General Marshall, General Arnold, and Admiral King to review military strategy in view of the bomb's now-proven power. Truman's advisers were unprepared at this juncture to recommend immediate use of the weapon against Japan and advised that, at least until the Trinity test could be further analyzed, America proceed with existing plans for Operation Olympic.

The Potsdam Conference of the Big Three leaders was centered on a large round table in one of the four wings of the Cecilienhof Palace, the former country estate of Crown Prince Wilhelm. For seven days, Truman, Churchill, and Stalin and their large delegations hammered through the difficult questions concerning the fate of tens of millions in Europe. From the perspective of the Americans and British, the war in Europe had been fought to secure the principles of the Atlantic Charter, which guaranteed democracy and human rights. For the Soviet Union, the Great Patriotic War had been an anti-Fascist crusade. Stalin's victorious armies had brought in their wake pro-Moscow socialist governments in exile. The case of the Moscow-installed client government in Poland was of particular sensitivity to President Truman because of the large number of Democratic Polish-American voters. But the question of how to resettle millions of displaced persons and repatriate vast numbers of prisoners of war was almost as troubling. The issue of war reparations to be imposed on the defeated Axis was also knotty and contentious.

As the days of the conference ticked by, the individual delegations met in camera or, in the case of the British and Americans, conferred apart from the Soviets. The senior American and British military staff at Potsdam was preoccupied with the ongoing war in the Pacific. One of the prime strategic considerations in defeating Japan was the ominous question that—even if a bloody invasion of the main Japanese islands brought about a collapse of the Imperial government—invasion might not necessarily "obviate the necessity of defeating Japanese forces elsewhere" in their far-flung empire. The several million members of the Japanese Imperial Navy and Army still stationed in bypassed garrisons in the Solomons, to Burma, all the way to the border of Siberia, might simply refuse to surrender given their warrior tradition. At Winston Churchill's behest, the British Army chief of staff, Sir Alan Brooke, suggested modifying the Allies' inflexible unconditional surrender terms so that Japanese resistance would not be "unduly prolonged in outlying areas."[26]

No doubt the British and their Australian colleagues were deeply concerned about dislodging stubbornly resisting Japanese forces from Malaya, as well as the adjacent Netherlands East Indies, territories where tens of thousands of Allied prisoners of war and civilian internees languished in captivity. In this regard, the British had to consider the projected high casualties of Operation Zipper, the recapture of Singapore and Malaya scheduled to begin in September.

But modifying strategic goals was a political, not a purely military, question, as General Marshall pointed out to his Allied colleagues.

Truman had planned to release at Potsdam a declaration from the three major Allied powers—the United States, Great Britain, and China— then at war with Japan, which would specifically inform the Japanese as to the terms they must meet to avoid utter destruction. This declaration, however, would not reveal the fact that America now possessed nuclear weapons. Instead, a draft text simply stated that Japan now stood on the "threshold of annihilation."[27] In effect, the multiple terms of the draft declaration already *were* a modification of the unconditional surrender imposed on Germany and Italy.

Small numbers of Americans at Potsdam, as well as Churchill and a few in his delegation, knew of the Manhattan Project and the success of the Trinity test firing. It was not considered practical, however, to either specifically warn the Japanese about the existence of the atomic bomb or to arrange a demonstration firing of a Trinity-type device in a remote area, as some concerned scientists in the Manhattan Project had recommended. Plutonium was still too scarce to expend in such a demonstration—and what was becoming available was destined for the tactical weapons Marshall planned to use during the Downfall invasions—and there was always the possibility a device would fail where the Trinity explosion had succeeded. Further, Japanese fighters might shoot down the bomber carrying the demonstration bomb. The prowar faction among Japanese militarists might also simply refuse to be impressed, no matter how devastating the demonstration. Or, following the revelations about the Bataan Death March, and atrocities against British prisoners on the Burma–Thailand railroad, some feared the Japanese might concentrate large numbers of Allied prisoners of war at the designated demonstration site.[28]

General George Marshall considered the atomic bomb a combat weapon that would hasten Japan's inevitable collapse and greatly reduce casualties by eliminating the need for the Downfall invasions—and possibly for the increasingly problematic Soviet intervention. Truman concurred.

However, there were influential members of the Truman administration who believed that any Allied declaration should include an explicit guarantee that Hirohito would remain on the throne. The draft declaration favored by Stimson stipulated that Japan would become "a constitutional monarchy under the present dynasty" but be freed of control by the militarists. This was a provision that Under Secretary of State Joseph C. Grew strongly favored. He was a former longtime ambassador to Japan with strong prewar ties to the Imperial Palace who felt it imperative that the Allies not try to compel Japan to abandon their national polity as a surrender condition.

But other presidential advisers were opposed to Grew's language in the Stimson draft. The Japanese, they said, might interpret calling for a "constitutional monarchy under the present dynasty" to mean the Allies planned to arrest or execute Hirohito—it had already been announced that the victorious Allies would try Nazi war criminals—and replace him with a puppet from the Imperial family; or that the Allies intended simply to preserve untouched the existing "institution of the Emperor and Emperor worship"—an act that would not be politically acceptable in any Allied nation.[29]

Meanwhile, the conference ground along, covering such far-ranging and diverse questions as postwar borders in the Middle East and access for the Western Allies to the "puppet" states the Soviet Union had installed in Eastern Europe. It became clear that Soviet intransigence in Europe might be a precursor to what the Allies could expect if Stalin's huge Red Army invaded Japanese-occupied Manchuria and southern Sakhalin Island in early August, as he had promised. The question facing Truman was whether the Soviet forces would be any more inclined to leave their Asian conquests than they were occupied territory in Europe. And he was determined to resist any permanent Soviet expansion that would follow a relatively easy defeat of Japanese forces already weakened by the long bloodletting in the Pacific. Truman's concern had been growing since presidential assistant Harry Hopkins had reported during a mission to Moscow that the Soviet Union would expect to share in the actual occupation of Japan just as the Allied powers had established their occupation sectors in Germany. American unease about eventual Soviet expansion into Japanese-occupied Chinese territory had been growing since 1943.[30] Now Truman's chief military advisers concurred that dropping the atomic bomb on Japan might obviate the need for Soviet intervention in Asia.[31]

The British delegation required what they hoped would be a brief recess so that Churchill and Foreign Secretary Anthony Eden could return to London to learn the results of the general election, a delayed process caused by the need to count the huge absentee military vote. (Winston Churchill and his Conservative ministers would not return to Potsdam. The British delegation that re-joined the conference on July 28 was led by the new Labour prime minister, Clement Attlee, and foreign secretary, Ernest Bevin.)

On July 24, Truman decided to reveal to Stalin that America now possessed the atomic bomb. But the President did so in a singularly oblique manner. When the plenary session adjourned that afternoon, Truman got up and approached Stalin near the big round table. There, as Truman would later write, "I casually mentioned to Stalin that we had a new weapon of unusual destructive force."[32] Other accounts state that Truman directed the words "a very powerful explosive which we are going to use against the Japanese and we think it will end the war" to Stalin's interpreter. In any event, the Soviet leader did not seem overly interested. He simply told Truman that he was glad to hear the news and hoped that the Americans would make "good use" of the new weapon against the Japanese. Truman did not specify the nature of the explosive, but other officials present verified that Truman's account was basically accurate.[33]

The reason for Stalin's reticence was probably the fact that the Soviets had an active espionage program in the United States that had penetrated the Manhattan Project. German-born Los Alamos physicist Klaus Fuchs, a naturalized British citizen, had been spying on the Project for Soviet intelligence for several years.[34] At the time Truman and Stalin spoke at Potsdam, the Soviet Union had already received considerable design information about the American weapon. When Stalin returned to the Soviet villa, he immediately told Soviet Foreign Minister Vycheslav Molotov about Truman's new weapon.

Molotov was scornful. "Let them," he said. "We'll have to talk it over with Kurchatov and get him to speed things up."

This was a reference to Igor Kurchatov, who had been secretly working on a Soviet atomic bomb for several years.[35]

Meanwhile, at Potsdam, a debate had been underway between two of Truman's principal advisers, Secretary of War Stimson and Secretary of State Byrnes. As late as Monday, July 23, Stimson was still strongly recommending language in the proposed Potsdam Declaration that would reassure the Japanese they could retain their emperor. Stimson suggested a revision reading that the Allies would "prosecute the war against Japan until she ceases to resist." But Byrnes vehemently defended unconditional surrender, reminding Truman of the earlier U.S. public opinion polls that only a tiny percentage of Americans thought Hirohito should stay on the throne.

Truman chose to eliminate any direct or implied reference to the Emperor in the Potsdam Declaration.

While these deliberations unfolded, Truman made firm his previous decision to use the atomic bomb against Japan as soon as the weapon was ready for combat. This decision coincided with the mounting Ultra intelligence reports that the Japanese military was reinforcing Kyushu with a steady progression of large, well-equipped formations. This undercut General Marshall's assurance to Truman at the June 18 White House meeting that the American Air Force and Navy could completely interdict enemy reinforcements to the island.

Secretary Stimson's staff had prepared a list of potential target cities. Truman ruled out one, Kyoto, the old Imperial capital of Japan, when Stimson himself indicated its great cultural and religious significance. The military staff now narrowed the list to four potential targets, arrayed by priority: Hiroshima, Kokura, Niigata, and Nagasaki. Truman had insisted that each city be a "military target," and a case was made that they fit this criterion.[36] Kokura, for example, had multiple large arsenals, while Hiroshima, headquarters of the Second Area Army, was crowded with soldiers and was the port of embarkation for troops reinforcing the Ketsu-go defenses of Kyushu. Nagasaki, however, was a minor port that had been all but blockaded by the American mining effort, and was also near a number of Allied prisoner-of-war camps.[37]

On July 25, 1945, Truman instructed General Marshall to send orders through the Air Force chain of command to the 509th Composite Group on Tinian to employ the atomic bomb against Japan. Marshall immediately contacted his deputy, General Thomas T. Handy, who wrote formal orders to General Carl Spaatz, Commanding General, United States Army Strategic Air Forces based in the Marianas. The message read in part that the 509th would "deliver [drop] its first special bomb as weather will permit visual bombing after 3 August 1945" on one of the four selected targets. "Additional bombs will be delivered on the above targets as soon as made ready by the project staff."[38] (The plutonium core for a third atomic bomb would be ready to fly to Tinian around August 15. Because "production was going up on a very sharp curve," about "seventeen" Fat Boy bombs would be available for combat by the end of the year.[39])

On the morning of July 16, 1945, the cruiser USS *Indianapolis* had left the Navy pier in Oakland carrying a special cargo to Tinian on the other side of the Pacific. A long, heavy crate was secured to the deck of the hangar bay and a mysterious steel canister disappeared into the confines of "officers' country," which was off-limits to enlisted sailors.

The crate contained the specially modified cannon barrel, the canister the uranium projectile for the Little Boy bomb's core. Ten days later the cruiser reached Tinian and proceeded to unload its vital cargo, slinging the crate and canister precariously into a landing barge rising and falling fifty feet below in the swell alongside the anchored warship's steep hull. The cruiser drew too much water to moor at the wharf in the inner harbor, which the Navy had dredged for shallower draft vessels. So for several anxious minutes the fruits of almost a billion dollars and tens of thousands of man-hours hung suspended over the Tinian lagoon by half-inch steel cable.

By the end of the torrid afternoon, Manhattan Project engineers on Tinian had taken possession of their crucial bomb components. The 509th Composite Group was finally prepared for its unique mission.

As Truman's biographer, David McCullough, has convincingly shown, the President "never seriously considered not using the bomb" if dropping it meant ending the war before the Olympic invasion. Even though it was well known that Japan had faced military defeat in the traditional sense of the term since its fleet was decimated in 1944, their resistance stiffened sharply as American forces neared the Home Islands: "In the three months since Truman took office, American battle casualties in the Pacific were nearly half the total from three years of war in the Pacific. The nearer victory came, the heavier the price in blood. And whatever the projected toll in American lives in an invasion, it was too high if it could be avoided."[40]

After rather laborious long-distance telegraphic consultation with Chinese leader Chiang Kai-shek, the Allies were prepared on the evening of July 26, 1945, to issue their Potsdam Declaration, which was actually transmitted from the Little White House in Babelsberg to Washington. There the Office of War Information immediately began to broadcast the message directly to Japan, in both Japanese and English. The State Department translated formal versions of the Declaration text to the government of Japan, using the diplomatic intermediaries of the Swiss and Swedish embassies in both countries. (August 3, 1945, the date Truman chose to release delivery authority for the first atomic bomb mission, was one week after the Allies issued the Potsdam Declaration.)

The Potsdam Declaration can succinctly be described as a mixture of encouragement and threat. Because the Soviet Union was still officially neutral toward Japan, it was not mentioned in the Declaration. After an introductory article in which it was stated that the United States, the Republic of China, and Great Britain had agreed that "Japan shall be given an opportunity to end this war," the Declaration continued that Japan faced the Allies' land, sea, and air forces, which would be employed against Japan "until she ceases to resist." The third article reminded the Japanese of the "futile and senseless German resistance to the might of the aroused free peoples of the world," which was now converging on Japan. The time had come for Japan to decide to continue under the control of the "self-willed militaristic advisers whose unintelligent calculations have brought the Empire of Japan to the threshold of annihilation, or whether she will follow the path of reason."

Next, the Allies stated their terms, adding, "We will not deviate from them. There are no alternatives. We shall brook no delay."

The terms called for a complete and permanent abolition of Japanese militarism that would help establish a "new order of peace, security and justice." Until that new order was established and Japan was disarmed, "points in Japanese territory shall be occupied to secure the achievement of the basic objectives we are here setting forth." Japanese sovereignty would be limited to the four major Home Islands. After being completely disarmed, Japanese military forces would be permitted to return to their homes "with the opportunity to lead peaceful and productive lives . . . We do not intend that the Japanese shall be enslaved as a race or destroyed as a nation, but stern justice shall be meted out to all war criminals, including those who have visited cruelties upon our prisoners."

The Japanese government would revive and encourage "democratic tendencies" among its people. Peaceful industry and trade would be permitted. The occupying forces would be withdrawn once these terms had been met and a peaceful and responsible government had been established "in accordance with the freely expressed will of the Japanese people."

The Potsdam Declaration's final term was forceful: "We call upon the Government of Japan to proclaim now the unconditional surrender of all Japanese armed forces, and to provide proper and adequate assurances of their good faith in such action. The alternative for Japan is prompt and utter destruction."[41]

There was no mention in the Potsdam Declaration's final text of Emperor Hirohito or of the atomic bomb.

CHAPTER FOUR

THE BOOMERANG
AND *ENOLA GAY*

O N   T I N I A N ,   T H E   5 0 9 T H   C O M P O S I T E   G R O U P   was installed in a separate, high-security area near the taxiways and hardstands of the veteran 313th Wing at the small island's North Field. As soon as the Group had arrived in early July 1945, it was clear from their highly modified Superforts and the fact that the unit did not fly regular combat missions that the 509th had a secret assignment. And the fact that the Group's planes disappeared almost daily on short practice runs did not endear the unit to the other aircrews that had to sweat out the long combat missions to the Empire.

Historian Peter Wyden has noted in *Day One, Hiroshima and After* that the newly arrived airmen were treated scornfully by their colleagues on the base. Soon other Superfort groups of the 313th and 58th Bomb Wings were serenading the men of the 509th with a scornful ditty:

Into the air the secret rose
Where they're going nobody knows . . .
Don't ask us about results or such
Unless you want to get in Dutch.
But take it from one who is sure of the score,
The 509th is winning the war. . . .

This derision was often accompanied by a hail of rocks thrown over the tall barbed-wire fence separating the 509th's compound from the rest of North Field.[1]

At the end of July, Paul Tibbets, now a full colonel, ordered the short milk runs to the battered Japanese garrison islands of Rota and Guguan replaced with combat training missions to the Empire. The 509th's modified Superforts flew twelve of these strikes in four days during the last week of the month, sending two to six planes against each target. The missions were meant to replicate as closely as possible the actual delivery of either Little Boy or Fat Man. Each mission was flown at high altitude (above 29,000 feet), and the drop of the single 10,000-pound blockbuster-type weapon, either cylindrical or spherical, was performed with visual sighting. The moment the massive bomb had dropped away, each aircraft commander executed a radical 155-degree banking downwind turn to achieve maximum "slant" distance from the exploding bomb, a maneuver that usually took the Superfort about fifty seconds and carried it ten miles from the aiming point.

For security reasons, Tibbets himself did not fly these strikes. He was the only airman in the 509th who knew the unit's true assignment. When he did fly to Japan, it would be on the first combat drop of an atomic bomb.

While the American airmen of the 509th Composite Group flew their practice missions, the Japanese press railed against the Empire's relentless enemies and called on the citizens of Japan to give their all to "protect the kokutai."[2]

The Japanese government received the official text of the Potsdam Declaration on July 27 with a marked lack of interest. At the direction of the Suzuki cabinet, the domestic press followed the lead of the Domei News Agency by publishing a heavily edited, abbreviated version of the Declaration. After almost a day had elapsed, War Minister Korechika Anami and his confederate, Navy Chief of Staff Toyota, convinced Suzuki to formally reject the Potsdam Declaration. Anami and the two service chiefs of staff were adamant that the Allies' terms were "too dishonorable."[3]

Premier Suzuki did so at a stage-managed press conference on the afternoon of July 28. He denounced the Potsdam Declaration as a virtual "rehash" of the Allies' unrealistic demands following the Cairo Conference. The government of Japan, he said, intended to "ignore" the Potsdam Declaration as not worthy of consideration. The term Suzuki used was *mokusatsu*, which literally means "to kill with silence."[4]

Prime Minister Suzuki believed that this was not an arbitrary or overtly hazardous diplomatic position from the Japanese perspective. His government was still awaiting word from Stalin and Molotov on the Emperor's request to send Prince Konoye as his special peace envoy. And the two Soviet leaders had not yet returned to Moscow from Potsdam.

But for Foreign Minister Shigenori Togo, the Potsdam Declaration represented the best terms that "Japan could hope for, the war situation being what it was." He also felt that, since the Potsdam Declaration covered such a wide area, the Japanese had room to negotiate and that it was unwise to reject the ultimatum out of hand.[5]

Navy Minister Mitsumasa Yonai, although an alleged pro-peace moderate, was inclined to wait the Allies out. He told his secretary, "Churchill has fallen. America is beginning to be isolated. The government therefore will ignore it [the Potsdam Declaration]. There is no need to rush."[6]

Yonai was tragically mistaken.

At Potsdam, Harry Truman did not publicly reveal any emotion over the contemptuous Japanese rejection of the declaration. Instead, he pressed on through the simultaneously tedious and tense negotiations with Stalin. Truman had issued his orders to the field commanders on the use of the atomic bomb. The Japanese action only seemed to confirm the validity of his decision.

While Truman was in Germany and the *Indianapolis* was en route to Tinian, the U-235 "target" section of the Little Boy bomb, consisting of three heavy rings, was loaded aboard a C-54 transport at Wendover Air Base to begin the long flight to the island.

After successfully delivering the Little Boy bomb components to Tin-

ian, the *Indianapolis* was torpedoed by the Japanese Imperial Navy submarine *I-58* on July 29. The American warship, which had survived a
kamikaze hit off Okinawa, was now en route to the Philippines. Struck by
at least two powerful Long Lance torpedoes, the *Indianapolis* sank in minutes—too quickly for the crew to transmit an SOS. After enduring four days
in the shark-infested tropical water, only 316 of the ship's crew survived,
leaving behind 883 dead sailors. The war in the Pacific was far from over.

In their book, *Enola Gay,* authors Thomas and Witts describe the events
before the first nuclear bomb mission. On Tinian, Manhattan Project technicians had completed the preliminary assembly of the Little Boy uranium
bomb. It would be flown to the target with its firing circuits "safed" from
accident, and Navy Captain William S. Parsons, the man who had greeted
Paul Tibbets in Colorado Springs in September 1944, would complete the
final arming of the bomb en route to the Empire. This was considered prudent because a takeoff accident involving the bombing aircraft might trigger a nuclear blast that would wipe out all of North Field and disable the
American B-29 campaign for months. But even with the bomb unarmed, an
accident on takeoff might still cause the atomic bomb to explode.

On August 2, 1945, Field Orders No. 13 selected Hiroshima as the primary target, with Kokura as the secondary. The bombing aircraft would be
part of a group of three B-29s. One of the others would be a photo plane,
while the third would drop instruments by parachute to measure the radiation and other effects of the blast.

Three days later, on the hot afternoon of August 5, technicians used
a tractor to tow a tarpaulin-draped trolley, guarded by heavily armed military police, to the hardstand of the *Enola Gay*, the Superfort Paul Tibbets
had selected as the strike aircraft and named for his mother. Takeoff was
scheduled for 0245 local time August 6, with bomb away at 0815 over
Hiroshima. Tibbets had briefed the crews of the mission aircraft that they
would be delivering a unique bomb with an unprecedented explosive blast.

As historians Thomas and Witts describe, Captain Parsons was more
explicit. "The bomb you are going to drop is something new in the history
of warfare," he said. "It is the most destructive weapon ever produced. We
think it will knock out almost everything within a three-mile area."

Yet even at this late hour, neither Tibbets nor Parsons revealed the
source of that explosive power.

At 0242 on August 6, 1945, Paul Tibbets swung the *Enola Gay* onto the active runway. With almost 7,000 gallons of fuel, the five-ton bomb, and twelve men on board, the bomber was dangerously close to exceeding its maximum possible takeoff weight. Tibbets's copilot, Captain Robert Lewis, was nervous, as was the rest of the crew. Tibbets had not told them that his intention was to hold the bomber down on the runway as long as possible in order to achieve maximum airspeed before attempting takeoff.

Tibbets advanced the throttles full forward and released the brakes. The big bomber trundled slowly forward, the four engines roaring. Jeep lights marked the end of the long runway. With the bomber careering through the darkness, those lights seemed to grow larger and larger without the plane gaining sufficient liftoff speed.

"She's too heavy!" Lewis yelled over the intercom.

But Tibbets remained silent, his eyes fixed on Jeep lights at the end of the runway.

Lewis's hands hovered over his own control wheel. But Tibbets ordered him away. With no runway pavement left beneath the wheels, Tibbets pulled his yoke toward his chest, the nose tilted gently upward, and the bomber cleared the ground. The *Enola Gay* was en route to Hiroshima.[7]

2320 HOURS, 5 AUGUST 1945

Three hours before the *Enola Gay* took off from Tinian, a stream of B-29Bs from the 315th Wing droned north through the summer night. The slender moon had set, but now heat lightning revealed the humps of the Japanese Home Islands ahead. Aboard *The Boomerang*, the ten young crewmen tried to shake off the fatigue of the seven-hour flight from Guam and prepare for the challenge of bombing their target in the face of possibly intense enemy resistance.

In the crowded compartment behind the two pilots and the flight engineer, First Lieutenant Tony Cosola leaned forward in the faint red glow of the chart table light, deftly plotting his last star sight. Then he double-checked the airspeed indicator and compass and squeezed his throat intercom microphone.

"Estimate landfall twenty-six minutes."

In less than half an hour, *The Boomerang* would reach the south coast of Shikoku, smallest of the Home Islands, and proceed northwest above the Inland Sea toward Honshu.

"Roger," the aircraft commander, First Lieutenant Carl Schahrer, acknowledged from the port-side seat in the greenhouse cockpit. "On the ball, everybody," he told his crew. "We're in long fighter range now, and we know they've got us on their radar."

As the bomber slowly climbed, tail gunner Sid Siegel crawled back to his lonely position at the plane's extreme aft end.

During the premission briefing at Northwest Field on Guam, the Wing intelligence officer had estimated that there would "probably" not be much Japanese night fighter resistance as the bomber stream entered the Inland Sea. This was because enemy air defense headquarters would not yet know American intentions, and thus the bombers' routes. But as the Superforts approached the Ube Coal Liquefaction Company synthetic oil plant, Intel had predicted that as many as twenty radar-equipped fighters would almost certainly rise to intercept the 110 American bombers. Further, the flow of the bomber stream required a breakaway from the bomb run and a route south to land's end on the coast of Kyushu for the 1,500-mile return leg of the mission that would expose the Superforts to thirty more minutes of fighter harassment and possible flak from the steadily growing Japanese ground forces there. The Japanese Second General Army Headquarters in Hiroshima, sixty miles north of Ube on the Inland Sea, received radio intercepts and radar-tracking reports that the 315th Wing was inbound well before the stream of B-29Bs neared the target.

Sergeant Jim Smith flexed his cramped shoulders and unsnapped the nylon-web seat belt. In the pale gleam of his radio dials, he sorted through the canvas bag on the vibrating aluminum deck that held his flak jacket, chest-pack parachute, and steel helmet. After groping in the dark to check that his one-man life raft pack was correctly snapped to his quick-release parachute harness, Smith pulled on the heavy, armor-plated flak vest and made sure his steel helmet was at the top of the bag. Satisfied that his equipment was ready for combat, he resnapped the seat belt and clamped on the earphones again. Under the weight of the flak jacket, spasms again seized his shoulders and back. In the tail, Sid Siegel tried unsuccessfully to adjust his flak jacket in the claustrophobic compartment, but he gave up and continued the painstaking task of tuning his APQ-15 short-range fire-control radar.

The Boomerang's crew was now ready for combat. Jim Smith sat in the noisy darkness, trying to stay alert but also to dampen the adrenaline spiking through his fatigue, which he recognized as the precursor of useless fear. Once they were into the searchlights and flak, and the Jap night fighters came slashing past, everyone on board would deal with his own nerves, and he knew no one would panic. They would all do their jobs. Now there remained about ten minutes before making landfall. And Smith had to keep his station, monitoring the VHF watch frequency to listen for distress calls from other bombers ahead and behind them out there in the darkness. If he did receive a Mayday call, he might be lucky enough to get those poor guys' ditching coordinates, which he could relay to the Super Dumbo search-and-rescue planes.

As *The Boomerang* continued its slow climb, burdened by more than 3,000 gallons of gasoline and nine tons of 500-pound high-explosive bombs, Smith removed one earphone and listened to the steady beat of the big engines. They sounded good, and he was able to purge his mind of images of flaming crankshafts slicing through the bomber's wing spars like a welder's torch and concentrate on his duty.

"Estimate IP six minutes," Ginster called, looking up from his radarscope. *The Boomerang* was approaching its Initial Point on the islet of Hime Jima for the run in to the target near Ube on the coastline ahead.

Jim Smith's vivid memories of *The Boomerang*'s first seven missions to the Empire pulsed and waned in sudden waves. Since that first night six weeks earlier, the 315th Wing had attacked oil targets north and south along coastal Honshu. Now they were back south above the Inland Sea, on their second mission to Ube to complete the destruction of the refinery begun on July 22, when eighty B-29Bs had battered their way through the turbulence of an intense weather front north of Iwo Jima. Because of that violent weather, the line of Superforts had become strung out, and bombing had not been as accurate as required. So the 315th was returning tonight to finish the job.

On the flight north that July night, Smith had switched his receiver to the Japanese propaganda frequency. The broadcaster had spoken perfect American English, describing the Imperial forces dug in on the homeland and ready for any threat the Americans might present. Then he had recounted the heavy losses Japanese air defenses had inflicted on the Far Eastern Air Forces' B-24s and B-25s striking Kyushu from the new U.S. bases on Okinawa. "And we will be more than ready for the so-called 'Superforts' we know are on the way from the Marianas tonight." He had proceeded to list the large number of B-29s from each wing and group that had supposedly been shot down in the previous several days. Smith had no way of knowing if any of this propaganda was true. His main responsibility in listening was to learn if the Japanese had discovered the 315th Bomb Wing's B-29s had been stripped of defensive armament. The broadcast had ended with the propagandist becoming progressively more arrogant. But he had made no mention of the 315th.

Now, on August 5, Smith left the radio operator's station, slid inside the tunnel, and eased his head under the navigator's astrodome. His combat position would be to act as the fourth observer, augmenting tail gunner Sid Siegel and the two side scanners. As Smith groped his way in the darkness, the eleventh man on board tonight, the gruff, taciturn colonel from XXI Bomber Command who had been sleeping with his back against the flight-deck bulkhead, roused himself, pulled on a flak jacket, and sat back again. *I just hope he's not a jinx,* Smith thought, thrusting his head under the Plexiglas dome.

Probing shafts of searchlights cut the scattered clouds ahead. Most were glaring white, but two had a cooler, greenish cast, reportedly the color associated with antiaircraft radar.

"Rope," Schahrer called to the scanners.

In the aft compartment, Leffler and Carlson thrust one cylindrical bundle after another through their flare tubes.

Everyone in the plane was tense. Radar-controlled flak was not good. Although *The Boomerang's* crew had not seen it, many of the Wing's airmen recalled the night of July 25–26, when radar-directed searchlights near Kawasaki pinioned Captain Henry C. Dillingham's plane. Despite the pilot's violent evasive action, the ship took a direct hit, exploded in flame, and fell from the sky. There were no survivors.

Now, approaching Ube, Smith swiveled beneath the curved Plexiglas. The night sky seemed remarkably transparent: CAVU (Clear And Visibility Unlimited). In the starlight, enemy fighters would have no problem spotting the stream of silvery bombers. But at least the Superforts had been given one modification to help even the odds. The bellies of the Wing's planes had all recently been painted flat black to cut down on searchlight reflection. That paint job, of course, meant nothing to radar.

A distinctly green searchlight stabbed the sky ahead. "Keep up the rope," Schahrer ordered, his voice now strained.

As Schahrer spoke, Smith saw his first enemy aircraft of the night. "Fighter, three o'clock high. A big one. Two engines. Could be a Nick."

"Roger," Schahrer said, his voice again dry and precise. "Heads up, everybody. Call the shot for Sid if he gets one."

Smith watched the big twin-engine fighter roll into its attack from high above the starboard wing. The plane was diving now. As it grew larger in the starlight, he saw that the fighter was indeed a Kawasaki KI.45 Toryu ("Dragon Slayer"), the premier night fighter of the Japanese Army Air Force. The fighter's armament included a single, slow-firing 37mm cannon and two 20mm cannons. Hits from any of those guns would be devastating to *The Boomerang*.[8] But tonight the Nick pilot was not lucky. He began firing at extreme range and had misjudged the bomber's speed. The stream of thick reddish tracers wobbled through the night, then disappeared harmlessly several hundred yards ahead. The fighter followed.

"I've got a single-engine job off the port wing, pacing us as usual," Leffler reported.

"He's out of range," Smith confirmed, his words almost squeaky from taut nerves.

"We've got another one to starboard," Carlson called. And then he added, "Make that two over here."

The lead Japanese fighter was definitely bigger than the other two, Smith realized. It was probably a radar-equipped B6N *Tenzan* that was guiding the two smaller planes. Suddenly all three fighters snapped on bright, down-facing white lights. They were keeping formation with *The Boomerang* and signaling its position to flak gunners ahead. As Smith studied the planes, he saw that one had now lit a standard red navigation light port and green light starboard, but the other two displayed the reverse. This was a clever tactic that would make it more difficult for American gunners to track them. *At least they think we still have guns*, Smith thought.

Then, a couple of miles ahead, Smith saw a bizarre sight: A single-engine Japanese fighter blazed with what looked like sheet lightning, then disappeared toward the head of the bomber stream. *What the hell is that?* he wondered. (Later, Intelligence reported that the Japanese had fitted some of their fighters with rocket-assist packs to increase their performance for high-speed attacks on the Superforts.[9])

After escorting the bomber for several minutes, the three fighters climbed away. Smith continued scanning the sky. Suddenly a big twin-engine fighter was on top of them again, boring in from the starboard beam level.

"Fighter, three o'clock, level," he called out.

The plane passed very close, just as a green rocket exploded with a dazzling chartreuse glare 500 yards ahead, filling the nose compartment and flight deck with a ghastly light. Smith was stunned and confused. Had the Nick fired that rocket, or had it come from the ground? He didn't have time to wonder. Flak was bursting exactly at their altitude, glaring blasts that were closing on the plane.

"More rope," Schahrer ordered the two scanners.

"We never stopped, Carl," Leffler reported, his tone confident.

Smith wondered if the stuffed-shirt colonel would take exception to a sergeant addressing his commissioned aircraft commander by his first name. Maybe the officer would become a little less stuffy if the crew had to bail out or ditch in the ocean and they all had to rely on one another to survive. Survival, of course, was a questionable matter. Instinctively, he patted the bulging pockets of the sweaty survival vest under the webbing of his Switlick quick-release parachute harness and the rubbery flap of his inflatable Mae West. In theory, the vest contained everything an airman would need to survive for a few days on land or sea: first-aid kit with morphine, sulfa powder to treat wounds, water-purifying tablets, an extra flashlight, fishing gear, even bird shot to use in his .45-caliber handgun to hunt.

Probing in the darkness, Smith's fingers encountered the coiled shape of the emergency saw. Then he remembered the crew's orientation briefing in June when a Wing intelligence officer had reminded them of the reality they faced. "You will be flying over Japan at night. If you're forced to bail out, chances are you'll be within walking distance of a rice paddy. Dig in for the night." The wide topographical map was painted with fluorescent colors. When illuminated with ultraviolet "black" light in the dim briefing room, the ridges and flatlands stood out in sharp contrast.

"The mud will hide you," the officer continued confidently. "If you're spotted, don't analyze the situation. Shoot first. If you don't, the fourscore and ten they promise you in the Bible will be a lot shorter." Smith understood that the officer was trying to ease the palpable tension in the briefing room with his joke. But Smith hadn't been able to laugh. "Find your way to the coast and steal a boat," the man had advised. "If the boat is chained, use the steel saw in your survival vest. Row out to sea. A U.S. Navy rescue submarine will find you. If the sub can't surface, throw a line around the periscope. The sub will tow you to an area where it's safe to surface. Just stay in the boat, and you'll be on the topside of the sub when it comes up." The crew had looked at each other in disbelief when receiving this officer's advice. But he'd insisted this survival technique was not something out of a Superman comic, and had been subjected to practical tests.

The intelligence officer had ended his briefing with another grim reminder. "If you are captured and interrogated, answer any questions that you can. It may save your life, and you've got to realize their intel people know almost as much about our operation as you do. However, we're gambling that they will not discover we're flying ships stripped of their guns." It was not pleasant for these young men to consider the prospect of Japanese interrogation. "Avoid the subject of the Wing's defensive armament at all cost," the officer continued. "One more thing: Never smile when you are being interrogated. To the Japanese, that means you are making fun of them."

Smith knew he would never smile during Japanese interrogation. He could imagine the techniques they used to extract information from downed American airmen. After months of firebombing, the Japanese would be in no mood to treat prisoners well. Now, wedged beneath the astrodome, he made certain his .45-caliber pistol was tucked inside its waterproof wrapper and buckled securely into the holster on his web belt. He stoically accepted the necessity of using that gun on enemy soldiers or civilians if it meant saving his own or a fellow crewman's life.

"Target bearing three oh five degrees, nine miles," radar operator Ginster reported. He was about to connect the Eagle's synchronous system circuits to Marshall's bombsight.

In the nose, bombardier Marshall saw the distinctive rectangular shape of the Ube Coal Liquefaction Company on a block of reclaimed land where the Utsube River entered the bay. Exploding bombs from the planes ahead rippled in incandescent shock waves, straddling the plant. But there wasn't too much smoke yet. "I can see the target perfectly," Marshall called. "I'm going to bomb visually."

"Roger. Radar standing by." Ginster flicked two switches on his console to disengage the linkage but kept his eyes focused inside the rubber collar of the APQ-7 radarscope, prepared if Marshall needed backup.

Carl Schahrer spoke to Marshall over the shrill noise of the open bomb-bay doors. "It's all yours, Dick."

Marshall leaned over the bombsight, adjusting his tracking knobs. Now the bombardier was flying the plane through the autopilot. The slipstream howled from the open bomb-bay doors as he fine-tuned his visual reticle. The bombsight indices converged, and the red light lit on the flight-deck indicator. The bombs dropped in a tight sequence.

"Breakaway," Schahrer announced, banking sharply left.

"Turning point, heading one nine two. Estimate eleven minutes," navigator Cosola called. This was the shortest route back south over the Inland Sea to landfall on the uninhabited coast of Kyushu between Yukuhashi and Nakatsu, a spot that Intelligence had deemed free of flak concentrations.

As the plane banked away south, Smith watched the tight pattern of their exploding bombs.

"It's a bull's-eye!" Dick Marshall sang out, his voice filled with professional pride.

Hank Leffler and Sid Siegel called exuberant confirmation. But Schahrer's calm, decisive voice immediately changed the mood. "Let's stay on the ball, everybody. We're still over the Empire."

As if arriving on cue, yet another twin-engine night fighter rolled out of the starry sky from high above. For a moment it seemed to be diving straight for them. But then Smith saw that the plane was lining up to attack the Superfort flying just ahead. A bright stream of tracers erupted simultaneously from both the fighter's nose and the bomber's tail guns. The attack ended in seconds.

"Watch that Superfort," Schahrer ordered. "He may be hit."

But the plane ahead droned on.

"Land's end," Ginster announced from his radarscope as *The Boomerang* passed above the dark, mountainous cape at Amae.

Cosola gave the flight crew their new heading: "One thirty five degrees Magnetic."

The Boomerang had begun its long southeast leg toward Guam.

0450 HOURS, AUGUST 6, 1945

The Boomerang's flight south from Ube was relatively uneventful. But Carl Schahrer had to give the headquarters colonel a full explanation of the inbound leg because the man had slept all the way from Guam to the Initial Point. Satisfied he could write his mission report, the Colonel crawled into the tunnel and slept again. This gave the crew their own opportunity to nap in brief, rotating shifts.

The crescent moon the crew had seen set the previous afternoon rose through the haze of false dawn.[10]

Faint light spread across the eastern horizon. Jim Smith had been deeply asleep for ten minutes when navigator Tony Cosola woke him. "Gotta work up some early-morning star sights," Cosola said tiredly. "Then I'm going to sack out for ten."

Cosola's sextant fix gave him an estimate that Iwo Jima lay sixty-two miles ahead. John Waltershausen roused Carl Schahrer from sleep. Fully awake in a moment, Schahrer asked Hank Gorder to confirm fuel status.

"We're in the green unless we hit unforecast head winds," the flight engineer reported.

"We'll take her back to Northwest," Schahrer announced, informing the crew there would not be any seat-of-the-pants landings on Iwo's soggy asphalt runway.

"Check those three 'Forts," Marshall called from the nose. "Twelve o'clock, right on a recip of our course, about fifteen hundred feet higher."

"Got 'em," Schahrer answered, studying the three farther B-29s that reflected the weak glow of the sunrise as they approached from the south in a standard line formation. As Marshall had observed, the bombers were on an exact reciprocal course to the returning 315th Wing's bomber stream. And like the B-29Bs, the Superforts flying north had no turrets on their bellies. "Photo recon ships headed for Ube," Schahrer reported confidently.

But the crew did not realize that these B-29s were not the usual stripped-down Superforts that the Army Air Forces had designated the F-13, which conducted very-high-altitude poststrike reconnaissance missions soon after targets were bombed. These planes were on another mission altogether.

As *The Boomerang* neared Iwo Jima, Tony Cosola called from the astrodome. "More photoreconnaissance ships. I guess we blew so much hell out of Ube they had to send a squadron of cameras to cover all the damage."

Jim Smith rose from his seat, shook the kinks out of his limbs, and stood behind Schahrer in the now-sunlit greenhouse. The three B-29s approaching from the south flew in a loose V, an unusual formation for photorecon ships, which normally favored a trail formation approaching the Empire because it presented a smaller radar profile. But no one on board *The Boomerang* doubted that these planes were retracing the 315th Wing's course of the previous night to make landfall on Shikoku and then turn northwest across the Inland Sea to photograph the bomb damage at Ube.

Good luck, Smith wished the recon crews, hoping they got sharp pictures. He did not want to have to return for a third time to the fighters and flak protecting Ube.

. . .

The Boomerang's crewmen were wrong about the nature of the two small formations of B-29s they had seen flying toward the Empire that morning. But there is evidence that Japanese early-warning radar operators were also confused about the six northbound B-29s, which they, too, mistook for either photoreconnaissance or weather aircraft that did not warrant a response from fighters or flak batteries.[11] The first three of these Superforts, *Straight Flush*, *Full House*, and *Jabbit III*, were in fact on a weather reconnaissance mission to verify the best target for *Enola Gay*. Major Claude Eatherly, flying the *Straight Flush*, would scout the weather over Hiroshima. Major John Wilson, commanding *Jabbit III*, would take the plane to Kokura on the island of Kyushu for weather reconnaissance. And the *Full House*, commanded by Major Ralph Taylor, would proceed on the same mission to Nagasaki near Kyushu's southern tip.

The Superforts of the loose V formation that Jim Smith had spotted were immeasurably more exotic. *No. 91*, under the command of Major George Marquardt, did carry cameras, but they were not the equipment of a standard recon plane. *The Great Artiste*, flown by Major Charles Sweeney, was crammed with a bizarre load of instruments that few outside of the world's most advanced physics laboratories even knew existed. And the 509th Commander Colonel Paul Tibbets's *Enola Gay* carried in her forward bomb bay a weapon unique in history.

Little Boy's dull steel cylinder was 10½ feet long from its blunt rounded snout to its boxy tail fins and resembled a larger variant of the British RAF's "Grand Slam" blockbuster. At 9,700 pounds, the American bomb was of similar weight. In Little Boy's heart, surrounded by batteries and a complex web of multiple-redundant radar and barometric fusing circuits, lay the length of modified five-inch bore cannon. Three "dense, purple-black" rings of uranium U-235 with a total weight of 39 kilograms were firmly mounted within a cylindrical hollow in a heavy spherical tungsten-steel tamper at the nose of the gun barrel. At the aft end of the six-foot gun, a 24-kilogram "bullet" of U-235 shaped like a deer hunter's shotgun slug was suspended by pins.[12]

(By some accounts, the total weight of U-235 was approximately 42 kilograms, divided in a similar proportion. Even today, the exact weight of the bomb's core and its design have not been made public, as the Little Boy type, although crude, remains the simplest bomb for a rogue state or terrorist group to assemble.)

Soon after the *Enola Gay* had strained into the air from Tinian, Navy

Captain William Parsons had crawled into the bomb bay and carefully inserted a four-section cordite explosive charge behind the U-235 slug.

When the charge was fired, the smaller U-235 chunk would blast through neutron-absorbing tampers lining the gun barrel, moving at the speed of a rifle bullet. This uranium slug would slam into the cylindrical cavity of the target rings and abut against the heavy armored-steel cap. The two sections of U-235 would be instantly pressure-welded to form a single solid shape.

A supercritical mass would occur, resulting in an uncontrolled nuclear chain reaction. Within millionths of a second, countless neutrons would be liberated to annihilate surrounding nuclei in the uranium core, which in turn would release more neutrons. Before the Little Boy was vaporized in a fireball thousands of times hotter than the surface of the sun, a small amount of U-235 would be converted from matter into energy in a blast equal to at least 10,000 tons of TNT.

At 0714, Major Claude Eatherly flew the weather scout *Straight Flush* high above Hiroshima. An all-clear siren had sounded in the predawn darkness after the last of the 315th's bombers had left Ube and headed south toward Guam. And, although an air-raid warning had again been issued when Japanese radar had detected this lone B-29, the alert would not remain in effect very long. From more than 30,000 feet, the port on the Inland Sea appeared calm and peaceful. In fact, Hiroshima was one of several Japanese cities that the Joint Chiefs of Staff had not yet targeted because—while containing concentrations of ground forces—they lacked aircraft industries, which were the priority of the relentless Superfort bombing campaign of the previous months.[13] Eatherly saw that the scattered cumulus clouds presented no problem to visual bombing, and there was a huge cloud-free hole above the city center. He radioed his report to the *Enola Gay*.

CLOUD COVER LESS THAN ³⁄₁₀ AT ALL ALTITUDES
ADVICE: BOMB PRIMARY

Aboard *Enola Gay*, Colonel Tibbets squeezed his intercom throat mike and called the crew: "It's Hiroshima."

PART II

ENDGAME

CHAPTER FIVE

"A RAIN OF RUIN"

A T P R E C I S E L Y 0 8 1 5 H O U R S Hiroshima time on that bright, calm Monday morning, Major Thomas Ferebee, the *Enola Gay*'s bombardier, aligned the crosshairs of his Norden bombsight on the distinctively T-shaped Aioi Bridge connecting two of the six fingerlike islands among the tributaries of the Ota River in the city center. Ferebee tripped a lever and the *Enola Gay*'s bomb-bay doors clanged open. From the altitude of 31,600 feet, Hiroshima was a flat expanse of pastel greens and browns, much softer than the stark black-and-white reconnaissance photos of the target that Ferebee had studied for days.[1] He hit another switch, engaging the automatic fifteen-second sequence to bomb release. At that moment, the aircraft's radio transmitted a continuous low tone, warning the crews of the trailing *The Great Artiste* instrument ship and *No. 91*, the photo plane, that the bomb was about to drop. The airmen in all three B-29s donned dark welder's goggles.

At 0815:16, the massive length of the Little Boy bomb fell free. *The Great Artiste* then dropped several blast-measurement instruments, which hung in the cloudless sky from large white parachutes.

Both *Enola Gay* and *The Great Artiste* immediately executed high-speed diving turns, calculated to provide the planes maximum slant distance from the bomb's detonation forty-three seconds after release.

When Little Boy dropped from the bomber, arming wires yanked free, starting the bomb's internal clocks. Then circuits tripped, preparing the next phase of the detonation process. As the bomb plunged toward Hiroshima, redundant radar-proximity devices came alive to measure the precise altitude above the ground. At 5,000 feet, Little Boy's barometric-pressure fuse circuit was armed.

At that moment in the city, thousands of people paused to gaze up at the spectacle of two shining B-29s diving steeply away toward the port. White·parachutes blossomed, a sight few of the city's residents had ever seen. Eight thousand schoolgirls, recently drafted into the civilian defense forces, worked in the humid morning heat clearing air-defense fire lanes. Elsewhere, Hiroshima's residents walked to their jobs along sunny sidewalks or crammed into overcrowded tramcars, unaware that their doom was hurtling toward them in the form of a 9,000-pound bomb.

At 0816:02 hours and an altitude of 1,900 feet directly above the courtyard of the Shima Hospital—just southeast of the Aioi Bridge aiming point—the bomb's final detonation circuit closed. The cordite charge fired, slamming the U-235 slug down the gun barrel and into the nestled uranium target rings. For an infinitesimal fraction of a millisecond, supercritical mass was achieved and sustained, converting less than 2 percent of the radioactive metal from matter into energy before the bomb was vaporized in a fireball with the stellar heat of 50 million degrees centigrade.[2] During that brief, hellish moment, the heat on the ground directly below flashed to more than 5,000 degrees Fahrenheit.

A silent, unearthly purplish glare filled the doomed city, blinding or dazzling countless thousands, followed almost instantly by the bomb's searing thermal pulse. Then the blast wave—traveling at two miles a second—ripped across Hiroshima. The parachute instrument packages that *The Great Artiste* had dropped automatically radioed "yield" data for the bomb: 12,500 tons of high-explosive equivalent.

According to the preeminent historian of the atomic bomb, Richard Rhodes, people caught in the open near the bomb's "hypocenter" (the spot immediately beneath the detonation) were either vaporized or "seared to bundles of smoking black char in a fraction of a second."[3] Distance from the hypocenter reduced injury somewhat, but burns were still generally widespread among those outdoors in the city center. The bomb's thermal pulse, which has been likened to a monstrous flashbulb, was so intense that it imprinted strange negative-image shadows on buildings and streets: A man pulling a handcart left his silhouette on the pavement before being carbonized; the dark patterns in women's blouses and kimonos seared tattoos in their flesh while the white fabric reflected the heat.[4] For people within 2.3 miles of the hypocenter who were directly exposed to the flash, the burns were horrific. Many who survived the blast wave stumbled naked through the pall of dust and smoke with their burned skin hanging in shreds and sheets from their limbs and torsos.

The blast itself was so powerful that almost all of the city's traditional wooden buildings were blown down before they were consumed in the ensuing firestorm that soon swept through the ruins. However, the heat, the blast, and the firestorm were not the only specter haunting the stricken city. The atomic explosion had released an invisible cascade of deadly gamma radiation across Hiroshima that penetrated the bodies of people not sheltered inside masonry buildings. Within twenty-four hours, victims of radiation sickness appeared at the handful of functioning hospitals in the area. Most had unexplained weakness, severe gastrointestinal symptoms, and strange, subcutaneous bleeding; many of these patients soon died of the disease Japanese doctors now called the *pika-don* illness, named for the "flash" (*pika*) and "boom" (*don*), of the atomic bomb.

Casualty estimates were difficult to obtain due to the utter devastation caused by the fireball, blast, and ensuing firestorm. One joint postwar American-Japanese study found that 80,000 people were killed on August 6 and another 80,000 were missing or wounded. Other estimates place the number of known dead at 100,000, while still later, more exact casualty counts cite the figure of 92,133 dead, including radiation victims in the weeks immediately following the bombing.[5]

Since World War II, the plight of the Hiroshima victims has been documented in great detail in scores of books, films, and television programs. The atomic bombing has come to symbolize the utter brutality of war. Ironically, this has blunted the impact of the far greater carnage Japan suffered during the nine-month American strategic bombing campaign of 1944–45.[6] The atomic bombings of Hiroshima and Nagasaki have also tended to cast

Japan in the role of victim, not an aggressor, and have often diverted the scrutiny of postwar generations from the wholesale atrocities Imperial Japanese forces committed throughout Asia (particularly China) in the name of the Emperor and the Greater East Asian Co-Prosperity Sphere.

But Hiroshima was far from the innocent civilian city it has come to symbolize in so many postwar accounts. And everyone on the ground certainly was not civilian. At the moment the bomb exploded, thousands of bare-chested Japanese soldiers were performing calisthenics on the parade grounds surrounding Hiroshima Castle, headquarters of the Second General Army, which was working feverishly on the Ketsu-go operation. In fact, according to Thomas and Witts, the chroniclers of the *Enola Gay*, the "largest single group of casualties" that morning was among those troops.[7] They burst into flame, and their ashes and charred husks were scattered by the blast wave.

Rather than being a purely civilian enclave untouched by war, as it has so often been portrayed since 1945, Hiroshima had earned its reputation among the Japanese as "an Army city." The sprawling Inland Sea port's wartime civilian population of perhaps 290,000 was augmented by an estimated 43,000 soldiers, which gave it the highest civilian-military density of any large Japanese urban area.[8]

(It is clear that President Harry S. Truman regarded Hiroshima as a military target. While at Potsdam on July 25, 1945, Truman wrote in his diary: "I have told Sec. of War, Mr. Stimson, to use it [the atomic bomb] so that military objectives and soldiers and sailors are the target and not women and children. . . . He and I are in accord. The target will be a purely military one. . . ."[9])

The city's flat estuary topography also made Hiroshima desirable for the first combat drop of an atomic bomb. The American military leaders wanted to achieve full "shock" value with the two nuclear weapons then available on Tinian, so one reason that Hiroshima was selected as the primary Little Boy target was that no deep valleys or ridges bisected the city's terrain. When the bomb burst above the aiming point, Manhattan Project leaders expected that blast and thermal-pulse effects would be at their maximum. It was thus hoped that the subsequent devastation would help convince the Japanese military, government, and people that further resistance was futile.[10]

Certainly the hapless few survivors among Field Marshal Shunroko Hata's shattered Second General Army headquarters needed little convincing. Hiroshima Castle had been leveled, effectively removing that headquarters from any effective role in the planned Ketsu-go operation.

Once the *Enola Gay* had recovered from the diving turn of the escape maneuver and survived the battering of the bomb's multiple shock waves, the crew had the chance to survey the horrible spectacle below. A roiling column of superhot flame and gases churned into the sky, its color changing from blast-furnace red to a molten purple none of the veteran American airmen had ever seen. Sergeant Bob Caron, the tail gunner, had perhaps the best view. To him, the flash had been "a peep into hell" and the growing pillar of flame that would quickly become a mushroom cloud was a "bubbling mass, purple-gray in color." Countless major fires sprang up across the city before the flames themselves were cloaked in the pall of dust and smoke. As the bomber circled at a safe distance, the boiling radioactive mushroom cloud climbed into the stratosphere, eventually reaching a height of over 50,000 feet.

Gazing out his cockpit window, Colonel Paul Tibbets was awestruck. He had missed the Trinity test of the plutonium bomb in New Mexico three weeks earlier. But for him, Little Boy "carried with it a connotation of destruction bigger than anything I really imagined."[11]

Navy Captain William Parsons, the Manhattan Project expert who had armed the bomb in flight, now sent a coded message to the Strategic Air Forces in the Marianas:

RESULTS CLEAR-CUT. SUCCESSFUL IN ALL RESPECTS. VISIBLE EFFECTS GREATER THAN ALAMOGORDO. CONDITIONS NORMAL IN AIRCRAFT FOLLOWING DELIVERY . . .

Parsons's message provided graphic proof that the atomic bomb was a practical combat weapon against Japan. In accordance with the White House–Pentagon orders of July 25, the senior Air Force commanders in the Pacific could continue to "deliver" nuclear weapons as their components arrived from Los Alamos. Fat Man, a fully assembled plutonium bomb, was already prepared for the next mission at the 509th's compound on Tinian. Other plutonium bombs would be available within days and weeks.

. . .

Perhaps due to the sensitive nature of Captain Parsons's message, it was carefully relayed as a Top Secret radiogram through Army circuits from Tinian to Guam and on to the Philippines before transmission to the Pentagon. In Washington that Sunday afternoon, Manhattan Project leaders and Chief of Staff General George C. Marshall waited anxiously for news of the mission's success or failure. But there was no word. Major General Leslie Groves was almost frantic with worry and repeatedly called the duty officer of the Pentagon code room. Even General Marshall, a normally imperturbable officer, revealed his gnawing anxiety as night fell with no news from the Pacific. Finally, after eleven that night, Groves got the "Results clear-cut. Successful in all respects" message. He took the unusual step of calling General Marshall at his quarters and waking him to report.

At a Pentagon meeting early the next morning, Marshall, Groves, and Air Force Chief of Staff General Hap Arnold discussed a more detailed description of the Hiroshima mission. The Little Boy uranium bomb was powerful indeed. Hiroshima had ceased to exist as a city.

Groves was elated. But Marshall cautioned everyone against "excessive celebration" because of the undoubtedly huge number of civilian casualties.

Groves pugnaciously replied that he "was not thinking so much about those casualties as I was about the men on the Bataan death march."[12]

President Harry Truman was aboard the U.S. Navy cruiser *Augusta,* one day from Newport News on his return voyage from the Potsdam Conference, when he received the message that Hiroshima had been successfully bombed. "I was greatly moved," Truman later recalled. To the sailors on the mess deck with whom he was having lunch, Harry Truman said, "This is the greatest thing in history." When he informed the ship's officers about the success of the Hiroshima bomb, Truman recalled, "I could not keep back my expectation that the Pacific War might now be brought to a speedy end."[13]

Truman now authorized the Pentagon to issue worldwide a statement in his name describing the awesome destructive force of the atomic bomb—"More than 2,000 times the blast power of the British 'grand slam'"—and to warn the Japanese leaders what they faced if they continued to defy the Allies' Potsdam Declaration.

"If they do not now accept our terms they may expect a rain of ruin from the air, the like of which has never been seen on this earth."[14]

. . .

Following the Ube mission, *The Boomerang* landed back at Northwest Field on Guam just before 0815 hours on the morning of August 6 after an exhausting flight that had lasted fifteen and a half hours. When the flight engineer, Hank Gorder, went through his postflight procedures, he found the fuel reserves well below 1,000 gallons. Had bad weather socked in Northwest Field and nearby North Field, it was unlikely the bomber would have had sufficient gasoline to divert to an alternate B-29 base and linger, "stacked up" in the clouds, waiting to land. It would have been nice to think that planes really low on gas would have received landing priority. But the fact was that there were often ten or more ships in equally bad shape, and they all had to wait their turn. The only thing that would get you down earlier than the other guys was having wounded on board or if the engines started dying from fuel starvation.

So, as the tired crew collected their flight equipment and climbed down to the asphalt hardstand, they once more fatalistically accepted their good fortune. They had learned that in combat flying it was best not to dwell on negative possibilities. Having survived this mission, they would not be concerned about the next one until they had to.

Even though it was not yet nine in the morning and many of the 315th Bomb Wing's airmen were not yet twenty-one years old, everyone who had flown the mission was issued his regulation two ounces of whiskey prior to debriefing. For Jim Smith and the others, the liquor made them a little giddy and added to their excitement in describing the absolute clobbering the bombers had inflicted on the Ube Coal Liquefaction Company at the mouth of the Kota River.

Later, reconnaissance photos would reveal that the target had not only been crushed, it had also been "destroyed and sunk," due to the breaching of dikes that had kept back the Inland Sea from the reclaimed land on which the sprawling plant was located. (The 315th Bomb Wing would receive a Presidential Distinguished Unit Citation for this mission.)

During the debriefing, however, few of the airmen thought to mention the two small northbound formations of "recon" planes they had seen near Iwo Jima after dawn.

Still relaxed from the whiskey, all Jim Smith and his fellow enlisted crew members wanted to do when they reached their barracks was peel off their sweaty flight suits and sink onto their cots for a fast eight hours of sleep through the heat of the day. In the crew's barracks, someone had tuned the radio to the base "Sack Rat" show. The soldier who had created this one-man program always announced the latest morning's news to the returning crews. Then, step by step, he'd talk his audience through the process of undressing in preparation for well-earned sleep. Usually this amusing diversion went along the lines of "Well, Sack Rats, you've had a busy mission and you're ready for some heavy ZZs. Now just sit down on your cot that you've fitted with that nice air mattress and take off those big old GI shoes. Umph, doesn't that feel good? Now, just stretch out and relax. That's a good GI."

Most mornings the announcer would lace his commentary with some vaguely lewd images of "Sack WACs" who were also undressing elsewhere on the island. But he always cautioned the tired young airmen, "Don't look," as their Women's Army Corps counterparts stripped down for bed. The sergeants and corporals, many of whom were only a year or two out of high school, loved this adolescent fantasy.

But this morning, the announcer's risqué script was interrupted when he was handed a news bulletin. The radio fell silent for a moment. When the man spoke again, his tone was somber:

"A superbomb was dropped on Hiroshima by a lone B-29 this morning, and the city was destroyed. The time of the explosion 0816 hours, Japanese time."

The men in the barracks exchanged incredulous looks, and then someone laughed. "This guy has really gone Asiatic!"

Jim Smith joined the laughter. "That's what happens when you stay on this island too long and drink too much of that 3.2 poison they call beer."

But apparently the announcer was serious. "This is no drill. A single B-29 dropped a superbomb on Hiroshima this morning, and the city was destroyed."

Now someone turned up the radio volume so that the announcer's voice echoed through the hut. "Repeating: One B-29 dropped a superbomb on Hiroshima at 0816 hours today and the city has been completely destroyed. The attacking B-29 was based on Tinian and took off at 0245 hours. Three weather ships and two technical support B-29s accompanied the lone bomber."

A guy spoke up from the end of the hut. "Tinian. Hell, we would have heard *some* kind of scuttle on this thing."

But Jim Smith turned to Hank Gorder, Sid Siegel, and his crew's two scanners. "Those two small flights of Superforts we spotted this morning . . ."

The crewmen were up to speed with him. "There was only one B-29 that bombed. Do you suppose the others were—?"

"You got it," Jim Smith interrupted. "The others must have been the weather planes and two supporting aircraft."

Still, for a while they retained a lingering suspicion that the super-bomb announcement might have been a morbid hoax. But the bulletin was repeated every five minutes with the sober warning "This is no drill." The news was not someone's idea of a gag. There was no punch line.

Jim Smith turned again to Hank Gorder and the others. "My God, one bomb and one city gone? This has *got* to shorten our stay here, friends. I'm going to start packing for the States."

The armed forces radio announcements did not indicate that the weapon that had destroyed Hiroshima had been an atomic bomb. And no doubt few of the airmen would have understood the meaning of the term had the broadcast employed it. But all the young airmen did believe the "superbomb" would help expedite a Japanese surrender.[15]

Finally, the excitement gave way to deep exhaustion. The men fell onto their cots to sleep.

While they slept, American shortwave radio was beaming the full text of President Truman's official announcement of the Hiroshima bombing to Japan in both English and Japanese. The Imperial Army's radio-jamming services received strict orders to overwhelm and smother this message whenever possible. They were not completely successful, and Truman's warning reached many Japanese:

"In their present form these bombs are now in production and even more powerful forms are in development," President Truman stated. "It is an atomic bomb. It is harnessing the basic power of the universe. The force from which the sun draws its power has been loosed against those who brought war to the Far East."

Although Smith and his fellow airmen would not learn the nature of the superbomb for several days, Smith was beginning to understand the significance of passing those Superforts as *The Boomerang* flew south and the other planes were en route to Japan. He now saw that the 315th's mission to Ube had not only destroyed the enemy's largest synthetic oil producer but had also served effectively as a diversion for the Hiroshima strike force, convincing the Japanese early-warning radar network that the two small northbound flights of B-29s were photoreconnaissance for the previous night's large-scale mission.

In fact, the Hiroshima flight of three aircraft had followed the exact reciprocal course as the returning 315th bombers, making landfall on the southwest tip of the Home Island of Shikoku before turning west over the Inland Sea. This course would have provided the optimum diversionary illusion that the atomic bomb strike force—whose planes were armed only with tail guns—was indeed a photoreconnaissance flight not worthy of interception.

Years later, the Japanese historians who wrote the definitive account of the war's final weeks, *Japan's Longest Day*, confirmed Smith's hunch. "At eight o'clock Hiroshima radar operators detected two B-29s. A warning was sounded. The planes mounted to an extremely high altitude; the radio announced that they were on a reconnaissance flight. Most of the city's quarter of a million people didn't bother to seek shelter, anticipating no bombing. Many gazed up into the sky to watch the maneuver."[16]

While the U.S. military was broadcasting President Truman's announcement to Japan, American planes were showering Japanese cities with leaflets warning civilians about the deadly potential of the atomic bomb.

> TO THE JAPANESE PEOPLE:
> America asks that you take immediate heed of what we say on this leaflet . . . We are in possession of the most destructive explosive ever devised by man. A single one of our newly developed atomic bombs is actually the equivalent in explosive power to what 2,000 of our giant B-29s can carry on a single mission . . . We have just begun to use this weapon against your homeland. If you still have any doubt, make inquiry as to what happened to Hiroshima . . . Before using this bomb to destroy every resource of the military by which they are prolonging this useless war, we ask that you now petition the Emperor to end the war . . .[17]

Over the next nine days, the Air Force dropped sixteen million copies of this and similar leaflets on forty-seven Japanese cities with a population of more than 100,000, reaching approximately 40 percent of the total population. The American planes also dropped 500,000 Japanese-language newspapers containing detailed articles on the atomic bomb and grim pictures of the attack on Hiroshima. Meanwhile, U.S. information-propaganda broadcasts from Radio Saipan went out around the clock, warning the Japanese of impending nuclear doom if their leaders continued to ignore the Potsdam Declaration.

After the war, the United States Strategic Bombing Survey estimated that urban Japanese workers and farmers understood little about the true nature of the atomic bomb and that this propaganda campaign did not influence them. However, the campaign to inform Japan about the dire threat of continued nuclear attack had a marked impact on government leaders.[18]

For many hours after the attack on August 6, the sheer magnitude of the catastrophe that had engulfed Hiroshima prevented senior Japanese military and government leaders in Tokyo from learning that their country had actually been struck by a nuclear weapon. This information gap was due principally to the virtual leveling of the city and the severing of almost every civilian telephone link and military radio circuit to the outside world. It was not until that afternoon that Japanese military units near Hiroshima were able to send the first reports about the scale of the disaster.

But the messages that reached Tokyo were confused. Japanese army messages initially described a new type of conventional bomb or bombs of extremely destructive force. When Foreign Minister Shigenori Togo heard the official American account of an atomic bomb having been dropped on Hiroshima, he immediately contacted his army counterparts on the Supreme Council for the Direction of the War. War Minister Korechika Anami and Army Chief of Staff General Yoshijiro Umezu told him that the matter of whether Hiroshima had been attacked with an atomic weapon was not yet established as fact and "needed to be examined more closely" in a thorough investigation.[19]

Togo replied that they'd better expedite their investigation because foreign governments were attaching a great deal of importance to President Truman's announcement that Japan had been attacked with an atomic bomb.

But the official Japanese description continued to downplay the bomb's destructiveness. On the morning of August 7, Radio Tokyo, the principal outlet of the Japan Broadcasting Corporation, told the country's listeners that a "small number of B-29s" had dropped a "small number of" a new type of bomb attached to parachutes, which exploded in the air. "As a result, a considerable number of homes were reduced to ashes and fires broke out in various parts of the city. . . . Investigations are now being made with regard to the effectiveness of this bomb, which should not be regarded as slight."[20] There was no mention that a single atomic bomb had brought almost instantaneous destruction to Hiroshima. And the description of bombs attached to parachutes exploding in the air made them sound like some form of high-power incendiary device. Moreover, as fragmentary reports reached Tokyo from Hiroshima, civilian officials tried to dampen panic by informing citizens that "those [in Hiroshima] who took refuge immediately in safe underground shelters escaped injury completely."

But the Japanese could not evade the horrible truth for very long. The Japanese military was well aware of the awesome potential of atomic weapons. In 1943, under the urging of Prime Minister Hideki Tojo, renowned physicist Dr. Yoshio Nishina led a concentrated Imperial Army effort to develop an atomic bomb. But the Japanese were unable to obtain the pitchblende uranium ore from Czechoslovakia, for which they had contracted for delivery by submarine. B-29 raids in March and April 1945 inadvertently destroyed the Japanese research facilities. But General Tojo's government took great stock in atomic weapons and Tojo personally believed they would prove to be Japan's salvation in the face of the Allied powers' industrial juggernaut.

The Imperial Army investigation team from Tokyo, which included Dr. Yoshio Nishina, did not reach Hiroshima until August 8. Flying over the charred and still-smoldering desert of a city, the physicist could see "at a glance" that only an atomic bomb could have inflicted such devastation. The head investigator, Assistant Army Chief of Staff Lt. General Seizo Arisue, reluctantly conceded that Hiroshima had been struck by "an unconventional type of bomb."[21]

Foreign Minister Togo, however, needed no convincing. He was certain that the Americans had used one atomic bomb, and would continue to drop them in the "rain of ruin" that President Truman's statement had described. At a meeting of select cabinet ministers on the morning of August 7, Togo stressed to his colleagues that American radio broadcasts were saying that the atomic bomb would revolutionize warfare and that more bombs would be dropped on Japan until she sued for peace by accepting the terms of the Potsdam Declaration. War Minister Anami tried to minimize the effect of the bomb by repeating that no one could be sure it was in fact a nuclear weapon. He insisted that the government wait for a full investigation report before further discussion.

That afternoon the Lord Keeper of the Privy Seal, Marquis Koichi Kido, told the Emperor of Hiroshima's fate and noted that the bomb had caused 130,000 casualties. In a postwar statement, Kido related to American interrogators that the Emperor said, "Now that things have come to this impasse, there is no other way. I don't care what happens to me personally, but we should lose no time in ending the war so as not to have another tragedy like this."[22]

Foreign Minister Togo, frustrated by the Army's unconcerned attitude toward the threat of the atomic bomb, sought an audience with the Emperor for August 8 in order to impress upon him the desperate nature of the situation. The tone of the American and British broadcasts had reached a new level of urgency. Togo was convinced that America did indeed have a growing arsenal of atomic bombs, just as President Truman's statement had warned, and would use them without hesitation unless Japan surrendered. The veteran diplomat's somber mood deepened as his official sedan approached the moat surrounding the Imperial Palace and the Double Bridge on that humid August morning. The stench of charred wood pervaded the Palace Grounds. The May B-29 raid in which several loads of incendiary bombs had gone astray had burned out the traditionally ornate tile-roofed residences of the Emperor, his mother, the Dowager Empress, the Crown Prince, and eight royal princes.[23] Even though Foreign Minister Togo realized that the Americans had not intentionally targeted the Palace—the grounds would have been littered with smoldering rubble had that been their goal—the sight of the ruined buildings reminded him that the U.S. Air Force was free to strike virtually anywhere in Japan. And now the enemy possessed this dreaded new weapon that was so much more powerful than conventional bombs.

Emperor Hirohito received Togo in the concrete-walled Gobunko, the Imperial Library, which had become his Palace residence after the May firebombing. Foreign Minister Togo did not waste time with the indirect and inconsequential conversation that traditionally began Imperial audiences. Instead, Togo presented the Emperor with an unvarnished summary of the information about the atomic bomb that the Foreign Ministry had obtained from Allied broadcasts and leaflets, as well as from cabled dispatches that Japanese embassies in neutral countries had sent. Foreign

Minister Togo told the Emperor that government and public opinion abroad was that the atomic bomb would revolutionize not only modern warfare but society and the daily life of the ordinary individual as well.

"The Americans will continue to use the bomb against Japan until we surrender," Togo concluded.

According to Foreign Minister Togo's postwar statement to Allied interrogators, Hirohito voiced the same opinion: "The Emperor indicated clearly that the enemy's new weapon made it impossible to go on fighting. I said that we should lose no time in ending the war to which His Majesty replied that I was quite right, [and] told me to try to end the war immediately, and requested me to convey his wishes to the Premier."[24]

The insightful Pacific War historian Richard Frank has noted that both the Kido and Togo statements to American officials came four years after the war and tended to place the Emperor "in a favorable light," while also lacking contemporary confirmation in the form of diary entries or notes from close Palace aides. But "even if the Emperor accepted the need for a speedy termination of the war," Frank has written, "he either still balked personally at simple acceptance of the Potsdam Declaration or perhaps he doubted whether the Imperial Army would comply with his command to end the war."[25]

However, Japanese historians who interviewed both Kido and Togo after the war have accepted their statements about the Emperor's position as accurate accounts.

But whatever the Emperor's stated opinion at the time, it is probable that both Kido and Togo did raise the issue of the atomic bomb's threat to Hirohito in separate audiences. Certainly the specter of the bomb now assumed critical importance among the three members of the "peace faction" in the Supreme Council for the Direction of the War. Before meeting with the Emperor, Togo had discussed the issue of the atomic bomb with Premier Suzuki. After his Imperial audience on August 8, Foreign Minister Togo returned to the Premier's office and the two men again conferred. Togo requested that Suzuki convene an immediate emergency meeting of the Big Six to discuss acceptance of the Potsdam Declaration. Togo told the Premier that the Emperor "agreed that the new weapon had made it impossible to go on fighting. . . . His Majesty felt that the atomic bomb made continuation of the war not only a political but a tactical impossibility."[26]

Since all the members of the Council were not immediately available, the meeting was postponed until August 9.

. . .

Historians William Craig, David Bergamini, and John Toland have separately described an important but long-overlooked event that occurred after the Hiroshima attack. At the Osaka *kempeitai* secret police headquarters on the night of August 8, a young American P-51 fighter pilot, Lieutenant Marcus McDilda, sat tied to a chair, undergoing brutal interrogation. He had been shot down earlier that day and captured in the bay as he floundered in his one-man dinghy. Already battered from the beating outraged civilians had given him as he was marched bound and blindfolded through the streets, McDilda now endured hours of additional punishment at the hands of the *kempeitai* interrogators, who demanded details of the American Air Force base on Iwo Jima. Whenever he was caught in a lie, McDilda received another round of punches.

The questioning changed tack when the Japanese officers demanded that the pilot reveal everything he knew about the atomic bomb that had struck Hiroshima. McDilda insisted that he knew nothing of the weapon other than the scant details that were in President Truman's official statement. But a Japanese general who now joined the interrogation would not accept that explanation. He slashed McDilda's swollen and bleeding lips with a sword.

"If you don't tell me about the bomb," the general shouted, "I will personally cut off your head."[27]

McDilda realized that the Japanese were perfectly capable of beheading American prisoners and that this might well be his fate unless he quickly invented a plausible description of the atomic bomb—a subject about which he knew absolutely nothing. Back on Iwo after President Truman's announcement, there'd been some scuttlebutt about "splitting atoms." So, starting with that, and hoping his Deep South Florida drawl—exacerbated by his battered mouth—would help further muddle his already murky description of the bomb, McDilda began.

"When atoms are split," he improvised, "there are a lot of pluses and minuses released. Well, we've taken and put them in a huge container and separated them from one another with a lead shield."

After the bomb—which McDilda claimed measured about thirty-six feet long and twenty-four feet wide—was dropped, the lead shield was "melted."

"All the pluses and minuses come together," McDilda went on.

"When that happens, it causes a tremendous bolt of lightning . . . ," which flattened the target city.

His bizarre description could possibly explain the *pika-don* weapon that had destroyed Hiroshima in the horrible flash and boom.

The interrogators now pressed McDilda for information on the bomb's next target. Still struggling for survival, he said, "I believe Kyoto and Tokyo. Tokyo is supposed to be bombed in the next few days."[28] Obviously, McDilda had no idea whatsoever when and where the atomic bomb would fall next. But the Japanese had been hoodwinked by his quick-witted bravado.

Word was flashed from Osaka to Tokyo that the Imperial capital might soon be subjected to atomic attack.

With senior civilian officials already anxious about a possible nuclear attack on Tokyo, panic over the atomic bomb spread through the Imperial Palace. The Empress Dowager demanded of her retainers that the Imperial Guards Division responsible for security dig a far more substantial bomb shelter beneath her residence. She refused to be mollified when Army officers indicated she had free use of the Emperor's own deep concrete shelter. Clearly, members of the Imperial family expected Tokyo to soon suffer the same fate as Hiroshima.[29]

Before dawn on August 9, the telephone rang at Foreign Minister Togo's bedside. It was the radio operator at the Foreign Ministry.

"Russia has declared war on Japan and her armies have invaded Manchuria," the stricken man announced.

Stalin had kept his promise to the Allies. Three months to the day after Germany surrendered, the USSR entered the war against Japan. As historian Richard B. Frank has noted, in a feat of strategic deception that ranks among the most effective in history, the Soviet Union had assembled more than one million troops and 5,000 tanks and artillery pieces on Manchuria's borders without arousing the suspicion of Japanese military intelligence. Now those forces were pouring into Manchuria to overrun the already depleted Kwantung Army.[30] The Red Army was also poised to attack Japanese-controlled southern Sakhalin Island. The Allies' noose was tightening on the Empire.

Prime Minister Suzuki conferred with the Emperor at 7 A.M. They agreed that it was critical to lose no more time in accepting the Potsdam Declaration. Suzuki convened an urgent meeting of the Supreme Council for the Direction of the War later that morning, to be followed by an emergency session of the full cabinet.

War Minister Anami's adjutant, Major Saburo Hayashi, brought the General the news just after sunrise, while Anami was practicing archery with a samurai long bow in the garden of his official residence near the Imperial Palace. "The inevitable has come," Anami said.[31]

In many ways, the shock of the Soviet action—when it had still been unrealistically hoped that Moscow would somehow use its "neutral" position to broker a peace on terms more favorable than those of the Potsdam Declaration—was as ominous as the atomic bomb to the members of the Council when they assembled at the prime minister's air-raid shelter near the Imperial Palace after 10:00. But the threat of additional atomic bombs, particularly the imminent attack on Tokyo that Lieutenant Marcus McDilda had "revealed" to save his life, also overshadowed the meeting.

(The American pilot was flown to Tokyo on August 10 for more detailed technical interrogation. There, when questioned in fluent English in a cordial, nonthreatening manner by a civilian graduate of City College of New York, McDilda admitted that his fantastic description of "pluses and minuses" had been a hoax.[32] But the seed of fear that his original account to the Osaka *kempeitai* had planted among the Japanese continued to grow.)

Foreign Minister Togo, the most energetic member of the peace faction, cited the Emperor's desire to end the war at once and spoke forcefully and at length about the need to accept the Potsdam Declaration.

"Since the present situation is so critical," he said, "and precludes all hope of victory, I feel it is essential that we sue for peace."

Prime Minister Suzuki and Navy Minister Admiral Mitsumasa Yonai, the only military member of the Council's peace faction, nodded their assent to Togo's words. War Minister Anami, Army Chief of Staff General Yoshijiro Umezu, and Navy Chief of Staff Admiral Soemu Toyoda sat coldly silent.

Continuing his argument, the Foreign Minister added that the "welfare of the Imperial Family must be maintained at all cost," a reference to obtaining from the Allies a guarantee that the national polity, or *kokutai*, system be retained following capitulation. Togo stressed that, given the Allies' inflexible position on unconditional surrender, they would no doubt refuse to negotiate if Japan tried to "exact a large number of concessions."[33]

Anami and his two military colleagues were not persuaded. The members of the war faction agreed that it went without saying that Japan would never sue for peace—the term "surrender" disgusted them—unless the Allies guaranteed that the Imperial system was maintained. But the officers were adamant that Japan also insist on three additional concessions.

The Allies must abandon their demand to occupy the Home Islands. The Japanese military and naval forces abroad would be demobilized and disarmed by Japan itself, not Allied forces. Finally, all alleged war crimes would be investigated and prosecuted by the Japanese government, not a tribunal convened by the Allied powers.[34]

The meeting, meant to be urgent and decisive, deteriorated into stubborn debate. When Foreign Minister Togo reiterated that the Allies were in no mood for negotiation, War Minister Anami countered that the occupation of the homeland—if this virtually unthinkable burden be accepted—at least exclude Tokyo and involve a minimum number of Allied troops at a few restricted locations. Togo told the three members of the war faction that he, too, would favor those conditions if there was any possibility that the Allies would accept them, but he knew there was not.

If Japan insisted on extensive negotiations at this point, Togo asked, and should those talks collapse, "can we expect to win the war?"

Each of the officers in the war faction admitted that he was not certain of "ultimate victory," but that Japan was definitely capable of one more campaign.

"If the Allies invade the homeland," Togo persisted, "can we ward them off?"

Army Chief of Staff Umezu now spoke: "All I can say with assurance is that we can destroy the major part of an invading Army. We can inflict extremely heavy damage on the enemy" (referring to the elaborate Ketsugo operation plan). General Anami added that Japan had 2.5 million battle-hardened soldiers in the Home Islands alone, men who were training to a peak of sacrificial readiness to defend the Empire. The Imperial forces also had ready thousands of kamikaze planes and pilots prepared to repulse the Allied invasion of Kyushu—or at the very least make that invasion so costly to the enemy that they would accept Japanese conditions for the end of the war.

But Foreign Minister Togo would not be persuaded. He pointed out that the Allies, who had fought with such tenacity on Saipan, Iwo Jima, and Okinawa, could surely be expected to stage another landing in due time. Their losses in ships, aircraft, and other equipment could be replenished, whereas Japan would not have the means to restore its own forces. In that situation, "our government's relative position would then be far worse than at present. The only thing to do under the circumstances is to try to end the war at once."[35]

His argument failed to impress the members of the war faction. For each point Togo raised, War Minister Anami and his colleagues took turns to present counterarguments. The hot morning dragged on.

As the Supreme Council for the Direction of the War continued their inconclusive debate in Tokyo, *Bock's Car*, a B-29 of the 509th Composite Group, approached the city of Kokura, flying at 31,000 feet. The aircraft's forward bomb bay held Fat Man, the plutonium implosion weapon similar to that tested at Alamogordo almost a month earlier. Unlike the virtually flawless mission of the *Enola Gay* three days before, this flight had been plagued with problems from its inception. Originally planned for August 11, the second atomic bomb attack had been urgently advanced two days because of a typhoon brewing in the Pacific between Tinian and the Empire. Working on only two hours' sleep, Major Charles Sweeney, the aircraft commander, and his crew had taken off from Tinian at 1:56 A.M., but a malfunctioning fuel pump and a missed rendezvous with one of the two camera planes near landfall on the Empire brought *Bock's Car* to its primary target dangerously short of fuel for the return flight to the Marianas.

At 0930 hours, Major Sweeney thought the jinx had finally been broken: The sky was beautifully clear, with excellent visibility. As the bomber approached the plains on the northeast coast of Kyushu, the crew could see the sprawling industrial area of Kokura and the adjacent cities of Tobata, Wakamatsu, and Yawata. Like Hiroshima, these cities made a vital contribution to the Japanese war effort. And the 610,000 people in this urban area had so far escaped heavy American bombing.

Bombardier Captain Kermit Beahan set up for the drop on the distinct shape of the arsenal that was his aiming point. But on the bomb run, roiling smoke from ranks of factory chimneys shrouded the image in his bombsight. Reluctantly, Sweeney circled for another pass at the target. He had strict orders that bombing had to be made by visual means. Once more, smoke and smog prevented Beahan from aligning his crosshairs.

On the third bomb run, the nervous crew announced that at least ten Japanese fighters were straining to reach the bomber's altitude. And dark puffs of heavy flak had already found the range and were bursting with alarming accuracy nearby. Sweeney banked sharply onto a southwestern course and headed for the alternate target, Nagasaki.

But even if bombing conditions were ideal at Nagasaki, *Bock's Car* was now so short of fuel that the plane could not even make it as far as Iwo Jima, and would have to attempt an emergency, "hot" high-speed landing on Okinawa.[36]

The mission's jinx continued as *Bock's Car* approached Nagasaki, a port on the southwest coast of Kyushu. The choice of the city as the third-priority target for the two atomic bombs ready for combat missions in early August was questionable. Nagasaki was best known as Japan's principal Christian enclave, where Portuguese missionaries had established a Western foothold in the early seventeenth century. The port had been all but strangled by the vigorous American aerial and submarine mining campaign, but had retained an active naval construction program at the Mitsubishi shipyard, which among other vessels produced suicide weapons for the Ketsu-go. The city's most promising target area for atomic attack was on the reclaimed land that stretched from the seafront to the nearby hills. Farther inland, the ridges and valleys around the Urakami River broke up the topography and created natural blast shields.

When *Bock's Car* reached Nagasaki just before 1100 hours, bombardier Beahan found his aiming point obscured by almost unbroken clouds. He called upon Staff Sergeant Edward Buckley, the radar operator, to assist on the bomb run, even though this was an explicit breach of standing orders. The Manhattan Project officer on board, Navy Commander Fred Ashworth, who had overall authority on the combat use of the bomb, initially refused Sweeney's request for a radar-assisted drop, but Beahan assured him, "I'll guarantee we come within a thousand feet of the target."[37]

This was combat, and the crew had to improvise. With *Bock's Car* so short of fuel, the plane could not carry the weight of the bomb even as far as Okinawa, nor could Sweeney risk landing with Fat Man, which was essentially a plutonium core surrounded by spheres of high explosive. Unless they dropped the bomb on Nagasaki, the crew would have to jettison it at sea, the least favorable contingency their briefers in the 509th had offered.

Ashworth approved the bombardier's request. With Sergeant Buckley giving radar bearings, Captain Beahan prepared to clutch in his bombsight to the radarscope. Suddenly Beahan sighted a stadium through a small break in the clouds. "I'll take it," he shouted over the intercom, aligning his crosshairs. At 1058 hours, Beahan dropped the bomb and *Bock's Car* dived into its sharp descending evasive turn. Behind the bomber, *The Great Artiste* released its parachute bundles of blast-measurement instruments and also dived for survival.

At 1102 hours, Fat Man detonated 1540 feet above the bowl-shaped valley of the Urakami, with the hypocenter near the Cathedral of Our Lady of the Immaculate Conception. The church, as well as the nearby Mitsubishi shipyard, was leveled. But Beahan's drop was badly off—by two miles, not the promised thousand feet from the aiming point. The valley absorbed the most devastating effects of the bomb, with the steep hillsides protecting much of Nagasaki from the thermal pulse, radiation, and blast. This spared countless thousands in the city because the parachute instruments transmitted a yield for Fat Man of twenty-two kilotons of high explosive, twice the power of the Little Boy bomb that had destroyed Hiroshima.

The number of dead in Nagasaki was difficult to estimate in 1945 because of its transient wartime population, and has remained so. Although destruction in the Urakami district of the city was complete, no firestorm swept across greater Nagasaki. It is probable that at least 40,000 people were instantly killed in the city on August 9, according to one Japanese estimate.[38] The United States Strategic Bombing Survey estimated in 1947 that more than 45,000 were killed with another 60,000 injured. As at Hiroshima, the churning mushroom cloud reached high into the stratosphere, and the crew of *Bock's Car* could see it behind them most of their way to Okinawa.

When Major Sweeney landed *Bock's Car* on Okinawa an hour later, he almost ran out of runway, even with the full braking power of the four big reversible propellers. Two of the engines died from fuel starvation as he taxied the bomber to its parking ramp.

The deliberations among the members of the Supreme Council for the Direction of the War had assumed an "extremely heated" tone but continued at an annoyingly languid pace, according to Foreign Minister Togo, and "nothing was accomplished."[39] The Council remained deadlocked between the peace faction, which favored immediate acceptance of the Potsdam Declaration—with the proviso that the Allies guarantee the Emperor's status—and the war faction, which insisted that Japan also negotiate for the three other conditions of capitulation. Before Prime Minister Suzuki stubbed out his cigar and called for the meeting to adjourn so the Council members could prepare for the full cabinet session scheduled for that afternoon, an officer entered the air-raid shelter and announced that Nagasaki had just been struck with an atomic bomb.[40]

Fifteen hundred miles to the south, Sergeant Jim Smith and his fellow crew members of *The Boomerang* had finished their lunch of rancid Australian mutton stew in the sweltering mess hall and were being briefed for yet another maximum-effort mission to the Empire. For the second time, the 315th Wing was striking the Nippon Oil Refinery at Amagasaki, one of the largest producers of aviation gasoline still functioning, which was located on the coast of Honshu, about 250 miles south of Tokyo.

The crews in the large briefing hut had been anxiously hopeful that Japan would accept the terms of the Potsdam Declaration after the bombing of Hiroshima. But Tokyo had remained silent on the subject of capitulation, so now the airmen faced the prospect of continued long missions, flown with their planes' worn-out engines, against targets the Japanese were defending with increased tenacity.

The briefing officer was noting the coordinates of search-and-rescue surface ships and submarines as well as the orbits of B-29 "Dumbo" aircraft that dropped large life rafts to ditched crews, when another officer stepped up to the rostrum.

"This morning," he said, tapping the ultraviolet-lit silhouette of the island of Kyushu on the large map with his pointer, "the city of Nagasaki was decimated with another superbomb. Initial results are reported almost the same as those at Hiroshima." The airmen in the room cheered and applauded.

We're going home now for sure, Jim Smith thought. They'll have to scrub this mission. But the intelligence major who had delivered the news about Nagasaki left the stage, and the original briefing officer resumed where he had been interrupted.

The night mission of August 9–10 would proceed.

While the airmen of the 315th Wing were being briefed on Guam, the fifteen members of the full Japanese cabinet met in emergency session at the Prime Minister's official residence in an unbombed neighborhood near the

Imperial Palace. The meeting, according to Foreign Minister Togo, was a "repeat performance" of the Supreme Council for the Direction of the War session held that morning.

After Suzuki briefly introduced the momentous subject under discussion—acceptance or rejection of the Allies' Potsdam Declaration—the elderly statesmen turned the meeting over to Foreign Minister Togo. Once more Togo spoke energetically for the peace faction; again General Anami made his strong case to continue the war unless the enemy acceded to all four conditions that the Big Six had delineated. The argument was protracted. Finally, Suzuki called for an individual vote, with each member of the cabinet being heard. Although postwar accounts of the session differ, all the ministers were in favor of demanding the sole condition that the Emperor's status not be changed. At least five sided with Foreign Minister Togo's peace faction. Another five favored acceptance of the Allies' terms but wanted to leave room for possible further negotiations.

Several ministers voiced the gloomiest possible picture of Japan's plight: The rice crop had been meager; American bombing and naval bombardment was virtually annihilating the coastal transport on which Japan depended to move food and war matériel. The country was dying.

But, while conceding the grim situation, War Minister Anami would not budge from his position: "We must face the war through to the end no matter how great the odds against us!"[41]

Home Minister Genki Abe stated frankly that civil obedience would not be certain if the government suddenly attempted to capitulate to the Allies. For almost four years, the military had assured the population that the war was going well. Abe also raised the specter of the bloody February 26, 1936, rebellion, during which young officer firebrands had led 2,000 troops against liberal members of the government, men they saw as exerting an unhealthy, nonbellicose influence on the Imperial Palace. Home Minister Abe was firmly against accepting the Potsdam Declaration.

Prime Minister Baron Kantaro Suzuki did not need reminding of the "26/2/37 Incident." His body and mind still bore the wounds of the assassins' three bullets that had almost killed him that day. The Army was known to still harbor fanatical young officers every bit as opposed to peace.

The cabinet was deadlocked. But once more, General Anami's deeply held conviction—that Japan must fight the final Ketsu-go battle and, in so doing, achieve the linked goals of maintaining the Imperial Army's honor and battering the Allies so badly on the beaches of Kyushu that they would accept the four Japanese conditions—had been thwarted.

By tradition dating back to the Meiji Constitution, a divided cabinet never presented its incapacity to resolve issues of state to the Emperor for his decision. But now there seemed to be no other recourse. At eight that night, Premier Suzuki asked Togo to accompany him to the Imperial Palace to consult the Emperor and request an Imperial conference for the Supreme Council for the Direction of the War. The Emperor called that conference for 11:30 that night in his small air-raid shelter near the Gobunko. The monarch and his two faithful ministers were confident that the fate of Japan would be settled that muggy Thursday night.

(In several postwar statements and interrogations, Japanese officials have tended to present the interaction among Premier Suzuki, Foreign Minister Togo, and Emperor Hirohito on August 9, 1945, as reasonably open, if unprecedented.[42] But some historians, among them the American William Craig, have unearthed evidence that the seemingly faltering and indecisive Prime Minister Suzuki and the aloof Emperor had skillfully outmaneuvered the Big Six war faction at this critical juncture. During the early-morning audience at the Imperial Palace on August 9, Suzuki reportedly convinced Hirohito that his intervention would be needed later that day to break the stalemate that Suzuki himself would stage-manage during the meetings of the Supreme Council for the Direction of the War and the full cabinet. "I will make sure there is no final vote taken in any meeting in the morning or the afternoon sessions," he allegedly told the Emperor.[43] Both Suzuki and Foreign Minister Togo were confident that the "mystic powers of the Emperor" would overcome all resistance from the war faction to demand unrealistic conditions from the Allies in order to prolong the conflict.[44])

2331 HOURS, 9 AUGUST 1945

As the members of the Big Six, dressed in their high-collared formal uniforms or long-tailed morning coats, assembled for the Imperial conference on the night of August 9, 1945, over 100 B-29Bs of the 315th Wing approached the Osaka urban area on the Honshu coast southwest of Tokyo.

The mission had begun normally, with the usual stressful takeoff at 1830 hours, Marianas time. The sun set as *The Boomerang* climbed to cruise altitude, followed seventy minutes later by the sliver of the new moon. But the plane soon encountered savage turbulence as aircraft commander Carl Schahrer tried to skirt the edges of the typhoon that had earlier threatened to scrub the Nagasaki atomic bomb mission. There were periods when the bomber seemed to slam into a solid wall, then drop with sickening speed. Sometimes the huge bomber rose uncontrollably in updrafts as the engines moaned and howled. Saint Elmo's fire static electricity danced and wove around the propeller disks, casting an eerie blue glow inside the airplane. In the surrounding sky, bolts of lightning flashed so close that the glare left the airmen momentarily blinded.

Smith could hear the bomb load of forty 500-pounders rattling and shaking on their release shackles, even through the padding of his earphones. And that was a noise that made everybody nervous.

Coming back from the mission on Shimotsu on the night of July 29, a 500-pound bomb had hung up when the load was dropped, then had finally torn loose to roll around, fully armed, inside the closed bomb bay. The doors had been damaged and jammed when that bomb fell. Smith had crawled inside the bomb bay through the forward pressure hatch but had been unable to open the doors with the emergency valve. Then bombardier Dick Marshall had entered the dark, swaying confines of the bomb bay, perched on the narrow catwalk, and somehow had managed to free the doors. Finally, Marshall had kicked the bomb out to fall 11,000 feet to the dark Pacific below.[45]

Now, ten days later, on the night of August 9, the sound of bombs jolting in the violent turbulence had the whole crew on edge. They were all worn out, at the end of their rope. Even the propaganda broadcast from Tokyo had assumed a frantic, desperate tone.

"You filthy, inhuman American pigs," the normally urbane announcer shouted through the lightning static. "You have exploded a new monster bomb on Hiroshima and Nagasaki." His tone rose to a scream of hatred. "You will pay. You will pay. You will *pay*!"

Unable to penetrate the storm front, Schahrer had called radar operator Rich Ginster to search for "clean air" among the towering thunderclouds. After another twenty minutes of turbulence, *The Boomerang* had broken free and was flying parallel to the edge of the typhoon in much smoother conditions. The crew checked the aircraft for structural damage, and to everyone's surprise, found none.

Four hours later, as *The Boomerang* flew northwest through the clear, moonless night, the sky was dense with unblinking stars. Occasionally there would be distant flashes of lightning over the southern horizon.

"Estimate eighteen minutes to landfall," navigator Tony Cosola announced over the intercom.

"Concur," Rich Ginster added, backing him up with a radar fix.

On this target, there would be a minimal run-in from landfall to the Initial Point to Bombs Away during which the Wing's long stream of aircraft would reach its most dense "compressibility" at altitudes between 14,600 and 15,800 feet. *The Boomerang* had been assigned 15,200 for its bomb run. It was time for everyone to forget the violence of the typhoon and prepare for the man-made storm ahead.

Flying into combat at this altitude required the crew to wear oxygen masks, because Hank Gorder depressurized the plane at the Initial Point to prevent explosive depressurization due to enemy fire. No one liked the discomfort of the masks, but everyone accepted oxygen as part of combat flying. And they hated the Japanese so much that they would put up with a lot worse to have the chance to bomb the Empire. Smith finished adjusting his flak jacket, steel helmet, and oxygen mask, then crammed himself awkwardly into the tunnel below the clear Plexiglas astrodome to assume his combat station, where he plugged in his intercom. The dark mass of Honshu was visible in the starlight. As always at his lonely perch, he said a quick but heartfelt prayer to be allowed to live into full adulthood, then concentrated on his job: watching for fighters and off-course Superforts.

As the bomber stream neared the target, a large number of night fighters bore in to meet it. The Japanese aircraft were both twin- and single-engine, big and small, agile and lumbering. They were the most aggressive *The Boomerang*'s crew had yet encountered. The enemy clearly intended to defend this target. In fact, the American Air Force would later learn that, following the bombing of Hiroshima and Nagasaki, the Japanese decided to commit the fighter force it had been hoarding as kamikazes for Ketsu-go into a more vigorous defense of the Home Islands.

Suddenly *The Boomerang*'s intercom was loud with fighter callouts:

"Big one, three o'clock level, making a run on us, I think . . . No, he's pacing us. . . ." Then bombardier Dick Marshall reported, "Two single-engine jobs, twelve o'clock low, climbing fast. . . ." Jim Smith added, "Three diving from two o'clock high. They're on us."

But the diving fighters might have been a diversion, because suddenly Marshall called out again, "Those two are still climbing . . . fast. . . . Here they come, right at us. They're going to hit us."

Smith watched through the thin Plexiglas dome as the two single-engine fighters flashed by just above his head. God, they were trying to ram us.

Three more fighters approached from astern but stayed well out of range of Sid Siegel's guns. Firing the tail guns was a last-ditch option: The muzzle flashes would betray the bomber's position. So Sid Siegel would not target the fighters passing nearby unless they actually attacked, and the crew could only hope that the Japanese would continue to believe that the B-29Bs were fully armed Superforts with the multiple gun turrets of the central fire-control system.

Apparently this illusion remained intact. For several minutes the fighters paced the bomber stream out of machine-gun range, then finally split off to climb away.

Now searchlights snapped on along the coast, first a pair, then eight, then a separate cluster of ten. Several had the distinctive green tint of German Wuerzburg radar fire control. Flak began bursting at the bombers' altitude. The first explosions were almost tentative. But soon the guns began to fire in salvos.

Suddenly a searchlight slashed across the length of *The Boomerang*, then crept forward to hold the bomber in its grip. Carl Schahrer banked sharply, his free hand on the throttles to climb and dive. But still the searchlight held the bomber. The flight deck and navigator's compartment were flooded with the searchlight's harsh glare. It was as if someone had switched on fluorescent tubes inside the aircraft.

Jim Smith was convinced that Tony Cosola had lit his navigator's lamp. "My God, Tony," he called irrationally, "turn off that light."

"The only light in here," the navigator shouted back, "is coming from down there."

"Keep dumping that rope," Schahrer told the two scanners. "There's no sense trying to save any."

At that moment, Smith looked forward to see the Superfort ahead of them caught in the searchlights. The big bomber also dipped and banked, trying to shake the glaring columns of light. Suddenly the plane took a direct hit in the fuselage. There was a flash, a puff of flame, and a billowing pall of smoke as the Superfort rolled to the left and fell out of the stream. Smith was certain he had just seen ten airmen killed.[46] In fact, the flak had not directly hit the bomber; the plane somehow survived the attack with damage and managed to return all the way to Guam.

The Boomerang's troubles were not yet over. Approaching Bombs Away, the flak intensified. Bombardier Dick Marshall had just called "clutch in" when an 88mm flak shell burst nearby. Shrapnel ripped into the nose of the aircraft, sounding as if hail were pounding the aluminum fuselage. There was a burst of static over the intercom. Later, Smith discovered, one of the radio antennas had been blown off the airplane.

"Anybody hit?" Schahrer asked, his voice incredibly cool.

No one had been.

"Bombs away," Marshall called, and the plane lurched as ten tons of 500-pound general-purpose bombs fell toward the flaming oil refinery below.

It was 0036 hours on August 10, 1945. *The Boomerang* banked into its procedural left turn off the burning target and headed southeast across the dark Pacific toward Guam.

As *The Boomerang*'s bombs were falling near Osaka, the members of the Supreme Council for the Direction of the War met in the Emperor's air-raid shelter twenty meters beneath the Fukiage Gardens of the Imperial Palace. Much to the displeasure of War Minister Anami, the Premier had invited Chief Cabinet Secretary Hisatsune Sakomizu and President of the Privy Council Kiichiro Hiranuma to attend the crucial meeting.[47] Sakomizu was Prime Minister Suzuki's closest adviser and could be expected to lend moral support to the peace faction, whereas Hiranuma was a known peace advocate.

The Imperial air-raid shelter was a narrow half-cylinder of reinforced concrete paneled in dark wood, only eighteen feet wide and thirty long. Ventilation was rudimentary. On this humid August night, the shelter was stifling. The members of the Big Six sat facing one another at two long, cloth-covered tables, joined by two aides and the two guests that Suzuki had invited. At the far end of the room stood a smaller table backed by a gilded silk screen. Here the Emperor would remain apart during the meeting. The officers and officials sat in their formal wear, uniform collars tightly buttoned, cravats tightly cinched. Everyone was sweating profusely as they waited for the Emperor.

After the men in the room had waited twenty-five minutes, the door to the shelter opened and the Emperor entered, followed by an aide. Everyone was on his feet, bowing deeply and holding his bow, until Hirohito took his place on a simple straight-back chair. According to historian William Craig, the men in the room "were dismayed to see their Sovereign's hair was unkempt, hanging down in disarray on his forehead. His harried look was hardly that of a godlike leader."[48]

After the Chief Cabinet Secretary had read the full text of the Potsdam Declaration, Prime Minister Suzuki summarized what the Emperor
already knew: The Big Six were stalemated three-to-three over accepting
the Allies' terms, while the full cabinet was even further divided. Now
Suzuki asked his younger colleague, Foreign Minister Togo, to resume the
presentation to the Emperor. Togo voiced the argument of the peace faction: that Japan must immediately accept the Potsdam Declaration, provided the Allies gave assurances that the *kokutai* would be preserved, and
explicitly that Hirohito remain Japan's Emperor.[49]

Instead of giving the war faction its turn, Suzuki asked Navy Minister Admiral Yonai his opinion. He rose and faced the Emperor. "I agree
with the Foreign Minister."

War Minister Anami realized that the elderly Premier was skillfully
undercutting his position in the presence of the Emperor. Anami jumped
up and energetically reiterated his argument that the outcome of the decisive Ketsu-go could not be known until the battle was fought. In any case,
General Anami said, it was imperative Japan insist on all four conditions.

By the protocol of rank, Premier Suzuki should have now called on
Navy Chief of Staff Admiral Toyoda to speak. Instead, the wily old statesman elicited the opinion of Privy Council President Baron Hiranuma. The
experienced politician—who was of Suzuki's generation and level of experience—now subjected the members of the war faction to a withering bar-
rage of questions.[50]

Ostensibly there to report back to the Emperor's Privy Council,
Hiranuma clearly relished playing the devil's advocate. He scornfully
addressed Anami and the other officers. "You said you had the means to
continue the war, but air raids now come every night and day. Do you have
the means to defend against the atom bomb? I wonder."

Resentful of the Baron's presence, War Minister Anami refused to be
baited and did not answer. But Army Chief of Staff Umezu spoke up in
defense of the military: "Regarding the atomic bomb, it might be checked
if proper antiaircraft measures are taken against the planes."[51]

But Hiranuma relentlessly bore in on the military, exposing their
failed assurances to prepare simultaneously adequate defenses of both
Kyushu and Honshu against the pending Allied invasion. It was obvious he
was scoring points against the war faction. The argument was protracted
and bordered on hot acrimony, an atmosphere unprecedented in the presence of the Emperor.

Finally, at almost 3 A.M., Prime Minister Suzuki called for an end of the debate. Noting that no conclusion had been reached and that the situation remained urgent, "I am therefore proposing to ask the Emperor his own wish and to decide the conference's conclusion on that basis. His wish should settle the issue, and the Government should follow it."[52]

When Hirohito replied, his voice was high-pitched and strained. "I agree with the first opinion as expressed by the Foreign Minister," the Emperor said, effectively demolishing the position of the war faction. He further undercut their stance by noting that the "military has frequently made statements contrary to fact" and that "we have lost confidence in the military's predictions of future success."[53]

The three members of the war faction sat rigidly in their chairs, their faces betraying no emotion.

Citing the traditions of his Imperial ancestors to bolster the nation's welfare and his own concern for "international world peace," Hirohito continued: "So, to stop the war on this occasion is the only way to save the nation from destruction and to restore peace in the world." He turned to face the members of the war faction and spoke with cold disdain. "Looking back at what our military headquarters have done, it is apparent their performance has fallen far short of the plans expressed. I do not think this discrepancy can be corrected in the future." The Emperor had just subjected these senior officers to the ultimate loss of face before their civilian counterparts. Their humiliation was complete.

Now Hirohito's voice assumed an anguished tone. "But when I think about my obedient soldiers abroad and of those who died or were wounded in battle, about persons who have lost their property by bombing in the homeland, when I think of all those sacrifices, I cannot help but feel sad. I decided that this war should be stopped, however, in spite of this sentiment and for more important considerations."[54]

Hirohito paused, then looked nervously around the room. Japan, he repeated, had lost the ability to defend its shores. "That is unbearable for me," he said. "But the time has come to bear the unbearable."

He rose and walked from the sweltering shelter. The men at the table sat wiping tears and sweat from their faces with damp white handkerchiefs.

After a pause, Suzuki stood. "The Imperial decision has been expressed. This should be the conclusion of the conference."[55]

No one voiced dissent.

But as the officers and officials climbed the narrow stairs to the garden above, Lieutenant General Masao Yoshizumi, Chief of the War Ministry's Military Affairs Bureau, lunged at Prime Minister Suzuki. "Are you happy?" Yoshizumi screamed. "Are you satisfied now?" The thick-chested General Anami pulled Yoshizumi away from the frail old statesman.[56] The outburst had been grotesque coming from a disciplined general officer. And everyone realized that countless fanatical junior officers, both in the Home Islands and abroad, shared his frustration and hatred for civilians such as Suzuki and Togo, whom they saw as traitors.

The full cabinet still had to ratify the Emperor's decision, and the ministers were waiting at Suzuki's residence to do just that. Once the cabinet had formally voted, the Foreign Ministry would transmit Japan's acceptance of the Potsdam Declaration to the Allies. As Suzuki had hoped and expected, the cabinet vote was unanimous for acceptance.

But as the Council meeting broke up, War Minister Anami took the Prime Minister aside. "Suppose the enemy refuses to give you any assurance that the Imperial House will be preserved. Will you go on fighting?"

Speaking softly, Suzuki reluctantly conceded that he was prepared to do so.[57]

Based on an extensive documentary record, there can be no doubt that—regardless of the Emperor's decision—Anami remained determined to conduct the final decisive Ketsu-go battle if the Allies refused to guarantee that *kokutai* would continue unchanged with Hirohito as sovereign following surrender. Before and after the Supreme Council meetings and the Imperial conference, the War Minister instructed the hot-tempered and bellicose Lt. General Masao Yoshizumi that Japan must continue the war if the Allies insisted on unconditional surrender. "In view of [the] considerable chances of victory in the decisive battle of the homeland, the war should not be given up at this time," Anami told Yoshizumi on the eve of the Imperial conference. And even after the Emperor had humiliated the Army leaders and rejected this idea, Anami sought to send Yoshizumi as an emissary to Lord Keeper of the Privy Seal Kido to further "the Army's view" on this matter within the Imperial Palace.[58] Kido refused to see the General. But Anami remained adamantly opposed to peace.

. . .

The cabinet unanimously voted to accede to the Emperor's wishes. Two hours after the predawn meeting on August 10, the Foreign Ministry transmitted a cable to the Allied powers via Swiss and Swedish diplomatic channels: The note was addressed to the United States, Great Britain, China, and the Soviet Union, and stated that the Japanese government "in obedience to the gracious command of His Majesty the Emperor, who, ever anxious to enhance the cause of world peace, desires earnestly to bring about an early termination of hostilities. . . ." The diplomatic fluff continued until the key provision:

"The Japanese Government is ready to accept the terms in the Joint Declaration which was issued at Potsdam, July 26, 1945 . . . with the understanding that said declaration does not comprise any demand which prejudices the prerogatives of His Majesty as a Sovereign Ruler."[59]

It had been Privy Council President Hiranuma who had insisted on this critical clause.

Now the members of the peace faction in Tokyo could only watch the sky and wait tensely for the Allies' response.

RUMORS OF PEACE

Never have I known time to pass so slowly.

—DIARY ENTRY, JAMES F. BYRNES, SECRETARY OF STATE

AT 7:33 A.M. EASTERN WAR TIME on August 10, American military radio-intercept monitors heard the unofficial text of the Japanese foreign ministry's cablegram, which was broadcast in plain language over the Domei News Agency's overseas service in an attempt to bypass sluggish diplomatic communication channels. The message reached President Harry Truman while he was finishing breakfast. The flowery court language—"In obedience to the gracious command of his Majesty the Emperor . . . ever anxious to enhance the cause of world peace"—contained the key phrase that Baron Hiranuma had demanded be inserted in the message concerning the understanding that the Potsdam Declaration not prejudice Hirohito's prerogatives as a sovereign ruler. The message concluded that the Japanese Government "desires keenly that an explicit indication to that effect will be speedily forthcoming."

It appeared that Japan was ready to surrender, provided that the

Allies would meet this one, albeit major, condition, which was yet another step beyond the already conditional surrender terms delineated in the Potsdam Declaration. Truman called a meeting of his top wartime advisers in the Oval Office at 9 o'clock that morning. When Fleet Admiral William D. Leahy, Truman's Chief of Staff; Henry L. Stimson, Secretary of War; James F. Byrnes, Secretary of State; and James V. Forrestal, Secretary of the Navy, gathered around the President's desk, each holding a mimeographed copy of the unofficial Japanese text, Truman addressed them one at a time.

Should they treat the Japanese message as an acceptance of the Potsdam Declaration? Many Americans (as evidenced in public opinion polls) saw Hirohito as "an integral part" of the Japanese system that America was pledged to destroy. Could Hirohito continue as sovereign while the "warlike spirit" of the Japanese was eliminated? And wasn't this Japanese demand incompatible with the long-held goal of unconditional surrender?

Truman's four senior advisers were surprised by the Japanese response and somewhat ambivalent about it. Given the time difference between Washington and Japan (which was on the other side of the international date line), there was an illusion that the Japanese had responded immediately after the atomic bombing of Nagasaki. Certainly none of the Truman administration's senior leadership was prepared to address the issue of imminent Japanese capitulation—with or without conditions—on the morning of August 10, 1945. Historian Richard B. Frank points out that the transition from total war to sudden peace was a momentous political and economic event for which the White House, the War Department, and the State Department were not prepared. Truman had issued no orders to smooth the process, despite the specter of mass unemployment and other economic upheaval. Huge war procurement contracts were still advancing as late as August 9. Secretary of War Stimson had no inkling that Japanese surrender was near: He was about to begin a vacation when Truman summoned him to the White House that morning. And Army Chief of Staff George Marshall had proposed direct discussions with the Japanese on freeing the tens of thousands of surviving Allied prisoners of war before serious surrender negotiations could proceed.[1]

Despite being caught flat-footed, Truman's advisers each had an opinion about the "conditional acceptance" clause concerning the Emperor in the Japanese message. Secretary of War Stimson repeated his position stated at the time that the Potsdam Declaration was drafted: The

Emperor would be needed to maintain discipline among the Japanese military. Only he could fulfill that function.

"Even if the question hadn't been raised by the Japanese," Stimson said, "we would have to continue the Emperor ourselves under our command and supervision in order to get into surrender the many scattered armies of the Japanese. Something like this use of the Emperor must be made to save us from a score of bloody Iwo Jimas and Okinawas all over China and the New Netherlands."[2]

(This was hardly an exaggeration: The casualty rate in the Pacific war had mounted steadily as American forces drew closer to Japan. "When Truman became President in April 1945, U.S. casualties were averaging more than 900 *a day*. In the Pacific, the toll from each successive battle rose higher," John T. Correll, Editor in Chief of *Air Force* magazine, wrote in the April 1994 issue, p. 30.)

Admiral Leahy and Navy Secretary Forrestal immediately concurred with Stimson. The foreboding with which the service secretaries and Admiral Leahy considered the prospect of trying to obtain the surrender of almost three million Japanese troops outside the Home Islands was based on reliable signals intelligence estimates of enemy strength. Even though the Soviet Army was rapidly decimating the undermanned Japanese Kwantung Army in Manchuria, the enemy remained strong elsewhere. Protracted military operations against Japan's intransigent forces distributed from the Solomon Islands through the Netherlands East Indies and Malaya, Indochina, the Chinese mainland, and Formosa would be extremely costly.

Having to dislodge disciplined Japanese forces from redoubts such as those they continued to hold in northern Luzon and the East Indies had already proven bloody challenges for the advancing Americans and Australians. Although Australian infantry had captured Japanese base areas in coastal Borneo in a series of sharply contested amphibious operations beginning in May 1945 during which a number of Allied ships were damaged or sunk, the surviving Japanese had regrouped and made disciplined retreats into the jungle hills, taking with them arms, ammunition, and even aircraft.[3] There were approximately 140,000 well-armed Japanese troops in bypassed garrisons in New Guinea and the Solomons alone. It would be the operational responsibility of Australian forces to dislodge the enemy from these jungle strong points.

Certainly Admiral Leahy was convinced that all of the more than five million Japanese soldiers, sailors, and airmen in the Home Islands and the overseas empire would fight to the death unless the Emperor ordered them to surrender. Leahy did not favor "little Hirohito" retaining all his power and prerogatives, but he knew the Emperor would be of practical use at this time.[4]

Secretary of State Byrnes differed from his colleagues on this matter. With the United States in such a strong position, he argued, it should be America and not Japan that laid down conditions. "I cannot understand," Byrnes said, "why we should go further than we were willing to go at Potsdam when we had no atomic bomb, and Russia was not in the war." Byrnes, an experienced Democratic Party politician who had been a U.S. Supreme Court Justice, President Roosevelt's director of war mobilization, and was a ten-year veteran of the Senate from South Carolina, instinctively tried to shield his new president from the political danger that a perception of leniency toward the hated Japanese Emperor might well spark.[5]

Navy Secretary Forrestal suggested a compromise: The Allies could inform the Japanese that they were willing to accept their surrender terms, but define the terms of that surrender clearly within the framework of the Potsdam Declaration, with which the American public largely agreed. If the Japanese accepted, Allied (American) policy would appear to have been consistent throughout the critical final weeks of the war. Truman asked Byrnes to draft a reply to the Japanese that would neatly thread the needle by accepting their request concerning the prerogatives of the Emperor, but couching this condition within the language of the Potsdam Declaration.

Byrnes returned to the White House just before noon to show the President both the Japanese government's official communication, which the Swiss legation had just delivered to the State Department (it was identical to the unofficial text the Domei News Agency had radioed earlier), and the draft of the proposed Allied reply to the Japanese. As Truman had requested, Byrnes had crafted the message in finely honed diplomatic language. But the meaning of the reply was unambiguous. Concerning the Japanese request on the Emperor's prerogatives as a sovereign ruler, the Allied position would be:

"From the moment of surrender the authority of the Emperor and the Japanese government to rule the state shall be subject to the Supreme Commander of the Allied Powers who will take such steps as he deems proper to effectuate the surrender terms.

"The Emperor and the Japanese High Command will be required to sign the surrender terms necessary to carry out the provisions of the Potsdam Declaration, to issue orders to all the armed forces of Japan to cease hostilities and to surrender their arms and to issue such other orders as the Supreme Commander may require to give effect to the surrender terms. . . ."

A provision on the immediate transport of Allied prisoners of war and civilian internees to places of safety followed. The next paragraph ran counter to the Japanese request that the Emperor and his heirs remain sovereign indefinitely:

"The ultimate form of government shall, in accordance with the Potsdam Declaration, be established by the freely expressed will of the Japanese people.

"The armed forces of the Allied Powers will remain in Japan until the purposes set forth in the Potsdam Declaration are achieved."[6]

To Harry Truman, Byrnes's draft reply was completely satisfactory. The President recorded in his diary that since the Japanese wanted to keep their Emperor so badly, "we'd tell 'em how to keep him."[7]

During an urgent cabinet meeting that afternoon, Truman's administration endorsed the draft reply. In the afternoon, the President also ordered that no more atomic bombs be dropped on Japan without his specific orders. As Truman told Secretary of Commerce Henry Wallace, he hated the thought of killing another 100,000 Japanese, including "all those kids," unless it was necessary. Truman's concerns were not abstract: Ultra signals intelligence intercepts had now made clear the extent of the carnage at Hiroshima.[8]

In any event, it would have been difficult to conduct another atomic bomb mission immediately, because Generals Marshall and Groves had agreed to delay flying the plutonium core of the third bomb, which would be available at Los Alamos by August 12 or 13, to Tinian by C-54 transport. In doing so, they were following the directions of Secretary of War Stimson, who believed that the bomb should be used only to force the Japanese to surrender. Should Tokyo refuse to capitulate and the President order the third bomb to be dropped, however, Colonel Tibbets's 509th Composite Group could possibly be ready to carry out the mission as early as August 17 or 18, but a more realistic date would be August 21.

And it was quite possible that, despite the obvious risk to the Imperial Palace, Tokyo would have been the target for the third atomic bomb. When Manhattan Project leaders considered possible targets that spring, Tokyo, including the Emperor's palace, had certainly been under scrutiny. However, the Manhattan Project target planners ruled out the Japanese capital, because Robert Oppenheimer and his colleagues "agreed that we should not recommend it but that any action for this bombing should come from authorities on military policy [i.e., senior administration officials or the President himself]."[9] By August 10, however, Strategic Air Forces commander General Carl Spaatz was advocating "placing" the third atomic bomb on Tokyo if that attack would hasten surrender through its "psychological effect on government officials."[10] But after consultation with his senior staff in the Pacific, Spaatz recommended a list of six other candidate targets, most well away from Tokyo.[11] However, these officers had not counted on the stubborn resolve of President Truman to shock the Japanese into surrender. As late as noon in Washington on August 14, when the long-anticipated official Japanese surrender message still had not arrived, President Truman sadly told the visiting Duke of Windsor and British ambassador Sir John Balfour "that he now had no alternative but to order an atomic bomb dropped on Tokyo."[12]

It seemed that Lieutenant Marcus McDilda's desperate and groundless prediction that Tokyo would be the next atom bomb target might prove valid after all. It is noteworthy that Truman considered annihilating the Imperial household and the headquarters of Japanese Imperial forces in this bombing, even though Secretary of War Stimson, Byrnes, and other key advisers saw the retention of the Emperor as crucial in implementing the surrender of the far-flung Japanese forces.

Meanwhile, on August 10 in Washington, Truman ordered that offensive air and naval operations against Japanese forces continue across the Pacific, in part because Japanese conventional bombers and kamikaze aircraft were still attacking American naval units near Okinawa and the coast of China. The strategic objective of the intense conventional bombing of the Home Islands was part of the ongoing preparation of Kyushu and southern Honshu for the Olympic Invasion, which was still scheduled to begin in November. This intense bombing was also meant to demonstrate American military superiority, which, in turn, might dampen the zeal of intransigent Japanese militarists still hoping to fight the suicidal Ketsu-go battle.

As soon as the cabinet secretaries left the White House that afternoon, the State Department circulated the draft reply to the Japanese to America's Allies. The British government quickly endorsed the message, with one exception. Prime Minister Clement Attlee cabled Truman suggesting it was inappropriate to require the Emperor personally to sign the surrender document. The British proposed replacement language by which the Emperor "shall authorize and ensure" the signature of the Japanese government and Imperial General Headquarters on the surrender rather than be required to sign it publicly. Truman agreed to the change.

By the morning of Saturday, August 11, Chinese Nationalist President Chiang Kai-shek had cabled his acceptance of the American draft message.

But the reaction of the Soviet Union was neither swift nor free of controversy. Soviet Foreign Minister Molotov told American Ambassador Averell Harriman that the Kremlin was "skeptical" toward the Japanese proposal, which Stalin did not consider unconditional surrender. Soviet forces, therefore, would continue to advance in Manchuria. When Truman's personal message requesting a quick Soviet response arrived, Molotov equivocated, promising an answer sometime later that night. But although Molotov did accept the draft Byrnes note, the Soviet foreign minister added the troublesome request that the Allies "should reach an agreement on the candidacies for representation of the Allied High Command to which the Japanese Emperor and the Japanese Government are to be subordinated."[13]

The Soviets were almost certain that Truman planned to designate General Douglas MacArthur to be Supreme Allied Commander, yet they attempted at this late juncture to split the high command between an American and a Soviet general, and specifically requested Marshal Aleksandr Vasilevsky, commander of the Soviet forces in the Far East. This was clearly an attempt to gain a foothold in Japan, against which it had been at war for only three days, just as it shared in the occupation of Germany, the intractable enemy it had battled for four years. Harriman understood that the Soviet position would be completely unacceptable to President Truman and so informed Molotov during "a most heated discussion."[14] When Harriman held firm, the Soviets backed down. On receiving the news, Truman was satisfied and later stated that he did not want "to give the Russians any opportunity to behave [in Japan] as they had in Germany and in Austria." America had conquered Japan with blood and technical superiority. Truman was not about to allow the Soviets to share the prize.[15]

On the afternoon of Saturday, August 11, the State Department handed the Swiss chargé d'affaires the official Allied reply to the Japanese to be cabled to Tokyo via Bern. Now it was the Allies' turn to wait. In the Far East, Admiral Chester Nimitz issued an order to the Pacific Fleet, warning his commanders not to drop their vigilance against Japanese attacks. "Take precautions against treachery even if local or general sur-render should suddenly be announced. . . ." As Nimitz sent his orders, U.S. Navy ships in the waters near the Home Islands, Okinawa, and the coast of China were under increasing Japanese air attack.[16]

The Allied reply was released to the international press, which would serve to deliver the message to the Japanese through unofficial radio-broadcast channels, just as they had done with the Domei announcement on August 10. This news created a peace frenzy in Washington, and Tru-man woke on Sunday, August 12, to find the White House "beleaguered" by press and radio reporters with large crowds waiting expectantly across Pennsylvania Avenue in Lafayette Park. That evening, a rumor swept Washington that the Japanese had formally surrendered. But the rumor was false.

Truman's closest advisers waited tensely. Secretary of State James Byrnes later summarized their shared sentiment: "Never have I known time to pass so slowly!"[17]

Because Tokyo was thirteen hours ahead of Washington, the deliberations in the American capital took place after equally crucial events affecting Japanese military leaders and government officials. During the early morning of August 10 in Japan, following the transmission of the official Foreign Ministry cable, War Minister Anami slept perhaps two hours, then ordered a meeting of his staff officers in the War Ministry's large air-raid shelter on Ichigaya Heights. He strode down the echoing concrete tunnel to the shelter and marched between the ranks of officers who stood at stiff attention to the briefing stage. Anami took his position to face his assem-bled officers and gripped his leather riding crop in apparent anguish. Only one or two men in the shelter realized what he intended to tell them. Most believed that the War Minister had called them to this conference to dis-cuss plans for the Ketsu-go or to assess the military situation in Manchuria. Instead, Anami recounted in detail what had happened during the Imper-ial conference. The senior officers were chagrined; the younger officers were stunned. Although many understood the growing power of the peace faction within the government, the finality of the Emperor's decision and the cabinet's action hit them without warning.

For months these men had worked tirelessly preparing the Ketsu-go defenses. They knew the strength of the Army units already in position to defend Kyushu. They recognized that the armada of hoarded kamikaze aircraft could inflict horrendous losses on the Allied invasion force. They also realized that Japan had a huge undefeated army in the field outside the Home Islands. Yet accepting the terms of the Potsdam Declaration meant that the Imperial Army, to which they had devoted their lives, would suffer the dishonor of being disarmed and disbanded by the enemy. Worse, demobilization would be followed by enemy occupation of the sacred homeland, a consequence of surrender that many feared was tantamount to the physical and spiritual extinction of Japan itself.

Although His Majesty was prepared to bear the unbearable, a large number of officers facing War Minister Anami were not. The humid atmosphere in the shelter churned with emotion as Anami spoke. Among the most deep-seated of these feelings were denial and the stubborn conviction that events had not yet progressed so far toward dishonorable surrender that they could not be reversed.

As Anami wearily described the events that led up to the Imperial decision, some officers grouped before the stage in a semicircle stepped forward to cry, "No!"

Anami held up his hands to silence the protests. "I do not know what excuse to make to you, but since it is the Emperor's decision, it cannot be helped. The important thing is that the Army shall act in an organized manner." He looked closely at his senior officers and those he recognized as leaders among the younger colonels and lieutenant colonels standing before him. Then Anami continued, "Individual feelings must be disregarded. This decision, however, was made on the condition that the upholding of our national polity be guaranteed. Consequently, it does not mean that the war has ended. The Army must be prepared for either war or peace."[18]

"What about the duty of the military to protect the nation?" a major protested. "Is the war minister actually considering *surrender*?" The foul word seemed to echo in the concrete chamber.

Normally a man of rigid self-discipline, General Anami was frustrated, embittered, and exhausted. He slapped his riding crop against the tabletop and silenced the grumbling. "Anybody who isn't willing to obey my orders will have to do so over my dead body."[19]

His vehemence stunned Anami's staff. They left the shelter in angry confusion. But, climbing the Ministry's sandbagged staircases, some began to speak furtively of rebellion. If Japan's civilian leaders persisted in exerting treasonous pressure on the Emperor, it would be up to the Army to save from dishonor both His Majesty and the sacred Empire he embodied.

One of those who had listened to Anami's remarks "with particular care and particular dismay" was Lt. Colonel Masao Inaba, a staff officer in the Ministry's Military Affairs Section. He now approached the War Minister with a bold plan to maintain the discipline and zeal of the Army. "Regardless of whether we end the war or not," he told the War Minister, "we must send out instructions to keep fighting, particularly with Soviet troops advancing in Manchuria."[20]

"Write it out," Anami ordered.

Lt. Colonel Inaba drafted the broadcast statement and cleared it through his section head in preparation for Anami's approval. But, after taking shelter from a daylight B-29 incendiary raid, War Minister Anami was preoccupied working on an entirely different statement that the Big Six had previously drafted for cabinet approval, to be broadcast to the nation and the armed forces later that day. This message was meant to prepare the Japanese people for either the eventuality of surrender or continued war. While this equivocal text was being edited, agitated officers at the War Ministry, fearful that the cabinet was about to issue a public appeal for surrender, decided to force the director of the Information Bureau, Hiroshi Shimomura, to broadcast the Army's "proclamation" and distribute it to the press under Anami's name, even if the Minister had not read the text.

Shimomura complied. That night at 7 o'clock on the regular news broadcast, Japanese in both the Home Islands and abroad listened to two conflicting statements. The official cabinet message to the people was unlike anything they had heard during almost four years of the Pacific war. For the first time the government announced that the enemy was using a barbarous "new type" of bomb with devastating effect. Although "our fighting forces will no doubt be able to repulse the enemy's attack . . . we must recognize that we are facing a situation that is as bad as it can be." This was the first reference that any Japanese cabinet had made that the war was not going well. The message was a shock to millions of listeners who, despite the widespread devastation of the American bombing, still believed that Japan was winning the war. "The government will do all it can to defend the homeland and preserve the honor of the country, but expects that Japan's hundred million will also rise to the occasion, overcoming whatever obstacles may lie in the path of the preservation of our national polity [kokutai]." It was unclear whether this was an appeal for continued resistance or for surrender if the Allies guaranteed the Emperor's status.

But the Army's inflammatory "Instructions to the Troops," issued over Anami's name, was anything but vague; it made no reference to military defeat or enemy strength. "We have but one choice," it read. "We must fight on until we win the sacred war to preserve our national polity. We must fight on even if we have to chew grass and eat dirt and live in fields—for in our death there is a chance of our country's survival. The hero Kusunoki pledged to live and die seven times in order to save Japan from disaster. We can do no less. . . ."[21]

(Masashige Kusunoki was a legendary fourteenth-century samurai who, through incredible feats of arms, defended the Emperor Go-Daigo against shoguns who had all but stripped him of authority. Ultimately, the Emperor forced Kusunoki into a battle in which he committed suicide rather than surrender.)

The War Ministry officers who had revised Lt. Colonel Inaba's already provocative draft included two men who harbored deep rebellious sentiments, Lt. Colonel Masahiko Takeshita and Major Kenji Hatanaka, both also of the Military Affairs Section, a hotbed of potential rebellion. Takeshita was General Anami's brother-in-law and a longtime colleague whose close relationship transcended their wide difference in rank. Hatanaka was slender but athletic, a pale, soft-spoken, and diligent staff officer known to be a "pet," or protégé, of the War Minister.[22] At 34, he looked much younger than his years, and, perhaps to compensate, his most distinguishing feature was a nearly constant serious expression.

The fact that these two officers enjoyed positions of special trust and confidence within War Minister Anami's inner circle made their involvement in the affair especially worrisome for civilian officials hoping for immediate surrender with no resistance from the military. To ensure that the Army proclamation—which was certain to have been intercepted by American radio monitors—did not derail the peace negotiations before the official Japanese government message reached Washington through diplomatic channels, Foreign Minister Togo bypassed military censors and had the Domei News Agency transmit the text of the foreign ministry message in Morse code in English.[23] This was the "unofficial" reply that President Truman and his advisers had discussed in the White House on the morning of August 10. Togo was also apparently motivated by the spreading rumor that Tokyo would be struck by an atomic bomb within days. (The *kempeitai* report that Lieutenant McDilda's revelations about the atomic bomb had been groundless had not yet reached key military or civilian leaders, and even when it did, they were still fearful.)

That night in Tokyo, a group of rebellious officers, reportedly including Lt. Colonel Inaba of the Military Affairs Section, hoping to see martial law declared, careered through the rubble-strewn streets throwing grenades from Army vehicles. Their act of defiance was futile.

It was significant that War Minister Anami did not discipline the officers involved in either broadcasting the fiery Army broadcast or the grenade-throwing incident, one a grievous overreaching of their authority, the other a gross breach of discipline bordering on rebellion. This convinced many young officers disgruntled with their government's acceptance of the Potsdam Declaration that General Anami was on their side.

And when the Emperor personally reprimanded the War Minister over the broadcast, Anami merely replied, "The Army will have to stand against the enemy to the very end; therefore the issuance of the instructions to the forces is necessary."[24] Later, he reportedly confided to his most trusted subordinates his bitterness at having been outmaneuvered by Prime Minister Suzuki, Foreign Minister Togo, and the peace faction during the Imperial conference on the night of August 9–10. "Perhaps there was some sort of scheme involved in absolutely disregarding our plan [to include all four negotiation conditions]."[25]

Although much of the historical record of this desperate period in Tokyo has been either accidentally or intentionally destroyed—diaries and contemporaneous minutes of meetings were burned together with secret documents—and surviving Japanese participants in the crucial events were often less than forthright when questioned by Allied interrogators (some of whom were gathering evidence for war crimes investigations), it is clear that War Minister Anami and his closest aides did everything they could to block the peace faction's maneuvers and the Emperor's "august wish" to end the war.[26]

The unofficial announcement that the Japanese government had notified the Allies they were ready to accept the terms of the Potsdam Declaration reached Northwest Field and the airmen of the 315th Wing on the afternoon of August 10. There was absolutely no doubt in anyone's mind that the official word of surrender would arrive at any moment.

Only hours before, they had been trapped in the greenish-white glare of the searchlights above Amagasaki as the flak burst along the length of the bomber stream. Some of the black smoke-balls looked close enough to touch. When he closed his eyes, Smith could picture the Superfort ahead of *The Boomerang* lit up by the flak burst. He could still hear the noise of the shrapnel, like marbles striking his airplane's skin.

And even after they had dropped their bombs and safely passed land's end, the danger of the mission wasn't over. Flight Engineer Hank Gorder had calculated their best fuel-saving cruise control for the return flight at an altitude of 27,000 feet. When the plane had reached that altitude, Smith was hunched at his table, having just prepared his strike report for transmission. Then there was a loud bang. *The Boomerang* had suffered explosive decompression. (It was later determined that the aft bomb-bay pressure door had failed to seal during the climb, and the mounting pressure differential blew the circular hatch into the rear bomb bay.)

Because the bomber only occasionally flew at high altitude, the crew rarely wore their oxygen masks. Now, with the pressurized air shrieking out of the cabin and aft compartment, the men had to scramble in the darkness to find their masks and hook up to their assigned oxygen outlets.

Carl Schahrer had called for a crew-oxygen check over the intercom. Everyone had reported in okay except the two scanners in their compartment aft of the bomb bay. Without hesitating, navigator Tony Cosola had plugged his oxygen mask to a little steel walk-around tank and crawled through the dark tunnel. He had found the two scanners, Henry Carlson and Hank Leffler, showing obvious signs of hypoxia: Their words were slurred, their movements clumsy. Then, in the beam of his flashlight, Cosola had found the cause of the problem. The two scanners had not connected the hoses of their masks securely and were trying to breathe an atmosphere almost as thin as the summit of Mount Everest. Cosola had corrected the problem and stayed with the men until he was sure that they had recovered. But crawling forward through the tunnel, Cosola's own portable oxygen tank was exhausted and he was slipping into hypoxia himself before he reconnected to the fixed outlet at the navigator's position.

After landing at Northwest Field, everyone was talking about the latest news. The Japs were ready to throw in the towel.

"You better pack your bag, Smitty," Crew Chief Sergeant Floyd Jennings told Smith. "They say the war's about over."

Jim Smith absorbed Jennings's words. It would be incredible if they were true. If Japan accepted the Potsdam Declaration, he had just flown his last combat mission.

Elsewhere in the Pacific Theater, American servicemen greeted the news with great joy that the Japanese were poised on the verge of surrender. On the American cruiser USS *Montpelier*, anchored in Buckner Bay on Okinawa, Seaman First Class James J. Fahey, a veteran of many hard-fought campaigns, joined his crewmates in cheering the report, which the ship's captain broadcast over the public address system. The crew compartments and mess hall echoed with yells and whistles. Men danced on the deck. On the nearby island, where Army troops were still mopping up pockets of die-hard Japanese resistance, soldiers began firing tracers in the air, and the hills were lit by multicolored flares and star shells. Ships in the anchorage turned on their searchlights to add to the illumination. A few ships fired their guns, while others blew their foghorns. For Fahey and his buddies, this was the "happiest day of our lives."[27]

But within forty-eight hours, the sailors' optimism had dampened. There was no news on progress in the peace negotiations. And Japanese planes had resumed their attack on American ships around Okinawa. At 2024 hours on August 12, the battleship USS *Pennsylvania*, which had survived the attack at Pearl Harbor, was hit in the stern by a torpedo launched from a Japanese bomber that had brazenly flown into the anchorage in the dark with its navigation lights lit, a ruse meant to convince the gunners on the ships that the enemy plane was actually American. Casualties aboard the *Pennsylvania* were heavy, with twenty men dead and many severely wounded.[28] The ship was so badly damaged that it could not move under its own power. The Japanese air attacks, including kamikaze raids, continued over the next three days. In fact, enemy air strikes on Okinawa grew so intense between August 11 and 14 that the Americans blacked out the entire island at night, except for a coral quarry run by U.S. Army engineers, which was kept lighted because the coral rock was urgently needed for airfield construction. This illuminated quarry was subjected to repeated Japanese air attack during this period.[29]

On August 10, while the 315th Wing was returning from the night mission to Amagasaki, the 314th Wing bombed the Tokyo arsenal in daylight despite the poor weather associated with the approaching typhoon that *The Boomerang* had dodged the previous night. Because this storm system was so large and violent, General Spaatz decided to cancel B-29 operations on August 11. When Spaatz told correspondents, "The Superforts are not flying today," they interpreted his remarks to mean that the Strategic Air Forces had received a cease-fire order. The American press published their correspondents' stories to this effect. Chief of Staff General Marshall was not pleased with this development, since the President had wanted to keep up the pressure of the B-29s on Japan. Marshall cabled Spaatz that his remarks to the press presented a "very delicate and critical problem to the President. Resumption of bombing would appear to indicate that preliminary negotiations had fallen through, giving rise to a storm of publicity and confusing views." He ordered Spaatz to stop all offensive missions and to avoid any further comment to the press. Army Air Forces Commander General Arnold took this directive one step further. He ordered Spaatz to "cease at once [all missions], and any missions which may now be in the air en route to targets will be recalled. This restriction will continue until such time as you may be directed to resume your operations."[30]

Inadvertently, President Truman had been obliged to reduce the bombing pressure on the Japanese while the Suzuki government waited for the Allies' response concerning Japan's acceptance of the Potsdam Declaration and their terms on the Emperor's future status.

On the morning of August 11, while the American military considered the appropriate degree of force to use against Japan at this stage of the negotiations, fifteen fanatical young officers from War Minister Anami's staff met secretly in the Ministry's air-raid shelter. They had come to plot a coup d'état that would disrupt the Japanese government's plan to surrender. This was a desperate, complex endeavor that required unswerving and tireless commitment. The War Minister's brother-in-law, Lt. Colonel Masahiko Takeshita, was the senior officer and presided at the meeting. Given his close relationship to Anami, he instilled confidence in his coconspirators.

"I can guarantee that the General will join with us," he assured them.[31]

With War Minister Anami firmly on their side, he said, the entire army would rally to them.

The key to success was bold action. A small cadre of brave and dedicated officers would move to isolate the Emperor from the traitorous civilian advisers, in particular Marquis Kido, Prime Minister Suzuki, and Foreign Minister Togo. Should these traitors resist, they would be arrested and even executed. Then the War Minister would try once more to convince the Emperor to continue the war. But if General Anami failed, the Emperor would be retained in protective custody within the Imperial Palace and a military government under the command of the War Minister would be established.

General Anami would then follow the only honorable course for the Army and the nation, the one he had long advocated: Fight the decisive Ketsu-go battle on the beaches and hills of Kyushu, inflicting such terrible casualties on the enemy invasion force that the Allies would sue for peace. If they did not, the Army would fall back to the mountains of the Home Islands and wage a protracted guerrilla war just like the one the Chinese Nationalist forces had conducted for years against the Japanese among the ridges and gorges of Szechwan.

The news of the Imperial decision to accept the Potsdam Declaration filled Takeshita and his colleagues with outrage. They were furious that the only condition that the Kido-Suzuki-Togo cabal had requested from the Allies was that the status of the Emperor (the national polity) remain unchanged. This meant that six million disciplined and well-equipped Japanese soldiers, sailors, and airmen would be forced to taste bitter surrender, that the long-victorious Japanese armed forces would be permanently disbanded, and that foreign troops would occupy the sacred homeland. With the Army stripped of its weapons, its authority, and its honor, those foreign occupation forces would be free to change the national polity in any way they desired, while loyal soldiers like the men in this dank concrete shelter would be forced to look on in shame as their leaders were tried as war criminals.

They had sworn a sacred oath to the Emperor to defend the homeland with their lives if called upon. Now they were willing to do just that, even if it meant defying the wishes of His Majesty and his legally constituted cabinet to end the war. Each man in the room recognized that the *kokutai* was unique and beyond the understanding of foreign nations. Should the Allies occupy the homeland, these foreign barbarians would transform the national polity simply by their presence. Therefore, the three additional conditions that War Minister Anami and Army Chief of Staff General Umezu had insisted on—especially the proviso that there be

no foreign occupation—were indispensable to the preservation of the
kokutai. Without these conditions, Takeshita later stated, describing the
desperate mood at the time, "it would be useless for the people to survive
the war if the structure of the State itself were to be destroyed."[32]

Although several of the plotters were staff officers who had never
commanded troops in the field, others, including Takeshita, had combat
experience. They quickly established a practical course of action. Once
General Anami had approved their plan, he would elicit the support of a
colleague, Army Chief of Staff General Umezu. In turn, they would bring
into the plot General Shizuichi Tanaka, Commander of the Eastern District Army, which had responsibility for all of Tokyo, and Lt. General
Takeshi Mori, Commander of the 1st Imperial Guards Division. This latter unit consisted of four regiments of infantry, artillery, and armored cav-
alry that guarded the Imperial Palace grounds. With General Mori's troops
on their side, the rebels could effectively seal off the Palace and hold the
Emperor incommunicado indefinitely. They would sever all telephone
lines from the Palace, take over broadcasting stations, occupy newspapers,
and seize control of the War Ministry and its communication links to
Japanese forces in the Home Islands and overseas. Once the lightning coup
had succeeded, General Anami could simply issue orders in the Emperor's
name to the armed forces to continue the war. The legal pretext for these
blatantly illegal actions would be the War Minister's constitutional authority to employ troops to maintain order during an emergency. The fact that
the rebels themselves would have provoked the emergency did not trouble
their consciences.

They were zealots, and reason was not their leading attribute. Among
the most passionate officers at this secret meeting were the Military
Affairs Section's Lt. Colonel Masao Inaba and Major Kenji Hatanaka, both
of whom had figured prominently in the "Instructions to the Troops"
broadcast.

The officers who had come to plot the coup had a common philosophy concerning their nation and its emperor. To them the Emperor was not
only a living god but the divine manifestation of Japan's unique essence,
the representative of the world's oldest dynasty, which stretched back
unbroken through the long succession of Imperial Ancestors with whom
Hirohito could commune through mystical means. Therefore, temporary
disobedience to the wrongheaded orders of the present Emperor might
well constitute a "wider and truer loyalty to the Throne in the final analy-

sis."[33] So the rebellious officers actually viewed their plot as an act of transcendent loyalty.

Several of the plotters were disciples of Professor Kiyoshi Hiraizumi, a deceptively soft-spoken ultranationalist firebrand who taught history and Japanese mythology at the Tokyo Imperial University. Emerging on the academic and military scenes in the mid-1920s, Hiraizumi had exerted a profound influence over two generations of Army officers. As a younger man, it was Anami himself who had first fallen under Hiraizumi's sway and given him entrée to his subordinate officers. Lt. Colonel Takeshita, Major Hatanaka, and their War Ministry comrade Lt. Colonel Masataka Ida belonged to a "research society" that the professor conducted at Tokyo's Shoin Shrine during the war.

As communism swept through Japanese universities in the 1920s (and took root among some discontented military officers), Hiraizumi had joined other nationalist academics in preaching the philosophy that every nation had its unique essence, which other countries must be forced to respect. Japan, he taught his military students, should be purified of all outside influences, including communism, individualism, and Western democratic values.[34] Japanese society was tantamount to a family; its citizens owed complete loyalty to their parents, the nation, and the Emperor, who embodied the sacred homeland's unique identity.

Mystical ultranationalist Professor Hiraizumi quickly developed a cult following. By World War II, he could count a significant segment of the Japanese officer corps among his devotees, including many kamikaze pilots who climbed into their cockpits speaking his aphorisms.

One crucial element of Hiraizumi's philosophy was that any given emperor, although the embodiment of the Imperial dynasty and the nation's destiny during his lifetime, might occasionally be led astray either through personal defect or by treacherous advisers. Then the nation's destiny would be in danger. Such extraordinary cases called for uncommon remedies. Placing the person of the Emperor under protection for the higher good of the nation was one of these remedies.[35]

The conspirators saw themselves as "young tigers," obliged by their destiny in these circumstances to take command, a dangerous tradition known in the Japanese military as *gekokujo* ("rule by juniors").[36]

This philosophy dovetailed perfectly with the desperation and frustration the rebellious officers in the air-raid shelter shared. Before disbanding, they decided to seek out a select group of colleagues to join their coup and then to approach War Minister Anami directly.

. . .

While the conspirators were meeting, Lord Keeper of the Privy Seal Kido met with Hirohito in the Imperial Palace. Kido had become convinced that when the time came—and he hoped that time was soon—for the Emperor formally to accept the Allies' surrender terms, His Majesty would agree to announce his decision to Japan and the world by radio. This would be unprecedented. Outside the Palace, few people in Japan had ever heard the "Voice of the Sacred Crane." (According to tradition, the Emperor's divine voice was as rare as legendary cranes that flew between heaven and earth, their cries never fading, but too indistinct for mortals to comprehend.)

However, Kido was convinced that it would be essential for Hirohito to address the military and the people directly for them to accept the ignominy of surrender without revolt or widespread civil disorder.

Kido had already conferred with Hiroshi Shimomura, the director of the Government Information Board, which controlled the Japanese Broadcasting Corporation, NHK. After confidentially consulting his technical staff, Shimomura recommended that, when His Majesty decided to address the nation, his words be recorded at the Imperial Palace, then broadcast from NHK's Tokyo studios.

Now Hirohito agreed to Kido's plan. The Voice of the Sacred Crane would be broadcast across Japan and her overseas empire once the acceptance of the Allied terms was final.[37]

Forty-five minutes after midnight on Sunday, August 12, 1945, Japanese civilian and military radio monitors began to receive an English-language broadcast in Morse code from San Francisco. It was the unofficial text of Secretary of State James Byrnes's reply to the message that Foreign Minister Togo had ordered to be sent through diplomatic channels to Washington two days earlier.[38] Before dawn, civilian and military translators were rendering the message in Japanese for their superiors.

The critical passages of the Allied reply were those that had most preoccupied President Truman and his advisers: "The authority of the Emperor and the Japanese government to rule the state shall be subject to the Supreme Commander of the Allied Powers." This sentence was so potentially explosive that the translators were at a loss to find the most suitable Japanese words to use, especially for the phrase "shall be subject to."

Fearful that this Allied condition would spark a coup d'état among zealous young military officers, Togo's foreign ministry translators finally worked up their own version to be circulated within the government: "The Emperor . . . will be under the limitation of the Supreme Commander . . ." This was an attempt to remove the dishonorable onus that the Emperor would be required to take direct orders from an American general.[39] But this was just semantics; there were enough fluent English speakers in the Army and the Navy to translate the exact meaning of the text for their superiors. And that meaning was clear: The Allies meant to place Hirohito, whom the Japanese people considered "a living god above whom there could be no earthly being," under the control of an enemy military officer.[40]

But almost as troubling was the paragraph in Byrnes's message that read: "The ultimate form of government of Japan shall, in accordance with the Potsdam Declaration, be established by the freely expressed will of the Japanese people."

Did the Americans mean to include the present Emperor and the entire *kokutai* within the word "government"? If so, no Japanese official could agree. But when Chief Cabinet Secretary Hisatsune Sakomizu (who exerted unusual influence over the Prime Minister) and Vice Minister of Foreign Affairs Shunichi Matsumoto (who exerted equal influence over his own minister) carefully read the text, they chose to interpret the word "government" as excluding the Imperial system.

By morning, however, the optimism of the night that semantic manipulation could make the Allies' harsh terms more readily acceptable, particularly to the military, had faded. As dawn bleached the ashes of bombed-out Tokyo, Vice Foreign Minister Matsumoto met Togo in his small private villa in the cool hills of Azabu. As expected, Togo saw through the attempt to dilute the meaning of the message when he compared the Japanese translation and the original English text. The "key provision," Foreign Minister Togo said, concerned the ultimate form of the Japanese government. Matsumoto suggested that the Foreign Ministry adopt a strategy of focusing the discussion on the phrase "subject to" in what promised to be heated meetings of the Big Six and the full cabinet in the coming hours. With any luck, that might deflect attention from the more troublesome issue of agreeing to the possible abolition of the *kokutai* through the "freely expressed will" of the Japanese people.[41]

As news of the Allied response spread through the long sandbagged corridors of the War Ministry on Ichigaya Heights, zealous young officers exploded in rage. But this emotion was not limited to junior ranks. War Minister Anami and Army Chief of Staff General Yoshijiro Umezu also expressed anger and chagrin. Following the Imperial conference on August 10, Japan had acted in good faith, informing the Allies that it was ready to accept the terms of the Potsdam Declaration provided they would guarantee that the Emperor remain the sovereign ruler of Japan. But it was clear from the Byrnes message that the Allies had made no such guarantee. The War Minister and the Army Chief of Staff were determined that the Japanese government reject Byrnes's note and press for additional negotiations, which they hoped would include the other conditions the Army deemed necessary to accept an honorable peace. While these negotiations unfolded, they believed they could fight the Americans and its Allies across the Pacific and on the mainland of Asia.[42] As the Foreign Minister, the Prime Minister, and their advisers had feared, the Allies' response had only stiffened the will of the Japanese military to resist.

Anxiety and confusion were rife. Rumors were incessant. As Japanese historians would later state concerning this bewildering period when Japan was suspended between possible sudden peace and the cataclysmic Decisive Battle for the Homeland, "No one's mood was of the kind to encourage accurate note-taking or sharp memory."[43] But the confrontations and meetings during this crucial period that have been documented reveal increasing anxiety and desperation among the Japanese civilians and military at the center of the turmoil.[44]

The Marquis Kido, who was probably the leading peace proponent in the Imperial Palace, took the Byrnes message to the Emperor in his emergency quarters at the Gobunko early on August 12. Kido was nervous. Japan had insisted that the Allies accept Hirohito and all future emperors as sovereign. But this reply was equivocal at best. As Lord Keeper of the Privy Seal, it was Kido's duty to delineate these problems to His Majesty.

Kido was stunned by the Emperor's serene reply. "That's all beside the point," Hirohito told him. "It would be useless if the people didn't want an emperor. I think it's perfectly all right to leave the matter up to the people."[45]

In his intramural struggle to make sure that Japan rejected the Allied terms, General Anami gained an unexpected ally, President of the Privy Council Baron Hiranuma, the acerbic old noble who had railed against the military during the Imperial conference on the night of August 9–10. It had been Hiranuma who had insisted on inserting the demand that the sovereign "prerogatives" of the Emperor be guaranteed. Now, with the Allies determined to make His Majesty "subject to the Supreme Commander of the Allied Powers," Hiranuma rejected this condition out of hand.[46] Together the Baron and the General went to pressure Prime Minister Suzuki not only on this condition but also on the issue of the people having the ultimate decision on the future of the Japanese Imperial House. After all, Premier Suzuki had promised War Minister Anami that Japan would continue the war if the Allies jeopardized the future of the dynasty. Now the aged Suzuki, more confused than usual by the recent turmoil, gave Anami his word that he would join them in protecting the Throne.

In historian Lester Brooks's descriptions of events, the Byrnes message had a particular impact on the young Army conspirators planning the coup d'état. As rumors flew around the War Ministry that General Anami had confronted the Emperor himself, the rebellious subordinates decided that they must immediately win the War Minister over to their plot. Led by Lt. Colonel Takeshita, the group tried to approach Anami through the Vice Minister on the afternoon of August 12 but were not allowed to enter Anami's office. Angry and frustrated, the young officers burst through the War Minister's door just as Anami was buckling on his sword, preparing to leave for an extraordinary cabinet meeting that the Prime Minister had called to consider the Allied response. General Anami had been discussing these matters with senior officers when the young officers forced their way inside. Obviously this was not the time or place to broach the subject of a coup. Lt. Colonel Takeshita adroitly changed tack. Now he spoke sincerely as the leader of these young staff officers deeply concerned with Japan's future. "General," he said, "it is our view that it is utterly inadvisable to end the war under the present conditions."

In a rush to leave, Anami nodded that he understood but did not commit himself. Sensing that the War Minister was on their side, Takeshita sought to press the advantage.

"General, under the present conditions, the Eastern District Army ought to be ordered to prepare to furnish troops to maintain order inasmuch as circumstances might well require such action."

War Minister Anami instructed the Vice Minister to pass on these orders to the army commander, Lt. General Tanaka.

Most of the officers in the room understood that Takeshita's words were a veiled preparation for irregular use of the military that could range all the way from an intimidating show of force to an actual coup d'état.

Colonel Hiroo Sato, a senior staff officer, glared at the younger men. "Do not act hastily," he said.[47]

Major Kenji Hatanaka stepped forward. "There are many Badoglios in the army," he said coldly, referring to the Italian General Pietro Badoglio, who had arranged the armistice between Mussolini's defeated Fascist army and the Allies in September 1943. Considered a hero to many Italians, Badoglio epitomized treachery to the traditional Japanese officer corps.

Now General Anami spoke in stern tones: "Military men must trust one another." His statement left no room for dispute. The crowded office fell silent.

A fellow conspirator took Takeshita aside and whispered, "Tell the Minister that the young officers trust him and intend to act as he directs." Although he felt awkward doing so, Takeshita made this statement. The Minister nodded silently, then departed hastily for the cabinet meeting.

Emotions were still running high among the conspirators. Many chose to believe that, since General Anami had agreed to place the Eastern District Army on alert, he was prepared to join them. But the officer who knew the minister best, his brother-in-law Lt. Colonel Takeshita, was unable at this point to judge Anami's real attitude. Nevertheless, the conspirators secretly proceeded with the necessary preparations for the coup.[48]

At 3 P.M., less than an hour after the tense confrontation in the War Ministry, the Japanese cabinet met at Prime Minister Suzuki's conference room in an extraordinary session. As he had planned with his close advisers, Foreign Minister Togo focused on the Allied condition that the Emperor's powers "would not be unlimited during the occupation, but that the Supreme Commander's authority would be paramount in order to make sure the Potsdam terms were carried out." Foreign Minister Togo initially avoided the issue of elections in Japan and assured the cabinet, "The Emperor's position is not destroyed nor changed in principle."

But eventually Togo was obliged to examine the troublesome paragraph concerning the "free will of the Japanese people" in determining the ultimate form of government. He tried to reassure his colleagues that this allowed the Japanese themselves to decide their own form of government free of intervention from the Allies, two of which—China and the Soviet Union—were known to be strongly opposed to the Emperor. "And who can believe that the Japanese people would choose anything but their Emperor system?"[49]

Before the merits of Foreign Minister Togo's case could be discussed, War Minister Anami argued energetically that the Allied reply was not satisfactory, that Japan must make further inquiries regarding the protection of the *kokutai*, and that, at the same time, the government should present the original three conditions concerning the trial of war criminals, the disarming of Japanese forces, and the occupation of the homeland. Togo was discouraged. It would be disastrous to submit multiple conditions to the Allies at this critical juncture. He told the cabinet that the Allies would interpret this as an indication of Japan's intention to break off negotiations. These matters had been "thoroughly debated" on August 9. It was the Emperor himself who had curtailed that debate and made his decision. Renewing the conditions now would show "disrespect" for the Emperor. And any attempt to continue fighting in the face of the Emperor's decision would result in the collapse of the negotiations.

Foreign Minister Togo's forceful words won over those in the cabinet who seemed to be moving toward Anami's position. But Home Minister Genki Abe and Justice Minister Hiromasa Matsuzaka stated that there could be no question of allowing the people to determine the future of the national polity: The Imperial system had been handed down by the gods.

Then the elderly Prime Minister, Kantaro Suzuki, who had been listening to the discussion half asleep, cold cigar clenched between his teeth, roused himself. The room fell silent. "The Allied reply is unsatisfactory," the old admiral proclaimed in his best quarterdeck voice. "To be disarmed by the enemy would be unbearable for a soldier, and under the circumstances there is no alternative to continuation of the war."[50]

Togo felt betrayed, but he retained his composure. He knew the Prime Minister had become increasingly confused in recent days. Instead of lashing out and causing the old man to lose face, Foreign Minister Togo said amicably that what Suzuki had said was worthy of careful consideration but that Japan should not continue the war irresponsibly without regard to the outcome. Unless there were some prospect of victory, the government must accept the Allied terms. But, sensing that the cabinet was deadlocked, and that the Prime Minister himself had become a wild card, Togo succeeded in having the meeting adjourned until Japan received the formal Allied reply.

Quietly furious at Premier Suzuki for derailing the cabinet meeting, Togo buttonholed him in a side room. It was "absurd" to take up the issue of disarmament of the forces after the Emperor had already made his decision, Togo told Suzuki, and Japan was in no position to make a strong stand on any issue unless there was some prospect of winning the war. "If you insist on this point," Togo said, "I will report to the Emperor alone." He left the room in a rage, fearing that the hard-fought peace negotiations had suddenly unraveled and that Japan teetered on the verge of disaster.[51]

While the cabinet was meeting, the conspirators plunged ahead with the practical aspects of their coup plot. Because winning the support of the Imperial Guards Division was vital, coup conspirator Major Kenji Hatanaka went directly to the unit's commander, Lt. General Takeshi Mori. Often referred to as the "Head Monk" by his fellow soldiers for his scholarly and solemn manner, Mori had dedicated his life to the Army. He was known to have spoken bitterly about generals whose blunders had brought Japan to the point of defeat. This was one of the reasons the plotters hoped to win Mori to their cause. But when Hatanaka visited the General at his headquarters in the north side of the Imperial Palace, Lt. General Mori stated that he was "absolutely opposed" to the coup d'état.

"I have been charged with the function of guarding the Emperor and the Imperial Palace," Mori told the junior officer. "I will perform the duty in direct accordance with the Imperial wishes regardless of the orders from the war minister and the chief of staff to the contrary."[52]

Conspirators Takeshita and Hatanaka did not consider the General's stance an insurmountable obstacle, however. They had already won over several battalion and company commanders in the division. When the time for the coup d'état came, they would simply call Mori to the War Ministry, try once more to persuade him to join the coup, and if he continued to resist, confine him in the Minister's office and use the division's troops to seize control of the Palace and isolate the Emperor as they planned. The elements were all falling into place. Now all they needed was the firm commitment of War Minister Anami.

While Hatanaka was at General Mori's headquarters, General Anami was nearby in the Palace grounds, calling on the Emperor's brother, Prince Mikasa. Anami hoped to convince the Prince to intercede with the

Emperor to reject the Byrnes note and resume negotiations with the Allies. Instead, Mikasa coldly rebuffed him. Hirohito had already convened a meeting of all members of the Imperial family, at which they had pledged to support the Emperor's decision to end the war. Before Anami was dismissed from the Prince's presence, Mikasa chided the Army for defying Imperial wishes in the past. "It is most improper that you should still want to continue the war when things have reached this stage," he said.[53]

That evening at 6:40, the official Allied reply finally arrived at the foreign ministry via the Japanese legation in neutral Sweden. But Foreign Minister Togo and his aides had already devised a ploy to gain time in their struggle to elicit support. Togo had arranged that the arrival time and date of the critical radiogram be stamped "7:10 A.M., August 13." This would give Togo almost twelve hours to stiffen the backbone of Prime Minister Suzuki and win over more cabinet ministers to his side.[54]

On that hot Sunday evening of August 12, War Minister Anami left his small official residence near the western moat of the Imperial Palace and was driven to his modest home in Mitaka, thirty-five kilometers west of central Tokyo. The previous weeks had given him almost no time to spend with his family. Anami still had three children at home, two daughters and a son. His oldest two children, both sons, had become soldiers. The second of the two sons, Koreakiri, had been killed in China on August 20, 1942, almost exactly two years before.

But Anami's plan for a quiet night at home was spoiled when a stream of visitors, including Lt. Colonel Ida and Major Hatanaka of the War Ministry's Military Affairs Section, called on him. There is no record that the two conspirators directly raised the issue of the coup, but it has been documented that they were still confident War Minister Anami remained their undeclared leader.

Exhausted but anxious, Anami could not sleep. Finally, before dawn, he summoned his adjutant, Major Saburo Hayashi, to carry an important message to Army Chief of Staff Umezu. Anami wanted the General to help convince Field Marshal Shunroku Hata, the commander of the Second General Army who had survived the atomic bombing of Hiroshima, to appeal directly to the Emperor to reject the Allied terms. But when Major

Hayashi reached Chief of Staff Umezu at sunrise, Anami's former ally said, "I'm sorry. I support the acceptance of the Potsdam Declaration."[55]

General Anami was devastated by the news but determined not to give up the struggle. And he was convinced that he could win Umezu back to his position. He was also hopeful he could sway the Emperor to side with the Army. On his way to an emergency meeting of the Big Six, Anami called on the Privy Seal, Marquis Kido, at his office in the Imperial Household Ministry. Fearing assassination—placards demanding "Kill Lord Keeper of the Privy Seal Kido" had appeared overnight across Tokyo— Kido had doubled his bodyguard and moved into the ministry, where he hoped his proximity to the Emperor would shield him from violence.[56]

Once more, Anami voiced his appeal. "We must by all means have the Emperor reconsider and conduct a final decisive battle in the homeland." Kido was silent. But War Minister Anami plunged ahead. "Pessimism in war never yields good results. If Japan makes one last effort, it will not be impossible to end the war more to our advantage."

Kido assured Anami that the Foreign Ministry had carefully analyzed the Byrnes message and found it acceptable. It was too late to resume negotiations. "Remember," Kido said, "Japan has already notified the Allies that we are willing to accept the Potsdam terms. If the Emperor should now turn his back on this official note, the Allies and the rest of the world would then regard him as a fool or a lunatic. It is unbearable to have His Majesty insulted that way."[57]

General Anami was forced to recognize Kido's logic. It was essential, however, that this close adviser to the Emperor understand the current mood of the military. As he rose to leave, Anami solemnly declared, "The atmosphere in the army is indeed tense."

In fact, the rebellious mood in the military was becoming widespread and widely known. News of a possible coup d'état reached Foreign Minister Togo on August 12. As early as July 1, he had conferred with Navy Minister Yonai about how best to prepare for disorders when the Army and Navy learned that Japan had begun peace negotiations with the Allies. From the outset of these negotiations, Togo had told Yonai, "We must be ready to risk our own lives." The assassin's bullet or dagger was a bitter legacy of the military uprising of February 1936 that every moderate civilian official or officer might have to confront. Yonai was confident he could keep the Navy loyal, but neither man trusted Home Minister Abe, so they bypassed his authority and issued an alert directly to the chief of the Tokyo Metropolitan Police. With tension mounting in the military, Togo realized he had to expedite the final cabinet approval of the Allies' terms. If matters continued to hang fire, the military was bound to revolt.[58]

And the degree of discontent within the military had reached proportions that would have stunned Foreign Minister Togo had he known them. While Anami and Kido were meeting at the Imperial Palace, Chief Cabinet Secretary Sakomizu received an unexpected and unwelcome visitor in the offices of the Prime Minister. Lt. General Sanji Okido, who commanded the feared *kempeitai* secret police, arrived in an obviously agitated state. Okido was known as a ruthless and bellicose officer. Soon after Anami was appointed War Minister, Okido had arrested 400 prominent Japanese civilians, including high-court judge Shigeru Yoshida, for their defeatist and allegedly pacifist thoughts.[59] Now Okido demanded to see Prime Minister Suzuki. But Sakomizu nervously explained that his superior was going directly to a Supreme Council for the Direction of the War meeting.

Okido heatedly noted that he was receiving "almost hourly" reports from military units across the country. "They all point to an insurrection." General Okido laid the blame for this explosive situation squarely on the peace faction. "If Japan surrenders, the army will rise."

Chief Cabinet Secretary Sakomizu was terrified. He could only listen as the dreaded *kempeitai* commander vented his spleen.

"The *kempeitai* urges that the war be continued. Tens of millions of lives may be sacrificed, but we must not surrender!"[60]

Sakomizu assured the general that he would relay this message to the Prime Minister. After marching to the doorway, Okido turned and glared at the cabinet secretary. "I know where you stand, you know where the troops and I stand. Be sure that the Premier understands this thoroughly also."

General Okido's message was clear. The *kempeitai*, which was the only unit within the military that could suppress a revolt without resorting to all-out civil war, was adamantly opposed to surrender, and, in fact—according to Okido's own words—stood in solidarity with the troops on the verge of insurrection.

Later that day, General Okido received a detailed briefing from an undercover *kempeitai* officer, Colonel Makoto Tsukamoto, who had infiltrated the circle of conspirators at the War Ministry and knew the details of their plot. He told Okido that coup plans were well advanced and that

The Boomerang, a B-29B Superfortress of the 315th Bomb Wing, on its hardstand at Northwest Field, Guam, in July 1945.

The Boomerang's battle stripes: eleven combat missions, a Prisoner of War emergency supply parachute drop near Tokyo on August 30, 1945, and the "V-J" symbol to mark Victory Over Japan on August 15.

Crew of *The Boomerang* (TOP) Standing, left to right: Sergeants Jim B. Smith, Hank Leffler, Hank Gorder, Sid Siegel, and Henry Carlson. Kneeling, left to right: First Lieutenants Carl Schahrer, Tony Cosola, John Waltershausen, Rich Ginster, and Dick Marshall. Enlisted crew members (LEFT): right front to left front: Henry Carlson, Sid Siegel, Jim B. Smith, Hank Gorder, and Hank Leffler.

Sergeant Jim B. Smith, Northwest Field, Guam, 1945.

The flight deck of *The Boomerang*, (LEFT) looking forward to bombardier's position in nose. (RIGHT) Aircraft commander's position on left (port side) of flight deck.

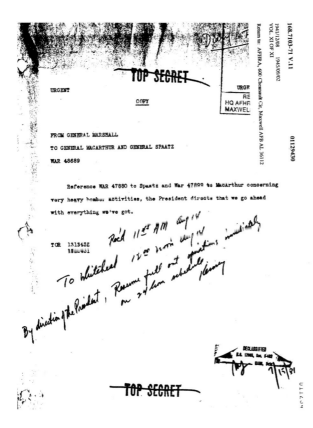

TOP SECRET

URGENT

URGE
RE
HQ AFHR
MAXWEL

COPY

FROM GENERAL MARSHALL
TO GENERAL MACARTHUR AND GENERAL SPAATZ
WAR 48689

Reference WAR 47880 to Spaatz and War 47899 to MacArthur concerning very heavy bomber activities, the President directs that we go ahead with everything we've got.

TOR 131343Z
14日44431

Rec'd 11⁰⁵ AM Aug 14

To Whitehead 12:00 noon Aug 14

By direction of the President, Resume full out operations immediately on 24 hour schedule Kenny

DECLASSIFIED
E.O. 12065, Sec. 3-402

TOP SECRET

WAR 48689, the Top Secret radiogram that launched the last mission and inadvertently ended the war. Transmitted on August 13, 1945, Washington date (August 14, 1945, in the Pacific), this message from Army Chief of Staff General George C. Marshall to Generals Douglas MacArthur and Carl Spaatz ordered the resumption of "very heavy bomber activities" (B-29 raids on Japan). The radiogram concluded, "The President directs that we go ahead with everything we've got."

(LEFT) War Minister Korechika Anami, Imperial Japan's most important military leader in August 1945, and a bitter opponent of surrender.

(CENTER) Prime Minister Baron Kantaro Suzuki, a retired Imperial Japanese Navy admiral and leader of the Supreme Council for the Direction of the War.

(RIGHT) Imperial Japanese Army Lt. Colonel Masahiko Takeshita of the Military Affairs Section of the War Ministry. Takeshita was War Minister Anami's brother-in-law and one of the original leaders of the conspiracy.

Japanese Imperial Army Major Kenji Hatanaka (LEFT) and Lt. Colonel Jiro Shiizaki (RIGHT), both ultranationalist firebrands in the Military Affairs Section of the Ministry of War.

Lt. General Shizuichi Tanaka, Commander of the Eastern District Army. General Tanaka finally quashed the coup d'état at the Palace around dawn on August 15, 1945, hours after rebel troops had begun their futile search for the recordings of the Emperor's Rescript, which was broadcast that noon, announcing surrender.

Artist's depiction of the critical Imperial conference of August 9–10, 1945, during which the Emperor met with the Supreme Council for the Direction of the War and other advisers to discuss accepting the Allies' Potsdam Declaration. The key figures are (third from left and moving clockwise) Admiral Soemu Toyoda, Chief of Staff, Imperial Japanese Navy; Foreign Minister Shigenori Togo; Admiral Mitsumasa Yonai, Navy Minister; President of the Privy Council, Baron Kiichiro Hiranuma; Chief Aide-de-Camp General Shigeru Hasunuma (near door, far left); Emperor Hirohito (seated separately, center); Prime Minister Baron Kantaro Suzuki (standing); War Minister Korechika Anami; Army Chief of Staff General Yoshijiro Umezu; Lt. General Masao Yoshizumi, Director of the Military Affairs Bureau, War Ministry; and Chief Cabinet Secretary Hisatsune Sakomizu.

The Nijubashi (Double Bridge) crosses the Imperial Palace moat and enters the granite-block wall (far left). This was one of the entrances the rebels sealed after midnight on August 15, 1945, isolating the Palace and holding the Emperor incommunicado.

The Imperial Palace, Tokyo (postwar aerial view). In May 1945, several Imperial pavilions (near moat, upper left) were burnt in an American incendiary raid. The Imperial Household Ministry (far right with smokestack) was not damaged. Near it is the Sakashita Gate, one of the Palace entrances the rebels seized and closed.

皇宗ノ神靈ニ謝セムヤ是レ朕カ帝國
政府ヲシテ共同宣言ニ應セシムルニ至レル所
以ナリ

朕ハ帝國ト共ニ終始東亞ノ解放ニ協力セ
ル諸盟邦ニ對シ遺憾ノ意ヲ表セサルヲ得
ス帝國臣民ニシテ戰陣ニ死シ職域ニ殉シ非
命ニ斃レタル者及其ノ遺族ニ想ヲ致セハ五
内爲ニ裂ク且戰傷ヲ負ヒ災禍ヲ蒙リ家業
ヲ失ヒタル者ノ厚生ニ至リテハ朕ノ深ク軫念ス
ル所ナリ惟フニ今後帝國ノ受クヘキ苦難ハ

固ヨリ尋常ニアラス爾臣民ノ衷情モ朕善
ク之ヲ知ル然レトモ朕ハ時運ノ趨ク所堪ヘ
難キヲ堪ヘ忍ヒ難キヲ忍ヒ以テ萬世ノ爲ニ
太平ヲ開カムト欲ス
朕ハ茲ニ國體ヲ護持シ得テ忠良ナル爾臣
民ノ赤誠ニ信倚シ常ニ爾臣民ト共ニ在リ
若シ夫レ情ノ激スル所濫ニ事端ヲ滋クシ或
ハ同胞排擠互ニ時局ヲ亂リテ爲ニ大道ヲ誤
リ信義ヲ世界ニ失フカ如キハ朕最モ之ヲ戒
ム宜シク擧國一家子孫相傳ヘ確ク神州ノ
不滅ヲ信シ任重クシテ道遠キヲ念ヒ總力ヲ將來ノ建
設ニ傾ケ道義ヲ篤クシ志操ヲ鞏クシ誓テ國體ノ
精華ヲ發揚シ世界ノ進運ニ後レサラムコトヲ期スヘシ爾臣
民

A page of the Imperial Rescript (TOP), which the Emperor recorded on the night of August 14, 1945. One of the four wax disks (two originals and two copies) of the Imperial Rescript that the Palace chamberlains hid from the rebels, who searched unsuccessfully for them in the blacked-out Imperial Household Ministry

A detonated "Kaiten" human torpedo hangs from a crane after the
U.S. Navy recovered it following an unsuccessful attack on American
vessels at Ulithi Atoll in July 1945. The warhead, forward oxygen and
fuel tanks, and the small crew compartment for the "special attack"
pilot were destroyed in the explosion.

Japanese "Kairyu" midget
suicide submarine. Two
men from the USS *Boston*
examine one of the hun-
dreds of midget suicide submarines prepared for the
Ketsu-Go battle and hidden
in shoreline caves, safe from
American bombing.

On August 27, 1945, the U.S.
Third Fleet draws near the coast
of Japan in preparation for the
official surrender ceremony to be
held on September 2. In the back-
ground is Mt. Fuji, the symbol of
Japan's "sacred" homeland, which
many in the Imperial military
had so long resisted being defiled
by the presence of occupiers.

The official surrender of Japan,
Tokyo Bay, September 2, 1945.
The Japanese delegation arrives
on board the battleship USS
Missouri. Leading this delegation
are Imperial Army Chief of Staff
General Yoshijiro Umezu (front
right) and Foreign Minister (of
the post-Suzuki cabinet) Mamoru
Shigemitsu (to Umezu's right,
with cane, wearing top hat).

Imperial Army Chief of Staff General
Yoshijiro Umezu signs the Instrument of
Surrender on behalf of Japanese Imperial
General Headquarters. Under the Allies'
original surrender terms, the Emperor
was required to sign this document personally. But the terms were amended to
read that he would "ensure" that his military and civilian representatives signed it,
thus guaranteeing compliance without
subjecting the Emperor to public embar-
rassment, which might have sparked a
revolt among the millions of Japanese
troops overseas who still had not been
demobilized.

General MacArthur and Emperor
Hirohito at the Dai Ichi Insurance
Building, Tokyo, September 27, 1945.
General MacArthur established his
headquarters in the building from
which Lt. General Shizuichi Tanaka
commanded the Eastern District
Army only weeks before and where
he committed suicide before the first
Allied occupation troops arrived.

the situation was dangerous.[61] Rather than order the immediate arrest of the conspirators, the commander of the *kempeitai*, acting under War Minister Anami's instructions, told Tsukamoto merely to keep them under surveillance. And Okido angrily dismissed the Colonel's suggestion that War Ministry Anami himself might be involved in the plot. But Okido's outburst lacked conviction, because he was not certain of the War Minister's true feelings.[62]

At 9 A.M. on Monday, August 13, 1945, the Supreme Council for the Direction of the War took up the debate on the Allied terms, which had left the cabinet deadlocked the previous day. As War Minister Anami had hoped, his colleague General Umezu had abandoned acceptance of the Potsdam Declaration terms and now stood solidly with the War Minister and their colleague Admiral Toyoda in favor of rejecting the Byrnes note. Anami now wished he could manipulate the growing confusion through stalling long enough that the Allies themselves would break off negotiations and resume the bombing; the Imperial armed forces would then be allowed to fight the cataclysmic final battle from which Japan could wrest honorable terms to end the war. At this point, Anami still was not convinced that America's atomic bomb was a serious threat to Japan's plans to fight the Ketsu-go battle. The preliminary report from Marshall Hata in Hiroshima had indicated that people protected in underground shelters had not been affected by the bomb's searing thermal pulse, the blast, or the frightening *pika-don* radiation.

Anami's optimism that the debate would continue indecisively past the breaking point of the Allies' patience grew stronger when the council meeting remained stalemated.

Then the Emperor sent word requesting that the two chiefs of staff, Army General Umezu and Admiral Toyoda of the Imperial Navy, come immediately to the Imperial office at the Gobunko. Hirohito reminded the two officers that the negotiations with the Allies were ongoing and let them know that he preferred to immediately minimize the level of violence during the negotiations. What was the status of current air operations? he asked. Umezu, as senior officer, recognized the implicit Imperial command.

"Our planes will only fire when fired upon," he said. The Emperor nodded and dismissed the two chiefs of staff.[63]

However, the Army Chief of Staff's reassuring words to the Emperor did not translate into practical orders. Both Air Force and Navy offensive operations continued, particularly against the Allied fleet near Okinawa. Even at this critical period in the negotiations, kamikaze planes, including at least one Baka carried by an Air Force bomber, attacked Allied ships in Buckner Bay on the southern tip of Okinawa.

Chief Cabinet Secretary Sakomizu—the Premier's principal adviser—had sources of deep anxiety other than General Okido's threats. For more than a day, American military and civilian radio broadcasts had accused Japan of intentionally stalling the peace negotiations. There was a common theme to these broadcasts: Japan could expect President Truman's threatened atomic "rain of ruin" to resume unless Tokyo quickly surrendered.[64]

Sakomizu avoided official channels and went directly to friends in the Domei News Agency with the story that the Japanese government had accepted the Allies' terms and was now merely discussing the correct procedure to reply. Later on Monday, August 13, an American station in San Francisco rebroadcast the story in English. Perhaps Chief Cabinet Secretary Sakomizu's desperate maneuver—which might well have landed him in a *kempeitai* cell—had spared Tokyo for a few hours from the atomic bomb.

That afternoon the full cabinet struggled once more to reach a unanimous decision on whether to accept the Allied terms. Again, War Minister Anami had only two allies—the Home Minister and the Justice Minister—in opposing the solid block of ten votes the Suzuki-Togo alliance had maintained.

The cabinet was hopelessly split, and the meeting dragged on inconclusively throughout the stifling afternoon, while General Anami and his two supporters made the same familiar arguments: Japan must insist that there be no occupation of the homeland, the military itself would disarm its own forces, and it would be the Japanese, not the Allies, who would investigate war crimes. Above all, the Emperor must not be subject to the authority of the Supreme Allied Commander and the future of the *kokutai* must not be subject to a plebiscite.

While the debate sputtered and flared, word reached the cabinet room through a Japanese journalist that Imperial General Headquarters was about to release an especially provocative communiqué:

"The Imperial Army and Navy having hereby received the gracious Imperial Command to protect the national polity and to defend the Imperial Land, the entire armed forces will single-heartedly commence a genuine offensive against the Allied enemy forces."[65]

This communiqué—which anonymous discontents somewhere in the vast headquarters of Imperial General Headquarters had drafted—would be sure to disrupt the negotiations. Anami claimed that he was completely unaware of the message because such press releases fell not under the jurisdiction of the War Ministry but under that of the Army general staff. But Army Chief of Staff General Umezu was dumbfounded when he heard the text read over the telephone. With less than ten minutes to go to broadcast time, Umezu's staff raced to contact radio stations before this inciting communiqué was released. They succeeded. Another crisis had been evaded.

The hot afternoon had finally faded through humid twilight, with the cabinet still stalled ten-to-three with two undecided. Although as clearly exhausted as the others, War Minister Anami seemed prepared to sit in this heat and support his position all night.[66] By tradition bordering on inflexible rule, the cabinet could only present a unanimous decision to His Majesty. Although appearing once again to have dozed through much of the stubborn debate, Premier Suzuki rose and called for a final vote on the issue. There were now twelve ministers in favor of immediate acceptance (two undecided had joined the original ten), with Anami and the Home and Justice Ministers opposed.[67]

Suzuki spoke with unusual passion. After carefully studying the Byrnes note, the Premier said, he had overcome his initial reservations. "At last I came to the conclusion that the Allied nations had not drafted it with any sinister purpose in mind. I know, and all of you know, that His Majesty's heart cries out for only one thing—the restoration of peace. . . . Therefore I have come to a most serious decision. I intend to report to His Majesty the hopeless result of this cabinet meeting, and ask him once more to give his most gracious opinion."[68]

General Anami and the war faction had once more been outmaneuvered by the shrewd old admiral. No one doubted what the Imperial decision would be. The Emperor had made himself clear in the hot confines of the air-raid shelter three days earlier. He would not reverse his decision now. But still the War Minister tried to delay the inevitable. He followed the Prime Minister to his office.

"Won't you please give me two more days before calling another Imperial conference?" Anami asked.[69]

"Impossible," Premier Suzuki replied with unusual firmness. "If we don't act now, the Russians will penetrate not only Manchuria and Korea, but northern Japan [Hokkaido] as well. If that happens, our country is finished. We must act now, while our chief adversary is still the United States."[70]

Observing the crestfallen War Minister leave the room, a navy physician who had come to attend Suzuki spoke up: "But, Mr. Prime Minister, General Anami may kill himself."

"Yes," Suzuki reflected sadly. "That is possible. I am sorry."[71]

Around eight that night, War Minister Anami received five younger officers at his official residence near the palace moat. The group, which included the zealous Lt. Colonel Jiro Shiizaki, also of the Military Affairs Section, and Major Kenji Hatanaka, as well as Anami's brother-in-law, Lt. Colonel Takeshita, was led by their superior officer, Colonel Okitsugu Arao. This section of the War Ministry harbored the deepest, most bitter opposition to the Allies' peace terms. And these men were the key conspirators in the planned rebellion, which they had hoped to stage at midnight. But those plans had been delayed when the conspirators had been unable to meet privately with War Minister Anami due to the protracted and deadlocked meetings that had required his presence all day.[72]

Now the officers, all of whom shared a deep loyalty to General Anami, presented their detailed plan for the coup d'état to the man they fervently hoped would be their leader.

Colonel Arao made the presentation, referring to a written operational plan. Arao was one of Anami's closest confidants, an officer in whom the War Minister had complete trust and with whom he shared his closest secrets.[73] As Arao crisply delineated the purpose, procedures, and exact measures to be taken, as well as the conditions and prerequisites for the coup, Anami sat on a plain woven mat, sphinxlike, eyes closed.

There could be no surrender, Colonel Arao stated, speaking for the War Ministry conspirators, until the Allies met all the conditions regarding the Emperor's status. The Army would have to reverse the Emperor's decision to end the war and continue fighting until the enemy met Japan's terms. The coup would be conducted by virtue of the War Minister's authority to use troops to control a domestic emergency. The Emperor would be personally isolated within the Imperial Palace. His advisers advocating peace—Marquis Kido, Prime Minister Suzuki, Foreign Minister Togo, and Navy Minister Yonai—would be arrested. Martial law would be declared throughout Japan. Arao concluded by noting that the coup could succeed only if the War Minister; Army Chief of Staff Umezu; General Tanaka, commander of the Eastern District Army; and Lt. General Mori, who commanded the 1st Imperial Guards Division, all agreed to participate. The fact that the conspirators already knew that Mori had refused to join them did not change the plan. They were confident that, with War Minister Anami as leader, he would sway the entire military to their side.

As he listened to the details, Anami occasionally grunted in neutral tones. Then he asked, "And when do you intend to put all this in motion?"

"At ten o'clock tomorrow morning," Arao explained, noting that the original midnight deadline had already been abandoned.

Arao continued his presentation, and Anami slipped back into silent meditation. But he again spoke words that the conspirators believed were clear indications that the War Minister approved of their plan. Once General Anami opened his eyes he said, "I will dedicate my life to your cause." He also spoke bitterly of his growing dissatisfaction with the peace faction's attitude and secret maneuvers since the Imperial conference on the ninth. A few moments later, he said, "I can well understand what Saigo felt."[74] (Takamori Saigo was considered by most officers to have been both the last great samurai and the father of the Imperial Army. He had helped overthrow the shogun warlords who ruled Japan and installed the Meiji Emperor in 1868. But only nine years later, convinced that the government around the Emperor had become corrupt, Saigo led a revolt, which was eventually crushed. Wounded, with his forces decimated, he ordered a subordinate to behead him to avoid the dishonor of surrender.) Now, as War Minister Anami compared himself to this legendary hero—and linked the conspirators' cause to those heroic times—the five junior officers in the room felt swelling confidence. Anami would lead the coup.

But he refused to commit himself openly at this point. "I can understand the feelings of Takamori Saigo on the one hand," he said. "But on the other hand, I have offered my life to the Emperor."[75]

This did not mean he disapproved of the coup. They had all dedicated their lives to the Emperor. Now Anami noted practical problems in their scheme. "The communications plan concerning the palace is too important. It needs work. I will give you an answer after I have thought about the matter."[76]

After the officers dispersed with Anami's promise that he would discuss the matter further with Arao in his ministry office at midnight, Takeshita remained behind. He asked the War Minister for his frank opinion of the coup plans. Enigmatic as ever, Anami simply replied, "One cannot reveal his true thoughts in the presence of such a large group."[77]

Takeshita was now convinced that the War Minister favored the coup d'état.

Foreign Minister Togo was at a dinner party to inaugurate his new official residence, which had replaced the villa that had been burned to the ground in an American air raid. But he was called away from the party by an urgent telephone message that Chiefs of Staff General Umezu and Admiral Toyoda needed to see him at the Prime Minister's office. This meeting was frustrating for the three men involved. Umezu and Toyoda virtually begged Togo to use his influence and renew negotiations with the enemy to achieve better terms. Togo refused to budge. About 11 P.M., Vice Admiral Takijiro Onishi, Toyoda's deputy and a man who was widely regarded as the "father" of the kamikaze corps, burst into the office. He was frantic, having learned that the decision to accept the "unsatisfactory" Allied reply might be made in the morning.

"We must formulate a plan for certain victory," Onishi said, "submit it to the Emperor, and then proceed to carry it through." His argument was brutally simple. "We will never be defeated if we are prepared to sacrifice twenty million Japanese lives in a 'Special Attack' effort."[78]

Foreign Minister Togo was shocked and dismayed as he recognized that even such senior officers as Onishi held this radical view. The negotiations had to be concluded quickly, before the military completely demolished the government's peace efforts and Japan committed collective suicide.

In Washington on August 13, the interminable wait for the Japanese response continued. The short Domei News Agency message, which Chief

Cabinet Secretary Sakomizu had managed to have transmitted despite military censorship, had been monitored earlier that day and had indicated that Tokyo had decided to accept the Allied terms. But no official reply had reached the Americans. President Truman and General Marshall both were doubtful that Japan was actually ready to surrender. And there were Ultra intercepts revealing that a probable "all-out banzai attack" was imminent.[79] The Strategic Air Forces headquarters on Guam was alerted to prepare to resume B-29 missions against Japan when ordered to do so.[80]

At their quarters on Northwest Field on Guam, the crews of the 315th Wing still waited restlessly for the final official announcement that Japan had surrendered. The end-of-the-war parties that had ignited on August 10 had now largely sputtered out. Negotiations had been hanging fire during the three tense days since the President had ordered the Air Force to stop all strategic bombing. But as each hour passed, pessimism grew that the war had not in fact ended, that the men would once more have to climb into their heavily laden aircraft and trust those worn-out engines to carry them all the way to the Empire and back.

Then, on the evening of August 13, word spread that three other B-29 wings stationed elsewhere in the Marianas—the 58th, 73rd, and 313th—had been placed on standby to fly missions against Japan in the morning. (Although the 315th crews did not know it at the time, the other wings' targets were the Hikari Naval Arsenal, the Osaka Army Arsenal, and the Marifu railroad yards. These bombers did in fact take off just after dawn in the Marianas to strike their targets on the early afternoon of August 14, 1945.) Rumor had it that Japan was finally on the verge of signing the surrender and that these missions had been ordered as grand finale insurance strikes to punctuate the process. But the 315th had *not* been alerted to fly.

When Sergeant Jim Smith heard the news, he was overcome with the same emotions—deep gratitude, joy, and disbelief—that he had experienced three days earlier on learning that Japan had notified the Allies that they were ready to accept the terms of the Potsdam Declaration. It definitely looked as if the 315th had flown its last mission. Apparently XXI Bomber Command had run out of oil targets for the B-29Bs equipped with the Eagle radar to attack. The men of the three other wings would have to risk their lives to expedite the surrender. But as Jim Smith discussed the situation with Hank Gorder and Sid Siegel, they agreed that it was unlikely that those crews would actually have to complete their missions.

"They'll get a hundred miles out and turn around," Smith predicted.

"They won't even get that far before the Japs surrender," Siegel said confidently.

Since the 315th was not on standby, there was no rule against the crews enjoying a little celebration drink. Slowly at first, then with increasing exuberance, the men began to break open their private caches of alcohol. Enlisted men dug out rusting cans of 3.2 "green" beer that they had hoarded from their weekly ration. Aging had not improved its quality. The only thing that this beer, which had been simmered in the holds of Liberty ships crossing the Pacific, was good for was producing a lingering headache. But other guys had smuggled bottles of whiskey, an indulgence denied enlisted men except for their postmission double shot. And a few of the aircrew had canteens of cloudy fermented coconut juice, a beverage of uneven potency and predicable effect on the digestive tract.

As the night progressed, the young airmen strolled among the barracks, whiskey bottles, beer cans, and aluminum canteen cups in hand, visiting friends from other crews, or pausing before battery-powered sets tuned to Radio Guam, hoping for the final word on the Japanese surrender. Instead, they heard a medley of big band favorites with an occasional Bing Crosby ballad.

The tropical night was soft. The new moon had set beneath the palms and the sky was full of stars. The music evoked peace.

As Tokyo remained locked in the debate on whether to accept the Allied terms or to continue the war, Harry Truman lost patience. General George Marshall now sent an urgent Top Secret radiogram to General MacArthur in the Philippines and Strategic Air Forces Commander Carl Spaatz on Guam: "Concerning very heavy bomber activities, the President directs that we go ahead with everything we've got."[81]

CHAPTER SEVEN

DECISION AND
INDECISION

IN TOKYO, TUESDAY, AUGUST 14, 1945, dawned clear and hot. A single B-29 circled high above the burned-out city. The American bomber dropped a string of canisters, which burst at around 8,000 feet, showering the rubble with tens of thousands of leaflets. On the coarse gray newsprint rectangles, the Japanese characters were not as crisply printed as those on earlier leaflets. This message had been prepared in haste and sent by radiophoto from Washington to Saipan.

Addressed "TO THE JAPANESE PEOPLE," the leaflet, which other American planes were scattering by the millions across Japan, explained that the cabinet had offered to surrender and went on to detail the Foreign Ministry's terms and the Allied reply. "Your government now has the chance to end the war immediately," the message stated.[1]

A soldier from the Imperial Guards took a leaflet, which had fluttered down near the Gobunko, to a Palace chamberlain, who rushed the scrap of paper to Lord Keeper of the Privy Seal Marquis Kido. "One look," Kido later recounted, "caused me to be stricken with consternation. . . . If the leaflets should fall into the hands of the troops and enrage them, a military coup d'état would become inevitable and make extremely difficult the execution of the planned policy for our country."[2]

Kido went immediately to the Emperor to discuss the ominous implications of this latest Allied tactic. The only course of action, Kido suggested, was a second Imperial conference during which His Majesty could directly impose his will on the restive military. Prime Minister Suzuki arrived to explain that both War Minister Anami and the two service chiefs of staff now wanted to postpone a scheduled ten o'clock meeting of the Supreme Council for the Direction of the War. Was the coup already in progress?

The Emperor acted without hesitation. He would break court protocol by calling himself for an Imperial conference, assembling the full cabinet and the service chiefs of staff in the Gobunko air-raid shelter at 10:30 that morning. Hirohito was determined to "command" the men at the conference to accept the Allied terms with no further debate. The cabinet would then draft an Imperial Rescript—a proclamation with both civil and religious authority—which the Emperor was prepared to broadcast to the nation by radio.[3] But Hirohito stressed that the conference must convene quickly. For the moment, at least, rebellious troops were unlikely to strike against the well-guarded Palace where the cabinet and senior military and naval officers had assembled in the presence of the Emperor.

While this decision was being reached, equally decisive events took place at the War Ministry on Ichigaya Heights. General Anami had promised the coup conspirators the night before that he would raise their plans with Army Chief of Staff Umezu. As the leaflets drifted across Tokyo, Anami and Colonel Okitsugu Arao, Chief of the Military Affairs Section, met behind closed doors in the Chief of Staff's office, trying to enlist his support in the planned coup. Umezu was not receptive to their appeal. The coup, he said, was doomed to failure as planned. For that reason, General Umezu was "unalterably opposed" to the plot. It appeared that the dream of a glorious rebellion had been crushed.

When War Minister Anami met with his brother-in-law, Lt. Colonel Takeshita, Major Hatanaka, and other young conspirators, his manner was calm.

"The coup d'état will have to be given up," Anami said, "because the Chief of the General Staff has expressed disapproval."

Arao, Takeshita, and the other senior conspirators in the Ministry had always recognized that the full support of the Army Chief of Staff was "an absolute requisite" for the coup's success. And Takeshita saw General Umezu's refusal to participate as the "final blow" that meant the conspiracy was defeated.

Now War Minister Anami himself told the conspirators that they would have to abandon the plot because neither he nor Colonel Arao had been able to convince Umezu to join them. Anami later confided in Takeshita that the Chief of Staff had opposed the coup because he believed deploying armed forces in the sanctuary of the palace would be a sacrilege. But Takeshita was not convinced by this explanation, because neither Anami nor Arao had discussed tactical plans with Umezu before he voiced his disapproval. Therefore, Takeshita was hopeful that fellow conspirators with better access to General Umezu could succeed in winning the Chief of Staff over.

But there was a more immediate problem at the war ministry. In anticipation of securing Anami's approval for the coup, the conspirators had summoned Eastern District Army Commander Lt. General Tanaka, Imperial Guards Division Commander Lt. General Mori, and *kempeitai* Commander Lt. General Okido to the War Ministry to be briefed on their roles in the plot. Now it appeared, however, that there would be no coup. Would Anami finally act decisively and brief the three generals about the plot and order the *kempeitai* to arrest the conspirators? This would have been the rational course of action for the War Minister to take had he been absolutely opposed to the coup and determined to prevent it from unfolding. Instead, Anami vaguely admonished the generals to pay "particular attention" to guard duties because the situation might become serious later that day.[4]

Before leaving to attend the hastily called second Imperial conference that had supplanted the scheduled cabinet meeting, General Anami assembled senior members of the War Ministry and spoke to them briefly. Although his statement was dramatic, he gave the impression that it lacked his full emotional commitment.

"Since we are confronted with a grave situation," Anami said, "all officers and men in the army should strengthen their unity and beware of any act of indiscipline."

But his words did not influence all the conspirators. The Japanese historians who wrote *Japan's Longest Day* after interviewing dozens of key participants in these events state that, following General Umezu's refusal to participate in the coup, "the young officers . . . persisted in their demands on Anami, and Anami persisted in his refusal to be explicit."[5]

Out of this murky record, however, several facts emerge: War Minister Anami did not directly order the conspirators to abandon the coup, and he did not have them taken into custody.

And it is evident that General Anami had not abandoned his own stubborn attempt to influence the Emperor to reject surrender. Anami had earlier tried to use Field Marshal Hata, just arrived from Hiroshima, to convince the Emperor that the atomic bomb was not as formidable a weapon as the defeatists had proclaimed. Instead, during an Imperial audience earlier that morning, Hata, crying openly, described the unprecedented destructive power of the bomb. Further, he said that he "had no confidence in repulsing" the enemy's Kyushu invasion landings. Hata raised no objection to the Emperor's plans to accept the Allies' surrender terms.[6] It seemed that Anami's last hope for support among senior military officers had been dashed.

But this was not the case. Just back from the brief Imperial audience for military leaders at which Field Marshal Hata had emotionally opted for surrender, Chief of Staff Umezu confronted two of his subordinate officers who had sided with the coup conspirators. Whereas General Umezu had been adamantly against the plot an hour earlier, he now stated that he "was not absolutely opposed to a coup d'état."

On hearing the news, Lt. Colonel Takeshita felt a surge of optimism. Umezu *did* back their cause! Certainly War Minister Anami would now commit himself fully to the coup. Takeshita quickly drew up his "Employment of Troops, Plan No. 2," which included a realistic new timetable— it was too late to meet the original start time of 10:00 A.M.—as well as the more substantive communication scheme that General Anami had requested to see the night before. Armed with this tactical document, Takeshita commandeered a staff car and sped toward the Prime Minister's residence, hoping to intercept General Anami before he departed for the Imperial conference in the Palace. As the car careered around heaps of bomb rubble, Takeshita throbbed with confidence. The coup would proceed. Chief of Staff Umezu was at last on their side. When General Anami learned of this and when he read the detailed new tactical plan, he too would finally commit himself to the sacred cause. The honor of the Army and the nation would be preserved.

Instead, having missed the War Minister at Suzuki's residence, Takeshita arrived just moments after General Anami and his cabinet colleagues had filed down the dank stairs to the Imperial air-raid shelter next to the Gobunko for the Imperial conference. The men who assembled at the hastily convened Imperial summons wore a motley collection of uniforms and civilian dress. Few in the cabinet had expected to have their scheduled meeting canceled and replaced by this Imperial conference. There had been no time for the cutaway morning clothes of formal court dress; many wore open-necked shirts and had to borrow suit coats from aides. A clutch of midlevel civilians, including Tokyo's police chief, the head of the government's planning board, and Chief Cabinet Secretary Sakomizu, joined the fifteen cabinet ministers and several senior military officers in the sweltering vault of the air-raid shelter. Some in this group wore the ubiquitous *kokuminfuki* wartime uniforms of the bureaucracy. They felt shame to appear before the Emperor in such drab attire. But they had no choice. His Majesty had commanded their presence.

To accommodate so many men, the palace chamberlains had arranged several rows of chairs facing the entrance. The Emperor's small table and wooden chair were positioned as during the first Imperial conference, before a gilded screen at the end of the narrow room.

With the small shelter so crowded, the heat and humidity soared, so that moisture actually dripped from the curved wood paneling of the concrete walls. For many this was more like a bathhouse than an Imperial conference. And, waiting for the Emperor to arrive, the men had to endure emotional pain every bit as severe as the physical discomfort. They understood that this would probably be the last conference that their revered Emperor would conduct before he was forced to face the dishonor of subjecting himself to the authority of the enemies' supreme commander.

Hirohito arrived twenty minutes late, accompanied by his chief military aide, and once more looking harassed in his sweat-soaked uniform that bore the single decoration of the Imperial chrysanthemum. The twenty-four men in the room bowed deeply and waited for the Emperor to take his place before they sat. Hirohito turned silently and faced Prime Minister

Suzuki. Chief Cabinet Secretary Hisatsune Sakomizu was anxious because the elderly statesman had often been so vague and vacillating that week that he might not be able to function decisively at this critical conference. Sakomizu feared that the premier would ramble incoherently or even reverse his position on surrender as he had two days earlier.[7]

But when Premier Suzuki rose to speak, his voice was clear and strong, his words direct and succinct. He explained to those assembled that His Majesty had brought them here to discuss the acceptance of the Allied note in his presence. He outlined the dissenting views, noting that War Minister Anami and the two service chiefs of staff, General Umezu and Admiral Toyoda, were the most firmly opposed.

Then he faced the Emperor squarely. "Thus, because support was not unanimous, I wish to apologize sincerely for the serious crime of troubling Your Majesty with this matter. Now, will you please listen to those opposing the terms and then grant us your Imperial decision?"

Army Chief of Staff General Umezu was the first to speak. He was not optimistic about changing the Emperor's mind and opened his remarks by also apologizing, in his case for Japan's recent military defeats. Umezu then summarized his stance against the accepting Allied note, concluding, "If our Imperial system cannot be preserved, I believe we must be ready to sacrifice the entire nation in a final battle."

When Admiral Toyoda addressed the Emperor, he spoke brilliantly, appearing to those in the air-raid shelter more as a skilled and experienced advocate than the rigidly bellicose naval officer he was thought to be. Toyoda linked the danger of Allied occupation with the threat to the Emperor's sovereignty. He summarized by warning that the Allies' demand for the "free will" of the people to determine the nation's form of government was the "most dangerous" term, which would "undermine the entire Japanese tradition."[8]

War Minister Anami rose to speak.* He brought up many of the same points as his colleagues, but, unlike Toyoda, Anami's logical argument gave way to emotion and he concluded by gasping between words, his face wet with tears. "If it is impossible to question the Allies again about the safety of the Emperor system, it would be better to fight on, for there are still chances to win. And if not to win, at least to end the war on better terms than these."

---

* Certain historians differ as to the sequence that Umezu, Toyoda, and Anami spoke on August 14, 1945. See: Brooks, op. cit., p. 265; Craig, op. cit., p. 171; Coffey, op. cit., p. 442.

After Anami spoke, Prime Minister Suzuki bowed deeply again and asked the Emperor to deliver his Imperial decision. Hirohito nodded to Prime Minister Suzuki, then stood to address the men who faced him in the sweltering chamber. With a damp handkerchief clutched in equally damp white gloves, he wiped sweat and tears from his face and glasses.

"I have listened carefully to all the arguments against Japan's acceptance of the Allied reply as it now stands," the Emperor began in a strained and halting voice. "My own opinion, however, has not changed." Having carefully studied the terms of the Allied message, he said, as well as the situation in Japan and elsewhere in the world, he had concluded that the Byrnes note represented a "virtually complete acknowledgment" of the Japanese position sent to the Allies on August 10. "In short," Hirohito continued, "I consider the Allied reply to be acceptable."[9]

Facing Anami, Umezu, and Toyoda, the Emperor spoke with deep emotion. "I appreciate how difficult it will be for the officers and men of the Army and Navy to surrender their arms to the enemy and to see their homeland occupied. Indeed, it is difficult for me to issue the order making this necessary and to deliver so many of my trusted servants into the hands of the Allied authorities by whom they will be accused of being war criminals."

The Emperor was almost overcome with emotion and was sobbing uncontrollably. Seeing the Emperor cry broke the traditional stoic reserve of several of the men he faced. Their chests heaved in anguish, and they also sobbed loudly.[10] Hirohito forced himself to continue. "I appreciate the people's determination to sacrifice themselves for the sake of their Emperor." He voiced his grief for those who had died on Japan's overseas battlefields and those who were victims of the cruel bombing of the homeland. "But continuing the war," he added, "would bring death of tens, perhaps hundreds of thousands of people. Our nation would be completely devastated and reduced to ashes. The reconstruction of a peaceful Japan will be a difficult and lengthy task. However, I believe it will be accomplished through the strenuous efforts and cooperation of our people. I am ready to do whatever I can do."

Regarding Allied motives concerning the power of the Emperor, Hirohito stated, "I agree with the Foreign Minister. I do not believe the note was written to subvert our *kokutai*." Once more, it seemed that Foreign Minister Togo had outmaneuvered his adversaries and that the war faction had been thwarted.

When the Emperor said, "I am not concerned with what happens to me. I want to preserve the lives of my people," the anguish in the room became general. Men who showed only stoic faces in public were now weeping openly. Education Minister Ota and Welfare Minister Okada trembled in spasms of grief. They slipped to the floor and wailed, hiding their faces in their hands.[11]

Before the conference lost the last semblance of order, the Emperor issued his instructions. "It is my desire that you, my ministers of state, accede to my wishes and forthwith accept the Allied reply. In order that the people know of my decision, I request you to prepare at once an Imperial Rescript so that I may broadcast to the nation."[12]

To many in the bomb shelter, the thought of the Emperor himself, the Voice of the Sacred Crane, submitting to the indignity of a radio broadcast like some politician or news announcer was more than they could bear. The sobs of anguish grew louder.

Before he turned to leave, Hirohito added, "I am also prepared to go anywhere to talk personally to the troops if requested."

Anami and the Chiefs of Staff lowered their heads in shame. The Emperor's implied fear that they could not control their own forces was the ultimate humiliation. He was putting them on direct notice that there could be no excuse for soldiers and sailors to blame manipulative politicians for the Imperial decision to end the war.

When Hirohito ended his remarks, Prime Minister Suzuki bowed and again offered a humble apology. Stifling his own tears, the Emperor nodded silently and left the bomb shelter. The decision had been made. Japan would surrender. The humid, narrow vault echoed with cries of despair.

The cabinet members drove from the Palace to the Prime Minister's official residence, where they would convene to ratify the Imperial decision and help draft the Imperial Rescript. Under the Meiji constitution, unanimous cabinet approval of the rescript was required before the document became official.

Coup conspirator Lt. Colonel Takeshita had been waiting with frantic impatience for his brother-in-law to emerge from the air-raid shelter. It was clear, however, that neither Anami nor General Umezu, who was also openly weeping, were in any emotional state to discuss the coup d'état.

Takeshita followed the convoy of cabinet sedans to the Prime Minister's residence, hoping to buttonhole Anami at the earliest possible moment.

Before the cabinet undertook their afternoon's work, they sat down for an austere lunch of black bread, dried whale meat, and pickled vegetables. Anami was unable to enjoy the food, although the Premier ate with relish. The War Minister left the dining room and, joined by his adjutant, Major Saburo Hayashi, went to the tiled lavatory. Anami's solemn demeanor suddenly gave way to a determined smile. "Hayashi!" he proclaimed. "You've heard the rumor that the enemy has a huge landing force near Tokyo Bay. I want to hit that hard while we're still talking peace—then maybe we'll get the kind of peace terms we want."[13]

Anami's aide was thunderstruck. There had been intelligence reports of an approaching American invasion fleet. But how could the War Minister seriously suggest attacking this enemy force after the Emperor had made his decision to accept the Allied terms? Was this some macabre joke? "Your idea is absolutely mistaken," Hayashi said boldly to his superior, reminding him that the Imperial decision had already been made and noting that the rumor of an American convoy near Tokyo Bay had not been confirmed by aerial reconnaissance.

"I still believe," Anami persisted, "that we should deal one decisive blow to the enemy before proposing peace."[14]

When Hayashi suggested that the War Minister raise this issue with Army Chief of Staff Umezu, Anami seemed to lose interest.

Most historians have dismissed this incident as a futile Bushido gesture on Anami's part. Supposedly, the existence of the close-in enemy fleet was indeed a mere "rumor." According to declassified American translations of Japanese documents, however, the War and Naval Ministries had already verified that American Third Fleet warships, including large, vulnerable fleet aircraft carriers, had "pulled close to the Japanese shore in what appeared to be an attempt to add impetus to the peace offensive. It was believed that they might attempt an intimidatory landing, depending on how the situation developed." To guard against this threat, Imperial Navy General Command had already alerted combined Navy and Army air units to prepare for planned Ketsu-go defensive operations (which called for massive kamikaze attacks).[15] These strikes would have been devastating both to the Japanese pilots and to the Allied fleet. Certainly, the no-quarter battle would have set back the peace negotiations. And War Minister Anami came precariously close to triggering that engagement.

Instead, he simply left the lavatory, only to find his waiting brother-in-law. In a small anteroom to the cabinet chamber, Anami and Takeshita conferred. The younger officer told Anami that General Umezu had reversed his earlier position and now supported the coup d'état. This of course was not fully accurate; Umezu had simply told his staff officers that he was not "absolutely opposed" to their coup plans. Anami smiled with a momentary flash of renewed confidence. "Is that so?" he asked eagerly. Then his face clouded. "But everything has already been decided. The Emperor has reached a final decision and an Imperial Rescript ending the war is about to be promulgated."

Takeshita would not be put off so easily. The War Minister could disrupt the peace process simply by tendering his resignation, and, in so doing, bring down the Suzuki government. Without a cabinet, the Imperial Rescript would remain an unofficial draft document. The collapse of the government would throw the country into upheaval at this critical moment. The Army could impose its own conditions on the future of the negotiations before it agreed to provide a candidate war minister to the cabinet, a process that could continue until a suitable designate prime minister had come forward, possibly even Anami himself.

Anami called in his adjutant, Major Hayashi. "Get me an ink slab and paper," Anami ordered, fingering a writing brush on the desk before him. "I intend to write my resignation. Check on the procedure."

Hayashi snapped to attention and turned to obey the order. But Anami stopped him in the doorway of the small chamber. "There's no need for that, Hayashi." Then he faced Takeshita with a mournful expression. "Now that things have gone this far, the Imperial Rescript will be promulgated whether I sign it or not." His eyes clouded with tears once more. "If I resign now, I can never see the Emperor again."[16]

It seemed unlikely that War Minister Anami would change his mind again. To Takeshita, Anami's last statement revealed his warm personal attachment to the Emperor as both friend and sovereign. But Takeshita also knew that Anami viewed the pending subjugation of the Emperor to Allied authority with deep fear and revulsion.

The tone of the cabinet meeting after lunch was almost perfunctory. Seated at a large round table in Prime Minister's Suzuki's inner conference room, the ministers discussed the draft language of the Imperial Rescript, on which Chief Cabinet Secretary Sakomizu had been working for two days in anticipation of this moment. Some ministers were too dejected to devote full attention to what would prove to be the most crucial document in Japanese history. Sakomizu reported that the Emperor's own words from the two Imperial conferences were being incorporated into the rescript. This would take perhaps an hour, after which the ministers could consider the text.

While they waited, the cabinet unanimously agreed to formally solicit His Majesty's pardon for the troubles they had caused him. They next took up the matter of whether it was most appropriate for the Emperor to broadcast directly to the nation or to record the rescript for rebroadcast from the NHK studios. Once more unanimous, the cabinet decided it was more appropriate for the Emperor to record the rescript at the Imperial Palace for later broadcast to the people in the homeland and, when possible, to the forces overseas by shortwave.

The cabinet agreed to reconvene that afternoon to review the draft of the rescript before it was submitted to the Emperor. His majesty would then sign the document, and so would the cabinet. Once they had done so, the rescript would become official, the Emperor would record the message, and the Foreign Ministry would send the Allies official notice through diplomatic channels that Japan had accepted the Byrnes note.

The war would be over.

While the cabinet was meeting, NHK Chairman Hachiro Ohashi received instructions from Information Bureau Director Shimomura to proceed to the Palace with a recording team led by Director of Engineering Daitaro Arakawa and set up their equipment in the Imperial Household Ministry. There the technicians met with Palace bureaucrats and selected the Imperial administrative office, or Goseimu, on the second floor of the central building, which, with its deep Western-style carpet and thick overlapping blackout curtains, was devoid of echo and would be the ideal place to install the microphone. The actual recording apparatus for the large wax disks could be conveniently placed in an adjoining room. Just as important, these rooms were wired to receive current from a small generator in the building should there be a citywide blackout due to an air raid.[17]

. . .

At Strategic Air Forces headquarters in Guam that morning, General Marshall's urgent radiogram relaying President Truman's orders to resume maximum B-29 operations against Japan triggered a flurry of activity. General Carl Spaatz immediately discussed targets with General Arnold by radio-teletype conference. Arnold wanted the maximum number of B-29s to bomb Tokyo "so as to impress Japanese officials that we mean business and are serious in getting them to accept our peace proposals without delay." Spaatz noted that Tokyo no longer represented a worthwhile target "except for the atomic bomb." Spaatz issued orders for four wings of B-29s to attack other Empire targets.[18]

When Allied Air Forces Commander General George Kenney received the Top Secret Marshall radiogram at 1145 hours in Manila, he hastily scrawled an order on the incoming message form to his deputy, Lt. General Ennis C. Whitehead: "By direction of the President, Resume full out operations immediately on 24 hour schedule."[19]

Kenney's Far Eastern Air Forces command included some of the new very heavy B-32 bombers, heavy (B-24) and medium (B-25) bombers, light bombers (A-26, A-20), as well as P-47N fighter-bombers flying from the new air bases on Okinawa against targets on the Home Island of Kyushu and shipping links between Korea and Japan.[20] Because Chief of Staff George Marshall had assigned General Spaatz an independent command in the Strategic Air Forces, his B-29s of the XXI Bomber Command in the Marianas concentrated on targets north and east of those assigned to Kenney's Far Eastern Air Forces' bombers.

The consequence of Kenny's handwritten order, which coauthor Jim B. Smith unearthed in the Kenney archives at the Air Force Historical Research Agency, Maxwell Air Force Base, Alabama, was that the entire combined U.S. Air Force in the Pacific was now committed to bombing Japanese forces both day and night, including raids on the afternoon of August 14, 1945, and continuing through the night. But at the time that one particular order—to the 315th Bomb Wing at Northwest Field on Guam—was issued, no one could foresee its historic significance.

On Northwest Field, Sergeant Jim Smith was nursing a hangover and kicking a football near his barracks on the humid Tuesday morning of August 14 when a jeep roared into the camp and the driver tacked an announcement to the order board. Smith yelled at *The Boomerang*'s two scanners, Henry Carlson and Hank Leffler, "Here's the news we've been waiting for, gang. It's surrender time."

Another sergeant reached the board first. "Jesus," he gasped. "It's not surrender time. It's briefing time."

Smith stared at the terse mimeographed order. "The 501st Bombardment Group will report to briefing at 1200 hours for a maximum-effort strike."

The briefing room reeked of alcohol, and many of the pilots, Smith saw, seemed in no condition to fly. Stateside, a trooper would probably pull them over for drunk driving. But that hadn't mattered to the Wing. Thank God Carl Schahrer is no drinker, Smith thought. *The Boomerang*'s pilot would be in shape to fly. But why do any of us have to fly again?

The briefing officers mounted the stage. A colonel announced, his voice hesitant, as if he could not believe his own words, "Gentlemen, your mission tonight is the Big Daddy of them all, the most significant of the war from the strategic standpoint. It will be the longest B-29 mission ever attempted from the Marianas, just under 3,800 miles, round-trip. You will carry a maximum bomb load and no bomb-bay fuel tanks." He pulled the gray curtain from the wall map and raised his long pointer. "Thanks to you, Japan is starved for oil. Tonight's target is the Nippon Oil Company refinery located on a little bay called Tsuchuzaki near the port of Akita on the Sea of Japan, approximately 277 miles northwest of Tokyo. The area around Akita is Japan's only indigenous source of petroleum, so normally they'd guard the refinery with heavy air defenses. But you shouldn't have to worry, because the Japanese have not believed that we could reach Akita from the Marianas and fortunately they have not concentrated flak sites around the target. You shouldn't encounter much opposition, unless, of course, the enemy has figured out that the Wing's Superforts have been stripped of armament. In that case, there will be plenty of fighters around."

The airmen warily examined the wall-size briefing map, starkly illuminated with its shimmering black-light emphasis. The first thing that struck Smith was that Akita lay near the northern tip of Honshu, far beyond any target they had ever bombed. In fact, it was much nearer Hokkaido and Soviet Siberia than were the refineries the Wing had previously hit. He studied the inbound and outbound course lines and realized that they would be threading their way among enemy fighter bases in north central Honshu for at least three hours between landfall near the port of Iwaki on the Pacific coast north of Tokyo and land's end at Ishinomaki, a heavily defended Imperial Navy base.[21]

"If you run into trouble at the target," the officer continued, "and suffer major battle damage or have seriously wounded on board, instead of trying to make it back to Iwo Jima, consider proceeding to Vladivostok in the Soviet Far East. It's roughly 480 miles from Akita, two hours closer than Iwo. The navigators will receive approach charts to Vladivostok at their briefing. But remember, the Russians might inter you . . . or worse, so look at Vladivostok as the very last resort."

And he cautioned the crews to treat an emergency abort to Vladivostok as "landing at an enemy field." They were to destroy all their sensitive equipment, especially the Norden bombsight and Eagle radar, before leaving their planes in the hands of the Russians.[22]

The men in Smith's crew glanced nervously at one another. There had been rumors—later confirmed—that Soviet forces had detained three B-29 crews and seized their aircraft. (The Russian authorities held the American airmen—who had been forced to land in Vladivostok late in 1944 or early 1945—for several months. But the Soviets never released the three B-29s. Using these aircraft, the Soviet Union began an ambitious reverse-engineering campaign that resulted two years later in the Tupolev-4, a very heavy bomber that was a virtual clone of the Superfortress.)

"If you can avoid Vladivostok," the officer said, pointing to glowing black-light spots on the map, "head for these ditching positions where American submarines will be waiting to pick you up."

The crew made careful notes of the coordinates, which were not just the sole responsibility of the navigator, who could be killed or wounded just as easily as any other crew member.

"The Wing has been ordered to mount a maximum-effort, 143 aircraft," the colonel continued. "And each aircraft will be carrying a maximum bomb and fuel load: either 164 100-pounders or an equivalent weight of 250-pound General Purpose bombs as well as 6,780 gallons of gas. With that bomb load, there'll be no room for bomb-bay tanks, so gas is definitely going to be a factor."

Again his long pointer tapped the map. "As I said, the flight to Akita and back will take you almost 3,800 miles and will be the longest mission ever attempted with a maximum bomb load and without auxiliary fuel tanks. You will have to stretch your cruise-control envelope to the absolute limit."

Groaning echoed through the briefing room. Beside Jim Smith, flight engineer Hank Gorder was shaking his head. "This is going to be close."

The briefer announced that the bombs would be set to explode on impact, spaced every thirty-five feet. Without delay fuses that allowed bombs to penetrate masonry structures, the ordnance would explode on contact, inflict maximum fragmentation damage, and ignite fires over a wide area among the thin-walled refinery structures and storage tanks.

Now the officer traced the inbound and outbound legs of the mission. He tapped the Pacific shore just east of Tokyo. "Chosi Point at the north end of the Boso Peninsula provides a prominent radar return [a clear image in the radar operator's scope]." He gave the point's coordinates, 38 degrees 27 minutes north, 139 degrees 14 minutes east, which pilots, navigators, and radar operators carefully copied.

"From there, you fly north to a smaller, but well-defined cape"— again the officer provided detailed coordinates—"and turn northwest, across Honshu to the small island of Awa Shima on the Sea of Japan. That is your Initial Point. From the IP, the approach north to the target is 81 nautical miles along the western coast of Honshu. Although the coast is fairly smooth, there are several useful radar navigation points. If necessary, radar operators can use the distinctive projection north of Akita as a landmark. The target is located at the mouth of the Omono Gawa River and gives a good radar return for direct synchronous bombing by individual aircraft."

He cleared his throat and hesitated a moment. The crews realized that the other shoe was about to drop. "Your target altitude will be 10,000 to 11,000 feet."

There was another rumble of discontent from the men in the room. As during the Amagasaki mission four days earlier, the bomber stream flying at these low altitudes would present easy targets for enemy fighters. And if intelligence had screwed up and the enemy had actually installed the German radar-controlled flak guns around this important refinery, some of the men in this room would not live to see the end of the war.

"Thanks to you," the briefing colonel said, "Japan is starved for oil, and Akita now represents the Empire's most important remaining oil target. Depending on the progress of the peace negotiations, this mission is subject to a scrub. You will be given coordinates for jettisoning your bombs if you receive that order. Your takeoff will be followed one hour and ten minutes later by one group of the 313th and the entire 314th Bomb Wing, as well as an element of the 73d. They will be hitting targets farther south."

The men knew that the three wings from Tinian and Saipan that had taken off just after dawn were already striking the Empire. With the addition of these night missions, XXI Bomber Command was launching a massive assault on Japan.

The mood of the airmen varied from repressed anger to stoic determination to get this job done. Hoping to raise the men's spirits, the briefing colonel smiled confidently. "Yours will be the last mission, since you will be bombing last and landing last after an estimated seventeen hours in the air. And I hope to God your mission will be the last one flown in World War Two."

At the separate briefing for radio operators, Jim Smith learned that he would have a vital role to play in the mission. The word "APPLE" would be sent in Morse code as soon as the United States received official notice of the Japanese surrender. That would be the order for the Wing to salvo their unarmed bombs over an ocean jettison point and return to base.

The officer briefing them ordered the radio operators to monitor their command frequency from the time their planes started engines. Then he added, "It's my guess that you'll receive the scrub signal 'APPLE' before you even reach Iwo."

When the cabinet adjourned to meet again that evening to review and sign the Imperial Rescript, War Minister Anami returned to his office on Ichigaya Heights. The tension and agitation in the building were palpable as word spread among the young conspirators that Anami was back. He immediately called officers from the section director level up to the minister's conference room to deliver his final address. But a number of younger men, including Takeshita, Hatanaka, and another conspirator, Lt. Colonel Ida, also crowded in with their superior officers.[23]

Gripped by emotion, Anami summarized the situation. "A council in the Imperial presence has just been held, and the Emperor has finally decided to end the war. The entire army must act in complete accord with this decision. Japan will face difficult times. Even if it means sleeping on grass and eating stones, I ask you all to do your utmost to preserve the national polity."[24]

The officers were stunned. Why had General Anami, the staunchest advocate against surrender and for fighting on, suddenly lost his resolve?

Lt. Colonel Ida stepped forward boldly. "Will the War Minister explain why he has changed his mind?"

This was a breach of military etiquette bordering on insubordination. But Anami chose to answer. "The Emperor told me he understood fully how I felt. With tears in his eyes, he asked me to persevere, however difficult the duty. I can no longer oppose my view to the Emperor's decision."

Many in the room were moved by Anami's words. But others stared back defiantly. To them, he now echoed the phrase he had first spoken on August 10, "Anyone who disagrees will have to do so over my dead body!"[25]

Troubled silence filled the room. Still, Anami's message was ambiguous. He might have meant that the conspirators would have to physically confront and kill him if they proceeded or that he would commit suicide in a gruesome samurai ritual called *seppuku*—which involved slicing open one's abdomen in three precise slashes—should they persist in their plot. But there was a third possibility: Anami's sudden public reversal of position might disguise his true decision to wait on the sidelines to see if the conspirators succeeded in their coup attempt before joining their cause.

At first, no one responded to Anami's fierce admonition. Then the frantic, unrestrained sobs of Major Kenji Hatanaka reached the level of a wail. His world was shattered; his idol, War Minister Anami, seemed determined to abandon both the nation and the Army they both loved.

Earlier, Anami and Imperial Navy Chief of Staff Admiral Toyoda had assured Marquis Kido that they could control the Army and the Navy and would not have to subject His Majesty to the humiliation of appealing personally to the armed forces to remain calm. And Anami had joined Army Chief of Staff Umezu, Field Marshal Hata, and other senior officers in signing a terse statement: "The Army will act in accord with the Imperial decision to the last."[26] It certainly appeared that he had committed himself to peace.

During that afternoon's cabinet meeting, convened to review and approve the draft Imperial Rescript, however, several ministers remained suspicious of Anami's sudden change of heart and apparent docility. On the surface he seemed calm and determined to implement the peace process. But they remained deeply troubled about what might lie beneath his impassive features.[27]

. . .

Once it became apparent that the cabinet would approve the language of the rescript at some point that afternoon, a person in the Prime Minister's office—probably Chief Cabinet Secretary Sakomizu—contacted the Domei News Agency announcing that peace was at hand. Just as the agency had unofficially broken the peace story that Sakomizu had planted the day before, Domei now transmitted an urgent broadcast on its overseas radio channels, including the shortwave frequencies beamed in English toward America and the American-held islands of the Pacific: "FLASH! FLASH! Tokyo, August 14—It is learned an Imperial message accepting the Potsdam proclamation is forthcoming soon." It was 2:49 P.M. in Tokyo.[28]

Most of the conspirators had left General Anami's conference room badly shaken and dejected. It now seemed that no senior officers would back the coup plot. But once Major Hatanaka had recovered his composure, he rallied several of his colleagues. Hatanaka's zeal was not diminished, even though his fellow conspirators Takeshita and Inaba now had urged him to abandon the coup. The conspiracy could proceed as planned, Hatanaka believed, because he and his comrades stood an excellent chance of seizing the Palace and isolating the Emperor. Two majors in the Imperial Guards Division remained solidly in their camp. One was Hidemasa Koga, the son-in-law of former dictatorial Premier General Hideki Tojo, who retained a great personal following in right-wing military circles. The other prominent rebel staff officer in the division was Major Sadakichi Ishihara. With their support, and that of other Division officers, the Emperor would be closely followed, placed in custody, and held incommunicado. Then, with the Imperial Palace isolated, the rebels could dictate their terms. The rest of the Army was certain to rally behind them.[29]

But Hatanaka also realized that the operation's tactical plan had a "new objective . . . of the highest priority." The conspirators and their allies in the Imperial Guards would have to seize the recording of the Imperial Rescript "before it was delivered to the NHK (Japan Broadcasting Corporation) building."[30]

With the Sacred Voice of the Crane silenced, Major Hatanaka and his comrade officers, exercising a higher form of loyalty to Japan's ancient throne, would instead speak for the Emperor and issue orders to continue the war in His Majesty's name.

.   .   .

The heat inside *The Boomerang* was terrible. Smith hunched, sweating at the radio operator's narrow table behind the flight deck, and winced at the sun glare reflecting through the Plexiglas nose from the asphalt runways of Northwest Field. He felt queasy. His hangover had not gotten much better since the briefing. As soon as he flipped the switches to warm up the big Collins radio set, Smith grabbed his oxygen mask and breathed in deeply for a couple of minutes to clear his head.

But Carl Schahrer seemed sharp and methodical as always as he worked through his checklists, so Smith knew they were almost certain to take off safely, as always. The briefing officer's words echoed in Smith's mind, *the longest continuous bombing mission of the war*, almost 3,800 miles—seventeen hours, most over water, with a bomb load of more than eight tons and 6,780 gallons of gasoline. This was the heaviest combined bomb and fuel load they had ever carried, and the plane would be right on the edge of the maximum allowable gross takeoff weight of 140,000 pounds. They were going to need every inch of the 8,500-foot left runway.

Suddenly he was gripped by the terrible image of the takeoff for the Ube raid on August 5 when that Superfort couldn't reach takeoff speed and ground-looped at the edge of the cliff, its brakes flaming.

Today they were even heavier than that '29. And the afternoon was even hotter. Flight engineer Hank Gorder frowned as he checked his gauges and worked his slide rule again. It was 1515 hours, about time for Start Engines.

Before boarding the plane, Carl Schahrer had asked Hank about fuel after he'd verified that the tanks had been topped off. "You sure we've got enough gas loaded for a round-trip to Akita?"

"That's what they tell us, Skipper." Hank sighed, double-checking his briefing notes.

The sweat was soaking through Smith's tropical flight suit, forming wet patches under the survival vest and floppy rubber collar of his Mae West. The parachute harness dug into his groin and shoulders. When he leaned close to his set to adjust the BFO (beat frequency oscillator), sweat dripped onto the radio logbook.

He mopped the mission notes with a square of toilet paper, careful not to smear the code word APPLE: the abort order to be sent in Morse code in the event of surrender. The officer had told the radio operators that they'd hear that signal in the first three hours of the mission. That was easy for him to say; he wasn't flying tonight. And he wouldn't have to try to land on Iwo Jima's short, soggy asphalt runways in the dark if gas ran low on the way home—or, far worse, to attempt ditching in the Pacific as one engine after another coughed dead, starved of fuel.

A captain drove a jeep down the flightline, stopping at each hard-stand to give the Start Engines hand signal. Carl relayed the command to Hank Gorder, who began the sequence. "Start number three."

"Starting number three," Hank echoed.

The tired engines sounded rough. The 315th had received few spare parts in recent weeks, thanks to those striking workers at the Wright-Cyclone plant in Cincinnati. So much for the Home Front, Smith thought bitterly.

Hank Gorder was working the levers and switches on his engine panel, trying to keep the mixture lean enough to conserve gas as they sat here idling, but not overheat the engines. Every minute those 72 big cylinders fired here on the hardstand, they burned another six gallons of precious gas. Along the line of planes, the engines were laying down black clouds of oil as they ran at low RPM.

"Let's do it or get off the pot," Dick Marshall, the bombardier, said gruffly over the intercom. He was normally one of the coolest heads on the plane, but the tension was getting to him too. But he spoke for all of them. After nine missions over the Empire, they were as exhausted as the engines.

At 3:49 Guam time, the U.S. Navy radio station on the island picked up the urgent Domei News Agency bulletin announcing that the Imperial message accepting the Potsdam Declaration was "forthcoming soon."[31]

The duty operator typed the short text on his Incoming form and a messenger rushed it to the headquarters of the Strategic Air Forces. Now General Carl Spaatz and his subordinates had to reach a command decision. Should the night B-29 missions proceed? One hundred forty-three B-29Bs of the 315th Wing had already started engines and were waiting for the order to taxi to the twin runways of Northwest Field. The 314th Wing and the group of the 313th that had not flown earlier that day were scheduled to take off in a little over an hour, the 313th's planes from Tinian and the 314th's from North Field on Guam.

But was this bulletin authentic or just another Japanese stalling tactic like the Domei message of August 13? It was late at night in Washington, hardly the time to wake the President or the Chief of Staff to advise these veteran field commanders on reaching their decision.

Spaatz and his staff faced a difficult problem. The lives of hundreds of young airmen were at stake. Simply taking off in a heavily loaded B-29 was hazardous. Some planes were bound to encounter engine trouble en route to their targets and abort to Iwo Jima or be forced to ditch. And the Japanese might have decided to aggressively intercept the bombers, just as they had resumed their kamikaze attacks against Okinawa. And what if the long streams of Superforts were dropping their bombs just as the Japanese government was about to reach its final decision on surrender? Would this act disrupt the peace negotiations?

The commanders struggled to reach their decision.

None of the 315th's airmen in their planes understood the reason for the unusual delay on the hardstand.

Although the aircrews most affected by the urgent Domei News bulletin never heard it, they quickly felt its repercussions. The line captain's jeep came racing along the hardstands, and he signaled the planes to shut down engines.

"It's a scrub," Jim Smith said.

Hank cut the master and ignition switches. The four big Cyclones coughed, and the throaty roar abruptly ceased. Beneath Smith's shoes, the deck stopped vibrating. The only sound was the creaking of the hot engine cylinders, the whirring spin-down of the turbo superchargers. It's over, he thought. We're going home.

Before climbing aboard the plane, Sid Siegel, the tail gunner, had bet Smith five dollars that they'd scrub before takeoff. Smith had gladly taken the wager, hoping to lose and not fly the mission.

"I owe you a fin, Sid," Smith called over the intercom.

Then a message crackled over the pilots' short-range VHF, breaking the normally stringent rule about radio silence. "All aircraft are to stand by for orders."

The mission wasn't over yet.

Farther down the line of hardstands, First Lieutenant Chuck Miller, aircraft commander of *For the Luvva Mike*, named for his infant son, sat rigidly in the left-hand flight-deck seat. He felt like a condemned prisoner waiting for the last-minute phone call from the governor that would spare his life. But as the leader of his crew, he could not reveal his emotions to the other men on the plane. And he was determined to fly this last mission as professionally as possible, should the Wing be ordered to do so. In fact, as the delay dragged on, the more determined Miller became.

Time passed. The 315th's crews waited in limbo.

. . .

After nearly an hour of discussion, Spaatz and his staff agreed: The night missions would proceed.

It is significant, however, that what would prove to be one of the most crucial command decisions of the Pacific war was reached in what might be called a historical vacuum. Jim B. Smith has spent years trying to locate any minutes, records, or references to the command discussions or consultations with Washington that took place after the Domei bulletin reached Guam.

Declassified records do not exist in open archives. Perhaps those involved were too preoccupied to take notes. It is also possible that the senior officers who reached the decision to proceed did not want a record that could document their role should the night missions end in disaster, either with needless deaths among American aircrew or widespread casualties among Japanese who were killed after their government had surrendered.

But there is another possibility. Historians at the Air Force Historical Research Agency suggested to Smith that Spaatz's decision might actually have been influenced by Chief of Staff Marshall, who wanted to end the war immediately, virtually at any cost, to prevent the Soviet Union from gaining a foothold in the Japanese Home Islands and forcing the Western Allies to accept a divided Japan, with separate occupation zones as in Germany. But such matters went beyond the authority of military commanders in the Pacific theater and broached that of Pentagon and civilian leaders in Washington. For that reason, any record of the debate on whether to launch the night missions might have been suppressed.[32]

Over the years that he has investigated this question, Jim Smith has found evidence that the 315th Bomb Wing's maximum-effort strike on the Nippon Oil Company refinery at Akita after the Domei News Agency broadcast reached Air Force commanders in Guam had more to do with emerging Cold War tensions than with World War II strategy. Had the war dragged on and the Soviets captured the northern island of Hokkaido, as many Japanese (and American) leaders feared, Smith believes that the Red Army would have also probably secured its foothold in northern Honshu well before the Americans could launch Operation Olympic to invade Kyushu.

Historian Richard B. Frank strongly supports Smith's thesis that the Russians had designs on northern Japan and the means to accomplish them: "The [Soviet Red Army's] seizure of Hokkaido would confer important military and political rewards: a springboard for attacks on Honshu and a right to participate in the occupation of Japan."[33] Further, rather than risk having Japan's only indigenous oil field and last undamaged refinery—which represented 67 percent of the Home Islands' August 1945 petroleum production—fall into Soviet hands, Smith has concluded, the United States ordered this unusual and dangerous mission.

It must be remembered that the Soviet Union, although it had rich oil fields around Baku on the Caspian Sea, had no natural sources of petroleum in the Far East and had to request large quantities of fuel from the Americans before the Red Army could launch its Far East offensive. But, even if the Soviets had occupied northern Honshu before the Americans, the island's oil reserves there would do them little good without a working refinery at Akita, which had been built specifically to process the output of the nearby fields. And the Red Army needed oil to run.

Strategic Air Forces Commander General Spaatz might have used the delay in launching the 315th Wing following the Domei News Agency bulletin to consult with his superiors in Washington—even though it was after midnight, eastern war time—in order to decide if the Akita mission should still proceed. What might have weighed in favor of proceeding was the fact that, although the American occupation forces in Honshu would have use for the oil products from the Akita refinery for both military and civilian requirements, it was more important to deprive the Soviets of the Akita refinery.

Without question, the American occupation forces could have benefited from the Akita refinery, which was probably why the 315th Bomb Wing had not struck the target earlier. But, now that it appeared the Soviet Red Army might capture Akita first, nascent American Cold War strategy probably leaned toward destroying the facility to keep it out of the hands of potential Soviet occupation forces.

And America's wartime leaders certainly wanted to avoid sharing the occupation of Japan with the Soviet Union if at all possible. Secretary of War Henry L. Stimson noted on August 14, "It was of great importance to get the [Japanese] homeland into our hands before the Russians could put in any substantial claim to occupy and help rule it."[34]

In an apparent attempt to confuse the matter of the Akita bombing, however, the Strategic Air Forces issued a press release later that day, stating: "The Tuesday–Wednesday raids were under way when the Tokyo radio broadcast that the Japanese would accept the Potsdam declaration."[35]

This was not true. Although there had been more than 400 Superforts from the Marianas bombing Japanese targets at midday on Tuesday, August

14, 1945, the 143 aircraft of the 315th Wing, as well as the 163 bombers of the 313th, the 314th, and the 73d Wings assigned to the night missions were all on the ground when the Domei News Agency bulletin reached Guam.[36]

At 1625 hours, the line captain's jeep stopped beneath the Plexiglas nose of *The Boomerang* again. He waved his hand in the Start Engines signal.

Ever the optimist, Carl Schahrer called Smith over the intercom. "It's my guess, Smitty, that we'll hear that code word 'APPLE' before we even run up the engines. So keep those earphones on."

Smith adjusted the phones tightly on his ears. "I'm a steel trap, Carl."

Finally, the tower fired two green flares and the Superforts began to trundle out onto the taxiway. As they turned, the crew saw the long line of huge silvery bombers, each with its belly painted flat black to dampen searchlight reflection, forming up behind them. They were taking off every thirty seconds, alternating between the two parallel runways. The plane swayed with the prop wash as they jolted slowly along the taxi ramp. Finally, the B-29 ahead turned onto the main runway and began to roll. Carl Schahrer taxied deftly into position, and he and John Waltershausen ran up the engines as Hank Gorder intently studied his gauges. A green light blinked in the distant tower. "Takeoff," Carl announced calmly.

He stood on the brakes and thrust the four throttle levers forward to the EMERGENCY WAR POWER setting. The roar inside the fuselage was deafening. The plane seemed to be shaking apart. He released the brakes.

From the right seat, John called out the ritual of takeoff airspeed as the dried mud and spiky grass beside the runway flashed by in a blur. "... ninety ... one hundred ... one-twenty ..." The cliff at the end of the runway was coming up fast. Still, Schahrer kept the yoke down, his arms straight ahead. "... one-thirty-five," Waltershausen announced, his voice tight.

Schahrer grimaced as he pulled back pressure on the yoke, willing *The Boomerang* to rise. Smith felt the first floating sensation of lift as the Plexiglas nose filled with the blue-green Pacific horizon. The landing gear had left the runway just before the drop-off of the cliff. Schahrer eased the yoke forward as Waltershausen carefully reduced the power setting. As always, they would fly low across the water for fifteen minutes to cool off the engines before climbing to cruise altitude.

It was 1651 hours, 14 August 1945. Once more, *The Boomerang* was on its way to the Empire.

PART III

"TO OUR GOOD AND LOYAL SUBJECTS . . ."

CHAPTER EIGHT

REBELLION

THE HOME ISLANDS OF JAPAN, toward which the 315th Bomb Wing flew on the afternoon of August 14, 1945, seethed with unease and thinly submerged rebellion, like the contents of a kettle kept too long on the flame. Over the previous two days, the millions of leaflets dropped by American aircraft that revealed the full extent of the peace negotiations had spread among both the civilian population and the Imperial armed forces. For many the startling prospect of peace was a dream they had never dared consider. But for many others, particularly the diehards in the military, the sudden awareness that their leaders were actively dealing with the hated enemy to bring about Japan's surrender in such a manner that the Emperor's authority would be "subject to the Supreme Commander of the Allied Powers"—a shameful concession that the war and navy ministers had explicitly confirmed to their senior officers—was a disgraceful and infuriating insult to Japanese sovereignty and a blasphemy against the divine person of the Emperor. The *kokutai,* and with it both the spiritual essence and the very physical existence of the Japanese people, were threatened.

On Pacific islands such as Saipan and Okinawa, where large numbers of Japanese civilians had participated in the defense against invading Americans, Imperial armed forces had inflamed the population with propaganda that wholesale rape was one of the enemy's priority objectives, meant to engender a mongrelized non-Japanese race. This propaganda had also been widespread in the Home Island as a means to rally support for the Ketsu-go. Now the population had to face the specter of Allied occupation, with its associated mass rape. And, under the shameful terms of the Potsdam Declaration, the Imperial armed forces, which still numbered over six million at home and abroad, would be forced to surrender their weapons and stand by, powerless, as the Yankees raped the soldiers' and sailors' wives, mothers, and daughters. Within five years, Japan would become a spawning ground for half-breed bastards. The warrior race of Yamato faced extinction.

But throughout the Imperial Army and Navy—principally among the thousands of aviators trained for the Ketsu-go battle—there were officers and enlisted men grimly determined to never accept surrender. They would fight on no matter what orders they received from their traitorous civilian and military leaders in Tokyo.

Admiral Mitsumasa Yonai was deeply concerned about the simmering discontent over pending surrender in his service. "During my long career as Navy Minister," he said after the war, "I probably never worried so much as I did during the period from the 14th to about the 23d of that month [August 1945]."[1]

He had reason to worry. There were numerous but isolated pockets of stubborn resistance to the Imperial decision to end the war. Fortunately, on the afternoon of August 14, the leaders of these groups remained ignorant of the others' existence. But they represented the proverbial tinder, lacking only a spark to burst into flame, flare into a conflagration, and consume the peace process by launching kamikaze and conventional air attacks on the Allied naval forces lurking offshore and on American bases from Okinawa all the way down to the airfields of the detested *B-san* in the Marianas.

According to the knowledgeable historians who wrote the definitive *Japan's Longest Day,* a particularly combustible nest of potential rebellion was the Imperial Navy's Atsugi Air Base, on the coastal plain, twenty-three miles southwest of Tokyo. Atsugi was huge, the Empire's most formidable installation. The airfield was a warren of deep, reinforced-concrete underground hangars, maintenance shops, and barracks for thousands of airmen and support personnel. Hundreds of combat planes of the Imperial Navy's 302nd Air Corps were also sheltered belowground, beyond the reach of American bombs. Although Atsugi's main runway had often been cratered during Allied carrier strikes, the base's other strips were successfully camouflaged from air attack and defended by concentrations of light and heavy antiaircraft guns.

The 302nd Air Corps was commanded by one of Japan's most experienced and fanatical officers, Captain Yasuna Kozono. Because of his competence as a combat leader, and his ability to rally the Navy's best surviving pilots to him, Kozono had been given the responsibility of protecting the seaward approaches to Tokyo from B-29 attack. And, despite the priorities of the Ketsu-go preparations, Kozono had received enough advanced Gekko night fighters and an adequate fuel allowance earlier that summer. His unit was now well prepared for combat.

On August 14, when Captain Kozono got word that the beloved homeland actually teetered on the brink of capitulation, he vowed to do all in his power to prevent this shameful calamity. He cabled Navy Minister Admiral Yonai and repeated the cable to the Chief of the Navy General Staff, just to make sure his message reached the highest leaders of the service in Tokyo. Continuing the war, Kozono wrote, offered Japan the only promise of salvation and the Navy the only chance to redeem its honor. But defeatist civilian "weaklings" were intent on stripping that honor from the nation and the armed forces. Those in uniform must unite to defeat both the enemy and the traitors at home.

"It is only natural that officers of the Imperial Army and Navy, who have been taught never to surrender, should come into conflict with those government officials who desire to accept the surrender terms," the cable said in part.[2]

And the fact that Atsugi's underground hangars were jammed with his country's most innovative warplanes—including rocket-powered fighters and a few prototypes of the four-engine G8N1 Renzan bomber, which had the range to strike as far south as the Philippines or to hit America's Marianas bases with heavy bomb loads—gave Captain Kozono confidence that he could deal the Allies a sharp blow when the time came to disrupt surrender.

Kozono's resolve would have been strengthened had he known there were even flag rank naval officers just as adamantly opposed to disgraceful surrender as he was. Among them was Vice Admiral Matome Ugaki, Commander-in-Chief of the Fifth Fleet on Kyushu and an ardent leader of the kamikaze effort. Even as the cabinet prepared to approve the draft Imperial surrender rescript, Ugaki planned for renewed war. He had multiple kamikaze squadrons available, which included hundreds of the latest D4Y4 Suisei dive-bombers that had been built as special attack aircraft. Carrying a combined bomb and fuel load of two tons, with a one-way range of almost 900 miles, Ugaki's planes represented a deadly threat to the Allied fleet.[5]

Had rebel Major Kenji Hatanaka known about such powerful undeclared allies, his renewed confidence in the wisdom of the coup would also have been bolstered that steamy August afternoon in the sooty streets of Tokyo. Hatanaka's confidence had nearly been shattered several hours earlier when War Minister Anami had told the staff on Ichigaya Heights that they must abandon any thoughts of continued resistance or ill-conceived notions of a coup.

But, from just such irrational conviction—or from a subtle, private communication with Anami—by 4 P.M. the fanatical young zealot had become convinced that the conspiracy *would* succeed and that it must proceed in order to save the nation. In what might have been either desperation or naïveté, Hatanaka frantically pedaled his bicycle through the humid heat to the monolithic block of the Dai Ichi Insurance Building near the southeastern moat of the Imperial Palace, and climbed to the sixth-floor headquarters of the Eastern District Army.

According to most later historical accounts, Major Hatanaka then brusquely demanded that an adjutant admit him into the office of the commanding general, Shizuichi Tanaka. Hatanaka and the adjutant had sharp words. Alerted by the loud voices, General Tanaka burst into the outer office and glared at the pale young major. Before Hatanaka had a chance to renew his appeal that the General bring his command into the conspiracy, Eastern District Army Commander Tanaka, fuming in rage, pointed at the door and ordered him to leave. Hatanaka could only silently comply.

This, at least, has been the commonly accepted version of Hatanaka's purpose at the Dai Ichi Building that afternoon. There is an equally convincing explanation, however, one that helps clarify several strange events that unfolded as the coup d'état proceeded. Perhaps it was not the commanding general of the Eastern District Army whom Hatanaka had come to see, but rather that army's Chief of Staff, Major General Tatsuhiko Takashima. After the war, one of the original conspiracy's key leaders, Lt. Colonel Masahiko Takeshita, gave Allied military intelligence a detailed account of these matters. A section of a Takeshita interrogation transcript is critical to understanding the complex final week of the war. Describing August 12, 1945, when the conspirators still believed General Anami was firmly in their camp, Takeshita stated:

"Since we had independently won over the regimental and subordinate commanders of the [1st Imperial Guards] Division, we decided that when the time for the coup d'état came we would call Mori [the Division commander] to the War Ministry, try once more to persuade him to join us, and, if he continued to resist, confine him in the Minister's office and use the Division's troops as planned."

Then Takeshita added a sentence that could better explain Hatanaka's presence at Eastern District Army headquarters on the afternoon of August 14: "We established contact with the Chief of Staff of the Eastern District Army as to the employment of its troops."[4] The officer in question was Major General Tatsuhiko Takashima, who would play a key role on the night of August 14–15, 1945.

So it is entirely possible that Hatanaka had come to see the Eastern District Army Chief of Staff and not the commanding general that sweltering afternoon.

But many Japanese have preferred to put such conjecture far behind them, along with other unpleasant memories of the war. The possibility that the leadership of one of the Imperial Japanese Army's major commands was actually flirting with an insurrection that would, in effect, defy the Emperor and imprison him on the eve of surrender evokes a widespread Japanese cultural trait: *haji*, an attribute that pioneering American anthropologist Ruth Benedict introduced to the West in the 1940s.

Haji can be translated as unacceptable shame at having broken traditionally inviolable norms of behavior. Certainly absolute obedience to His Majesty's commands was just such an inviolable form of conduct. Any admission detailing plots against the Emperor's authority would confront a wall of *haji* on the part of the conspirators. The results would likely be distortion or silence.

So it is no wonder that many Japanese historians have preferred to interpret the coup d'état that Major Hatanaka and his colleagues sparked on the night of August 14 as the desperate act of a few junior officers, which never involved senior military leaders and certainly never put the person of the Emperor or his dignity in jeopardy.

Whatever Hatanaka's motives for visiting the Eastern District Army, he was far from defeated on leaving. He quickly pedaled clockwise around the edge of the Imperial Palace moat, as the massive dark gray granite blocks of the outer walls radiated back the afternoon heat. Within minutes, Hatanaka climbed the road to Ichigaya Heights and reached the War Ministry. Sweating and winded, he mounted the stairs to the office of his former ardent coconspirator, Lt. Colonel Masataka Ida of the Military Affairs Section. On War Minister Anami's orders, Ida had abandoned the coup, and was now setting his office in order before committing suicide in the morning.[5]

While Hatanaka had continued his attempts to rally support for the coup, Ida had decided on a less grandiose, more spiritual course of action, one befitting a true samurai. He had tried to persuade as many War Ministry colleagues as possible to join him in a mass act of seppuku. This would be a persuasively dramatic gesture, especially in Japanese cultural terms, meant to be both the deepest expression of apology to the Emperor at losing the war and also to convince the world that the Imperial Army, and not His Majesty, was responsible for that war. So far, however, Ida had found only a handful willing to join him in this agonizing final act of Bushido.

Ida and Hatanaka, who had been close friends at the Imperial Military Academy in the 1930s, now needed each other. Hatanaka was charismatic and popular; he could help sway those in the Ministry still wavering about ritual suicide. And for Hatanaka, Ida's maturity and expertise at staff work would help solidify the still-fragile heart of the plot. Ida was also a kinsman of Lt. General Takeshi Mori, commander of the 1st Imperial Guards Division, whose support was essential to the success of the planned coup d'état.

Hatanaka found Ida's office an unsatisfactory site to discuss the conspiracy, however. For one thing, acrid smoke was drifting up from a huge bonfire as soldiers burned mounds of classified documents on the grounds below. The two officers adjourned to the Ministry roof.

There, overlooking the blackened desolation of Tokyo, from which a few undamaged buildings close to the Imperial Palace rose like islands, was a damp breeze. Ida explained in detail his plan to lead all the Ministry's officers in seppuku, then asked Hatanaka his opinion. Hatanaka replied that this action "would indeed be a beautiful and correct thing to do." However, he added, the plan was "doomed to failure" because fewer than half of the Ministry officers would support it.

Ida challenged Hatanaka to present a more attractive alternative, which was just the opening the Major sought. Even at the risk of being called a traitor, Hatanaka said, "I would rather fight the enemy than entrust my Emperor and my country into his hands!"

Ida pointed out that it was the Emperor himself who had commanded surrender and that General Anami had ordered all on his staff to obey that command. The Army would follow the General's lead, the Colonel added. A small band of rebels did not stand much chance.

"Heaven may favor either side," Hatanaka said, his eyes gleaming with emotion. "That is something no human being can say."

Hatanaka detailed his latest refinements on the original plan to cut off the Imperial Palace from all outside contact, thus holding His Majesty incommunicado. "I want us to concentrate all our efforts on helping the Emperor preserve Japan. Liaison with the Imperial Guards Division has already been made," Hatanaka explained, adding that key staff officers and battalion commanders had joined the plot. After the Palace had been isolated, the soldiers would occupy the Imperial Household Ministry, where spies in the Division had reported that the NHK engineers had already set up their equipment to record the Emperor as he read his surrender rescript. Once troops loyal to the coup had occupied the Ministry, the building could be sealed and the Emperor prevented from recording the dishonorable rescript that the traitorous elements in the government were preparing at that very moment, according to General Anami's earlier announcement. To make doubly sure the Japanese people and armed forces never heard the rescript, the conspirators would also occupy the NHK broadcasting center near the Imperial Palace. It was a foolproof plan.

"If just a few officers start the uprising now," Hatanaka said enthusiastically, "the whole Army will follow. Heaven will favor us. Join us, Colonel!"

Ida remained doubtful that the plot would succeed and retained his intention to commit suicide. But he did not try very hard to dissuade his colleague. "Go ahead with your plan. I won't try to stop you. But I won't join you, either."[6]

Hatanaka left the Ministry to continue mustering support for the coup, all the elements of which he hoped to have in place as soon as possible after nightfall. He was disappointed that Ida had not joined him, but remained committed to the plot.

While Hatanaka was preparing a covert offensive, War Minister Anami was conducting a stubborn retreat. Meeting with the cabinet at the Prime Minister's official residence near the Palace walls, Anami was trying to buy time. He argued that the Emperor's Privy Council would have to review and approve the draft rescript before it became official. The General who had fought many straightforward battles had also mastered the subtle art of court politics: Accepting the Potsdam Declaration was tantamount to signing a treaty, he announced, an act that must involve the Privy Council. This was a clever rearguard action, because it would take at least twenty-four hours for the full council to meet on the matter, and Anami would have won the delay he had earlier requested in vain from Prime Minister Suzuki.

Haji notwithstanding, it is significant that he took this step in opposition to the Emperor's express wishes and fully aware of the smoldering plans for a coup d'état among members of his own staff.

The cabinet session meant to quickly approve the draft rescript was forced to recess, while legislative advisers to the Premier considered the legal complications of Anami's request.

At the Palace, NHK technicians had set up their microphone and recording equipment in the second-floor administrative office of the sprawling Imperial Household Ministry. Their superiors had told them to be ready to record the Emperor's reading of the rescript no later than 6:00 P.M. Naturally, they had arrived earlier and tested the equipment to be certain everything was ready. Now they waited in the heat, gripped by excitement that they would soon be in the Imperial presence and that they would be required to perform the most important assignment of their lives.

Had the recording technicians dared to leave their posts to seek some cooler air on nearby Maple Leaf Hill, they might have seen a sight that turned their excited anticipation into fear. Some 400 soldiers of the 1st Imperial Guards Division, a full battalion, carrying long Arisaka rifles and Model 11 Nambu light machine guns, marched in a column behind an officer with the fierce military bearing common to the Guards. The battalion belonged to the Second Regiment, responsible today for Palace security. What was unusual was the fact that these soldiers had entered the walls of the inner grounds, even though the regular battalion was already on duty along the Palace's outer perimeter. Further, the officer who led this new battalion was the regimental commander himself, Colonel Toyojiro Haga.

Seen from the air in August 1945, the Imperial Palace would have had the appearance of an early-autumn leaf, most still green, but with dark, shriveled edges. The Palace was a little over a mile long and about three-quarters of a mile at its widest point. Surrounded by a serpentine moat from which rose the gray granite blocks of the outer walls, the grounds had retained much of their dense stands of pines and hardwoods. And the Fukiage Gardens near the Gobunko were lush. The greenery of the trees and gardens was one of the most striking features, because the Palace was surrounded by the burned-out flatlands of central Tokyo. Despite the accidental damage the Imperial pavilions had suffered during the American incendiary raid of May 25, most of the hilly grounds and ornate traditional buildings had been untouched by bombs.

For the soldiers of the Imperial Guards Division's Second Regiment, the dense stands of trees and luxurious gardens, as well as structures such as the Imperial Household Ministry, presented a tactical challenge. Normally only one battalion at a time was deployed from the Guards' barracks on the northern Palace quadrant to fixed positions just inside the gates. The troops did not usually infringe on the sanctity of the inner Palace.

Now Colonel Haga was placing companies and platoons along paths near the Calabash Pond in the Fukiage Gardens and among the stands of trees at the edges of the road that connected the Gobunko with the Imperial Household Ministry. For the moment, the soldiers were in full sight of the nervous Palace Chamberlains who happened by. Soon, however, the troops would be ordered to conceal themselves in the foliage.

All this was puzzling. But Japanese soldiers, especially the hand-picked, disciplined troops of the Imperial Guards Division, knew better than to question orders.

And Colonel Haga did not reveal the reason for his actions.

Even as the soldiers deployed, Lord Keeper of the Privy Seal Marquis Kido met with Prince Konoye (on whose shoulders hopes for Soviet assistance in ending the war had earlier rested) at Konoye's suburban Tokyo residence. The Prince was a sophisticated, West-leaning former premier in his mid-fifties who had tried hard to limit Japan's military adventures in the 1930s—causing him to run afoul of Army hard-liners—and had struggled to keep Japan out of the disastrous current war with the Allies.

Now Konoye was worried and had called for Kido's advice on a matter too sensitive to discuss by telephone. "I have heard a rumor that I do not like the sound of at all," he told Kido. "I am afraid of what might be happening at the Imperial Guards Division. Do you know anything about it?"

Kido shook his head. "Nothing."

"Well," the prince said, "let's hope it ends as a rumor."[7]

At 1910 hours, *The Boomerang* flew northwest with the sunset's afterglow highlighting the distant thunderheads off the port wing.

"Anything on that scrub signal, Smitty?" Carl Schahrer called Jim Smith on the intercom.

Smith had sat tensely at his station for three hours after takeoff, earphones pressed painfully to his head as he listened for the Morse code word "APPLE": *dit dah, dit dah dah dit, dit dah dah dit, dit dah dit dit, dit.*

But all he had heard above the droning engines was the endless Japanese jamming: *dah dit dah dit, dah dit dit dit,* the mindless, grating "BC . . . CB . . . BC" that squeaked and warbled in his earphones until his head was ringing.

"Nothing, Carl," Smith said. "I would have heard it if they'd sent the message to scrub. And I'll sure tell you the minute that they do."

The plane's flight rations this evening were especially good, tender roast beef with mashed potatoes and gravy. But Smith was concentrating so hard on the radio that he couldn't enjoy the food.

At 1800 hours in Manila, General George C. Kenney, commander of Allied Air Forces, instructed his deputy, Lt. General Ennis C. Whitehead, to cancel the Far Eastern Air Forces missions scheduled for the night of August 14–15, 1945, including those already under way. In Kenney's hand-scrawled wartime diary, at "6:00 PM" he told Whitehead "to lay off nite missions for nite of 14/15."[8]

However, General Carl Spaatz at the headquarters of the Strategic Air Forces on Guam chose not to recall the XXI Bomber Command B-29s en route to Japan, as Kenney had recalled the planes under his command, even though Spaatz could easily have done so. Even by 1800 hours Guam time, the last of the 315th Wing's 143-plane maximum effort still had not taken off for Akita, the longest and, everyone hoped, the last mission of the war. And the long bomber columns from the later missions were making equally slow progress departing the Marianas' bases. So Spaatz certainly had ample time to cancel that mission as well as the later B-29 raids.

Why didn't Spaatz order those planes to scrub their missions?

(The 315th Bomb Wing's aircraft took off for the Akita mission from Northwest Field, Guam, between 1642 and 1858 hours August 14, 1945. B-29s from the 313th Wing on Saipan and the 314th Wing at North Field on Guam took off to bomb Kumagaya northwest of Tokyo between 1752 and 1839 hours that afternoon. Superforts of the 73rd Bomb Wing on Saipan that had not flown the earlier daylight missions and another group of the 314th Bomb Wing from Guam took off to strike Isesaki on central Honshu between 1845 and 2005 hours August 14, 1945. The timing of these takeoffs placed the 315th Bomb Wing's aircraft first in the vicinity of Tokyo at approximately 2300 hours that night.[9])

As Jim Smith has surmised, it is certainly plausible that the leaders of the Strategic Air Forces—acting on unwritten instructions from Chief of Staff General George Marshall to end the war as quickly as possible, so that the Soviet Union would not gain a foothold in Japan (and capture the Akita oil refinery)—decided to proceed with the night missions to pressure Japan to surrender. General Spaatz's command also chose to disguise the fact that the 315th's Bomb Wing had begun the mission takeoffs from Northwest Field almost an hour after the Domei News Agency's Flash announcement of imminent Japanese capitulation.

For whatever reason, *The Boomerang* and the 315th's bomber stream now droned steadily toward the Empire, none of the radio operators having received the scrub word "APPLE," as had the bomber crews of General Kenney's Far Eastern Air Forces received their recall signals.

Darkness engulfed the 315th Wing's bombers around 1920 hours. They passed the blacked-out speck of Iwo Jima and about 2100 hours were flying about fifty miles west of another volcanic island in the Bonin chain, Chichi Jima. Japanese early-warning radar, land-based variants of the

Imperial Navy's obsolescent but still serviceable Type 14 system, began detecting the B-29Bs. U.S. Navy electronic countermeasure aircraft operating in the area eroded much of the Japanese radar's effectiveness. But as the long bomber stream continued north, the early-warning operators eventually gathered enough data to send the bombers' heading, altitude, and speed by undersea telegraphic cable to the Home Islands. Up and down the coast of Honshu and Kyushu, Japanese air defense forces prepared for renewed night attacks by the hated American bombers.

(Although no major battle was ever fought at Chichi Jima, the small island does figure large in American history. On September 2, 1944, almost a year before the 315th's planes passed west of the Bonins en route to Akita, a teenage U.S. Navy pilot named George Herbert Walker Bush, who would go on to become America's forty-first president, flew his Avenger bomber on a raid against a Japanese communications center on Chichi Jima. Bush's plane was struck by antiaircraft fire, but he managed to remain airborne until it was over the sea again. After parachuting into the Pacific, Bush and a surviving crewman were rescued by the American submarine *Finback*. Bush was awarded the Distinguished Flying Cross.)

After hours of debate, during which Chief Cabinet Secretary Sakomizu vigorously argued that there was no constitutional obligation for the Privy Council to review the Imperial Rescript before the cabinet signed it, War Minister Anami changed tack and agreed.

But he quickly went on the counteroffensive, attacking the phrasing of the draft rescript, which each minister studied on mimeographed sheets with varying degrees of comprehension. Written in the obscure Chinese-based language of the Imperial Court known as *kanbun*, the draft was difficult to follow. Chief Cabinet Secretary Sakomizu, the rescript's principal drafter and no mean Chinese scholar himself, had relied on an academic expert in Chinese to provide the required nuances.

Once deciphered, the text of the message did in fact closely follow the Emperor's own statements made in the Palace air-raid shelter in the early-morning hours of August 10 and during that Tuesday morning's Imperial conference. A few of the ministers recommended alternative wording, but most felt constrained not to even indirectly criticize the Emperor in this manner. War Minister Anami was not so constrained.

"I would like to point out one sentence which I must say I find unacceptable. Halfway into the second paragraph, you will notice the sentence, 'Despite the best that has been done by everyone—the gallant fighting of military and naval forces, the diligence and assiduity of Our servants of the State, and the devoted service of Our one hundred million people, the war situation grows more unfavorable to us every day.'"[10] Speaking with his familiar resolve, Anami insisted that this sentence implied that every official announcement the military had made had been false.

"In any case," he said, "we still have not lost the war—the situation has merely not turned in our favor."

The cabinet was tense. War Minister Anami had the advantage. He could still walk out of this meeting, publicly submit his resignation, bring down the government, and rally the Army to his side. Most ministers were inclined to accommodate him. Navy Minister Yonai, Anami's longtime nemesis on the Big Six, was not.

"Japan," Navy Minister Yonai said heatedly, was on the "verge of destruction," having lost its recent battles in Okinawa and Burma. If Anami was still proposing the Ketsu-go, Yonai said, "we will lose that too. We have been defeated, we have clearly been defeated."[11]

But on this point, Anami would not budge. The cabinet had reached a stalemate.

Inside the granite block walls of the Imperial Palace, the humid night was falling. The members of the NHK recording team waited, spent with the heat and drained by their anticipation.

At 1950 hours, the low crescent moon provided enough shimmering light for the northbound pilots of the 315th's planes to see the long lines of converging Superforts flying south on almost a reciprocal heading and at about the same altitude. *The Boomerang*'s commander, Carl Schahrer, was intrigued.

"Did those guys get the recall signal?" he asked over the intercom. "Smitty, are you sure you haven't heard 'APPLE'?"

The *dit dah, dit dah* of the Japanese jamming was the only signal he had received. "Nothing, Carl."

Aboard *For the Luvva Mike*, Lieutenant Chuck Miller was absolutely convinced that the bombers flying south had to have received the scrub signal. He repeatedly questioned his radio operator, Sergeant Leonard van Driel. "Lenny, with the Japs' jamming, could you have missed the scrub signal?"

"No, sir," van Driel said formally. Like Jim Smith and every radio operator in the 315th that night, he fully understood the importance of the message. Still, how could the crew explain all these Superforts on a recip back to the Marianas?

Then, even in this weak moonlight, it became clear that the scores of Superforts flying south toward Saipan and Tinian were the bombers of the 58th and 73rd Wings returning from the daytime raids on Honshu that had taken off around dawn from northern Marianas bases. But these B-29s appeared not to have maintained enough altitude separation from the 315th's planes. The commander of the Wing's 501st Bomb Group, Colonel Boyd Hubbard, made the decision to turn on his landing lights to avoid a midair collision. Back along the line of northbound bombers, other aircraft commanders followed his lead. Carl Schahrer chose not to do so because planes ahead and behind them had illuminated the bright lights in their wing roots. He certainly did not want to collide with another Superfort, and he also wanted to preserve as much night vision as possible. But Schahrer had another motive. Intel had reported that Japanese night fighters, flying one-way kamikaze missions, had enough range to strike the inbound bombers far out to sea. So he chose to avoid giving them any better target than they already had.

In the airless cabinet room, Chief Cabinet Secretary Sakomizu proposed compromise language that he hoped War Minister Anami would accept. The offending phrase now read, "The war situation has developed not necessarily to Japan's advantage, while the general trends of the world have all turned against her interest." This was an astute means of relieving the Army of responsibility for Japan's defeat. "General trends of the world" was a veiled reference to the Soviet declaration of war and the Red Army's juggernaut campaign on the Asian mainland. The Army (and the Emperor) were exonerated even further by Sakomizu's next clever turn of phrase, "Moreover, the enemy has begun to employ a new and most cruel bomb, the power of which to do damage is indeed incalculable, taking toll of many innocent lives."[12]

As expected, Anami gladly accepted this revision. Navy Minister Yonai acquiesced once Prime Minister Suzuki also backed the wording. But Anami's initial challenge gave other ministers latitude to try their hand at editing the archaic language of the text. Several found fault with words and phrases that seemed either to elevate the Emperor to a divine abstraction with whom no average Japanese could empathize or, conversely, to portray him as a mere workaday political and military leader.

Hours passed in painful wordsmithing, made all the more difficult by the nature of the ritual language involved.

But again it was General Anami who pushed the discussion beyond empty semantics. The War Minister had always found the very concept of enemy forces occupying the sacred homeland intolerable. And he knew that this would also be anathema to most of the troops and to millions of civilians. So, by dint of his strong personality, Anami was able to secure unanimous agreement to an introductory clause to the Emperor's concluding statement. These added words, meant to assure the restive armed forces and the people that their homeland and their Emperor had been protected, were "Having been able to safeguard and maintain the structure of the Imperial State . . ."

The original draft language then continued, ". . . we are always with ye, our good and loyal subjects, relying upon your sincerity and integrity. Beware most strictly of any outbursts of emotion which may engender needless complications, or any fraternal contention and strife which may create confusion, lead ye astray and cause ye to lose the confidence of the world. Let the entire nation continue as one family from generation to generation, ever firm in its faith in the imperishableness of its sacred land and mindful of its heavy burden of responsibilities, and the long road before it. Unite your total strength to be devoted to construction for the future. Cultivate the ways of rectitude; foster nobility of spirit; and work with resolution so that ye may enhance the innate glory of the Imperial State and keep pace with the progress of the world."

Following the place for the Imperial seal, the document was dated: "The 14th day of the 8th month of the 20th year of Showa."

Finally, after tense hours of carping over major wording and minor nuance, the cabinet approved the draft Imperial Rescript.

Almost physically ill with fear that the Americans would drop an atomic bomb on Tokyo before the Emperor could sign the document, the cabinet could formally ratify it with their own signatures, and the Foreign Ministry could so inform the Allies through the sluggish diplomatic channels, Chief Cabinet Secretary Sakomizu ordered his driver to speed up the potholed street toward the Palace. It was after 7:00 P.M. in Tokyo. The sun had set and the crescent moon was dipping toward the cloudy western horizon. Dim, jerry-rigged streetlamps lit the road, casting shadows across the worst of the debris piles and the intersections. But the Palace grounds themselves were somewhat brighter, with the traditional five-globe cherry cluster lamps lighting the bridges across the moat and the road to the Imperial Household Ministry.

Chief Cabinet Secretary Sakomizu delivered the blotted, marked-up rescript draft that the cabinet had approved to a pair of skilled calligraphers so that they could make one clean copy for the Emperor's signature and the cabinet's approval and one for His Majesty to read before the NHK recording microphone. Despite the time pressure, court etiquette required that the Emperor be presented with a flawlessly transcribed *kanbun* document. This process would require an estimated additional two hours.

Meanwhile, Sakomizu paced anxiously. The Domei FLASH message announcing Japan's imminent acceptance of the Potsdam Declaration had been broadcast at 2:49 P.M., almost five hours earlier. How long would the Americans wait?

Another question was equally disturbing: How long would the rebellious elements in the military hold back?

In the Prime Minister's cabinet room, General Anami still tried to forestall the inevitable surrender. Now his ploy was to request that the broadcast of the Imperial Rescript be delayed at least one day to ensure that orders issued to the troops overseas were obeyed. Foreign Minister Togo and Navy Minister Yonai, suspicious that War Minister Anami was playing for time to accommodate rebellious troops here in Tokyo and not the overseas forces, refused his request.

Another compromise was reached: At 7:00 A.M., NHK Radio would alert the country of the upcoming Imperial message. At noon, the recording of the Imperial Rescript would be broadcast.

Premier Suzuki asked General Anami if he would make sure the frontline troops in the far-flung armies received advance notice of the broadcast.

"I'll do my best," Anami replied, his face devoid of emotion.[13]

The cabinet recessed and was due to reconvene at 9:30 P.M. to sign the Imperial Rescript, on which the Emperor would have already affixed his signature and seal. Once ratified, His Majesty could finally stand before the microphone and make the historic recording. Meanwhile, the court calligraphers sweated through their tense assignment.

General Anami returned to the War Ministry to find the once-teeming building all but deserted. The rats had indeed fled for drier ground. With his own hand, he prepared a joint War Ministry–Imperial General Headquarters radiogram for all units. The message that would reach Imperial Army forces from the Kuril Islands in the north, across the Home Islands, to bypassed Japanese garrisons such as Rabaul in the Solomon Islands near the equator, and throughout mainland Asia was seemingly unequivocal.

War Minister Anami detailed his and Chief of Staff Umezu's vigorous efforts to oppose surrender, preserve the national polity, and to maintain the "Imperial domain" free of Allied occupation. But Anami said that the enemy's demands had made it nearly impossible to meet those conditions. Then he noted that "His Imperial Majesty nevertheless has decided to accept the terms of the Potsdam Declaration. . . ." Therefore, the entire Army had to act so that no dishonor sully its "glorious traditions and splendid record of meritorious service. . . ." The message concluded with an admonition: "It is earnestly desired that every soldier, without exception, refrain absolutely from rash behavior and demonstrate at home and abroad the everlasting fame and glory of the Imperial Army."[14]

This radiogram was open to interpretation, however. Very few of the officers who received it had previously understood the full extent of the peace negotiations. For many, the only official word they had heard of their government's position was that it planned to "kill with silence" (*mokusatsu*) the Potsdam Declaration. Now the commanders of more than six million Japanese soldiers were suddenly told that they had to prepare for immediate surrender.

The subtext of the message was clear to any experienced Japanese officer: Their courageous military leaders had struggled to protect the *kokutai* and the sanctity of the homeland from the boots of the lustful enemy. But the Emperor had apparently listened to other, traitorous civilian counsel. And now the undefeated Army had been ordered to accept defeat.

This would not be an easy order to accept or to see followed by subordinates, as evidenced in messages Anami had already received from loyal senior officers overseas who had heard troubling reports of the peace negotiations in Allied propaganda broadcasts. General Yasuji Okamura, who commanded the vast and powerful Imperial Japanese Expeditionary Forces in China, for example, had sent Anami an urgent cable: "We should fight for the realization of our war aims even if it means the death of all our troops."[15]

But Anami dutifully told the Army that the Emperor himself would broadcast his rescript ending the war at noon on August 15. All troops were to listen and obey. The net effect of Anami's order was to freeze the Army in place—aside from the troops still fighting the Americans in the Philippines, the Australians in Borneo, and the units involved in the desperate struggle against the Soviets from Sakhalin Island to Manchuria and northern China.

The Army remained ready, poised, waiting to hear the Emperor's own words that the war had ended in defeat.

On that broadcast hung the future of Japan.

While General Anami waged his final retreat, trying to slow the advance of his opponents in the cabinet, the young leaders of the conspiracy conducted their own campaign. Major Hidemasa Koga, the staff officer on the Imperial Guards Division whom Hatanaka had recruited early in the plot, joined by another rebel officer, brazenly sought information on the status of the Imperial Rescript's recording. The two as-yet-undeclared rebels pushed their way into the Imperial Household Ministry office of the Emperor's Chief aide-de-camp, General Shigeru Hasunuma. Announcing that they were staff officers of the Imperial Guards Division, Koga added that he and his colleague had been told that the Emperor planned to record the rescript that evening. "Can you tell us what time the recording will be made?" Koga asked.

Both the General and his assistant refused to comment, but the officer with Koga persisted. "Has the recording already been made?"

General Hasunuma did not like the tone of this. "No, not as far as we know," he said, pleading ignorance.

"That's hard to believe," the officer with Koga snapped. Coming from a junior officer, this remark was both an insult to the General's honor and blatant ill discipline.

But Koga defused the situation. "They're telling the truth," he said. "Let's go."[16]

The officer who accompanied Major Koga has never been positively identified. This may be due to both reasons of *haji*—the questioning of General Hasunuma implied a plan to hunt the Emperor and waylay him before the recording could be made—and to more practical considerations that emerged in postwar Japan. After the surrender, the Japanese government prosecuted several surviving members of various rebel factions. It is possible that this officer was Koga's colleague on the Division staff, Major Ishihara, a staunch supporter of the conspiracy who did survive the war. But it is equally possible that the officer with Koga was Major Hatanaka, who had arrived at the Palace to consult with confederates already in place in the Imperial Guards Division.

What evidence has emerged concerning Hatanaka's movements on the evening of August 14 is filled with intriguing gaps. It is clear that he managed to reassemble several members of the original coup plot, including Captain Shigetaro Uehara of the Air Academy and Lt. Colonel Jiro Shiizaki of the War Ministry, both of whom he would work closely with that night. But Hatanaka was also in contact with dissident ultranationalist civilians he had met through Professor Kiyoshi Hiraizumi. This was a diverse group that included business leaders, bureaucrats, and members of the aristocracy. Most important, they had far-ranging personal connections in the military. Once Hatanaka's coconspirators had seized the Imperial Palace, these civilian supporters could use their influence to help solidify the rebels' position.

Aboard *The Boomerang*, at 2156 hours, navigator Tony Cosola leaned intently over his chart table, working with dividers as he compared his airspeed-time-and-distance calculations with Rich Ginster's latest radar sighting from small islands below.

"Recommend you come right five degrees, Carl," he told Schahrer.

"Coming right," Schahrer said. "What's that going to do to our cruise control, Hank?" he asked flight engineer Gorder.

Hank Gorder already had his slide rule out and was working in the dim glow of his instrument panel. "We'll have to wait and see."

Jim Smith followed this intercom exchange through the piercing distortion of the Japanese jamming signal. Honshu lay about two hours ahead. Wing headquarters' navigation experts had plotted landfall on the Home Island's Pacific coast near the port of Sendai, ninety miles north of Tokyo. They had also carefully charted the route across Honshu and the eighty-one-mile run up from the Initial Point at Awa Shima just offshore the Sea of Japan to the Nippon Oil Company refinery at Akita, a route that combined the best fuel efficiency while avoiding the worst concentrations of flak and fighter bases. Now *The Boomerang* might have to sacrifice the fuel efficiency of optimal cruise control by flying east to avoid the danger of premature landfall above the heavily defended Kanto Plain around Tokyo.

Jim listened to the annoying Japanese *dah dit dah dit* signal.

"No 'APPLE,' Smitty?" Carl Schahrer asked yet again.

"Nothing, Carl. Just the Japs."

The historians of Japan's Pacific War Research Society have documented the drama unfolding at Atsugi Air Base. Captain Yasuna Kozono was fighting a sudden bout of malaria, the disease he had contracted flying in the Solomon Islands earlier in the war. Weakened by chills and fever, Kozono remained resolved to continue the battle to protect the sacred homeland, no matter what the weaklings in Tokyo had proclaimed to be the Emperor's wishes.

He assembled his executive officer and the twelve commanders of his air groups, each of whom led several squadrons. Word was spreading that the Emperor himself would order the armed forces to surrender. There had been rumors that Army squadrons at other bases had actually removed the propellers and drained fuel from special attack aircraft in anticipation of the surrender. But Captain Kozono meant to quash any such action at Atsugi.

"I am determined to fight to the end no matter what happens," he told these officers. "I hope you have all decided to cooperate with me."

For a moment the officers remained silent, which Kozono interpreted as the standard Japanese form of agreement in questions involving sensitive matters.

But a group commander now stepped forward. "How do we reconcile our policy with the order to obey the Emperor's decision—whatever it may be?"

Captain Kozono had been expecting this. "That's an easy question to answer," he said. "How can we be disobeying the Emperor's decision if what we do is for His and the country's good?"[17]

As he had hoped, this logic was persuasive. Now he turned his combat leaders to more practical matters: planning an early-morning attack on the Allied Third Fleet that employed every available combat plane in Atsugi's underground hangars.

On dispersed smaller air bases that had been built for the Ketsu-go, Japanese airmen of both the Imperial Army and Navy also prepared their planes for combat the next day.

. . .

When Emperor Hirohito reviewed the clean copy of the rescript, he told Marquis Kido that he would like five small changes made for purposes of semantics and rhythm. To the chagrin of the calligraphers, making these changes would normally require recopying both documents, another two hours' work. In order to preclude this laborious process and speed the rescript's official promulgation, Palace officials broke tradition by allowing the calligraphers to paste thin strips over the sections the Emperor wished changed. Then, carefully maneuvering their narrow-tipped brushes, the calligraphers added the *kanbun* characters to the patchwork. On reviewing the "final" copy of the rescript, it was found to be missing an entire phrase. By now the document had almost acquired the look of an indifferent student's sloppy examination paper.

Nevertheless, the Emperor brushed his signature on the rescript and a chamberlain stamped the broad Imperial seal beneath it.

No one waited with more impatience for the cabinet to sign and ratify the final rescript than Vice Foreign Minister Shunichi Matsumoto, who had already done so much through unofficial communications with the Allies to hasten Japan's surrender before the Americans unleashed more atomic bombs, as President Truman had threatened to do. Now Matsumoto had prepared Japan's official message of capitulation. The radiogram was ready to transmit via Stockholm and Bern. All he needed was Foreign Minister Togo's instructions to proceed.

The message referred to both Japan's note of August 10 and Secretary of State Byrnes's reply of August 11 and stated that "the Emperor has issued an Imperial Rescript regarding Japan's acceptance of the provisions of the Potsdam Declaration." The Emperor was also "prepared to authorize and ensure the signature by his government and the Imperial General Headquarters of the necessary terms for carrying out the provisions of the Potsdam Declaration. His Majesty is also prepared to issue his commands to all the military, naval, and air authorities of Japan and all the forces under their control wherever located to cease active operations, to surrender arms and to issue such orders as may be required by the Supreme Commander of the Allied Forces for the execution of the above-mentioned terms."[18]

There was nothing ambiguous about this message. When it arrived in Washington, London, Moscow, and Chunking, the Allies would know that Japan had unequivocally accepted the Potsdam Declaration, that the power of the Emperor was now subject to the control of General Douglas MacArthur, the Supreme Allied Commander, and that Japan's military was prepared to lay down its arms.

The only possible interpretation of the message was that, for Japan, the war had ended in defeat.

It is unclear exactly why Colonel Toyojiro Haga, commander of the Imperial Guards Division's Second Regiment, unexpectedly added a battalion of troops inside the Palace walls earlier that evening. Perhaps he was merely taking a wise precaution in light of the rumored unrest in the Army. However, Japanese and Western researchers have discovered that just after 9 P.M. two of the chief conspirators of the pending coup d'état, Major Hatanaka and Lt. Colonel Shiizaki, entered the Imperial Palace at the Nijubashi (Double Bridge) and spent over an hour in confidential discussion with Colonel Haga.

The two conspirators described in detail their operational plan to isolate the Palace, to "protect" the Emperor from the traitorous civilians around him, to either prevent His Majesty from recording the rescript or prevent the message from being broadcast, and to supplant the recording with orders to Japan's armed forces to continue the war.

Hatanaka and Shiizaki were adamant that the top Japanese military leaders had endorsed the plot. These included War Minister Anami, who would lead the military government once martial law was declared; General Umezu, the Army Chief of Staff; the "two commanders" of the Eastern District Army (a reference that would include both General Tanaka, the Commander, and also Major General Tatsuhiko Takashima, the Chief of Staff); as well as Haga's own superior, Lt. General Takeshi Mori, Commander of the First Imperial Guards Division.

Colonel Haga found their case compelling. Had he suspected treachery—or had he not personally endorsed the goals of the plot—Haga could have easily had Hatanaka and Takeshita arrested and delivered to the *kempeitai*. Instead, the three officers apparently discussed the important tactical details of the operation. Each of them understood how dangerous it could be to employ almost one thousand infantrymen, armed with rifles and machine guns, inside the Palace walls, many dug in along the thickly wooded hillsides and the curving roads.

Fratricide—what today are known as "friendly fire" casualties—would be an imminent danger. Infinitely worse was the hazard that the troop deployment in the dimly lit Palace grounds posed to His Majesty. The purpose of the coup was to save the Emperor, not to put his life at risk.

There were myriad details to discuss: passwords and visual recognition signals, as well as safe fields of fire for riflemen and the automatic weapons. Each platoon and company had to stockpile an adequate reserve of ammunition at central locations. Medical aid stations had to be set up, field telephone wire strung. The fact that almost none of the regiment's rank-and-file soldiers were familiar with the inner Palace grounds made this task even more challenging.

One of the most straightforward problems was how to distinguish the regiment's *loyal* soldiers from any outsiders who might, out of misdirected motives, oppose them. Each soldier under the command of Colonel Haga—and eventually every member of the Imperial Guards Division—would wear a white sash across his chest and shoulders, a mark easily distinguishable even in the murky shadows of the Palace grounds.

The two rebels from the War Ministry assured Colonel Haga that he would have time to thrash through these details. And he would have detailed orders from General Mori himself before the actual operation began at 0200 hours.

Hatanaka and Shiizaki left just before 10 P.M., promising to return as soon as possible.

At Premier Suzuki's cabinet room, most of the ministers had arrived for the scheduled 9:30 signing ceremony. But by 10 P.M., Suzuki realized that some of the members were going to be late—not, thankfully, War Minister Anami—so the Premier took the patched document that bore the Emperor's signature and seal, raised an inked brush, and signed his own name.

Then, with painful slowness, the other ministers each read the four-page rescript to make sure the wording they had labored over for hours had not been substantially changed. As the sweat-damp pages were passed down the table, each minister bowed deeply in his chair as if in the presence of His Majesty, then set about to read carefully. This was, after all, probably the last time these officials would ever serve their Emperor or their country's government. Several undoubtedly faced prosecution for war crimes once the Allied occupation force arrived in Japan.

Around 10:20 P.M., Hiromasa Matsuzaka, the Minister of Justice, read the rescript several times at the meticulous pace of a jurist. Finally, he wet his brush and signed.

As Matsuzaka passed the rescript to War Minister Anami, the men at the table sat in rigid silence. Would Anami walk out and topple the government at this late stage? With a mere glance at the rescript, the General turned to the last page and affixed the large characters of his formal signature: "ANAMI KORECHIKA."

One by one, the cabinet ministers continued to slowly read and sign the Imperial Rescript.

At the Foreign Ministry, Vice Minister Shunichi Matsumoto waited for the call from Minister Togo at the Premier's residence that would be his authorization to transmit the formal surrender message to Washington.

He scanned his watch and the wall clock every half-minute and began to pace his office. What was taking so long?

Although tired, the crew of *The Boomerang* were working smoothly. By now, 2233 hours, it appeared they were going to pass closer to Tokyo than anyone would have liked. Everyone had been briefed on the flak and fighters around the Japanese capital and didn't want to confront these defenses on what was supposed to be the last mission of the war. But Cosola and Ginster were now confident that they could intersect the original landfall point more or less on schedule.

Matching time-on-course "dead-reckoning" navigation with radar fixes on small volcanic islets, Cosola and Ginster estimated that *The Boomerang* was 290 miles south of the mountainous Boso Peninsula that formed the eastern arm of Tokyo Bay.

Rich Ginster's radar returns helped provide Cosola with a reasonably accurate ground speed, which in turn gave flight engineer Hank Gorder a better estimate on the fuel situation.

Jim Smith's back was beginning to spasm again from sitting so long hunched at his set. Putting aside his earphones for a moment, Smith stood up, grabbed the bulkhead, and slid down beside Hank Gorder to scan the engine and fuel-quantity instruments. Everything looked good to Smith, so he grinned and did a thumbs-up.

Hank smiled back and held up crossed fingers on each hand.

Returning to his seat, Smith wondered if Hank had been crossing his fingers for the engines or the fuel supply, or still hoping that they would receive the coded scrub signal, "APPLE."

Japanese early-warning radar stations on the mainland and the tiny off-shore islands began detecting the 315th Wing's long bomber stream as the B-29Bs crept over the curvature of the earth and moved relentlessly north northwest. The offshore stations had been mercilessly shelled by Allied naval forces and bombed by carrier planes for weeks. But, showing their stubborn resolve, the radar operators repaired their equipment in mainte-nance shops dug in to the volcanic hillsides and repositioned their anten-nas each night. The tracking sensitivity of this radar was far below Allied standards. And the electronic radar countermeasures of the U.S. Third Fleet made it especially difficult for Japanese air defense planners to estab-lish the enemy planes' precise destination.

But one fact became obvious as more and more bombers cleared the southern horizon and continued on a basically northern course. These B-29s were not veering west toward Nagoya or Osaka. It was very possible that the bombers were once more headed toward Tokyo.

By now the early-warning radar station at Chichi Jima had identified a bomber stream more than 200 miles long, numbering more than 100 air-craft. Of the 143 B-29Bs that the 315th Wing had launched between 1642 and 1858 hours on Guam, 132 were still proceeding toward the Empire, the other nine having aborted with mechanical problems. Japanese air defense coordinators had no way of guessing that this extended string of bombers was headed all the way north to Akita. As the planes flew north through the night, the Japanese became increasingly convinced that Tokyo would once more be the American target.

According to Lt. Colonel Masataka Ida's postwar statements, he had fallen into an exhausted sleep on his cot at the War Ministry, oddly serene in the knowledge that he would climb to the building's roof in the cool dawn, kneel toward the rising sun, and slice open his belly in the act of seppuku. He was at peace, and all obligations had been met, even though he had not been able to rally anyone else to this ritual sacrifice.

In the streets below, Major Hatanaka and Lt. Colonel Shiizaki panted as they pedaled their clumsy bicycles up the rough pavement to Ichigaya Heights. The thin moon had set, and cloying mist swirled up the hillside, further dimming the glow of the isolated emergency streetlamps.

They finally reached the War Ministry, winded, their uniforms clammy with sweat, and bounded up the stairs to Ida's cell-like bedroom. Ida was not pleased at being rousted from what he had hoped would be his last untroubled sleep on earth. Now Shiizaki and Hatanaka were carrying on about their hopeless scheme to continue with the coup d'état.

"The Imperial Guards are with us!" Hatanaka proclaimed, assuring Ida that Colonel Haga had brought the entire Second Regiment into the conspiracy. But there was a key figure still uncommitted among the Guards officers—Lt. General Mori, the Division Commander. Ida, however, had influence with the General. If he spoke with him persuasively, Mori would join them. "And once he does," Hatanaka added, "our success is certain."[19]

Lt. Colonel Ida was torn with ambivalence. When he had initially become involved with the plot, it had been clear to all the conspirators that General Anami endorsed their motives and plans. The War Minister knew them all well and recognized that they would not be easily dissuaded, even though Anami himself had ostensibly withdrawn his support. So why hadn't the General ordered the *kempeitai* to place Hatanaka and all the other suspected conspirators into custody until the shameful surrender process was completed? Was it possible that the War Minister, the Chief of Staff, and the leaders of the Eastern District Army and of the *kempeitai* itself secretly wanted the coup to succeed?[20]

But Ida realized that the entire issue pivoted on winning the support of Lt. General Mori, the man who had sworn a sacred oath to protect the person of the Emperor and the sanctity of the Imperial Palace. What if Ida was unable to sway him? Ida now raised the issue of the practicality of an attempted coup with several colleagues preparing for sleep nearby. They were pessimistic and urged him not to attempt any rash action. He told Hatanaka and Shiizaki that the chances of persuading General Mori were faint indeed.

"I'm sure God will help us," Shiizaki said. "We must attempt a coup."

Hatanaka was more blunt. "If Mori doesn't agree with us," he said coldly, "I'll kill him."[21]

Although Hatanaka's fervor shocked Ida, he understood and empathized with the younger man's guiding philosophy. They had both been acolytes of Professor Hiraizumi at the Shoin Shrine. There, they had learned that the life of any individual was vastly less important than the preservation of the *kokutai*, through which Japan maintained its unbroken link to Heaven and the sacred line of Imperial Ancestors who guided and protected the nation. If the Emperor was reduced to a mere secular figurehead whom the victorious Allies stripped of mystical authority, the nation as Ida understood it would be extinguished.

But, before he finally agreed to join Shiizaki and Hatanaka, Ida extracted a promise from the Major. Would he abandon the coup if Ida could not win Imperial Guards Division Commander Lt. General Mori to their side?

Hatanaka softened his stance and gave his word of honor that he would do so.

With stoic determination, the three officers mounted their bicycles and set off down the curving road toward the Imperial Palace.

In the cabinet room, the rescript signing ceremony proceeded at the same ponderous speed. It was nearing 11 P.M. and there were still two ministers who had not yet read and signed the document.

The Emperor waited with steadily fraying patience in his private quarters on the second floor of the Gobunko, dressed in a perfectly tailored uniform of a generalissimo in the Imperial Army. Beside him stood Impe rial Chamberlain Sukemasa Irie, who would escort His Majesty in the massive, armor-plated Mercedes-Benz limousine for the short ride to the Imperial Household Ministry, where Hirohito would record the rescript.

The entire process was running hours late, which did not please His Majesty. He had always demanded punctuality from his personal aides and government officials. Now it almost seemed that those bureaucrats were intentionally delaying procedures on this historic night.

In the administrative office on the second floor of the Imperial Household Ministry, a group of Palace officials and technicians waited for the Emperor. They included Hiroshi Shimomura, director of the government Information Bureau, and NHK Chairman Hachiro Oashi. Awed by the presence of these important men, and virtually stunned by the now-imminent arrival of His Majesty the Emperor, the recording technicians set about once again to verify that their equipment and the broad wax recording disks were ready.

.   .   .

By 2257 hours, *The Boomerang* was approximately 186 miles south of the Boso Peninsula, flying thirty-odd planes from the head of the long column of the 315th Wing's Superforts.

By a quirk of radio-wave propagation, the Japanese jamming had temporarily weakened, giving Jim Smith the chance to listen with renewed intensity for the mission scrub signal.

After getting the latest navigation report from Tony Cosola, Carl Schahrer asked Smith, "Anything on APPLE?"

"Nothing yet, Carl."

"If you don't hear it by the time we get to the Tokyo area, forget it," Schahrer said. "We're not flying all this way for nothing."

"Roger," said Smith, his voice so loud with determination and anger at the Japanese that Schahrer almost heard him without the intercom.

In the Eastern District Army Air Defense command post, officers had studied the mounting evidence that a major American B-29 force was approaching Tokyo. The lead aircraft of that formation were now headed directly for the Boso Peninsula, which the enemy had frequently used as a turning point for night attacks on the capital.

Although the Japanese did not know it, these bombers were the first of the 315th Bomb Wing's aircraft that had begun taking off from Guam almost seven hours earlier. Beyond the first bombers, one aircraft after another slowly appeared above the moonless southern horizon and crawled up the radar screens.

At 11 P.M., the Eastern District Army ordered a complete blackout of Tokyo. Officers went to their telephones and telegraphic relays to command the city's power plants to cut current to Tokyo for the duration of the air-raid alert.

Sirens began to moan and wail. The scattered emergency lighting in the streets flickered out and the few buildings that still drew power from the central grid went dark. It was 11:05 P.M.

In the cabinet room of the Premier's official residence, Transportation Minister Naoto Kobiyama, the last member to sign the rescript, had just raised his brush when the familiar howl of the air-raid sirens filled the room. The overhead lamps faded, then blinked out. Aides drew the heavy blackout curtains and the building's auxiliary generator chugged to life to provide enough wavering light for Kobiyama to sign.

"Gentlemen," Chief Cabinet Secretary Sakomizu announced, his voice tense, "the Imperial Rescript is now in effect."[22]

In the Foreign Ministry, Vice Minister Matsumoto snatched up the telephone on the first ring. This was the word he had waited for all day: The cabinet had finally signed the rescript. He immediately told the cipher room to transmit the prepared diplomatic radiogram so that the Allied powers would understand as soon as possible that Japan had capitulated. Thank Heaven the Ministry had its own auxiliary generator to power the radios.

As he listened to the air-raid sirens, Matsumoto realized how tragic it would be if the Americans, their patience finally broken, had decided to continue their campaign to break Japan's will with more atomic bombs.

This dread also seized Chamberlain Irie as he and the Emperor left the Gobunko for the blanketing darkness of the Palace grounds. From where they stood, the last sirens still echoed off the granite walls. Hirohito strode toward the limousine in the faint glow of the chauffeur's blackout lamp. The Mercedes-Benz would carry the Emperor the half-mile to the Imperial Household Ministry to record the rescript.

But Chamberlain Irie stepped forward. "Your Majesty," he said, daring to challenge the Imperial will, "the air-raid alarm of a few minutes ago is still in effect."

"I would like to go anyway," the Emperor insisted.

"May I advise that we wait in the shelter at least until we have some indication of the enemy's targets?"[23]

Obviously irritated, Hirohito allowed the chamberlain to light the way to the nearby shelter with his dim blackout light.

The unexpected scream of the sirens threw rebel Major Hatanaka and Lt. Colonel Shiizaki into panic.

Major Hatanaka had convinced Lt. Colonel Ida to go directly to Imperial Guards Division headquarters while he and Shiizaki conferred again in the inner Palace grounds with rebel officers. On arriving back at the Palace they had learned that the Emperor still had not left the Gobunko for the Imperial Household Ministry, so the tactical problem remained choosing the safest manner of either barricading him in the Gobunko or intercepting His Majesty's limousine on the dimly lit road.

Suddenly even those faint lights went dark.[24] With no moon, the night was devoid of texture and dimension.[25] They waited almost half an hour, but the Emperor's limousine did not appear at the Imperial Household Ministry. Could he have possibly diverted to another recording site? This sudden blackout was maddening. They even might have missed the Emperor's limousine in the absolute darkness.

Hatanaka recognized that the rebels would need all of the Imperial Guards Divisions regiments—not just the 1,000 men of Colonel Haga's unit—earlier than anticipated to completely seal off the Palace perimeter and patrol the dark, sprawling grounds. But the best way to gain control of the division was still to convince its commander, Lt. General Mori, to join the rebellion. Obviously, Ida had not yet been able to do so. Now Hatanaka himself had to act decisively.

He had wasted too much time already, stalking His Majesty like a cat who preyed at night. Hatanaka could no longer delay facing General Mori.

A Palace military aide telephoned the Eastern District Army's Air Defense Section for the latest information on the enemy bombers that had triggered the air-raid alert. At the Air Defense command post, Lieutenant Tsune Fujii announced that the B-29s seemed to be headed north up the coast, but flying just to the east of Tokyo. The alert and its automatic blackout would remain in effect, but there did not seem to be any danger of immediate attack on the capital.[26]

Accompanied by Chamberlain Irie, Hirohito returned to the limousine and drove across the dark grounds of the inner Palace toward the Imperial Household Ministry, completely unaware that the clumps of pines and maples concealed the heavily armed, but confused and anxious, soldiers of the Imperial Guards Division's Second Regiment.

Hirohito arrived at the front entrance of the Imperial Household Ministry at 11:26 P.M. and immediately climbed to the second-floor Goseimu.

The Ministry was a strange building, even by the eclectic standards of twentieth-century Japanese urban architecture. In effect, the structure was a string of older and newer buildings, some built around open atria and connected by covered walkways and narrow corridors. Sections of the Ministry dated back decades; others were of much more recent construction. Building styles and furnishings varied from classic Japanese to modern Western design. The corridors in some of the side wings were twisting and narrow. In places the building sharply descended the steep slope toward the moat. The names on the doors of offices and living quarters of the major and minor Palace bureaucracy were virtually cryptic, familiar to only a few.

Hirohito himself had rarely visited the Imperial Household Ministry, but he had been assured that the Goseimu would be the perfect room to record the Imperial Rescript. Indeed, when he entered the room, blinking at the bright lights provided by the Ministry generator, he grasped the wisdom of the officials' choice. The thick drapes and carpet almost completely muffled the faint chug of the distant generator. The room was hot and airless, but the Emperor felt the recording could be quickly made, as he had practiced reading the text several times while waiting in the shelter.

The entourage of Imperial Household Ministry and NHK officials, as well as the technicians, all dressed in formal clothes despite the stifling heat, bowed to the waist. The Emperor went to the microphone and turned to Shimomura, director of the Information Bureau. "How loudly should I speak?"[27]

Shimomura assured the Emperor that the NHK team was prepared to capture his regular tone.

In the adjoining room, the technicians were gripped with a mixture of wonder and anxiety. They had just heard the voice of a living god. And he sounded remarkably like any well-born gentleman in his fifties. The technicians were thankful that they had prepared the "voice" settings of their equipment properly, based on prompting from Shimomura as to the Emperor's normal speech level.

Shimomura signaled the Emperor to begin speaking and nodded through the door of the adjoining room to make certain the technical team was recording His Majesty's words. They were.

"To Our good and loyal subjects," Hirohito began. "After pondering deeply the general trends of the world and actual conditions in Our Empire today, We have decided to effect a settlement of the present situation by resorting to an extraordinary measure.

"We have ordered Our government to communicate to the governments of the United States, Great Britain, China, and the Soviet Union that Our Empire accepts the provisions of their Joint Declaration."[28]

Holding the stiff, hastily patched sheets of the hand-corrected Imperial Rescript, the Emperor read on despite the sweat streaming down his face and neck to soak the stiff collar of his formal uniform. He cited his "solemn obligation" to strive for the "common prosperity and happiness of all nations," a duty that had been "handed down by Our Imperial ancestors, and which We keep close to Our heart." Noting that it had been his "sincere desire to ensure Japan's self-preservation and the stabilization of East Asia," which had caused the nation to declare war on the United States and Britain, he added that it had been "far from Our thoughts" either to infringe on the sovereignty of other nations or to embark upon territorial aggrandizement.

Now Hirohito launched into the face-saving explanation as to Japan's defeat, noting as General Anami had insisted that "the war situation has developed not necessarily to Japan's advantage." He cited the unfavorable "general trends of the world," and added that the enemy had begun "to employ a new and most cruel bomb, the power of which to do damage is indeed incalculable."

With Japan and the rest of human civilization on the brink of extinction, the Emperor said, he had to save his millions of subjects. If he failed to do so, he could never excuse himself "before the hallowed spirits" of his Imperial ancestors. "This is the reason why We have ordered the acceptance of the provisions of the Joint Declaration of the Powers."

Hirohito added a note of compassion for Japan's "allied nations of East Asia" (Japanese collaborators in Malaya, Indochina, and the Dutch East Indies, which would certainly be treated as traitors by the victorious Western Allies) and for the millions of Japanese military and civilians who had died or otherwise suffered in the war.

"We are keenly aware of the inmost feelings of all ye, Our subjects. However, it is according to the dictates of time and fate that We have resolved to pave the way for a grand peace for all the generations to come by enduring the unendurable and suffering what is insufferable."

Again, relying on language provided by General Anami, the Emperor began his conclusion: "Having been able to safeguard and maintain the structure of the Imperial state, We are always with ye, Our good and loyal subjects." He cautioned them to avoid any outbursts of emotion or "fraternal contention and strife which may create confusion, lead ye astray and cause ye to lose the confidence of the world."[29]

When he finished, the Emperor lowered the stiff sheets of the rescript and stepped back from the microphone. Although the recording was technically acceptable, the Emperor wanted to make another because he was dissatisfied with his tone of voice. Once more, he approached the microphone. "To Our good and loyal subjects . . ."

Some in the room thought His Majesty's voice was now too high-pitched, almost squeaky. Clearly he was in distress from the heat and the anguish of the message. Although he was willing to make a third recording, the NHK technicians and Information Bureau Director Shimomura were disinclined to heap this additional strain on their already overwrought sovereign. His Majesty's subjects in the crowded Goseimu once more bowed deeply. The Emperor left, again followed by Chamberlain Irie.

They climbed into the Imperial limousine and drove through the darkness at a walking pace, the weak glow of the blackout headlights casting pale shadows on the cobbled roadway. At the Gobunko, the Emperor quickly entered the main door, while servants drew aside the heavy blackout curtains.

In an atmosphere bordering on a mystical experience, the NHK technicians under Director of Engineering Arakawa played the two recordings. The second had a better quality, even though the Emperor had inadvertently skipped a character. This was no major stumbling block given the obscure nature of *kanbun*, which most Japanese would not be able to follow when they heard the Emperor's recorded words; the Information Bureau planned to broadcast a plain-language version of the Imperial Rescript read by a professional radio announcer immediately after the first. Information Bureau Director Shimomura consulted with the senior chamberlains present and decided that the second recording would be the one broadcast, with the Emperor's initial recording held in reserve.

To be certain the precious six-minute recordings were protected, the technicians made copies of the broad wax-disk originals. They then diligently listened to each disk and carefully packed all four, each double set neatly labeled and wrapped in corrugated paper. These in turn were put into motion-picture film canisters. But, with the protective cardboard covering, the metal canister lids would not close tightly. So the recording team decided to place each can into a khaki cotton bag, originally intended to hold air defense helmets and gas masks.

Now it was time for another decision. Who should guard the recordings, NHK or the Palace? No one wanted to take the responsibility, and the NHK team even suggested that carrying them to their studio so late at night bordered on *lèse-majesté*. Moreover, everyone in the room knew of the unrest in the Army; whoever held the recordings might be in danger.

Finally, Chamberlain Yasuhide Toda reluctantly took possession of the sacks. But he quickly turned them over to Chamberlain Yoshihiro Tokugawa, descendant of a long samurai line and veteran Palace functionary. Tokugawa knew of a secure hiding place, a safe in a tiny office where one of the Empress's ladies-in-waiting sometimes stored jewelry and documents related to the Imperial family. But since the American fire-bombing, that jewelry and those documents had moved to deep underground shelters. The safe would be empty, and Chamberlain Tokugawa knew the combination.

The closetlike office lay off a twisting corridor in an older section of the Ministry that had not been connected to the building's auxiliary generator. The narrow room was a black oven. But Tokugawa used a flashlight to work the safe combination. After storing the cotton bags inside, he hid the safe door behind a toppling pile of out-of-date administrative notices. He cast his flashlight beam around the office, which looked like the shabby cubbyhole of a minor clerk. The Imperial Rescript recordings would be safe here for the night.

While the Emperor had been recording the rescript, the cabinet had finished its final business. Members rose, made their formal farewells to each other, and left to make their way home through the blacked-out streets of the capital.

War Minister Anami bowed to Foreign Minister Togo, with whom he had repeatedly clashed over the preceding days and weeks. Earlier, Anami had seen a draft "solicitation" message to the Allies that Togo intended to send as soon as the surrender was official. The message contained many of the points in the four conditions for which Anami had been ready to fight the Ketsu-go battle. Although there was no request that Japan be allowed to prosecute its own war criminals, Togo had asked that "occupation points be limited to the minimum number and selected to leave cities unoccupied and occúpation forces as small as possible at each point." The Foreign Minister had also requested that the Japanese forces be allowed to disarm themselves, just as Anami had requested. He had even asked the Allies to ship food and medical supplies to distant Japanese forces and to transport the wounded safely home.[30]

For this, General Anami was profoundly grateful. He thanked Togo, and the two antagonists turned away, if not amicably, at least with apparent mutual respect.

Now Anami entered Premier Suzuki's private office, where the old man was conferring with Chief Cabinet Secretary Sakomizu. General Anami apologized to the Prime Minister for his intransigence during the Supreme Council for the Direction of the War, full cabinet meetings, and Imperial conferences that had led up to this night.

"I expressed the opinions I held as representative of the Army," he said solemnly. "I may have expressed them overstrongly at times, but my intention was always to assist the Prime Minister to the best of my ability."[31]

Premier Suzuki assured Anami that he understood the General's motives and added that the *kokutai* would be preserved.

Before he left, War Minister Anami presented the Premier with a box of cigars, a precious gift in wartime Japan.

When Chief Cabinet Secretary Sakomizu and Suzuki discussed the General's visit a moment later, the Premier said, "I think the War Minister came to say goodbye."[32]

"Smitty," Rich Ginster said at 2400 hours, looking up from the green glow of his radarscope's rubber collar, "we've got Tokyo just off the port wing."

"Come on up and take a look at the Nips' capital, Smitty," Carl Schahrer said over the intercom.

Carl had increased the power setting so that *The Boomerang* was in a slow climb from 7,500 to 9,000 feet. The plane bumped and shuddered as it rose through the scattered clouds. Jim Smith gripped the edge of the bulkhead and swayed forward.

Schahrer took his hands off the throttles and pointed to the left. Below, the darkness was absolute. The moon had disappeared two hours earlier, and Smith could not see any fires in any direction still burning from the B-29 raids that had taken place earlier that day. All of Tokyo was a sea of black, not a spark of light or shimmer visible.

Smith felt a weird sensation, as if the Japs were nearby listening. He leaned close to Schahrer's right ear and said softly, "Did you ever see anything this black?"

"Nope." Schahrer shook his head. "Their radar probably picked up the Wing an hour ago and most of the folks in Tokyo are no doubt sitting in bomb shelters, worrying about that third superbomb that General Spaatz said we were going to drop on them if they didn't surrender."

"Well," Smith added, "I bet their War Cabinet is down there signing the surrender right now."

Carl Schahrer grinned in the weak glow of the instrument panel. "Maybe so, Smitty," he said, shaking his head. "But we haven't heard the scrub signal, so we're heading to Akita. I just wish they'd signed the surrender yesterday. We'd be back at Northwest Field watching a picture show instead of giving the Japs another chance to shoot us down."

BLACKOUT

M AJOR KENJI HATANAKA WAS FURIOUS. It was well after midnight, and General Mori had kept the young rebel officers who had come to see him on urgent business waiting for almost an hour. The General was supposedly in "conference," but Hatanaka knew from Major Koga that the only man in Mori's private office was his brother-in-law, Lt. Colonel Michinori Shiraishi, a staff officer who had survived the atomic bombing of Hiroshima. Now Hatanaka paced the dimly lit outer office, while fellow rebels Shiizaki, Ida, and Air Force Captain Shigetaro Uehara—who had helped deploy the Second Regiment troops—waited with varying degrees of impatience.

Then, just as an adjutant announced that the General would admit them, Hatanaka abruptly stopped pacing and proclaimed, "There's no time, there's no time. I've remembered something I've got to do!"[1] He nodded to Captain Uehara, and the two officers departed.

Lt. Colonels Ida and Shiizaki now had to face the stern Lt. General Mori and his brother-in-law, Colonel Shiraishi, without Hatanaka's fanatical support. Mori and his relative regarded the two rebels coolly.

(It should be noted that Lt. Colonel Masataka Ida was the only man in the room who would survive until the arrival of General MacArthur's occupation force. So postwar Allied Military Intelligence interrogators and historians in later years had to rely solely on his account of exactly what took place that night in General Mori's office.)

Overcoming his misgivings, Ida began to speak.

"General Mori," he began. "We have come to ask your help. We think there is still a chance to save Japan from an ignominious surrender. We believe that with the support of the Imperial Guards we could yet free the Emperor from the people who are influencing him and—"

"Are you asking me," Lt. General Mori interrupted, "to use my men in an unauthorized operation? I have no permission from the Eastern District Army to send my men into such an action."[2]

Ida attempted to be logical: When the Imperial Guards rallied to the cause, the Eastern District Army, and soon the entire Army, would join the effort. But Mori dodged the issue by launching into a turgid philosophical discourse that flitted from a soldier's duty to questions of mystical destiny. Even at this critical moment, Ida later reported, military etiquette prevented him from rudely interrupting the General. When he had the briefest moment to speak, Ida tried to interject his own philosophy, which had been nurtured during years of study with Professor Hiraizumi. But General Mori again dominated the discussion so that no concrete decision could be reached.

Time passed. Ida and Shiizaki listened with mounting frustration.

The urgent errand that Hatanaka had suddenly remembered had taken him to the billet of his former coconspirator, Lt. Colonel Masahiko Takeshita, in an ornate mansion in the hilly Surugadai district near the Imperial Palace that the military had appropriated as officers' quarters.

As with Lt. Colonel Ida's postwar account, Takeshita's later statements would be the only description from a surviving eyewitness of many of that long night's crucial events.

Takeshita was sleeping deeply when Hatanaka roused him and shined a flashlight about the tiny bedroom, disregarding the open blackout curtain. "The Second Infantry Regiment of the Imperial Guards Division has decided to start a coup d'état and completed preparations for it," Hatanaka said. "It will be done as previously discussed between us. Please use your influence to win over the War Minister."[3]

Takeshita urged Hatanaka to reconsider. The two men argued both the wisdom and the practicality of the coup, with Takeshita remaining pessimistic, as he emphasized that all of the senior officers—War Minister Anami, Army Chief of Staff Umezu, Eastern District Army Commander General Tanaka, and Lt. General Mori, Commander of the Imperial Guards Division—whom the conspirators had considered essential to the success of the enterprise, now opposed it.

But Hatanaka's enthusiasm would not be dampened. He insisted that Takeshita, the War Minister's brother-in-law and close friend, could sway him back to the cause. And once Anami was with them again, the entire Army would follow.

Still, Takeshita remained unconvinced. But when Hatanaka announced that he was returning to the Palace to continue the rebellion, Takeshita pulled on his uniform and followed.

Since Hatanaka had said the coup was scheduled to begin at 2 A.M., in about one hour, Takeshita commandeered a staff car and rushed to the War Minister's residence.

The long line of B-29s of the 315th Bomb Wing continued north, skirting the Boso Peninsula. As the planes in the bomber stream passed Tokyo, thirty-six fighters, guided by several radar-equipped Ki.45 Toryu of the 27th Air Corps, took off from their base at Kodama west of the capital, seeking the long column of American planes. People from the small city flocked to the base at the powerful growl of the aircraft engines. They yelled, "Banzai!" while the fighters taxied into position and one by one roared down the runway into the moonless sky. The leaders of this unit, like those at Atsugi, were determined to continue the battle, even though their effort ended by squandering irreplaceable aviation gasoline in what would prove to be a fruitless hunt for the American bombers.

Aboard *The Boomerang*, navigator Tony Cosola was working with focused precision, timing the distances run between landmarks that radar operator Rich Ginster had identified on the coastline below. The aircraft had made landfall at 0034 hours. Carl Schahrer crossed the invisible coastline below and turned left onto a new compass heading of 330 degrees. Once more, he began adding power to the engines for the most fuel-efficient climb rate possible to their assigned bombing altitude of 10,500 feet.

Navigation responsibility now shifted to radar operator Rich Ginster. If the plane was on course, he should soon pick up the coastline of the Sea of Japan and the clear land–water contrast of the little blade-shaped island of Awa Shima, fourteen miles off the beach. That was the Wing's Initial Point. From there they would turn northeast onto a new compass heading of 012 degrees.

While Tony Cosola and Rich Ginster sweated over their navigation, bombardier Dick Marshall opened the forward pressure hatch of the bomb bay and swung gingerly onto the narrow catwalk. This swaying aluminum bridge stretched thirty feet between the stacks of shackled 100-pound General Purpose bombs, which the plane's electromechanical interval-ometer would automatically drop in the proper sequence when Marshall's Norden bombsight sent the command. Using his flashlight, he proceeded to arm each bomb by pulling the cotter pin from the little propeller at its nose. As he worked, he couldn't help but remember the terrible night of July 29, returning from Shimotsu, when the armed 500-pounder had broken loose and rolled around the bomb bays. Even though it was pleasantly cool at this altitude, Marshall was sweating by the time he finished arming the entire load of 164 bombs.

He would fly his missions along with everyone else and work as well as the next guy. But, just like the next guy, he sure as hell would be happy when this war was over.

By 0053 hours, radar operator Rich Ginster had a solid fix on Awa Shima, the mission IP. *The Boomerang* would soon be swinging right, northeast, on its 81-mile run to the target.

At his headquarters on Atsugi Air Base, Imperial Navy Captain Yasuna Kozono, commander of the 302nd Air Corps, assembled his group leaders for a late-night meeting. Still feverish, Kozono had worked himself into a state of manic agitation after receiving official word from the Navy Ministry that the Emperor had signed an Imperial Rescript surrendering to the Allies. According to the Japanese historians of the Pacific War Research Society, Captain Kozono now decided to transform his personal intention to resist capitulation into overt rebellion:

"As long as I am commander here," he cried, "the Atsugi Air Corps will never surrender! There is a supply of food underground that will permit us to hold out for two years. Are any of you with me?"

The officers bellowed their assent.

"Let them call us traitor!" cried Kozono. "It doesn't matter. Surrender is not only against our traditions, it's against our law. Japan *cannot* surrender! Are you with me?"

The group leaders again shouted their response. "Yes, yes! Banzai! Banzai! Banzai!"[4]

In General Mori's stifling little office at the Imperial Guards Division headquarters on the northern Palace quadrant, the tense confrontation had deadlocked. It was apparent that these rebellious junior officers would not have tried to win over the Division commander unless they had already found sympathy among some of his subordinates. This was a volatile situation, and Mori could only continue to stall Ida and Shiizaki.

"I sympathize with you," Mori said. "I appreciate your objectives and—confidentially—I respect them. I might even say that under other circumstances I would share them, but that is no longer possible: I am sworn to abide by the Emperor's decision. . . .

"However," Mori went on, "and I speak now as a plain, ordinary Japanese, my present intention is to go to the Meiji Shrine. Prayer may give me the answer to my problem."[5]

Ida was now convinced that this ploy was just another tactic to delay the inevitable. General Mori would never agree to join the conspiracy. In fact, he shunted Ida off to discuss the matter with the Division Chief of Staff, Colonel Kazuo Mizutani. As Ida left Mori's office, Hatanaka and Captain Uehara arrived, their uniforms dark with sweat, streaked with ashes and dust. Hatanaka had a strange gleam in his eye. When Ida explained the General's intention to meditate in the Meiji Shrine, Hatanaka flared with anger.

"This is all a waste of time!"[6]

He and Uehara pushed their way into General Mori's office. Undeterred by the General and Colonel Shiraishi's glaring indignation, Hatanaka demanded that Mori declare his intentions once and for all. Mori, however, reiterated his desire to consult the gods.

According to postwar accounts, Air Academy Captain Uehara snapped.

He sprang toward the General, brandishing his samurai sword. Mori's brother-in-law tried to protect him. But Uehara chopped into Lt. Colonel Shiraishi's torso, driving the blade through his shoulder and neck. Bright arterial blood spouted in the lamplight. General Mori half rose in his chair, but Hatanaka aimed his pistol directly at his heart and fired once. The General slumped to the bloody floor and died with his kinsman.

'I did it because there was no time left," Hatanaka muttered. "I'm sorry."[7]

In the crowded hallway outside the office, Ida stood dazed and gripped by chagrin. Hatanaka had given his word that there would be no violence if General Mori refused to join them. Now two men were dead.

Through his muddled shame and fear, Ida reluctantly agreed to Hatanaka's request to accompany Imperial Guards Division Chief of Staff Colonel Mizutani to the Eastern District Army to announce that the rebels were now in control of the Palace and to ask once more for General Tanaka's support. The two officers, visibly shaken, left in a headquarters car.

Division staff officer Major Hidemasa Koga, with whom Hatanaka had conspired for much of the previous week, now laid down the rebels' hidden trump card: "Imperial Guards Division Strategic Order No. 584."

This was a totally convincing forgery, drafted on an official form right here in the Division's headquarters. Koga and Hatanaka had intended to have General Mori sign the document and affix his seal to it. Now the seal alone would have to suffice.

The printed order would mobilize all the regiments of the Imperial Guards Division. To briefly inform the Division's subordinate commanders as to the purpose of the extraordinary order, the document began:

"1. The Division will smash the strategy of the enemy and uphold the Emperor to safeguard our country."[8]

Each of the regiments and smaller units was given a specific mission. The First Regiment was to occupy the Palace and deploy a company of troops to NHK's main station and prevent it from broadcasting. The Second Regiment was ordered to seal off the Palace perimeter. The Sixth Regiment would remain on reserve alert in the barracks, while the Seventh Regiment would block the Nijubashi Gate and prevent any entrance into the Palace. Smaller units would take up over-watch and blocking positions near the principal thoroughfare leading to the Palace, Daikan Street. The Signal Unit was to cut off all communication to the Palace except the line to the Palace from Division headquarters, where the Division commander would supposedly remain. Ominously, the Mechanized Battalion, whose tanks were armed with cannon and heavy machine guns, was to guard the Palace with the unit's "full strength."

Major Koga stamped the orders with General Mori's official seal and dispatched the copies to the dispersed units by runner. Within minutes, tank and armored car engines were revving and the clatter of hobnailed boots echoed across the cobbles of the Imperial Guards Division's barracks compound as the disciplined troops assembled.

None of the officers questioned the authenticity of Strategic Order No. 584.

For years after World War II, Western—and most Japanese—historians were led, or chose, to believe that it was General Mori's "chop" (seal) that gave the false orders this authenticity.

Again, however, American historian Richard Frank, a combat infantry officer in Vietnam with particular insight into the process of military orders, has recently unearthed startling new information about the coup. In his masterly account of the Pacific war's end, *Downfall*, Frank states that "Anami's role in these events [the coup conspiracy] seems to have been central but remains unclear," and relates that he has discovered a "bombshell" in Hirohito's postwar soliloquy, *Showa Tenno Dokuhakuroku* (The Showa Emperor's Monologue).[9] The Emperor dictated this long statement, which included details on the turbulent final months of his wartime rule as the Allies were preparing war crime trials in 1946. Perhaps, Frank suggests, Hirohito intended to serve as a friend of the court and help the prosecution. In any event, the Monologue did not come to light until after Hirohito died in 1989. What Frank—and apparently the Emperor—found quite revealing in the Monologue was the information that the Imperial Guards Division order was not merely stamped with General Mori's seal; that seal was countersigned by Colonel Okitsugu Arao, one of War Minister Anami's closest advisers. (The Emperor's Monologue does not disclose how Hirohito obtained a copy of the false order, but obviously, the Palace would have conducted a thorough investigation of the coup attempt after the surrender.)

Surely, Arao's peers among the regimental commanders in the Imperial Guards Division would have understood his unique relationship with the War Minister, as they were of equal rank and moved within the same elite Tokyo military circles. So Arao's signature on the order would have been tantamount to Anami's endorsement, which, perhaps, it actually was.

Frank notes that at least one Japanese historian, Kazutoshi Hando, who wrote commentary on Hirohito's Monologue, has observed that the plot to seize the Imperial Palace was "not the fleeting dream of a few young officers but a plan in which some central figures [plural] in the Army were participants."[10]

It was Hatanaka himself who carried the false order to Colonel Haga at the Second Regiment's temporary command inside the walls. Hatanaka explained that both General Mori and War Minister Anami had backed the operation. The fanaticism that still gripped Hatanaka prevented him from recognizing that the murder of General Mori would no doubt come to light before the night was out. He could only hope that he could find and destroy the recordings of the Imperial Rescript, then finally and unequivocally rally the War Minister to the rebellion. Through his forceful will, General Anami could then override any objections to the earlier unfortunate, but necessary, bloodshed that Colonel Haga or other Imperial Guards Division officers might raise.

After reading the order in the light of a hooded blackout lantern, Colonel Haga found no reason to doubt his persuasive younger colleague. Hatanaka even added that Mori had appointed him and Shiizaki staff officers of the Division.

Now the mission of the Second Regiment was to recall the platoons and companies ineffectively scattered among the dark hills and gardens between the Gobunko and the Imperial Household Ministry, to regroup and concentrate the troops at the now-sealed Palace gates, and then to begin searching for the recording of the Imperial Rescript.

But with the normally dim wartime lighting of the Palace grounds completely extinguished due to the continuing air-raid alert and the auxiliary generators located around the Palace shut down to save precious fuel, the rebels' missions would be especially difficult.

When Lt. Colonel Takeshita reached War Minister Anami's residence at 1:00 A.M., the military police guards and the maid who met him seemed relieved.

"We are glad you have come, Colonel," a *kempeitai* sergeant said, saluting. "The minister seems to us to be preparing for suicide."

"Yes," Takeshita said, thanking them for their concern.

He was not surprised. Ever since Anami had become War Minister, Takeshita had felt that the General was secretly determined to kill himself at the last stage of his duty, during the Ketsu-go, or certainly before the victorious Allies arrived to occupy the homeland.

Takeshita went straight in and found Anami seated on a mat in his small rear bedroom, writing at a low table in the flaring light of a kerosene pressure lamp. The billowing mosquito net hung ready above his sleeping mat. A dinner tray had been placed near him. Takeshita paused, immediately sensing that the minister was writing his will. As Takeshita approached, Anami rolled up the paper and put it on a shelf.

Then he breathed deeply to compose himself and spoke. "I am thinking of committing suicide tonight."[11]

"It may be all right for you to commit suicide," Takeshita said, "but it doesn't have to be tonight, does it?"

Anami seemed relieved. "To tell the truth, I thought you were going to give me trouble by trying to dissuade me. I'm glad you approve."

Once more, Takeshita's description of all the events that took place at War Minister Anami's residence on the night of August 14–15, 1945, represent the account of the sole surviving eyewitness. As General Anami was married to Takeshita's sister, it is important to remember that the Japanese trait of *haji* might well have colored his version of Anami's motives and actions, so that the legacy of the War Minister was that of an officer loyal to the Emperor to the last, a Japanese soldier who chose to die rather than join a rebellion against the Throne.

Takeshita bowed silently, the appropriate response to such a statement.

"I decided on tonight because the fourteenth is the anniversary of my father's death. The twentieth is just as good a day because it is the anniversary of my second son's death, but I can't bear to listen to the Emperor's broadcast tomorrow, so I better do it tonight. [That son, Koreakiri, an Imperial Army pilot, had been killed in combat in China two years earlier.] That is why the will was dated fourteen August."[12] He nodded toward the rolled document on the shelf.

At the War Minister's elbow, the dinner tray held a plate of cheese and a bottle of sake, from which he had been sipping in a small ceramic cup. After Takeshita sat, Anami called the maid for another bottle and two larger beer glasses. The two men drank deeply. Just as the clock reached 2:00 A.M., they heard the sound of shots in the direction of the Imperial

Palace. It was at that moment, Takeshita later told Allied Intelligence officers, that he "first informed" the War Minister that the coup directed by Major Hatanaka and Lt. Colonel Shiizaki was under way.[13]

Takeshita's explanation conveniently exonerates War Minister Anami, leaving him innocent of any prior knowledge of the revolt. However, Takeshita's continuing description of events does raise questions about Anami's motives: Specifically, was the War Minister sitting on the fence, waiting to learn the outcome of the ongoing rebellion in the Palace before he decided whether to go through with his suicide, or, alternatively, to assume the leadership of a postrebellion military government as the conspirators wished?

On hearing that the coup was finally under way, Anami remained "surprisingly calm," and merely added, "even though the Imperial Guards Division has risen in arms, the Eastern District Army probably will not join it. If it doesn't, there is nothing to worry about."

Taking this statement at face value, one phrase stands out: "The Eastern District Army *probably* will not join it." (Emphasis added.) In other words, War Minister Anami was ambivalent at best about the coup and the likelihood that the conspirators would find—or had already secured—support in the Eastern District Army. If Anami truly had been worried that the coup would spread from the Palace to the Eastern District Army, the War Minister could have simply telephoned that unit's commander, General Shizuichi Tanaka, or Lt. General Sanji Okido, commander of the *kempeitai*. Either officer would have followed Anami's orders and taken immediate action to put down the coup, or at least contain it. But Anami made no phone calls.

(It is interesting to note that the Japanese historians of the Pacific War Research Society—by necessity depending on Takeshita as a source—quote Anami as saying, "But the Eastern [District] Army will never join a revolt." This is perhaps an attempt to protect the War Minister's reputation.[14])

Earlier, however, Anami had taken no action to place suspected conspirators into preventive *kempeitai* detention, even though the War Ministry's Director of Military Affairs Bureau, Lt. General Masao Yoshizumi, had urged him to do so.[15]

According to Takeshita, he and the General simply continued drinking, "one beer glass full of sake after another."

"If you drink too much," Takeshita cautioned Anami, "won't your suicide attempt be a failure?"

Anami shrugged. "No man who has reached the fifth order in *kendo* [samurai fencing] needs to worry about that, but if I should make a slip, please act as my second. The liquor in my system will cause such heavy bleeding that my death will be certain."

As they steadily consumed their sake, Anami asked Takeshita to deliver detailed messages to his family, friends, and colleagues. (Takeshita has not revealed the nature of those messages.)

While they spoke, Anami shared with his brother-in-law the will he had been completing earlier. Then War Minister Anami unrolled one of two other papers. According to historian Lester Brooks, this was a *waka*, a thirty-one-syllable poem:

> Having basked in the limitless benevolence
> > Of the Emperor,
> I cannot find words to express my gratitude
> > In my final hour.
> > > [s] *Korechika*[16]

This was a samurai's death poem that Anami had carried with him as a regional army commander in Manchuria in 1942. He could find no better way to express his sentiment at having had the privilege to serve His Majesty. But now Anami raised his brush again and somewhat unsteadily assumed the full burden of shame that *haji* required of a man in his position:

"For my supreme crime, I beg forgiveness through the act of death."[17]

The maid timidly announced that one Captain Uehara of the Air Academy had arrived with a message. Takeshita met him at the door.

"The plan is succeeding as scheduled," Uehara reported.

Takeshita was not convinced. "Do you mean that General Mori has agreed to it?"

"Actually, no," Uehara said. "He didn't agree. He had to be killed."[18]

Uehara asked if General Anami had any message for the rebels. Takeshita said there was nothing "yet."

When Takeshita told the War Minister of Mori's murder, Anami nodded.

"My suicide is to atone for his assassination, too," he said.

The "too" in this statement raises the question as to the nature of the "supreme crime" in Anami's apology. Was he admitting guilt for allowing the coup to progress, or even for taking an active role in it? At the very least, it seems that Anami's passivity while his fanatical young subordinates seized the Palace and effectively held the Emperor incommunicado could only be judged a criminal act.

At 0112 hours, Jim Smith leaned awkwardly backward, gripped the handholds, and hauled himself into the tunnel to assume his combat station. *The Boomerang* was approaching the IP at Awa Shima. Radar operator Rich Ginster had his face pressed against the rubber collar of his scope as the powerful Eagle set scanned ahead.

Ginster looked down briefly to the folded chart at his elbow, glanced over at the dimly lit dial of Tony Cosola's airspeed indicator, then peered into his scope again.

"Estimate IP in seven minutes," he said.

"Concur," Cosola added.

"Roger," Carl Schahrer replied. "Let's stay on the ball, everybody. There could be fighters anywhere along here."

Smith swiveled his head. The sky around them was thick with shredded cloud layers. Then, as Schahrer banked right onto the eighty-one-mile northbound run to Akita, Smith saw the distant horizon explode with a molten red glare and billowing columns of dense smoke, underlit by the spreading inferno from below. It seemed as if a volcano were erupting up there. The smoke had already mounted past 20,000 feet. And with each B-29B that dropped its load, the rippling fires intensified.

"It looks like the lead ships are on the target," Smith announced.

"It sure does," Schahrer said.

At the headquarters of the Eastern District Army, Lt. Colonel Ida and Colonel Mizutani arrived to inform Army Commander General Shizuichi Tanaka that the coup was under way at the Palace and that General Mori was dead. According to most later accounts, Mizutani was completely unnerved at declaring this shocking news and fell into a faint. Ida allegedly could no longer stomach the plot. His request for support made to Chief of Staff Major General Takashima (the same officer who Lt. Colonel Takeshita later stated was privy to and supported the conspiracy) was unpersuasive. The words were zealous but the tone weak. "The Eastern [District] Army must act at once. It will be too late after the noon broadcast,"[19] Ida said.

Takashima said he would report to the commander and dismissed Ida.

. . .

The rebels were now fully in control of the Imperial Palace. All the heavy, iron-bound wooden gates had been bolted, and automatic weapons were positioned to sweep the approaches to the bridges over the moat. Hatanaka, Shiizaki, and the other leaders of the revolt were now ready to hunt for the recording of the Imperial Rescript. But first they had to verify that the crucial object was still within the Palace walls.

Now luck turned in the rebels' favor. As Information Bureau Director Shimomura and the NHK officials reached the Sakashita Gate to leave the Palace, armed troops arrested them. Soon most of the group that had been in attendance while the Emperor recorded his rescript were jammed into a black and airless wooden shed that served as a temporary command post for one of the Second Regiment's battalions.

Shining weak blackout flashlights, soldiers ransacked the cars they had stopped. The search was made that much more difficult by the need to employ these faintly glowing lights inside the cars. The soldiers were reduced to groping beneath seats and in the cars' trunks like blind men.

The situation was no better at the Imperial Household Ministry. The sprawling, labyrinthine structure remained as dark as the blacked-out grounds, and the initial search of the central rooms revealed nothing. Hatanaka realized that they would need a member of the NHK team to tell them where the recording had been placed for safekeeping. Eventually an officer returned from the detention shed, accompanied by a platoon of soldiers and Kenjiro Yabe, head of Domestic Broadcasting. As Yabe arrived, soldiers inside the ministry, commanded by Shiizaki and Uehara, were ransacking rooms, their heavy boots pounding up and down the staircases. Enraged at finding so many Western furnishings, which the rebels considered unsuitable for the Imperial Palace, they smashed French armoires and the glass doors of cabinets. But this violence did not yield the recording the men sought.

Yabe was terrified by facing the armed troops and the zealous young major in his blood-splashed uniform. The NHK official explained that the recording of the Imperial Rescript had been made as an original and a copy version, and that each had a reserve set of disks wrapped, placed in film cans, and stored inside air defense uniform bags.

"Where are the records now?" Hatanaka demanded.

The NHK's Yabe honestly replied that he had no idea because he had turned the khaki sacks over to one of the Palace chamberlains, whose name he did not know, wearing one of the ubiquitous dark blue *kokuminfuku.*

While the search for the records continued frantically through the darkened rooms and narrow hallways of the Imperial Household Ministry, Hatanaka and his fellow rebels began to hunt for the chamberlain who had the information they needed. As they seized these terrified officials, they brought them to display to the NHK's Yabe in the glare of flashlights. Was this the one? What about him? Even though Yabe did recognize Chamberlain Toda, he insisted that none of the men looked familiar.[20] One by one, the rebels paraded the bewildered and frightened chamberlains and officials at bayonet point before Yabe, as the increasingly frustrated and angry troops continued to smash and rampage through the dark maze of the Ministry, searching for the recordings.

At the headquarters of the Eastern District Army, the commander, General Tanaka, was committed to driving at once to the Imperial Palace "to prevent the insurgent officers from going on with their plan."[21] But Chief of Staff Takashima was reportedly strongly opposed to the General's taking this risk—especially with the blackout in effect—and was able to convince the reluctant General Tanaka to remain at headquarters while subordinate officers were dispatched to assess the actual situation at the Palace. Major General Takashima assured his commander that he would assemble the most detailed picture possible of the confusing events.

This is a plausible enough account, one that appears in the authoritative *Japan's Longest Day*. But it does not take into consideration the fact that the Eastern District Army made no effort to mobilize or even to place on alert an adequate body of troops to surround the Imperial Palace and thus prevent the rebels from receiving reinforcements. Nor did Takashima contact *kempeitai* commander General Okido; instead, the Eastern District Army Chief of Staff merely requested that the Army's own *kempeitai* unit send a company of guards to the Dai Ichi Building "to accompany General Tanaka when he decided that his own presence was required at the scene of the rebellion."[22]

Eastern District Army Chief of Staff Takashima's actions can be fairly viewed as either the cautious response of a veteran staff officer concerned about the safety of his commander, or obstruction by a covert rebel sympathizer maneuvering for enough time for the Imperial Guards Division to solidify its hold on the Imperial Palace.[23]

. . .

0141 Hours, 14 August 1945

The Boomerang shook and wobbled in the thermal updrafts from the spreading inferno ahead. The Nippon Oil Company refinery was a churning mass of flame and dense black smoke.

Jim Smith sat at his perch and swung his shoulders first right, then left to scan for fighters and other Superforts converging on the target in this rough air. From the edges of the boiling smoke, a pair of searchlights probed the sky and found the plane, as always filling the flight deck with a frightening and dazzling glare.

"Rope," Schahrer ordered. "Just keep it coming."

"It's coming, Carl," Hank Leffler replied.

Momentarily blinded by the searchlights, Smith closed his eyes. When he opened them again, the lights were stabbing the sky behind them and he saw another gleaming, black-bellied Superfort bank steeply to dodge the searchlights. He hoped it wasn't Lieutenant Miller's *For the Luva Mike*. But his speculation was interrupted when he saw two small aircraft streaking toward them from dead ahead.

"Fighters," he called, "twelve o'clock, level."

By the time the two fighters had slashed by, they were far out of range of Sid Siegel's tail guns. "Dirty bastards," Siegel cursed. "I almost had a shot at them."

Smith knew everyone had to be breathing easier with those fighters gone. He certainly was. No one stood a chance of bailing out into *that* flaming mess. Then he suddenly saw a pair of pacing night fighters, one on each side.

"Single-engine fighter, three o'clock," he said. "He's just out of gun range, as usual."

"Another one at nine o'clock," Hank Leffler added, his voice rock steady. "Same deal, just beyond gun range. At least they still think we *have* guns."

"Clutch in," Dick Marshall called. *The Boomerang* had turned onto the bomb run and crossed the coast.

The plane rumbled as the bomb-bay doors opened. They all heard the familiar noise of the slipstream. But now there was something else— the choking stench of a massive petroleum fire. The thermals were much worse as the flames ballooned and swelled into long streamers. Carl Schahrer and John Waltershausen fought their yokes and rudder pedals to keep the bucking aircraft straight and level. Smith was pushed down hard on his perch, only to float up suddenly as the savage G-forces competed. If the pilots lost control and the plane snap-rolled over on a wing and inverted, the crew was dead.

"There's a fighter coming fast from six to three o'clock!" Sid Siegel yelled.

"Keep your guns on him, Sid," Carl answered, his voice thick with anxiety for the first time. "When he's in range, get on him."

"I've got him—"

Henry Carlson's voice broke in. "I think it's a Twenty-nine, Sid," he said. "Don't shoot. Don't *shoot.*"

Smith swung his head in time to see an off-course Superfort plowing toward their tail.

"He's going to hit us," Siegel shouted.

But the huge bomber roared past from right to left, missing *The Boomerang* by perhaps fifty vertical feet.

No sooner had *The Boomerang* survived the near midair collision than a line of four heavy flak shells burst below the right wing with a flash and solid thump. They're tracking us, Smith realized.

Radar operator Rich Ginster called course corrections to Dick Marshall. They had drifted slightly left in these thermals. "Fifty-five degrees," Ginster said. "Fifty degrees . . ."

Carl Schahrer and John Waltershausen struggled to maintain the exact altitude and airspeed that Marshall needed for synchronized radar bombing. At precisely 10,490 feet and 210 miles per hour airspeed, Schahrer called, "Dick, it's all yours."

Bombardier Marshall engaged the Norden bombsight through which he would now steer the plane. The refinery structures seaward of his aiming point were already blazing. His crosshairs crept relentlessly toward a line of intact storage tanks visible among the smoke and flames below. That was where *The Boomerang* would lay down its string of bombs.

The plane was over the center of the target now, and the thermals were much more treacherous than they had been. Suddenly more searchlights cut across their flight path. But Marshall held the plane on course despite the incredible turbulence.

Smith looked up to see another B-29B directly above *The Boomerang.* The plane was perfectly silhouetted in the glare from the exploding oil tanks and the probing searchlights. It was so close that Smith thought the narrow wing of its Eagle radar antenna must have already sliced into their own tail. The plane's bomb bays were open, and Smith saw the nestled stacks of 250-pounders. He flushed with adrenaline at the mental picture of those bombs ripping into his plane.

Smith squeezed the switch of his throat mike and yelled, "Carl, there's a Twenty-nine right on top of us."

A moment later, Sid Siegel called out the same warning. Then Tony Cosola squeezed into the tunnel beside Smith's knees to look up.

Carl Schahrer gazed above through his overhead greenhouse window. The other bomber was only thirty feet away. He could see the red glow of the four engines' turbo-superchargers. That plane was also on the bomb run, with its bombardier guiding it. But he was aiming ahead and could not see *The Boomerang* just below. It was as if the planes were stuck together.

"Dick," Schahrer said to Marshall as he overrode the autopilot to break the link to the bombsight. "I've got it."

Schahrer put *The Boomerang* into a shallow left bank to pass safely away from the other Superfort. Then he gave control of the plane back to Marshall. The moment he did, the synchronous system tripped the bomb release and their 100-pounders began dropping in their precise sequence. To the right they could see the heavier bombs of the other plane streaming down toward the burning target. Had they not banked left, that plane's bombs would have struck them.

If anything, the air was even rougher on the other side of the target. The smoke columns had converged and were lifting intense heat from the blazing petroleum tanks. Schahrer held his heading through this turbulence, then followed Tony Cosola's prompts to begin the briefed turns back toward land's end.

Smith's fingers shook as he tapped out the strike report and received the brief three-letter confirmation that the message had been received: *dit dah dit, dit dah, dit dah dit.* With the rest of the crew invisible around him, he sat silently in the darkness for a while. There was no post-target banter or funny chatter on the intercom tonight. Everyone was thinking the same thing: They had come within seconds of death on what was meant to be the last mission of the war.

Then Carl Schahrer broke the intercom silence. "You saved our bacon tonight, Smitty."

Smith shook off the lingering vision of the near midair collision, the blazing cauldron of the target, with its thermals that almost inverted *The*

Boomerang, and he nearly succeeded in erasing the horrible picture of that Superfort just above them, poised to release its bombs.

Then Smith swelled with youthful pride at Schahrer's compliment and tried to sound nonchalant. "Anytime, Skipper."

As *The Boomerang* flew southeast toward land's end, the 315th Wing's long column of Superforts still streamed past the Boso Peninsula, en route to Akita. These northbound bombers were a seemingly endless procession on Japanese radar screens, which kept the blackout in effect in Tokyo.

In the Imperial Household Ministry, that blackout drove the frustration of the rebel troops and their leaders to new levels of fury. Soldiers slapped and manhandled cowed chamberlains and minor functionaries. Troops knocked open doors with their rifle butts and ripped desks apart with their bayonets. Meaningless court documents were scattered on the floor. But the sacks containing the film cans with the recordings of the Imperial Rescript could not be found.

To add to this mounting frustration, flashlight batteries were failing and runners had to be dispatched to the Guards' supply rooms at the other side of the Palace to search for more.

Major Kenji Hatanaka was frantic. He *had* to destroy those recordings before any Guards officers discovered the true nature of Strategic Order 584 and challenged his authority. But, once he had crushed the wax disks and surrounded the Gobunko even more tightly with troops loyal only to him and his closest comrades, so that the Emperor was completely isolated, War Minister Anami would finally recognize the need for him to intervene, take control of the Imperial armed forces, and issue orders in the Emperor's name to prepare the nation for the Ketsu-go.

THE LAST MISSION

B^{Y 2:50 A.M., THE SCENE} in the Imperial Household Ministry was approaching bedlam. Major Hatanaka and Lt. Colonel Shiizaki had fed increasing numbers of soldiers into the chaotic search for the Imperial Rescript recordings. Majors Hatanaka and Koga also sought another prize, His Majesty's Imperial seal, which they knew would be essential for use on forged orders for the armed forces to continue the war.[1]

But in the black, constricted halls of the structure's multiple linked side wings, the troops collided with one another, provoking angry exchanges and shouted outbursts from platoon-leader lieutenants and squad sergeants trying to keep their soldiers focused on the mission.

To worsen the confusion, terrified chamberlains and Palace functionaries fled their sleeping chambers, waving flashlights in panic as they climbed or descended staircases so that the soldiers clomping toward them in the darkness would not shoot. The rebels herded the frightened officials into the Ministry's central rooms to be interrogated. But Sotaro Ishiwatari, Minister of the Imperial Household Ministry, and several aides managed, with the help of the resourceful Chamberlain Tokugawa, to descend through the darkened building via a secret passage to a steel-doored air-raid shelter unknown to the rebels.

Later it was surmised that, as the frantic search continued, at least one group of rebels probed the small office of the Empress's lady-in-waiting, where Chamberlain Tokugawa had locked the sacks with the recordings in the small safe. Soldiers kicked apart a desk and splintered a wooden filing cabinet. In the dark, stifling confines of the office, however, the troops apparently did not see the safe hidden behind the heap of meaningless Palace paperwork. The soldiers moved on to pillage another of the endless array of tiny offices.

The rebels had won several vital tactical victories, however. Hatanaka had sealed off the Imperial Palace's outer perimeter with heavily armed troops. Soldiers from the First Regiment had already left to take control of the main NHK studios. And, equally important, two companies of rebels had ringed the Gobunko so that the Emperor had become a prisoner in his own Palace. He could not leave; nor could any outsiders enter the building without provoking a firefight that would endanger His Majesty.

Once Major Hatanaka's men found and destroyed the recordings of the Imperial Rescript, there would be no way for the Emperor to record another or to leave the Palace to broadcast his rescript in person to the nation and the world. Instead, General Anami would have to step forward to fulfill his true destiny. Then, as the War Minister issued orders in the Emperor's name (bearing the essential codes of Imperial General Head-quarters), the Army and the Navy would be sure to obey. The entire nation, the rebel officers were confident, would follow.

Despite later reports that the Emperor had slept through the night in his Gobunko bedchamber, oblivious to the ineffectual coup attempt sputtering around him, he was very much awake and acutely aware of the dramatic and threatening events in the Imperial Palace the night of August 14–15, 1945.

When rebel troops closed in on the Gobunko, servants and a handful of bodyguards used all their strength to roll down rusty steel typhoon shutters that had not been locked in place for years. Once these steel-slat curtains had been secured—with the expected metallic screeching—the Emperor was relatively safe. But sleep was no longer possible, and he spent the night fearfully watching the combat-equipped troops prowling among the tall trees outside.[2]

But, again, the image of the Emperor being stalked and virtually caged within the Gobunko was too shameful for a culture so steeped in *haji* to accept. It was less painful for postwar Japan to imagine that His Majesty had merely slept through the night.

Lt. Colonel Masataka Ida—one of the most ardent original War Ministry rebels—returned to the Palace from the Eastern District Army headquarters sometime around 3 A.M. (It must be noted that the rebels did not keep logs noting the precise times of officers' movements, as would be the case during normal operations.) According to Ida's postwar accounts, he found Major Hatanaka at the Second Regiment's temporary command post. Later descriptions of this encounter appear to closely follow the version found in *Japan's Longest Day*.

"Eastern District Army won't go along," Ida told Hatanaka.

Moreover, Ida said, once the Imperial Guards Division discovered that Lt. General Mori, their commander, had been killed, "they'll refuse to continue [the coup]. If you try to force this thing through, there will be chaos. There's no other alternative: withdraw all your troops before dawn." Hatanaka tried to interrupt, but Ida held up his hand. "Face the facts; the coup has failed, but if you pull out all the troops quickly the people will never know it happened." It would pass like "a midsummer night's dream."[3]

Hatanaka's shoulders sagged (again according to Ida's later account), and he whispered, "Yes, I understand," leaving Ida to believe that the coup had ended.[4]

Ida then said he would deliver a situation report to War Minister Anami and drove off in a staff car.

Hatanaka, however, had not lost his taste for rebellion. The Palace was in rebel hands; the Imperial Guards Division was following the spurious order. The only unforeseen problem was this interminable blackout, which rendered even the simplest troop movement difficult and made the search for the recordings of the Imperial Rescript in the multistory warren of the Imperial Household Ministry almost impossible. But Hatanaka was not ready to admit defeat. He consulted with fellow conspirators Major Koga and Lt. Colonel Shiizaki. They decided to continue occupying the Imperial Palace, to maintain holding the Emperor in the Gobunko, and to press on with the hunt for those damned sacks until they found them.[5]

As the rebels held the Imperial Palace, the last of the 315th Bomb Wing's Superforts, *Horrible Monster*, passed east of the Boso Peninsula around 0240 hours, northbound toward landfall and Akita. Like the crew of *The Boomerang*, some of the men aboard *Horrible Monster* wanted to catch a glimpse of Tokyo. The pilot, First Lt. Roger B. Jensen—who had been Jim Smith's first pilot during training at Fairmont, Nebraska—indicated the black void where Tokyo should lie to his radio operator, Staff Sergeant Clyde Hussey, and Flight Engineer Master Sergeant Boyd F. Ludewig. Hussey and Ludewig took a moment away from their combat stations to stare out the port-side cockpit windows. But there was nothing to be seen. Tokyo was still fully blacked out. And the crew had not come here for sightseeing; it was time to prepare for combat. Even though *Horrible Monster* had been the last plane to take off and would be the last on the target, they were determined to make every bomb count. Aircraft Commander Captain Perry J. Hickerson kept the bomber on its northbound course. (The Superfort dropped the last B-29B bombs of World War II on Akita at 0339 hours.)

Ten miles seaward and 1,500 feet lower, the first of the Wing's B-29Bs to have bombed the target were streaming south toward Guam. The continuing presence of this extended column of enemy aircraft so near the capital—as well as the later arrival of Superforts from the 313th, 314th, and 73rd Bomb Wings, which were striking Kumagaya and Isezaka, west and northwest of Tokyo—caused the Eastern District Army to maintain the blackout that the first northbound planes of the 315th had initially triggered.

In part because of the confusion this blackout engendered, and also because of his youthful features, which masked his true authority, Chamberlain Yasuhide Toda had been allowed to slip away. Toda courageously went to rescue Lord Keeper of the Privy Seal Marquis Kido. Because Kido was unfamiliar with the Imperial Household Ministry, having previously occupied the more commodious Chamberlain's Palace, Toda led the Marquis through the dark corridors to the physician's room, where Kido put on a white doctor's coat as a disguise. Then the two men decided that Kido would be safer taking refuge with Household Minister Ishiwatari and the others in the hidden basement air-raid shelter.[6] Chamberlain Toda and the men already in the room had agreed that they would open the heavy steel door only at the sound of five sharp raps repeated in sequence. For now, the most important Palace officials other than the Emperor had managed to escape the rebels in the darkness and were safely hidden.

At Eastern District Army Headquarters in the Dai Ichi Insurance Building, the situation was tense. Colonel Teisaku Minami, commander of the Imperial Guards Division's Seventh Regiment, had arrived at 2:45 A.M., suspicious of the instructions he had ostensibly received from the Division Commander, Lt. General Mori. The full extent of the coup under way at the Imperial Palace soon became clear.

Impatient of waiting for the situation to be further clarified, the Eastern District Army's commanding officer, General Tanaka, again wanted to go directly to the Palace to confront the rebels. But, once more, his Chief of Staff, Major General Takashima, convinced him not to take such a step during the moonless blackout.

"Day will break soon, Your Excellency," Takashima said. "It is very difficult to control men during the dark."

"Oh, I see," Tanaka said.

The General agreed to wait.[7]

As General Tanaka waited, officers from his headquarters delivered orders to the Imperial Guards Division commanders stationed outside the Palace walls to report immediately to the Dai Ichi Building. Several did and were informed that their division's Strategic Order 584 was spurious. They were now ordered to return their men to barracks. The officers complied.

But inside the Imperial Palace the massive gates remained barred, with Major Hatanaka, Lt. Colonel Shiizaki, and Colonel Haga in control. The frantic search for the recordings of the Imperial Rescript continued through the pitch-dark maze of the Imperial Household Ministry.

About 3:20 A.M., a *kempeitai* guard showed Lt. Colonel Masataka Ida into General Anami's bedroom. Ida wore a summer dress uniform and carried his sword.

According to one of rebel Lt. Colonel Takeshita's later statements to Allied Intelligence, Ida said to the War Minister, whom he idolized, "I will join you in death."

General Anami, however, perhaps because of the esteem in which he held Ida, admonished him harshly, "Survive me and serve your country."

Ida abruptly abandoned thoughts of glorious suicide and agreed. The two then wept in each other's arms. Ida allegedly left soon afterward.[8]

There is no evidence in Takeshita's account that Ida and Anami discussed the failure of the coup d'état, which was ostensibly the reason for Ida to have come to the War Minister's residence. Ida also knew that the Eastern District Army had not joined the coup and did not appear likely to do so, yet, again according to Takeshita, he did not relay this important information either.

This raises intriguing questions. What were Ida's true motives for visiting War Minister Anami? Had he come merely for sentimental reasons, as Takeshita suggests, or rather to relay important operational information about the progress of the coup? We will probably never know. Takeshita and Ida were destined to survive the war. Anami and Hatanaka, and his key fellow conspirators, were not.

The import of both Takeshita's and Ida's postwar accounts is that they played no active role in the conspiracy once it began to unravel with the murders of Lt. General Mori and Lt. Colonel Shiraishi at Imperial Guards Division headquarters. But the actual situation is likely to remain murky. Takeshita and Ida have presented descriptions of events that not only exonerate themselves but, equally important, absolve War Minister Anami from any involvement in the coup attempt.

However, one thing is reasonably clear from statements of others who observed War Minister Anami that night: Whether or not Ida brought a report that the coup was failing, at about 4:00 A.M., Anami began his ritual suicide preparations. He wrapped his torso in a wide band of white cotton. Then he put on a freshly laundered white shirt.

"The Emperor himself gave me this when I was the Imperial aide-de-camp," Anami explained proudly.

He made certain that all of his campaign ribbons and decorations were correctly fixed to the blouse of his dress uniform, which hung on a wooden kimono stand nearby.

He selected an ornate short sword from the matched pair that lay before him in their lacquered scabbards in a velvet-lined case. "Here," he said, handing it to Takeshita. "I want you to have this."

Anami also chose a dagger with a keen double-edged blade, which he would use to cut his own throat after the seppuku belly slices. Then he began to mull over the most appropriate place to perform the act of seppuku. Japanese and Western historians have indicated that the choice of the suicide spot held special significance in Japanese culture. By tradition, if the man felt deep shame for intolerable acts—i.e., an overwhelming sense of *haji*—he would spill his blood on the naked earth. A guiltless, honorable man forced by circumstances beyond his control into seppuku would take his own life indoors, kneeling on a straw mat or a "low dais." Now, Anami, wishing to reveal himself as one who had sinned, but out of pure motives, was considering the slatted wooden bedroom veranda—midway between the sanctity of the household and the anonymous earth of the garden—as the appropriate spot to die.[9]

By 3:45 A.M., Major Hatanaka had become as frantic as the harried troops who were stumbling through the black labyrinth of the Imperial Household Ministry searching for the recordings of the Imperial Rescript. All of the Palace chamberlains they had interrogated claimed to have no knowledge of the recordings—other than the fact that the Emperor had indeed recorded his rescript.

(Hatanaka had no idea that the rebel officers had already questioned Chamberlain Yoshihiro Tokugawa—the one man in the entire Palace who knew the exact whereabouts of the recordings—before releasing him into the night, because Kenjiro Yabe of NHK had sworn that the chamberlain who had taken the recordings was "taller with a bigger nose" than Chamberlain Tokugawa.)

So the maddening hunt continued in the Imperial Household Ministry, with both soldiers' and officers' anger now exploding. Once more, flashlights grew dim because of spent batteries, and the troops were reduced to cupping candles as they waded through the splintered furniture and heaps of papers.

When Hatanaka went to consult Major Koga at the Second Regiment command post, Colonel Haga impatiently confronted the two rebel officers. As described in *Japan's Longest Day*, the encounter was not pleasant. By now, Hatanaka had hoped to have received word from Lt. Colonel Takeshita that the War Minister had finally decided to back the coup. But there had been only silence from that quarter. And with every Palace telephone line but one at Guards Division headquarters cut, Hatanaka would have to go there to call Anami or leave the Palace and take a staff car to his residence. But Hatanaka wanted to stay here to make sure that the recordings were destroyed should they be discovered—and not preserved out of some misguided sense of reverence toward the Emperor.

"Where is the War Minister?" Colonel Haga demanded. "Why hasn't he come? What has gone wrong?"

From Koga's expression, Hatanaka saw that the War Minister had not called over the line to Division headquarters. Hatanaka had no choice but to continue stalling. The troops stumbling through the dark jumble of the Imperial Household Ministry might find the recordings at any time. "I'll telephone at once," Hatanaka said, "to see whether General Anami has left yet or not."

Koga, who knew Colonel Haga better, realized that they could no longer stall him. "General Mori is dead," Koga now admitted. "The Colonel must take command of the Guards division."[10]

Colonel Haga demanded to know how Mori had died, but Koga and Hatanaka were evasive. The confrontation ended in a tense standoff, with Haga still accepting the ruse that the rebellion had the backing of War Minister Anami.

At 0320 hours, *The Boomerang* made land's end on the Pacific coast of Honshu just below Ishinomaki on schedule. Luckily, no more Japanese fighters had intercepted them. Navigator Tony Cosola gave Carl Schahrer an over-water heading almost due south to Iwo Jima, approximately 840 miles—or four hours—away.

The plane's engines ran smoothly as flight engineer Hank Gorder patiently checked his instrument panel and wrote detailed notes in his logbook. Once more, he worked his slide rule and adjusted fuel mixture to optimize the cruise control's gas consumption. It was a demanding task that would require his constant attention until they reached Guam. But after the exhaustion of the long trip north, and the adrenaline flood of the target, the rest of the crew was winding down.

Jim Smith woke abruptly with his head flat on his radio table. He did not remember dropping off to sleep. Rubbing his eyes, Smith shook himself further awake and drank some water. It had the heavily chlorinated taste from the big canvas Lister bags of potable water that hung between the barracks at Northwest Field. As grubby as that base was, with its alternating mud and coral dust, rats, and rancid mess hall chow, the thought of reaching there safely from yet another mission was very appealing. He sat in the darkness, listening to the terse intercom exchanges among Carl, John, and Tony. The two pilots were taking turns dozing. And Tony Cosola would actually slip into a real nap for fifteen minutes before Hank would wake him. Then Tony would snap fully alert and give Carl or John an update on the heading before falling back to sleep.

Smith heard the engines throb steadily. As always, his headset was filled with the Japanese jamming signal, *dah dit dah dit, dah dit dit dit*. If this really was the last mission the 315th had to fly, he would be quite happy never to have to listen to *that* again for hours on end.

The 315th Wing's homebound course took the bomber stream about ten miles farther seaward than the northbound route had. But the planes were still well within range of Japanese radar, so the Tokyo blackout continued as they returned.

In War Minister Anami's residence, he and Takeshita were still drinking sake after 4 A.M. But Anami had reached his decision. Although there is no record of his having made or received a telephone call, and Lt. Colonel Ida had allegedly not reported that the coup d'état was unraveling, General Anami seems to have decided he could wait no longer.

Stripped to the waist, his torso wrapped in the multiple layers of the white cotton band, he prepared to drink his final brimming glass of sake with his brother-in-law.

Anami wanted Takeshita to carry a message to his wife, Ayako, Takeshita's sister, whom he had married thirty years earlier. "I have absolute confidence in her. She has done well." He admonished Takeshita to make sure his older surviving son, Koretaka, "do nothing rash" (a reference to suicide), adding that Anami himself was going to join his son, Koreakiri, the Army pilot who had been killed in China, in the Yasukuni Shrine, where the souls of warriors rested.

The two men drank deeply, and Takeshita refilled the glasses as etiquette demanded. Anami did not stay his friend's hand on the bottle, but instead checked Takeshita's notes to make sure he had written all the names of those to whom Anami wished to send his death greetings, an important formality in samurai tradition. Not surprisingly, Anami wanted to extend his compliments to Army Chief of Staff Umezu and Admiral Suzuki, both of whom he honored for their long military service to Japan.

"How about Yonai?" Takeshita asked.

As described in *Japan's Longest Day*, "The War Minister's face, flushed with drink, turned a deep angry color. 'Kill him,' he cried. 'Kill Yonai!'"[11]

His bitterness and hatred toward Navy Minister Admiral Mitsumasa Yonai were boundless. Yonai had treacherously sided with Foreign Minister Togo, allowing him to manipulate the civilians of the peace faction within the Supreme Council for the Direction of the War. For this Anami wanted to extract retribution, although he would not live to see it.

Even a zealot like Hatanaka had to recognize that the coup was crumbling. As the pale light of false dawn gave texture to the clouds, an outraged Colonel Haga ordered Major Koga and Hatanaka to Imperial Guards Division headquarters. Over the damaged but usable telephone line to the Eastern District Army that the rebels had inadvertently left open, Haga was now speaking directly to Chief of Staff Major General Takashima.

Had the Eastern District Army's Chief of Staff been a possible covert supporter of the rebels earlier that night—as suggested in Lt. Colonel Takeshita's postwar statements to Allied Intelligence interrogators, and by Takashima's own actions in delaying General Tanaka from quashing the rebellion—he now came out firmly against the coup. This might have been because Takashima realized that it was unlikely War Minister Anami would back the rebellion. Or, equally plausible, Takashima might have always been acting out of loyalty to the nation and the throne. Again, the situation was murky. Many of the key participants in these events were destined to survive the war and present their versions of what transpired. Others would soon be dead and could never reveal the actual complexity of the intrigue.

But, according to Colonel Haga and Major General Takashima, as related in *Japan's Longest Day*, the telephone call between the Imperial Guards Division and the Eastern District Army headquarters at approximately 4:25 A.M. was critical. Despite the echoing static over the line caused by the rebel troops' sabotage of the Palace communications center, Takashima was able to convince Colonel Haga that Division Strategic Order 584 was false. He ordered Haga to disperse his troops and send runners to the Dai Ichi Building for new orders. Then Takashima asked Haga, "You're not alone there, are you?"

Haga shouted over the scratchy line that Major Hatanaka was at his side.

"Let me talk to him," the Chief of Staff demanded.

When Hatanaka took the phone and identified himself, he immediately begged Takashima "to try to understand our position—"

"I understand," Takashima interrupted. "But it makes no difference. Your situation is hopeless, you are alone, the Eastern [District] Army will not join you. You think you are succeeding because you hold the Palace temporarily, but you are defeated, you are like soldiers trying to defend a hopeless position in a cave with no way out. Listen to me carefully! Don't do anything rash—you will only sacrifice more lives uselessly. I respect your feelings as a private individual, Hatanaka, but as an officer in the Army you must obey the Emperor. Japan's supreme virtue is obedience! Are you listening to me, Major?"

Hatanaka saw the hopelessness of his position, but he still fanatically persisted, requesting that the rebels be given ten minutes over national radio before the Emperor's recording was broadcast in order to tell the world "the reasons for what we have done and the goals we still hope to win. . . . Ten minutes, that's all, only ten minutes to talk to the people."[12]

Eastern District Army Chief of Staff Takashima adamantly refused. Again, this might have reflected his own deeply held convictions. Or there might have been a more practical reason. By now he could no longer restrain his commander, General Tanaka, who was finally about to depart for the Palace.

Colonel Haga reacted with fury. "Now I understand," he said, glaring at Hatanaka, Koga, and Shiizaki, "why General Anami never came. You've been lying to me the whole time."

Haga ordered the rebels out of the Palace. But the young major merely stared boldly at the superior officer and strode away in defiance.[13]

Eastern District Army Commander General Shizuichi Tanaka arrived at Imperial Guards Division headquarters at dawn accompanied only by his adjutant, Major Kiyoshi Tsukamoto, and a staff officer.[14] General Tanaka encountered the First Regiment commander, a colonel named Watanabe, marching his combat-equipped troops out of the barracks to deploy them inside the Palace in accordance with the specious Strategic Order 584 the rebels had issued earlier.

"Watanabe!" Tanaka said. "I'm lucky to be in time. That order you received was false. Call back your troops and let's go to your headquarters."[15]

Tanaka now confronted the rebel leaders—Hatanaka, Shiizaki, Koga, and Uehara—whom he harangued and berated, demanding that they give up the plot and "expunge the stain they had made on the honor of the army by disobeying the Emperor's will." But instead of having the officers arrested, Tanaka released them with the implicit understanding that they would commit suicide in the "true bushido spirit."[16]

General Tanaka and his small entourage then drove to the Inui Gate, where Tanaka personally told Colonel Haga and his battalion commanders that they had been duped by the false order. Seeing that they had acted in good faith, General Tanaka instructed the officers to regain control of their men and return to barracks.

But at that moment another staff car arrived from which emerged Colonel Arao and Lt. Colonels Ida and Shimanuki, all of the War Ministry's Military Affairs Bureau—the seat of the rebellion—none of whom had legitimate business at the Palace. Glowering at them over his bristly mustache, Tanaka demanded to know why they were there.

"General," Colonel Arao said, "we have come to lead the Guards Division."

Tanaka exploded, ordering the men to leave at once.[17]

This incident raises more intriguing questions. If Colonel Arao had in fact been involved in the rebellion, as his signature on the false Imperial Guards Division order would seem to indicate, his arrival along with Ida might imply that he wanted to see the coup through to its conclusion, acting as an emissary of War Minister Anami. Yet again, however, the record remains murky. Arao and Ida survived the war to prosper in peacetime. General Anami and the three officers Tanaka had banished from the Palace did not.

Major Kenji Hatanaka left the Imperial Palace en route to the NHK studios, obviously unrepentant. He might well have bitterly reflected on the reasons the coup had failed, which had been a classic example of "for want of a nail, a shoe was lost" logic.

The long blackout, coming after four nights during which there had been no air raids, was foremost in the chain of events that had undercut the operation. When the already dimly lit Palace grounds were suddenly shrouded in absolute darkness, the tactical problem of safely deploying the troops of Colonel Haga's two battalions became almost impossible. The officers could not risk setting up barriers with armed infantry across the short road linking the Gobunko and the Imperial Household Ministry to block the Emperor's limousine for fear of accidental gunfire and injury to His Majesty. And coming when it did, at 11:05 P.M., and forcing the Emperor into his shelter just as he was leaving the Gobunko, the blackout caused the rebels to lose at least thirty precious minutes from their already strained schedule, as they waited trying unsuccessfully to determine his whereabouts.

In turn, this delay caused Hatanaka and Shiizaki to panic and rush to Imperial Guards Division headquarters. Their agitation ignited the bloody fury of Captain Uehara. This led to the murders of Guards Division commander Lt. General Mori and his brother-in-law, Lt. Colonel Shiraishi.

With the rebel leaders otherwise occupied, the Emperor was able to record the Imperial Rescript and return to the Gobunko, and a chamberlain was able to successfully hide the recordings—all virtually under the noses of the rebels.

None of that would have mattered had the blackout not transformed the Imperial Household Ministry into a pitch-dark hive of tiny, confusing offices and bedchambers, spilling down the steep hillside toward the moat. Even with those scores of rooms brightly lit, it would have taken a battalion of patient soldiers hours to meticulously search them. In the blackout, which also allowed key chamberlains and high officials such as Marquis Kido to slip free, the task of effectively searching the multistory, multiwing building was all but impossible.

So, before Eastern District Army Commander General Tanaka arrived to crush the coup, Hatanaka had been unable to report to General Anami that he had successfully destroyed the recordings, a report that no doubt would have finally spurred the War Minister to action. He would have imposed his forceful manner on the armed forces, taken charge of the nation, and defied both the traitorous civilians around the Emperor and the hated Allies who intended to subjugate the nation and mongrelize the Yamato race.

Now this cause seemed lost. All Hatanaka could hope for was the chance to broadcast to the nation himself, not just to state the rebels' grievances but to announce to the world that the entire Japanese Army was in revolt. He hoped this would inflame other nests of rebellion in the Home Islands and across the Empire. In fact, the rebels had already prepared a long newspaper article proclaiming the general Army rebellion against "the submissive and cowardly government," which they had ordered the Tokyo press to publish the next morning. (They had no way of knowing that the Prime Minister's office had also given the press a detailed article to run on newspaper front pages in special editions after the Emperor's noon broadcast. This one was to confirm that the Emperor had signed the rescript of surrender and that the war had ended in defeat.[18])

No one in Japan could realize, of course, why the air-raid sirens had howled and Tokyo was gripped by blackout at 11:05 P.M. This was a crucial moment: Transportation Minister Naoto Kobiyama had just signed the Imperial Rescript, which allowed Vice Foreign Minister Shunichi Matsumoto to send the surrender cable to the Allies via the Swiss. And the blackout fell just as the Emperor left the Gobunko en route to the Imperial Household Ministry, causing him to seek shelter and thus to escape the waiting rebels. The reason the sirens sounded at 11:05 P.M. was directly connected to the Domei News Agency FLASH! bulletin transmitted from Tokyo at 2:49 P.M. on Tuesday, August 14. The message had arrived in Guam at 3:49 P.M. local time, causing the B-29Bs of the 315th Wing, already warming up their engines for takeoff, to shut down and wait, while their commanders decided if the mission should proceed.

That wait lasted fifty-three minutes, and the first of the Wing's bombers did not take off until 4:42 P.M. (1642 hours). This placed the 315th's bomber stream near enough to Tokyo to trigger the air-raid alarm at almost exactly 11:05 P.M. Tokyo time, as the Emperor and Chamberlain Irie stepped out of the Gobunko toward the waiting limousine to record the Imperial Rescript of surrender. The sudden blackout, which was the lost nail causing the lost shoe that toppled the coup d'état, inevitably ensued.

General Anami reverently pulled on the fine linen shirt that had been a gift from the Emperor. Once more he reminded Takeshita of the garment's value.

"I can think of nothing I prize more highly—so I intend to die wearing it."

He folded his uniform blouse and made sure the multiple decorations were properly arrayed. Then he placed a handsomely framed photograph of his dead son Koreakiri atop the uniform.

"When I am dead," he asked Takeshita, "will you drape the uniform over me?"[19]

There are conflicting reports of what occurred next in War Minister Anami's residence. The exact sequence of events has always been confused but is of crucial importance to a proper understanding of the incident. Based on postwar interrogations of surviving witnesses, American historian David Bergamini states in *Japan's Imperial Conspiracy* that at 5:30 A.M. *kempeitai* Commander Lt. General Sanji Okido came to call on Anami to inform him that the coup had failed and that the Eastern District Army commander, General Tanaka, was in the Palace to take matters in hand. Anami refused to see Okido, but Takeshita accepted the report. According to historian John Toland, Anami then proceeded to complete the gruesome act of seppuku.

And, as reported in *Japan's Longest Day*, General Okido came to the War Minister's residence "around five-thirty to report on the insurrection among the Imperial Guards."[20] Again, the authors state that Anami refused to see him and sent Takeshita instead. This description, in both its timing and its sequence of events, creates a firebreak between the War Minister and the Palace rebellion, disconnecting Anami's suicide from the news that the coup had failed and that Eastern District Army Commander Tanaka had the situation in hand.

But Toland notes in *The Rising Sun* that "around four o'clock"—well before General Tanaka went to the Palace to crush the revolt—the commander of the *kempeitai* arrived at the War Minister's residence. In this account, the purpose of Okido's visit is not clear.[21]

The question remains unanswered: Did War Minister Anami kill himself before or after hearing that the coup d'état had failed?

The principal witness to these events was Lt. Colonel Takeshita. He told Allied Intelligence after the war that Anami's suicide and the failed rebellion were not related. Despite his statement that the War Minister believed General Tanaka's command would "probably" not join the rebels, Takeshita also said, "Anami always had complete confidence in the Eastern District Army and the Guards Division."[22] From his statements to Allied interrogators it appears that Lt. Colonel Takeshita wanted to prevent the posthumous reputation of his brother-in-law from being tarnished by the public perception that General Anami had participated—in even a passive manner—in an armed rebellion against the Emperor, a shamefully dishonorable act for a loyal Japanese soldier.

Takeshita told Allied Intelligence officials in February 1950 that at 4 A.M. Anami ordered him to deal with General Okido in the vestibule of the residence when the *kempeitai* commander arrived. According to Takeshita's statement, Okido reported on the insurrection of "the Guards Infantry Regiment" at the Palace, then apparently left, neither requesting nor insisting on instructions from General Anami.

When Takeshita returned to the rear bedroom, he found the War Minister "sitting in the corridor [bedroom veranda] facing the Imperial Palace." He had just slashed his abdomen in the prescribed seppuku cut— left to right, and then up. Now he was groping with the sharp dagger in his left hand, trying to slash the right side of his throat.

Here Takeshita offers an interesting observation: "After briefly conveying Lt. General Okido's report, I asked, 'Shall I serve as [your] second?'"

If accurate, this would mean that Anami finally decided to end the long night of indecision and begin the ritual of suicide *before* knowing the purpose of General Okido's visit and learning if Hatanaka and the others had succeeded.[23] This would mean that the War Minister had not been sitting on the fence all night, delaying his suicide to learn if the successful rebels would call upon him to lead a military government, reject surrender, and continue the war.

After slashing his belly, Anami drew the razorlike blade of the dagger across his neck, feeling for the right carotid artery. Blood poured in sheets across the white expanse of the Emperor's shirt and onto the scrubbed wood of the veranda.

Again, Takeshita asked if he could help administer the coup de grâce that was the privilege of every samurai to request.

"No," Anami grunted through his agony, weakened but still kneeling upright. "Leave me."

(Although mortally wounded, General Anami did not quickly die. Around 8:30 A.M., Takeshita and other staff officers had to command a medical orderly to administer a fatal overdose of morphine to the War Minister.)

At the Imperial Palace, General Tanaka quickly took control. He ordered the gates barred once more and made sure the NHK and Information Bureau prisoners were freed from the stifling guardhouse shed where they had been caged all night. Sometime before 7 A.M., General Tanaka convinced anxious Palace chamberlains that he was indeed a loyal soldier.

Slowly, with lingering terror, they emerged from their hiding places, not quite sure whether this fierce-looking mustachioed general might be part of the coup.

Tanaka drove across the Palace grounds in his staff car, his wide commander's flag fluttering in the early-morning sunlight. At the Gobunko, he was able to deliver the Emperor a detailed report on the near-disastrous events of the night. The General then continued his thorough reconnaissance of the Palace grounds and buildings to make sure all the rebel troops had returned to barracks.[24]

He found the Imperial Household Ministry a shambles, the offices and hallways littered with broken glass and splintered furniture. But chamberlains assured him that the rebels had not discovered the precious recordings.

Major Hatanaka went directly to the NHK Building, taking with him a junior officer and a pair of soldiers. They reached the broadcast house just before 5 A.M. and encountered white-sashed troops of the Imperial Guards Division First Regiment, who still believed the rebellion was unfolding, surrounding the building. Hatanaka provided the correct password and went directly to the windowless Studio 2, where announcer Morio Tateno was jotting notes for a news broadcast.

The startled announcer looked up at the sound of someone shoving open the soundproof studio door and saw a sweaty and desperate Army major brandishing a pistol. Hatanaka carried a bunch of notes in his left hand, the manifesto he intended to read to the people and the Army.

"I will take the microphone and speak to the entire nation," Hatanaka said, pointing his pistol directly at Tateno.

From the side of his eye, the announcer saw large characters brushed onto the Major's handwritten script: "Our troops are now guarding the Imperial Palace . . ." In a few minutes, NHK was scheduled to alert all of Japan to stand by to listen to the Emperor at noon. Now this fanatic wanted to make an inflammatory and unauthorized statement before His Majesty's rescript was broadcast that would invalidate the Emperor's remarks. Tateno was a professional journalist. He could never permit NHK to be misused in this manner. So he would follow regulations to the letter, even at the risk of death. At least the continuing air raid gave him an excuse to refuse this fanatic.

"But the air-raid warning is still in effect," he told Hatanaka. "We cannot broadcast during an alert without special permission from the Eastern [District] Army."[25]

Even though it was full daylight, that blackout still plagued him. Hatanaka set out to threaten station managers into cooperation. As he prowled about the unfamiliar offices, the employees telephoned ahead to warn their colleagues. Tell him the same story: NHK could not broadcast during an air-raid alert without the specific permission of the Eastern District Army.

Hatanaka swooped between rage and despair. Finally a phone rang in the manager's suite. It was headquarters of the Eastern District Army, demanding to speak to the rebel major. The voice on the other end of the line was loud and authoritative. Hatanaka could only reply with a timid "*Hai* . . . Yes, sir. I understand, sir. . . ."

His shoulders sagged. His eyes clouded with tears, and he holstered his pistol. Limp with disappointment, Hatanaka motioned to the rebels who had accompanied him to the studio. "We've done everything we could. Let's go."

They left in the direction of the Imperial Palace.

At 7:21 A.M., NHK announcer Tateno, his confidence restored now that the rebels had left, read a special announcement to the Japanese Empire: "His Imperial Majesty the Emperor has issued a rescript. It will be broadcast at noon today. Let us all listen respectfully to the voice of the Emperor." Then he solemnly repeated for emphasis, "Let us all respectfully listen to the Emperor at noon today."[26]

He added that locations in Japan that did not normally receive electrical power during daylight would have current at noon today, Wednesday, August 15. Radio receivers would be installed in places of employment and where the public gathered.

Japan's Longest Day describes dramatic events unfolding elsewhere in Tokyo: While Major Hatanaka was making his final effort at the NHK Building, an Imperial Army captain named Takeo Sasaki from the elite Yokohama Guards was frantically prowling the capital in a staff car, followed by a truck jammed with his own rebellious troops and zealous ultranationalist university students whom he had armed. Unaware of either the Imperial Palace rebellion or the mood of tense defiance at Atsugi Air Base—

both of which efforts he would have gladly supported—Captain Sasaki had assigned himself a violent mission: assassinate Premier Kantaro Suzuki and other "traitorous elements" that he was convinced had led the Emperor toward disgraceful surrender. By so doing, Sasaki believed, the Suzuki cabinet would fall and the Imperial armed forces would step forward to take control of the country and lead it into the Ketsu-go. Sasaki's group had adopted the name National Divine-Wind Corps (*Kokumin Kamikaze Tai*).[27]

These rebels surrounded Prime Minister Suzuki's official residence and began to pepper the broad façade of the Western-style building with 6.5mm rifle and light-machine-gun fire. Fortunately for Suzuki, he had decided to spend the remainder of the exhausting night after the last endless cabinet session at his small private home in the hilly Maruyama district. Frustrated at not finding Suzuki at the official residence, Captain Sasaki's rebels doused the building's entrance hall with oil and set it alight. But even as they sped off toward Maruyama, servants were able to smother the blaze.[28]

Over the next two hours, the aged Premier —whose body still carried bullets from the February 1936 military coup attempt—managed to stay just ahead of the pursuing rebels. Sasaki's men eventually lost their blood lust and returned, bitterly disappointed, to Yokohama. There can be little doubt that they would have continued their murderous quest in Tokyo had Major Hatanaka succeeded in broadcasting his call to rebellion earlier that morning at the NHK studios.

At Atsugi Air Base, Imperial Navy Captain Yasuna Kozono had heard the early-morning NHK announcement that the Emperor's rescript would be broadcast at noon. Since before dawn, he had been preparing his air groups for an attack on the American Third Fleet, which had now been positively sighted prowling just beyond the normal combat radius of most of his planes. This meant that the aircraft could carry only enough fuel for a one-way flight, which would transform the entire attack into a mass kamikaze mission.

Despite the rumors that had circulated wildly in the past two days, the NHK announcement that the Emperor had signed "a rescript," which would be broadcast to the nation at noon, was the first firm indication Kozono had received that decisive action was pending. But that morning's NHK broadcast had not even hinted at the nature of the Imperial Rescript.

Some of the younger pilots were already speculating that His Majesty would command the entire nation to rise up against the Allies and to continue the war through the Ketsu-go. On this base, as elsewhere in the nation, there were even men who believed the Imperial Rescript would announce that Japan had dropped an atomic bomb on Washington.

Captain Kozono canceled the early strikes. He would wait until noon, then decide if the 302nd Air Corps would be forced to defy their Emperor to help save the *kokutai* through massive kamikaze attacks on the Allied fleet.[29]

While the Empire of Japan braced itself to hear the Imperial Rescript, officials at the Palace prepared a ruse to deliver the recordings of the Imperial Rescript safely into NHK custody. The cardboard-wrapped pair of records labeled "Copy" was placed in an ornate lacquered box—one of only a handful of such precious objects to have survived the rampaging search of the rebel troops through the blacked-out Imperial Household Ministry. A chamberlain was given the cardboard-wrapped records labeled "Original," and he slipped them into a nondescript shoulder sack in which he normally carried his lunchbox. Both sets of recordings were brought together at the second-floor administrative office of the ministry where the Emperor had stood before the microphone the night before.

The separate sets of wax disks that the rebels had sought to destroy for much of the night left the Palace in two different cars. An Imperial Household Ministry sedan bearing His Majesty's chrysanthemum carried the "copy" set in its decorative box—accompanied by a Palace administrator named Motohiko Kakei, suitably dressed in court morning clothes—directly to the NHK studios. Meanwhile, Susumu Kato, another senior ministry official, dressed in the baggy trousers and puttees of a workingman, rode in a police car to a reserve underground NHK studio. No matter what tactic any lingering rebels might now attempt, it was likely the broadcast of the Imperial Rescript would proceed at noon.

Across Japan civilians and members of the Imperial armed forces had received their orders as to where to assemble to listen to the Imperial Rescript at noon. At the Imperial Navy's Oita Air Base on the Bungo Strait on Kyushu, Vice Admiral Matome Ugaki faced the same dilemma as Captain Kozono at Atsugi. Ugaki, too, had heard the NHK morning broadcast alerting the nation to await the transmission of the Imperial Rescript at noon. He delayed plans for launching a massive daylight kamikaze mission on the American fleet offshore and south toward Okinawa.

At 4:05 P.M. Eastern War Time (daylight saving time plus one hour) (5:05 A.M. on August 15 in Tokyo) in Washington, Secretary of State James F. Byrnes called the American legation in Bern, Switzerland, to confirm a Magic radio intercept that the Japanese government had finally sent their surrender message. (This was the radiogram that Japanese Vice Minister of Foreign Affairs Shunichi Matsumoto had ordered transmitted just after the Imperial Rescript was signed at 11:00 P.M. Tokyo time on August 14.) The answer was positive. Even as Byrnes spoke, the Swiss government was preparing to cable the official Japanese diplomatic note to its own legation in Washington.

Byrnes immediately telephoned President Truman. In typically pragmatic Missouri fashion, Truman chose to wait to see the note itself before announcing to the world that the long war had finally ended. But he did agree to schedule a press conference for 7:00 P.M. on that hot Tuesday evening of August 14, 1945.

Just before 6 P.M., the Swiss chargé d'affaires, Max Grassli— after having had his car stopped by a traffic policeman for making an illegal U-turn on Connecticut Avenue— delivered the Japanese note to Secretary of State Byrnes. The key statement was "His Majesty the Emperor has issued an Imperial Rescript regarding acceptance of the provisions of the Potsdam Declaration." The note continued, stating that the Emperor was prepared "to ensure the signature by his Government and the Imperial General Headquarters of the necessary terms for carrying out the provisions of the Potsdam declaration." Hirohito, the note added, was prepared to command all Imperial armed forces wherever located "to cease active operations, to surrender arms" and to await the orders of the Supreme Commander of the Allied Forces.

Harry Truman was satisfied. At 7 P.M., he stood behind his desk in the Oval Office and read the White House correspondents a brief note:

"I have received this afternoon a message from the Japanese Government in reply to the message forwarded to that Government by the Secretary of State on August eleventh. I deem this reply a full acceptance of the

Potsdam Declaration which specifies the unconditional surrender of Japan. In the reply there is no qualification.

"Arrangements are now being made for the formal signing of the surrender terms at the earliest possible moment."[30]

The newsmen rushed from the Oval Office to the telephone banks in the pressroom. Within minutes, radio announcers were interrupting scheduled programming around the world. Teletype machines at newspaper city desks chimed with the rarely heard double sequence of five bells proclaiming an incoming story of the highest priority. The Japanese had surrendered. The war was over.

The celebrations began.

It was just after 8 A.M. in Tokyo on August 15, 1945.

Due to a mix-up in orders, a company of troops attached to Eastern District Army headquarters had not reached the NHK studios to guard the building from possible further rebel intrusion—the captain in charge had been given the wrong address. Finally, around 11 A.M., the soldiers loyal to General Tanaka and the Emperor ringed the building, steel helmets in place, bayonets gleaming on their Arisaka rifles.

While these soldiers secured the NHK Building, the rebels were still attempting to spread sedition. Major Hatanaka drove a motorcycle and Lt. Colonel Shiizaki galloped his chestnut stallion across the wide Palace Plaza near the Double Bridge, on which crowds were gathering to hear the Imperial Rescript over loudspeakers erected on poles. The two rebels showered the people with leaflets. But these papers were far different from any dropped by the American airplanes. These were the words they had hoped War Minister Anami himself would have read to the Empire in place of the Imperial Rescript:

"We, officers of the Imperial Japanese Army, who, this morning of August 15th, 1945, have risen up in arms, declare to all officers and soldiers of the Armed Forces and to the Japanese people:

"That our intention is to protect the Emperor and to preserve the national polity despite the designs of the enemy;

"That our prime concern is neither victory nor defeat; nor are we motivated by selfish interest;

"That we are ready to live, or die, for the sole just and righteous cause of national loyalty; and

"That we devoutly pray that the Japanese people and the members of the Armed forces will appreciate the significance of our actions and join us to fight for the preservation of our country and the elimination of the traitors around the Emperor, thus confounding the schemes of the enemy."[31]

When they had no more leaflets, the two rebels met in a cool, shady beechwood grove at the far side of the plaza. Major Kenji Hatanaka sat down and raised the pistol with which he had murdered Lt. General Mori and used to threaten unsuccessfully the NHK broadcasting staff. Hatanaka put the muzzle of the pistol against his forehead and fired. Beside him, Lt. Colonel Jiro Shiizaki knelt toward the Palace, unbuttoned his uniform blouse, and slashed open his belly with a short sword, making the ritual cuts of seppuku. He delivered his own coup de grâce by shooting himself in the head.[32]

Both men died facing the Palace, as penitents, spilling their blood onto the naked earth. It was 11:10 A.M.

On the parade ground outside Imperial Guards Division headquarters, Major Hidemasa Koga, Hatanaka and Shiizaki's close associate, knelt in the hot morning sun. As with his comrades, it was Koga's time to accept defeat. He slashed open his belly, facing the Emperor's quarters in the Gobunko.

(Two days later at the Air Academy, Captain Shigetaro Uehara shot himself on the grass margin beside a runway. On August 25, 1945, Eastern District Army Commander General Shizuichi Tanaka also shot himself, apparently out of mixed remorse that his command had neither been able to defend Tokyo from B-29 attacks nor stop the rebels from penetrating the sanctity of the Imperial Palace.)

Near dawn, *The Boomerang* had flown beneath a broken cloud deck, which made it impossible for Tony Cosola to take early-morning star sights. But he was an adept time-and-distance dead-reckoning navigator, and he also had backup from Rich Ginster's radar returns from the string of volcano islets east of their track.

"Estimate Iwo ninety-seven miles, Carl," Cosola said. "About thirty-four minutes."

Carl Schahrer was minding the autopilot, but everybody else was either sound asleep or catnapping. The crew had been flying for twelve hours, and no one had gotten much real sleep since the Japanese peace overtures had begun on August 10.

Schahrer leaned back in his seat and called to flight engineer Hank Gorder, "Are we going to have to set down at Iwo?"

Gorder finished his latest fuel calculation and put aside his slide rule. "We won't have much of a fuel reserve left at Northwest Field, but the cruise control's good right now. With that old wing and a prayer, we'll make it."

Schahrer nodded and grinned. "Good, Hank. We'll take her home."

Forty minutes later, *The Boomerang* was nearing Iwo Jima, and Hank Gorder reported that all four engines were still running well and that gas remained "in the green."

Having caught up on some sleep through several short naps, Jim Smith tuned his big Collins receiver to Radio Saipan, the U.S. armed forces' most powerful station in the Marianas. He knew that any official bulletins on the surrender would be announced first over that station.

Smith climbed up into his combat position beneath the tunnel astrodome. An incredibly beautiful sunrise spread across the eastern sky. The Pacific below was smooth and soft blue, absolutely peaceful. He yawned deeply and worked his stiff limbs. He had never seen the ocean this pleasant shade of blue, the surface so tranquil.

The war has to be over now, he thought. This had to be it. None of them could fly another mission and operate at the demanding level of proficiency needed for survival. They were just too spent, physically and emotionally.

The Boomerang was passing Iwo Jima at 0646 hours. Still perched beneath the astrodome, Smith could see small gleaming B-29Bs circling below to make emergency landings on the island. Either they had battle damage or were short of gas—probably the latter. (Thirteen of the Wing's bombers were forced to land at Iwo Jima on the morning of August 15, 1945.)

He slid out of the tunnel and moved around the forward bulkhead to stand beside Hank Gorder. Just as Smith reached the flight engineer, Carl Schahrer again asked Gorder, "Hank, are you *sure* about our gas?"

Gorder tapped the fuel gauges to make sure they were not stuck. Then he consulted his mission notes. "We've used 4,240 out of 6,785 gallons, Carl. That doesn't give us much of a gas reserve at all. But in theory, with good cruise control, we should make Northwest."

Smith knew that they all had to trust Hank and Carl on this one. Iwo's single thinly paved runway was lumpy and pocked with cave-ins that the engineers had a hard time keeping filled due to the rain-sodden volcanic-ash substrate. No one wanted to land there—or to take off again—unless it was a true emergency.

"Well," Schahrer said, "we'll take her home."

Smith drank some still-warm coffee from the thermos and buckled himself back into the radio operator's seat. He fine-tuned the Radio Saipan frequency through the endless warbling of the Japanese jamming. But it was hard to concentrate. All he could think of was the two-ounce shot of booze at the debriefing. And today he would even clomp over to the muddy showers for a good scrub-down before falling on his air mattress for twelve hours of untroubled sleep.

But before they reached the base, they still had almost four hours of Pacific Ocean to cross.

0814 Hours Marianas time (Tokyo time plus one hour). Jim Smith was growing drowsy again when a strong voice message exploded over the Radio Saipan frequency. It was a relay of a civilian broadcast from San Francisco announcing Japan's surrender, repeating the phrases President Truman had delivered to the White House correspondents. But the announcer ended with his own words: "This, ladies and gentlemen, is the end of World War Two."

The bulletin was repeated again and again. Smith turned the intercom switch to the "Liaison" position, which allowed the entire crew to hear the incredible message. Suddenly, all the crew's earphones were filled with whoops and bellows of unrestrained, exploding joy. No one thought of sleep now.

Carl Schahrer, normally the most conservative of pilots, rolled and dipped *The Boomerang* in a series of wild "cowboy" maneuvers.

"It's stateside, gang," Smith yelled.

Even louder laughter echoed in the earphones.

But at that moment the engines began to backfire, a sharp, nasty crackling that sounded like small-arms shots. No one was laughing now. Everyone stiffened, realizing that the engines' fuel mixture was dangerously lean.

"Can you do something, Hank?" Schahrer asked, his voice tense again.

"I just can't go to Full Rich, Carl," he said, "not until we're on Final."

All Hank Gorder could do was advance his fuel-mixture control from Lean to Rich on one engine at a time as it backfired so violently it seemed about to shake apart.

Now the dry pops from the engines had become a crushing weight on the crew's mind. It was as if they were being pummeled in the solar plexus. Some men prayed; others just waited stoically for the backfiring engine to roar to life again as Hank riched up the mixture, only to have the snapping backfire begin again when he was forced to lean the engine back down to save gas.

If Gorder was not successful, Schahrer would have to attempt to ditch the aircraft, even as one engine after another quit from fuel starvation—an impossibly challenging feat of airmanship.

The sudden exuberance at the news of the surrender had been completely smothered.

At 1105 hours Hank Gorder was still milking everything he could out of the cruise-control mixture, while retaining a minimum fuel reserve to go to Full Rich for Final Approach and landing, when the bomber could stall and crash if an engine failed. Tony Cosola estimated that *The Boomerang* had about thirty-seven minutes flying time remaining before reaching Northwest Field.

Although no one said anything, Jim Smith knew that, like him, the whole crew was mentally reviewing ditching procedures. The two scanners and the tail gunner would crawl through the tunnel and lie on the deck in the navigator's compartment, as would the navigator himself. Jim Smith would sit, his back cushioned by his parachute pack and one-man life raft, against the forward bulkhead. Rich Ginster, the radar operator, would swivel and lock his seat facing aft. On the flight deck, bombardier Dick Marshall would move aft to sit, braced against the center console between the two pilots.

Smith hunched on his seat, again trying to concentrate on ditching procedures as the engines backfired, all but starved of fuel.

The crew had all heard about B-29s ditching off Iwo or Tinian. Sometimes the bombers seemed to set down gently and float for five minutes or longer. Other ditchings weren't so pleasant. The planes slammed into the water, broke apart, and sank within a minute.

No one wanted to test what kind of ditching they themselves might encounter on this last day of the war.

"What's the fuel status going to be when you go to Full Rich, Hank?" Schahrer asked, his voice betraying some of the strain they were all feeling.

"It's going to be close" was all Gorder could answer.

At 1131 hours *The Boomerang* was about nine miles from Northwest Field and the crew had now assumed ditching positions. Schahrer had *The Boomerang* on a slow descending course toward the runway, hoping to nurse the last of the fuel reserves into the landing.

Jim Smith sat against the bulkhead and unsnapped his parachute harness. He could always buckle it quickly enough in the unlikely event that Carl ordered them to bail out. If they didn't make Northwest, it was going to be a ditching, and the chute harness would just get in the way of inflating his Mae West.

Beside him on the deck the two scanners and Sid Siegel lay, listening, as he did, to the backfiring engines. After a while everyone felt the plane bank and settle onto a new course.

"Downwind," Carl told his crew. "We're in the pattern, about to turn onto Final."

"Carl," Hank Gorder said, "I'm going to Full Rich mixture now, but I think you ought to know that we could run out of gas on Final Approach. That's how tight the fuel is."

"Thanks," Carl said, his voice once again calm and determined. "I understand." The plane banked again. "Turning onto Final."

He was nursing his throttles and waiting to call out orders to Waltershausen for full flaps and landing gear until he was sure *The Boomerang* was going to clear the 500-foot cliff ahead.

Jim Smith and the crewmen jammed into the compartments around him did not have to be reminded of what could happen if the fuel was exhausted and the engines began to choke and die just then. The huge plane flew poorly on fewer than four engines. And if Schahrer was forced to try gliding now, they would smash into that rock wall ahead.

Schahrer issued a series of precise commands. Waltershausen dropped flaps and landing gear. The bomber seemed to shudder in the air as the airspeed bled off. The soft blue Pacific flashed by, then the chalk-white face of the limestone cliff.

They were over the end of the runway. Schahrer eased back his throttles and the main gear squealed against the asphalt. As they rolled out toward their hardstand, Number 3 engine coughed and sputtered to a stop, completely deprived of fuel. Using the throttles of the three good engines and manipulating the brakes expertly, Schahrer trundled the huge aircraft onto the asphalt hardstand.

As soon as they came to a stop and the engines were shut down, Tony Cosola unbuckled and went up to the flight deck with his mission notes. "What's the time and distance, Tony?" Schahrer asked.

"Three thousand seven hundred and fifty miles, Carl," Cosola said, glancing at his pad. "Sixteen hours, fifty minutes. A helluva long ride."

Carl grinned widely at his friend and tiredly replied, "Yep."

The Boomerang had just completed the longest nonstop combat mission of the war.

The unrestrained joy the crew had felt on hearing the surrender broadcast came flooding back. Everyone was talking at once; the plane was again loud with laughter.

There was a group of uniformed war correspondents and newsreel cameramen gathered around *The Boomerang* as the crew climbed down the nosewheel ladder and stepped onto the hardstand. The hand-cranked cameras whirred and flashbulbs popped. A red-haired older guy thrust a microphone at Carl.

"How does it feel to have flown the last mission of the war, Lieutenant?"

Schahrer grinned broadly again, happy to cooperate. "Well," he said, "I thought we'd flown our last mission after coming back from Amagasaki on August tenth, but I was wrong. The way things are going these days, it wouldn't surprise me if we had to fly another one."

Jim Smith stood exhausted in the heavy midday sun, trying to grasp the true meaning of this mission. Carl had been joking, of course. The war was over. Smith, still a few days short of his twenty-first birthday, would be going home alive.

At the Imperial Palace that stifling Wednesday morning, an exhausted Premier Kantaro Suzuki, who had fled his bed at dawn, pursued by the murderous rebels from Yokohama, now prepared to submit his cabinet's resignation at a plenary session of the Emperor's Privy Council. The old man had done his duty. Since taking charge of the government in April, he had somehow managed to lead the country from war to peace. Others would have to lead Japan into the bewildering world where the guns were finally silent and no bombs fell.

(Two days later, following the recommendation of Marquis Kido and Kiichiro Hiranuma, President of the Privy Seal, the Emperor appointed Prince Higashikuni Prime Minister. This noble had deep connections to the Imperial family through both blood and marriage. He was untainted by politics, and certainly had never flirted with the ultranationalist beliefs of the militarists. Further, the selection of the Prince served notice to the Allies who would soon arrive as an occupying power that the *kokutai* was a thriving institution with which they would have to deal.[33])

Across the Home Islands of Japan and throughout Asia where the Imperial Japanese armed forces flew the banner of the Rising Sun, tens of millions paused at noon to listen to the broadcast of the Imperial Rescript. Chief of Staff General Yoshijiro Umezu had assembled scores of staff officers at Imperial Army Headquarters. Many had just come from passing before the flag-draped bier of War Minister Korechika Anami, who, they believed, had committed seppuku rather than hear this broadcast.

In an underground chamber beside the Gobunko air-raid shelter, the Emperor sat next to a huge, varnished prewar RCA radio that aides had placed there for him to listen to his own words.

Veteran NHK announcer Nobukata Wada, who had brought the nation news of so many victories early in the war, now spoke again. "A broadcast of the highest importance," Wada said, "is about to be made. All listeners will please rise."[34]

After pausing for the unseen millions to come to their feet, Wada continued, "His Majesty, the Emperor, will now read his Imperial Rescript to the people of Japan. We respectfully transmit his voice." Engineers cued in the reverent strains of the Japanese national anthem, "Kimigayo." Then they delicately placed the playback arm on the spinning black disk.

"To Our good and loyal subjects," Hirohito began. "After pondering deeply the general trends of the world and actual conditions in Our Empire today, We have decided to effect a settlement of the present situation by resorting to an extraordinary measure."

At military bases across Japan, officers and men listened with mixed shock and grief. For the first time, they heard the actual voice of a living god, His Majesty the Emperor, who commanded them to join him in "enduring the unendurable and suffering what is insufferable." The Emperor also commanded them to "beware most strictly of any outbursts of emotion which may engender needless complications, or any fraternal contention and strife which may create confusion, lead ye astray and cause ye to lose the confidence of the world."

Although Imperial Navy Captain Kozono and a few other commanders at Atsugi Air Base would be able to muster a handful of die-hard supporters willing to continue the war in defiance of the Emperor's explicit instructions, the broadcast of the Imperial Rescript had effectively undercut the fighting spirit of Japan's armed forces.

At the Imperial Japanese Navy air base near Oita on Kyushu, Vice Admiral Matome Ugaki faced a dilemma. That morning, he had perhaps hundreds of young pilots willing to volunteer for kamikaze missions. But, after hearing the Emperor's words broadcast in the Imperial Rescript, the fighting spirit had dissolved. A number of flight and squadron leaders approached Ugaki, reminding him that His Majesty had just called on the nation to bear the unbearable as he himself was and to lay down their arms. Ugaki had to cancel the mass kamikaze attack on Okinawa.[35]

Discontent was still widespread, but overt action was not.

The situation would not have been the same had Major Hatanaka and his comrades been able to destroy the recordings of the Imperial Rescript, to hold the Emperor prisoner in the Gobunko, and to make sure the inflammatory message they had printed on their leaflets was broadcast—preferably by the leader of Japan's military government, War Minister Anami himself.

But the plot *had* failed, ultimately due to the long blackout in Tokyo. Japan was forced to endure disgraceful defeat. In so doing, however, the Empire that had caused so much bloodshed and agony throughout Asia and the Pacific was eventually able to return to the ranks of peaceful nations.

PART IV

A VERY NEAR THING

THE MIGHT-HAVE-BEENS

If there had actually been a coup d'état, the peace negotiations would

have been blown sky-high, but fortunately, we were spared such a development.[1]

—FOREIGN MINISTER SHIGENORI TOGO

History is not merely what happened; it is what happened in the

context of what might have happened. Therefore it must incorporate,

as a necessary element, the alternatives, the might-have-beens.[2]

—PROFESSOR HUGH TREVOR-ROPER; REGIUS PROFESSOR
OF MODERN HISTORY; OXFORD UNIVERSITY, 1980

IT WAS A VERY NEAR THING," historian Samuel Eliot Morison states, describing the final day of World War II. "That night [August 14, 1945] a military plot to seize the Emperor and impound his recording of the Imperial Rescript (which was to be broadcast on the 15th) was narrowly averted." Morison continues that, had the rebellious Japanese military succeeded in seizing power, "the war would have resumed with the Allies feeling that the Japanese were hopelessly treacherous, and with a savagery on both sides that is painful to contemplate."[3]

Is Morison's view worthy of consideration? Definitely.

History is the chronicle and interpretation of events known to have occurred. Speculative history is logical conjecture on events that *could* have occurred if circumstances had been different. The discipline has become quite developed, with historians exploring such themes as:

What if Xerxes' triremes had broken the fragile line of Greek vessels at the Battle of Salamis in 480 B.C.? The Classical Age of Greece would not have flourished to cast its long shadow over Rome, which, in turn, stood as the foundation of contemporary Western civilization.[4]

What if the Spanish Armada had not foundered but had instead successfully invaded and conquered Elizabethan England? Would all of North America have become a domain of Spain?

What if Napoleon's Grande Armée had held Moscow and western Russia in 1812 and not retreated through the decimating blizzards? Would Imperial France have continued unchecked as continental Europe's dominant power? If so, for how long? And what would have been the impact of this on the industrial revolution and the future history of Russia?

Historical speculation has always been a fascinating exercise.

And it is equally absorbing to surmise what *might* have happened if certain crucial, interrelated events had occurred, beginning on the night of August 14–15, 1945:

Suppose Major Hatanaka, Lt. Colonel Shiizaki, and their fellow conspirators had succeeded in their desperate plot to destroy the recordings of the Imperial Rescript, hold the Emperor prisoner in the Gobunko, issue orders in his name, and spark a much wider rebellion in the Japanese armed forces.

Imagine that rebellion had sparked martial law and the establishment of a military government, perhaps led by War Minister Anami, who did not commit seppuku but instead finally reached the decision to take command of the rebel forces.

What if the Japanese military launched the type of massive, "sharp" (kamikaze) blow against the Allied fleet off Honshu that General Anami had considered on the afternoon of August 14?

What if the United States had responded to this treachery with more atomic bombs, the first dropped on Tokyo itself?

How would this sequence of events have affected the combatant nations and, indeed, the people of the entire world?

It must be recalled that the Japanese diplomatic cable officially accepting the Potsdam Declaration, which Vice Minister of Foreign Affairs Shunichi Matsumoto had transmitted from Tokyo at 11 P.M. on August 14, 1945, reached President Harry Truman's desk just before 4 P.M. Eastern War Time on that same date (due to the thirteen-hour time difference). Truman announced the Japanese surrender in his White House office at 7 P.M. That was 8 A.M. on Wednesday, August 15, in Tokyo.

But, had the coup d'état succeeded, and had the rebels been able to rally the Imperial armed forces to revolt and to attack the enemy— following the instructions outlined in the leaflets Major Hatanaka and Lt. Colonel Shiizaki distributed as their last act—waves of kamikaze planes would have been striking the U.S. Third Fleet's Task Force 38 off Honshu and Allied ships at Okinawa at virtually the same moment President Truman announced that Japan had surrendered. As Morison suggests, the world would have judged the Japanese as "hopelessly treacherous."

And what would have been the upshot of such developments? Here it is appropriate to employ the "might-have-beens" that Hugh Trevor-Roper states are essential to placing events within the correct historical context.

First, is it reasonable to assume that the Japanese armed forces would have followed the rebels' call to arms? Again, it must be recalled that War Minister Anami's message of August 14 basically left the Imperial Army suspended, prepared to hear the command of the Emperor to surrender. But what if that command never came, and the millions of men in the Imperial forces spread across Asia heard instead an order issued in the Emperor's name to renew the attack against the enemy?

Certainly the Imperial armed forces (both Army and Navy) were not predisposed to end the war in defeat, demobilization, and Allied occupation. Soldiers, sailors, and airmen were extremely restive. As noted above, Admiral Mitsumasa Yonai told Allied Intelligence after the war, referring to the potential for rebellion in the Navy (especially among kamikaze squadrons), "During my long career as Navy Minister, I probably never worried so much as I did during the period from the 14th to about the 23rd of that month [August 1945]."[5]

And the threat of a mass kamikaze attack on the Third Fleet off the Home Islands was especially grave on the morning and afternoon of August 15. Even though many Imperial Army aircraft had been grounded and drained of fuel, a spirited call to defend the homeland would have seen hundreds of these disarmed planes (some of which had already had their propellers removed) quickly prepared once more for combat—had the Imperial Rescript not been broadcast and in its place a false order issued in the Emperor's name to attack the enemy.

And how successful would this combined Army-Navy kamikaze attack have been? There is operational success and psychological victory. Before the broadcast of the Imperial Rescript, at the Imperial Navy's Atsugi Air Base alone, Captain Yasuna Kozono probably could have mustered six to eight hundred kamikaze planes. Several hundred more would have come from other Navy bases following a general appeal for the armed forces to rise in revolt and defend the homeland.[6] The Army could have added at least 1,000 more from dispersed and hidden Honshu airstrips.

However, even though Captain Kozono remained intransigent, refusing to disarm the one thousand warplanes of the 302nd Air Corps, he did not unleash them against the enemy fleet following the broadcast of the Imperial Rescript. The closest the Atsugi aviators came to open rebellion after noon on the fifteenth was to fly over Tokyo, showering the ruined city with leaflets railing against the traitorous "government officials and senior statesmen" who had enticed the Emperor to issue the rescript ending the war. But, the leaflets added, "there is no such thing as surrender in Japan. There is no surrender in the Imperial forces." The message assured the population that the aviators were certain of victory.[7]

Even though some would later dismiss Kozono as an ineffective zealot, one of the leaders of the Imperial Navy's kamikaze corps, Captain Mitsuo Fuchida, saw him as extremely dangerous and considered killing him because "his revolt could spark nationwide rebellion."[8]

When—following the Imperial Rescript broadcast—Captain Kozono failed to rally support from elsewhere in the Imperial Navy, he became increasingly agitated and depressed, and worked himself into a state of nervous exhaustion. Within forty-eight hours, he had lost contact with reality and had to be taken from the base in a straitjacket, ranting about the ultimate victory of the Yamato descendants of Amaterasu, the Sun Goddess.

On the night of August 15, like Kozono, Vice Admiral Matome Ugaki had been unable to rally the numbers of kamikaze pilots he had hoped for to deliver a significant strike against the Allied fleet anchored at Okinawa, 350 miles to the south. Again, like Kozono, the Emperor's words had undercut the Bushido spirit of the kamikazes. So Admiral Ugaki planned to lead a symbolic kamikaze raid of three D4Y4 Suisei dive-bombers. But as historian John Toland recounts, when Ugaki reached the Oita Air Base runway, he found eleven aircraft warmed up and waiting. This was not the hundreds he had wished for before the broadcast of the Imperial Rescript to deliver an overwhelming blow, but he hoped the eleven aircraft would make their numbers count.

"All so willing to die with me?" he asked his airmen.

They raised their hands in unison and shouted, "Banzai!"

The dive-bombers took off into the sunset and banked south toward Okinawa. Around 7:30 P.M., Oita Air Base received a report from Ugaki citing his intention to "crash into and destroy the conceited enemy in the true spirit of bushido."[9]

Then the planes simply disappeared.

There is no American record of having engaged enemy aircraft that night. It is possible that the Japanese suffered vertigo on this over-water flight and crashed into the sea. It is also possible that they missed their targets completely in the darkness and the impact of their aircraft went unnoticed amid the bright and noisy pyrotechnic celebration sweeping the U.S. fleet anchorage and the military camps on the nearby hills.

However, the final strike of the kamikaze campaign would have been much more decisive had Admiral Ugaki been able to muster several hundred pilots and launch them on a daylight mission against Okinawa.

Nearer the Home Islands, given that Admiral William F. Halsey's Third Fleet fast-carrier task force (supplemented by British aircraft carriers) was operating so close to Honshu between August 13 and 15, carriers such as the USS *Ticonderoga* and USS *Randolph* would have definitely been priority targets of any mass kamikaze attack beginning with the rebels' call for revolt on the morning of the fifteenth. There had already been sporadic but increasing kamikaze strikes against this task force.[10]

A truly mass kamikaze attack on the Third Fleet—which was always envisioned under the Ketsu-go battle plan—would have been possible because, even with the pounding American air strikes had inflicted on Japanese airfields, most of the kamikaze planes were dispersed, and they still numbered about 10,000 operational aircraft by mid-August.[11] Although there were not sufficient reserves of aviation gasoline for extended conventional combat operations, there were adequate fuel reserves for at least one mass kamikaze attack provided for under the Ketsu-go operational plan.

So it is reasonable to assume that enough kamikaze planes would have broken through the defenses of the Third Fleet and the Allied vessels anchored at Okinawa to have inflicted heavy casualties, probably as grave as those suffered during earlier kamikaze campaigns. It is also possible that these casualties—especially given the presence of the large carriers whose flight and hangar decks were crowded with fueled and armed aircraft—could have reached a combined total approaching the more than 2,000 U.S. servicemen killed in action during the Japanese attack on Pearl Harbor in December 1941.

The kamikaze attack force, of course, would have suffered crippling losses en route to their targets. But probably enough aircraft would have struck those targets to justify these losses to the Japanese military who wanted to prolong the war.

And it is more than likely that the kamikaze campaign would have been extended on a smaller scale elsewhere, employing aircraft in Japanese-occupied territory overseas. In Indochina, for example, Lt. General Yuitsu Tsuchihashi, commander of the 38th Imperial Army, had at least 250 aircraft ranging from obsolete trainers, to small amphibians, to a handful of first-line fighters and fighter-bombers. Due to fuel shortages, these planes had been grounded for most of 1945. But had General Tsuchihashi received a forged order to launch his remaining aircraft on kamikaze strikes against the Allied fleet in the South China Sea, there is little doubt that he would have complied, using the last of his stockpiled fuel. In a similar manner, Japanese commanders elsewhere in Southeast Asia would have obeyed orders to throw the last of their aircraft into a kamikaze Armageddon.[12]

But would all the thousands of available trained conventional and kamikaze pilots have volunteered to die in order to inflict heavy losses on the enemy? There is persuasive evidence that the fighting spirit was seeping out of the kamikaze corps by mid-August 1945. The broadcast of the Imperial Rescript ending the war no doubt came as a welcome reprieve to many young Japanese pilots. However, the corollary to this is that a direct appeal from "the Emperor" (i.e., rebellious officers acting in the Emperor's name) might well have rekindled flagging devotion among the members of the kamikaze corps. The result would have been an unexpected wave of suicide attacks, launched not only from the Home Islands but also from bases on the Chinese mainland, Formosa, Indochina, Malaya, and the Netherlands East Indies. Even hours after the broadcast of the Imperial Rescript, Army General Staff in Tokyo had to order combined Army air and Navy air forces on Formosa to cease "positive action" (including kamikaze attacks) against Okinawa.[13] Had rebel orders instead reached these air units, they would have launched large-scale missions against the Allied fleet at Buckner Bay and air bases on the island.

The Imperial Army 13th Air Division in China, for example, had a standing order by August 1945: "Every opportunity will be taken to attack enemy transport convoys at sea, and should the opportunity arise, special attack planes will be used to attack enemy aircraft carriers."[14] It would not have taken much persuasion to convince the commanders of this powerful unit that the attack orders coming from Tokyo (in lieu of the Imperial Rescript) were legitimate.

Even without the hypothetical military rebellion of the might-have-been scenario, the Japanese remained a threat to Allied forces. On August 17 and again on August 18, Japanese radar-controlled flak and fighters attacked four of the new B-32 bombers of the Far Eastern Air Forces flying reconnaissance missions over Tokyo. During the second attack, an American crewman was killed and two Imperial Navy Zero fighters from Atsugi Air Base destroyed.[15] Fearing just such unauthorized attacks on Allied aircraft and vessels, the Imperial Navy had issued General Order No. 48 on August 16. The message was a clear command to cease hostilities.

Transmitted to all Imperial Navy regional commanders, the order required them to "halt hostile actions at once."[16]

To make sure that the armed forces did in fact honor the cease-fire after hearing the broadcast of the Imperial Rescript by shortwave radio or receiving the text of the document by radio-teletype, the Emperor felt obliged on August 17 to issue a separate "Rescript to Soldiers and Sailors" serving in the Home Islands and overseas. Addressing "Our beloved offi cers and men of the armed forces" who had fought gallantly on "barren fields and on the raging ocean," Hirohito expressed his deep appreciation. But "the Soviet Union has now entered the war, and in view of the state of affairs both here and abroad, We feel that the prolongation of the struggle will merely serve to further the evil and may eventually result in the loss of the very foundation on which Our Empire exists. Therefore, in spite of the fact that the fighting spirit of the Imperial Army and Navy is still high, we hereupon intend to negotiate a peace [with the Allies] for the sake of maintaining our glorious national polity."

Once more, Hirohito did not use the word *surrender*. To reinforce this second rescript, the Emperor dispatched three members of the Imperial Family—Prince Takeda, Prince Asaka, and Prince Kaiin—to Manchuria, central China, and the southwestern Pacific respectively, to make sure the regional commanders-in-chief carried out the Imperial cease-fire order. As Navy Minister Admiral Mitsumasa Yonai later recounted, this was a prudent action because Imperial headquarters in Tokyo found it "difficult to hold down front-line forces who were all 'raring to go.'"[17]

Still, Hirohito felt the need to again directly address the Imperial armed forces, especially those stationed overseas. Beginning this third message "To Our trusted soldiers and sailors on the occasion of the demobilization of the Imperial Army and Navy," he expressed his "fervent wish" that surrender be conducted rapidly and systematically, and explicitly ordered the members of the armed forces to comply with his wishes. Even as he sent this message, isolated bands of fanatics, including a few kamikaze pilots from Atsugi and other air bases, threatened to attack the Allied fleet offshore. Such unrest also spread among ultranationalist paramilitary student groups and restive bands of soldiers who seized radio stations to urge the people to resist surrender.[18]

It goes without saying that the second Imperial Rescript to the military, the explicit Imperial cease-fire order, and the delegations of Imperial princes (who did convince the regional commanders to lay down their arms) would not have happened had rebel forces in Tokyo succeeded in holding the Emperor incommunicado, even for a few days, and issuing false orders in his name to launch massive attacks on the Allies near the Home Islands and overseas.

But how real were the conspirators' chances of success? Again, the record is not clear. The role that War Minister Anami played is murky. It is definite, however, that he flirted with the rebellion for several crucial days and that he protected the conspirators from preventive detention. On the night of the Palace coup, Anami delayed his final act of seppuku for an inordinate time, and then completed the suicide only after the revolt had failed (even though his brother-in-law, Lt. Colonel Masahiko Takeshita, later reported that General Anami first plunged the sword before learning that the coup had unraveled).

But, in Trevor-Roper's spirit of historical speculation, let us assume that Anami was sitting on the fence during the long hours of that night, drinking his sake, waiting to see what would develop within the walls of the Imperial Palace. Would the rebels succeed, and would they call on him to unify the country, save the honor of the military, and lead the country through the cleansing fire of the Ketsu-go? It should be remembered that only the day before—even after the Emperor had ordered the cabinet to prepare the surrender rescript—Anami had suggested to his adjutant, Major Hayashi, that Army and Navy aircraft attack the U.S. Third Fleet cruising offshore. Given War Minister Anami's actions in the week before his death, it is reasonable to assume that he would have been capable of declaring martial law, assuming the constitutional powers granted him as War Minister in such an emergency, and leading a military government.[19]

Continuing to follow the line of speculative history, one can surmise what the reaction in Washington would have been had mass waves of kamikazes risen from their hidden airstrips across Honshu and Kyushu to strike the Allied fleet offshore and to attack the dense ranks of new U.S. air bases on Okinawa, employing the reserves of kamikaze aircraft on Formosa. The shock of this assault would have been heightened had the Japanese unleashed smaller but even less expected aerial attacks from Indochina, Malaya, and the Netherlands East Indies. The overall impact of such aggressive action—which, after all, was exactly what War Minister Anami had contemplated as late as August 14—coming several hours *after* the official Japanese surrender message reached Washington would have been confirmation of the lingering American suspicion that the enemy never seriously intended to capitulate.

That suspicion had been partly engendered by a number of Ultra intercepts in the final days of hostility, between the headquarters of the Imperial armed forces in Tokyo and regional commands, that exhorted the overseas forces to "prosecute our holy war to the last man," among other similar inflexible instructions.[20] So, even after War Minister Anami's August 14 instruction to the forces, a widespread attack coming after the Japanese foreign ministry had officially announced that the country had surrendered would have been viewed as a form of treachery tantamount to the bombing of Pearl Harbor.

There is no doubt that American commanders were wary of such Japanese deceit. On August 15, 1945, Admiral Chester Nimitz, Commander-in-Chief, Pacific, ordered Admiral William F. Halsey to suspend his Third Fleet's offensive operations but to maintain a defensive posture "at highest level and beware of treachery or last moment attacks by enemy forces or individuals."[21] In fact, Halsey's carrier aircraft were strafing and bombing in the Tokyo area between dawn and 7:25 A.M. when the

American planes received the order to return to their ships because Washington had just learned that the surrender message was forthcoming via Swiss diplomatic channels. This final naval aviation combat action placed the American carriers—maneuvering to recover their short-range fighter-bombers—close enough inshore to make them vulnerable to mass kamikaze attack.

The handful of four-engine Renzan heavy bombers and more numerous GM-4 "Betty" twin-engine bombers at Atsugi and other bases had the range to strike all the way south to Okinawa and even the crowded airfields on Tinian, Saipan, and Guam. Again, casualties among the Japanese attack force would have been disastrous, but the shock of their attack would have been a severe blow to Allied morale, which had anticipated Japan's imminent collapse since the first exchange of diplomatic messages concerning acceptance of the Potsdam Declaration had begun on August 10.

How would the United States, as the leader of the alliance, have reacted? First and most obviously, the surviving U.S. Third Fleet ships would have steamed out of effective kamikaze range, as would have other Allied warships elsewhere in the Pacific. Around-the-clock bombing of the Home Islands by both the B-29s of the Strategic Air Forces and the bombers of General Kenney's Far Eastern Air Forces—that is, all the aircraft surviving the hypothetical mass kamikaze attacks—would have resumed. And it is doubtful that there would have been much mercy shown by preparing targeted cities with leaflets warning the population of imminent attack, as had been the case on many targets in the final days of the war.

The big question, of course, is whether the United States would have now resorted to using more atomic bombs, both to punish the Japanese for their treachery and to batter them into final surrender. Given his view of the weapon, it seems certain that President Harry Truman would have resorted to the bomb to bring the war to a conclusion as quickly as possible. It must be remembered that Truman had told the visiting Duke of Windsor on August 14 that he was planning to drop a third atomic bomb—this one on Tokyo—only a few hours before the surrender message finally reached the Oval Office on August 14, 1945.[22]

Following the treacherous Japanese reversal of their surrender decision, Truman would have proceeded with that plan. The plutonium core of the third Fat Man–type bomb had been ready for delivery to Tinian by

C-54 transport as early as August 13. That material could have been delivered and the bomb quickly assembled—as had the Nagasaki Fat Man—by
August 18. The 509th Composite Group would have had a third bomb, and
there would have been more arriving for assembly on a regular basis as
the scientists and engineers at Los Alamos worked around the clock to produce them.[23]

But would Tokyo in fact have been the target for the third bomb?
That depends in part on the political pressures in the United States to exact
revenge. Had there been a general revolt among the Japanese armed forces
followed by the establishment of a military government (led, perhaps,
by War Minister Anami) that issued false and bellicose orders in the
Emperor's name, it definitely would have appeared to Washington that
Hirohito had resorted to his old, treacherous ways. The Emperor himself
would have appeared to sit at the center of evil, as would the die-hard militarists around him. Thus, even though General Carl Spaatz had earlier
judged Tokyo to be a poor target from a purely military perspective, the
Japanese capital—that is, the Imperial Palace (with the Emperor inside)
and the nearby Imperial armed forces headquarters—would have now
become important strategic targets. And, without question, striking Tokyo
and wiping out Hirohito and his generals would have answered Allied lust
for revenge after Japan's August 15 treachery.

But is it just empty conjecture to imagine that Truman would have
dropped more atomic bombs on Japan if the coup d'état had succeeded?
Although Stanford University professor Barton J. Bernstein faults the Truman administration for not immediately accepting Japan's diplomatic note
of August 10, which requested guarantees on the future of the *kokutai,*
Bernstein does note that during the "critical five-day period" between
August 10 and August 14, "Japanese militarists almost triumphed . . . [and]
had they regained control of the government and escalated demands, the
United States might well have used a third atomic bomb."[24] He based this
assumption on the proviso that militarists would have gained control of the
Japanese government and simply escalated demands (added new conditions) to the August 10 note. If that alone would have provoked a third
atomic bomb, what would the American response have been had the Japanese deceitfully attacked on August 15, following their apparent capitulation?

It is not unreasonably speculative to assume that Truman would have
continued using the atomic bomb. But Japanese air defenses would have
stiffened to a much-heightened alert posture, trying to prevent just such an

atomic bomb attack. Even though thousands of aircraft would have been expended in mass kamikaze attacks, a shrewd tactician such as War Minister Anami—assuming he headed the military government as well as commanded the Imperial armed forces—would have made sure Tokyo was strongly defended. However, the 509th Composite Group could well have overcome these defenses through high-altitude night bombing, relying on a combination of radar and aerial flares to designate the bomb's aiming point, probably the Imperial Palace itself.

Once Tokyo was bombed, Truman might have sought further vengeance—and appeased American public opinion—by dropping the next atomic bomb on the old Imperial capital of Kyoto. This would have gone a long way toward satisfying America's thirst for revenge.

But on a tactical and strategic level, the physical elimination of the Emperor and the highest officers in the military government might also have imposed practical problems in rapidly securing Japan's surrender. Already in the Imperial armed forces, there were advanced plans for extensive guerrilla warfare throughout the Home Islands as part of the Ketsu-go.[25] In a similar manner, the hundreds of thousands of troops preparing for the Decisive Battle on Kyushu would have retreated to their warrens of mountainous fortifications, which, given the terrain, would have been relatively resistant to attack from atomic bombs.

So the nuclear-weapon decapitation of Japan's civil and military leadership actually might have resulted in a largely disorganized, but still well-equipped, enemy force determined to defend the homeland. Of course, Anami and his staff could have escaped Tokyo and commanded the army in the Home Islands from a remote area.

This turn of events would have hardened Japanese resistance overseas, particularly in those parts of China and Southeast Asia where large military formations had not yet been subjected to Allied ground attack. In short, even if Tokyo, Kyoto, and large cities did suffer atomic attack, there would have been at least three million Japanese troops in the Home Islands and an equal number overseas prepared to continue the war. As Chief of Staff General George C. Marshall had planned, the use of atomic bombs would have now shifted to tactical targets in support of the long-planned Allied invasion of the Home Islands. Between September and December 1945, there would have been approximately twenty Nagasaki-type plutonium bombs, with a yield of 20 kilotons each, available to drop on the Japanese.[26] Again, however, if Japanese forces were widely dispersed in mountainous territory, the tactical value of these weapons would have been compromised.

But Truman would have been determined to continue using atomic weapons if they appeared to provide the Allies a tactical advantage in the planned invasion of the Japanese Home Islands. General Marshall and other military advisers had already convinced him that the atomic bomb would reduce American causalties. Truman believed until the end of his life that "dropping the bombs [on Hiroshima and Nagasaki] ended the war, saved lives."[27] He would have been even more persuaded that the use of atomic bombs was justified had the Palace coup succeeded and the Japanese established a military government determined to continue the war.

How would a successful coup, the subsequent mass kamikaze attacks, and the American response with nuclear weapons have affected the several hundred thousand Allied prisoners of war in Japanese captivity, both in the Home Islands and overseas? In the Home Islands and nearby Manchuria, the Japanese held approximately 65,000 Allied POWs, including about 15,000 Americans. On the eve of Japanese surrender, scores of Allied prisoners were dying daily, victims of malnutrition, illness, sadistic treatment, and outright execution.

For example, after the broadcast of the Imperial Rescript, Japanese officers near the industrial city of Fukuoka on Kyushu drove sixteen captured B-29 crewmen into the country. The Japanese forced the Americans to strip and then beheaded them one by one at the scene where they had massacred eight American prisoners a few days earlier. But this massacre was a minor affair compared to the wholesale beheading of more than fifty American airmen POWs carried out at the Osaka *kempeitai* headquarters after Japanese soldiers heard the broadcast of the Imperial Rescript.[28]

It was common knowledge among Allied prisoners that the Japanese planned to kill them all the moment invading enemy forces set foot on Japanese soil. One B-29 officer held prisoner in Tokyo, First Lieutenant Glenn McConnell (no relation to the co-author), recalls this Japanese threat: "We were told that if there was invasion we would be executed to simplify their problems."[29] Such threats were not the idle taunts of a few sadists but rather official Japanese policy. In March 1945, the War Ministry issued this policy statement to prison camp commandants: "Prisoners of war must be prevented by all means available from falling into enemy hands. . . . [But] they should be kept alive to the last wherever their labor is needed." Always meticulous in their staff work, the Japanese War Ministry's officers even delineated how prisoners were to be "destroyed individually or in groups . . . with mass bombing, poisonous smoke, poisons, drowning, decapitation, or whatever, dispose of them as the situation dictates."[30]

From this document, it is clear that the Japanese regarded enemy soldiers and airmen who surrendered as having relinquished their humanity and right to live. Surrender was so shameful in the tenets of Bushido that there were very few Japanese soldiers captured on the battlefields of the Pacific. And the Japanese had no compunction about working to death, starving, or butchering the Allied soldiers, sailors, marines, and airmen whom they captured. To the Japanese, these prisoners were men without honor, a soldier's most sacred attribute.

If Japan had entered the final cataclysmic phase of the war, with its remaining cities incinerated by atomic bombs and its armies dug in for a protracted struggle, it is doubtful the Japanese military would have found it necessary to keep any Allied prisoners of war alive. Already by mid-August 1945, 38 percent of the Americans Japan had captured were dead. Had the war continued, the remainder would have quickly followed.

Although the American Office of Strategic Services did not have an agent network in the Home Islands to report POW massacres, Ultra radio intercepts between Imperial headquarters and overseas commands would have revealed the extent of the atrocities. And in areas such as China and Manchuria, where the OSS and British Special Operations Executive did have espionage agents, Allied military intelligence would have quickly learned that the liquidation of prisoners of war was under way. At least outside the Home Islands, the American, British, and Australian forces would have undertaken risky Ranger, commando, and airborne-unit rescues, many of which would have suffered heavy casualties.

During that weird, hazardous interlude between the broadcast of the Imperial Rescript and the official surrender ceremony two weeks later, this fear that the Japanese would slaughter Allied POWs led to a number of daring rescue missions.

The OSS's Team Pigeon, commanded by a twenty-four-year-old airborne infantry temporary major named John Singlaub, was offered the chance to "volunteer" to parachute into a notorious Japanese camp at Bakli Bay on Hainan Island off China's southwest coast on August 25, 1945. Singlaub was a veteran of OSS combat behind Nazi lines in France in 1944.

He understood and accepted the risks involved: Should the Japanese at the camp refuse to recognize his authority, he and his men faced capture, interrogation under torture, and execution.

Singlaub and his eight men made up one of eight OSS POW rescue teams that were sent into China, Indochina, and Manchuria. They were all hastily organized, improvised operations—Singlaub gave his men impromptu parachute training while their C-47 transport was en route from Kunming in China to Hainan. When they jumped onto a field near the camp, they found that the Japanese either had not heard of the Imperial Rescript and the Emperor's surrender rescript to the armed forces, or had chosen to ignore these messages.

The hundreds of Australian, Dutch, and Indian prisoners of war at the Bakli Bay camp were all suffering from malnutrition and disease. Many had already been executed or had died as a result of brutality. Major Singlaub took charge and, almost by force of personality alone, cowed the Japanese into accepting his command authority. The field near the camp became a drop zone for desperately needed food and medical supplies. Soon American aircraft were landing to evacuate the most dangerously ill and starving Allied prisoners.[31]

(*The Boomerang* and hundreds of other Superforts of XXI Bomber Command dropped thousands of tons of food and medical supplies to Allied prisoners of war languishing in camps across Japan and Manchuria.)

Had the OSS prisoner rescue teams not performed their hazardous missions, the Japanese probably would have massacred or allowed to die an unknown number of POWs following the broadcast of the Imperial Rescript.

And had the Tokyo coup succeeded and the war entered a new and more vicious no-quarter stage, it is virtually certain that the Japanese would have murdered all the remaining Allied prisoners.

When the Japanese accepted the Allies' surrender terms on August 14 and the Imperial Rescript was broadcast on August 15, General Douglas MacArthur and Admiral Chester Nimitz's staffs were completing work on the Operation Olympic plan for the invasion of Kyushu, scheduled to begin on November 1, 1945. The Japanese capitulation, of course, caused that plan to be canceled. The grim estimates of casualties never had to be weighed against reality on the beaches and hills of the southernmost Home Island.

However, had the Japanese armed forces risen in revolt and toppled the civilian government, it is probable that the Olympic invasion would have proceeded, even had there not been mass kamikaze attacks on the American fleet off Honshu and around Okinawa. The landings no doubt would have been delayed, perhaps as long as six weeks, by the typhoon that swept north from Okinawa on October 9 with winds of more than 140 miles per hour—sinking or grounding a number of supply vessels staging for the invasion at the island's exposed anchorages. But the operation would have eventually proceeded.

Carrying out Olympic that autumn and the subsequent Operation Coronet assault on the Kanto Plain near Tokyo in March 1946 would have required an unprecedented number of Allied forces, principally American Army and Marine Corps ground troops. Almost 400,000 would have had to redeploy directly from the European Theater of Operations to the Pacific. Approximately 477,000 would have transitted from Europe through the United States for leave, retraining, and reequipping. Many of these ground and air units were composed of veterans who had seen more than their share of combat in Europe.[32] A large proportion of the men sent from the United States to Europe for garrison duty that summer had no combat experience, and most were young draftees a few months out of basic training.

And the soldiers and airmen transitting American bases from Europe en route to the Far East would have found a war-weary country, dissatisfied with the stagnant military situation in the Pacific and stringent wartime rationing. Labor unrest was growing. Even as workers struck the B-29 Wright-Cyclone engine plant in Cincinnati, the government was forced to take control of a B-29 tire plant in Detroit to keep the assembly line moving. In short, the nation was deeply apprehensive that the war in the Pacific would continue with the unacceptably high casualty rate our forces had suffered on Iwo Jima and Okinawa.

Issues of fairness toward men who had faced months and years of combat in units such as the 97th Infantry Division, the 20th Armored Division, and the groups of the 8th and 15th Air Force had to be weighed against those of unit cohesion. Some men who had accrued less combat time in Europe were discharged to seek civilian work, while men who had faced the enemy for longer periods were assigned to Olympic/Coronet forces to maintain these units' levels of critical skills and experience. The same situation, of course, prevailed in the Navy.

This difficult and complex issue became embroiled in a highly emotional and widely misunderstood demobilization and redeployment plan involving an intricate system of "points" that affected each man. Those waiting in European ports for troopships to take them to the Far East had no choice but to accept orders. But veteran combat units returning from the ETO and passing through the United States on their way to the Pacific became openly angry at the unfairness of their lot. As military historian John Ray Skates indicates, the veteran 95th Infantry Division, which had fought in Europe from June 1944 until VE-Day on May 7, 1945, was being retrained in Camp Shelby, Mississippi, in transit to the Far East to prepare for the Coronet invasion. Morale plummeted and insubordination rose as the departure date approached. Division Commander Major General Harry L. Twaddle later commented, "There was a continuing and growing opposition to being ordered to the Pacific. A very disturbing situation arose approaching open sedition and mutiny."[33] These conditions prevailed to a greater or lesser degree among the almost 900,000 members of the armed forces being reassigned from Europe to the Far East.

It is impossible to judge how this morale problem would have affected the combat performance of the redeployed units. But evidence suggests that the fighting spirit of the huge American forces was being stretched by August 1945. And, had the two invasions of the Home Islands gone ahead, the Americans would have faced the stubborn resistance of Japanese soldiers, sailors, and airmen as well as militia—determined to inflict maximum casualties on their enemy, as the Ketsu-go battle required. Further, even if the Japanese had already expended the bulk of their kamikaze aircraft during a military revolt, they still would have retained their thousands of suicide boats and Kaiten human torpedoes. The Japanese also had huge reserves of ammunition, as the Allies discovered after the war, so the Imperial armed forces could have fought a stubborn and protracted defensive action, falling back from one line of prepared fortifications to the next, just as they had on Okinawa, where Americans suffered the worst casualties of the war.

Therefore, it is safe to say that had Japan not surrendered when it did and had the Olympic invasion gone ahead, America and its Allies would have faced the most bloody and difficult period of the war. And similar problems would have confronted the Allies in their attempt to dislodge stubbornly resisting Japanese forces on an arc from Shanghai to the Solomon Islands. Already by August 1945, Australian forces fighting to capture the oil fields of Borneo were encountering increasingly fierce Japanese opposition. If none of the redundant Imperial surrender orders had reached these and other Japanese garrisons in Southeast Asia and the Southwest Pacific, U.S. Secretary of War Henry L. Stimson's fear that America would face "a score of bloody Iwo Jimas and Okinawas all across China and the New Netherlands" would have been realized.

One offshoot of a protracted war would have been the impact of that seemingly endless struggle on the people of the European colonies in the region. Great Britain, with hundreds of thousands of troops and airmen stationed on the Indian subcontinent, was in a strong position to attack Japanese forces occupying Malaya. However, the British plan to reconquer their colony, Operation Zipper, anticipated a large number of casualties, presenting a dilemma to the Labour government, given the prevailing war weariness in Great Britain in the summer of 1945, which was even deeper than that in the United States—as witnessed by the ouster of the Churchill government.

But France and Holland were even less militarily prepared to dislodge stubborn Japanese forces from Indochina and the East Indies, even though both war-ravaged countries needed the rubber, tea, tin, oil, and spices of these rich colonies.

The colonial powers faced another problem in 1945. During almost four years of Japanese occupation, the indigenous people of Southeast Asia had seen their white European colonial masters vanquished by Asian soldiers from Japan not so different from themselves. The myth of unassailable European superiority was destroyed when a farmer in Java, a rubber mill worker in Malaya, or a *cyclo* driver in Saigon witnessed a white soldier marching with his hands raised at the point of a Japanese bayonet.

Had the armies of the former colonial powers been forced to fight the Japanese in months of bloody combat to regain their lost territories, incipient but growing independence movements would only have been strengthened. There was a mood of boldness in the air, stretching from the Spice Islands to Hanoi. Following the Japanese surrender, when British troops occupied Java with the intention of holding the colony until Dutch troops and administrators could arrive from Europe, the local people rose in revolt. It was only when the British rearmed disciplined Japanese units and employed them against the local rebels on Java that the uprising was put down.

In French Indochina, where Japanese commanders intended to fight a suicidal last-ditch battle rather than surrender to the returning Europeans, a surprising number of people in what is now southern Vietnam developed pro-Japanese sentiments.[34] The issue of France's Indochina colonies was among the most pressing that General Charles de Gaulle presented during his first meeting with President Harry Truman in August 1945 in Washington the week after Japan capitulated.

Suffice it to say that the history of Southeast Asia would have been significantly different had the hundreds of thousands of well-armed and -equipped Japanese forces stationed there not been convinced to surrender, but had instead engaged in a protracted rearguard struggle against the Allies.

Another intriguing line of speculation concerns the increasingly precarious relations between the Soviet Union and the United States in the final weeks of the war.

By August 14, 1945, the Soviet Red Army was on its way to cutting Manchuria in half along the access of the Chinese Eastern Railway, thus separating the Japanese Kwantung Army into two unequal and isolated sections. Japanese resistance was fierce, with air commanders hurling kamikaze planes at Soviet armored columns passing through constricted valleys and gorges. Soviet forces on Sakhalin Island were advancing south, also against stubborn and mounting Japanese opposition.[35]

These Soviet operations followed almost to the letter agreements the Allies had reached earlier. To conduct their Far Eastern campaign, the Soviets had requested that the Allies provide them aircraft (the P-39 fighter-bomber, C-47 transports), trucks, food, and thousands of tons of gasoline. The Western Allies had complied.[36]

It was obvious by August 15, however, that the Soviet forces had become a juggernaut and that Red Army commanders had no intention of stopping their advance with a cease-fire in place, particularly the sweep south on Sakhalin Island. Their goal was to crush the fierce Japanese resistance, then to stage an amphibious assault on Hokkaido, the northernmost Home Island. Fighting continued throughout the last two weeks of August, with the Red Army branching out to attack the well-defended Japanese ports on the nearby Kuril Islands.[37]

The planned Red Army assault on Hokkaido was a flagrant breach of Allied agreements and confirmed the worst fear of American civilian and military leaders: The Soviet Union intended to seize a foothold on Japan, which it would parlay into a zone of occupation. After the long and bloody battle for Sakhalin and the Kurils, it did seem possible that the Russians were poised to accomplish this objective.

After the August 15 Japanese capitulation, there was little the United States could do militarily to prevent the Red Army from moving into northern Japan before significant U.S. occupation forces could arrive in Honshu.

But in a secret addendum to the Potsdam agreement, the Americans and the Russians had placed all of Hokkaido within the American zone, while granting the Soviet Union the occupation of Sakhalin Island. There was a proviso, however, that allowed the Allies to plan for military operations across the line separating the zones. This seemed to give the Red Army the justification it needed to move on Hokkaido and stake a claim to an occupation zone.

But on August 15 (U.S. date), President Truman cabled Stalin a copy of General MacArthur's specific orders on the occupation of Japan, which placed all of Hokkaido within the American zone. Stalin tried a countermove, offering to occupy northern Hokkaido in order to neutralize Japanese forces there once the Red Army had captured Sakhalin. Truman would not budge, and he forced the Soviets to abide by the Potsdam agreement they had signed. Meanwhile, the savage Japanese resistance on Sakhalin slowed the Soviet advance until August 29, when American occupation forces were already establishing their own foothold in southern Japan.[38]

Naturally, had Japanese resistance in one form or another continued in the southern Home Islands after August 15, the Soviets might well have advanced from Sakhalin into northern Hokkaido, and even farther south, perhaps to the burned-out ruins of the Nippon Oil Company refinery at Akita.

And had the war in the Pacific dragged on, exacerbated by growing friction between the Soviet Union and the western Allies, there might well have been unforeseen ramifications in the devastated countries of Western Europe. Most of the veteran combat units in the U.S. forces that had fought in Europe had lost their experienced troops through the point system or redeployment to the Pacific by June 1945. "Trained, experienced veterans were replaced overnight with green soldiers," historian John Ray Skates notes.[39] In the summer of 1945, the ostensibly combat-ready American regiments and divisions facing the Soviet Red Army across the Occupation

Zones' lines of demarcation in Germany, Austria, and Czechoslovakia were, in fact, "hollow," largely staffed by recruits, and facing chronic equipment and supply shortages because most of the tens of thousands of tanks and artillery pieces that had helped with the war against the Nazis were on their way to the Pacific to fight the Japanese.

Had the United States and its Western Allies become bogged down in a seemingly endless war—especially a bloody campaign to defeat the Japanese on their Home Islands—Stalin's Soviet Union might well have been tempted toward military adventures in the West. Despite the massive weight of the Red Army on the Far Eastern Front, Soviet forces in west and central Europe remained both numerically stronger and more experienced than their Western counterparts.

But Red Army tank divisions and artillery regiments did not represent Stalin's only assets in Europe. The anti-Nazi resistance movements in France, Italy, and the Low Countries often had communist leaders who answered directly to Moscow.[40] After the war, many of these former *partizans* became influential in labor unions, the press, and government. One of their favorite tactics was the general strike intended to destabilize bourgeois governments. Between 1945 and the start of the Marshall Plan recovery effort in 1947, the situation in western Europe was grave. Hunger was widespread, and industry and transport lay in heaps of charred brick and twisted steel. The Utopian dream of communism with food and employment for all offered promise to millions.

Had a Moscow-inspired "popular" uprising struck France, Italy, Belgium, or Holland during this period—and had American armed forces been bogged down still fighting the endless costly campaigns against the Japanese five or even six years after Pearl Harbor—the Red Army in Germany might well have been able to smash through the token Allied garrison force in western Europe and come to the aid of its guerrilla comrades on the streets of Paris or Rome.

In reality, of course, the United States did have the deterrent of the atomic bomb. The 509th Bomb Group, whose B-29s were armed with Fat Man-type weapons, was stationed in New Mexico after the Japanese surrender. The unit could have quickly deployed to old 8th Air Force bases in England to put its aircraft in range of the Soviet Union, a move the 509th did make in July 1949. But, had the Japanese not surrendered, and had the U.S. Strategic Air Forces expended all its limited stock of nuclear weapons against Japan in 1945 and 1946, America would not have been able to prevent Soviet aggression in Western Europe with the bomb. The nascent Cold War in Europe might have ignited into a full-blown conflagration.

None of these terrible scenarios was realized. The Imperial Rescript of Emperor Hirohito was broadcast at noon on Wednesday August 15, 1945, in Tokyo. With repeated further prodding from the throne, Japanese forces eventually did lay down their arms and surrender to the Allies.

Only decades after that humid August morning back at Northwest Field would Jim Smith begin to amass evidence that the 315th Bomb Wing's mission on the night of August 14–15, 1945, had been not only the last mission of World War II but the first of the Cold War.

And in the decades since then, Smith also began to assemble the startling connection between the blackout that the 315th Bomb Wing imposed on Tokyo and the failure of the attempted coup d'état.

On September 2, 1945, a delegation of Japanese military officers and civilian officials faced Allied officers on the deck of the battleship USS *Missouri*, anchored in Tokyo Bay, and signed the formal instruments of that surrender, ending the most costly conflict in history.

Army Chief of Staff General Yoshijiro Umezu signed for Imperial headquarters. Had it been possible to follow the protocols of rank, this shameful task would have fallen to War Minister Korechika Anami. But General Anami's body had been cremated the evening following the long night of sake drinking before his final Bushido gesture, seppuku.

As General Douglas MacArthur announced the proceedings closed, formations of American warplanes, ranging in size from hulking B-29s to small Hellcat fighters off carriers, flew low overhead, filling the sky with thunder.

CHRONOLOGY OF MAJOR WARTIME
EVENTS IN THE PACIFIC: 1945

February 19, 1945: U.S. Marines invade Iwo Jima.

April 1, 1945: U.S. forces invade Okinawa, experience massive Japanese kamikaze attacks.

April 12, 1945: President Franklin D. Roosevelt dies; Harry S. Truman assumes office of the presidency.

June 15–16, 1945: *The Boomerang*'s (501st Group, 315th Bomb Wing [Very Heavy]) first combat mission was from Northwest Field, Guam, against Moen Airstrip on Truk Atoll.

June 26–27, 1945: *The Boomerang*'s second combat mission—first to the Empire— was against the Utsube River oil refinery, Yokaichi, Honshu Island, Japan.

June 29–30, 1945: *The Boomerang*'s third combat mission was against the Nippon Oil Company refinery at Kudamatsu on Japan's Inland Sea south of Hiroshima.

July 2–3, 1945: *The Boomerang*'s fourth combat mission was against the Maruzen oil refinery at Shimotsu/Wakayama, 266 miles south of Tokyo, near Kobe.

July 9–10, 1945: *The Boomerang* returned to the Utsube River oil refinery near Yokaichi, south of Tokyo.

July 16, 1945: Fat Man plutonium atomic bomb successfully tested at Alamogordo, New Mexico.

July 17–August 2, 1945: The post–VE Day Potsdam Conference of the United States, the United Kingdom, and the Soviet Union, which took place in a suburb of Berlin, was the first meeting among wartime leaders Truman, Churchill, and Stalin.

July 19–20, 1945: *The Boomerang*'s sixth combat mission was against the Nippon Oil Company refinery at Amagasaki, near Osaka, on Honshu.

July 22–23, 1945: *The Boomerang*'s seventh combat mission was against the Ube Coal Liquefaction Company near Ube on the coast of Honshu south of Tokyo.

July 25, 1945: President Truman's letter to U.S. Strategic Air Forces Commander Carl Spaatz giving authority to release atomic bombs on Japan.

July 26, 1945: Potsdam Declaration issued.

June–July 1945: Imperial Japanese armed forces intensify Ketsu-go operational plan to defend the Home Islands, "the decisive battle of the homeland."

July 28, 1945: Japanese Premier Kantaro Suzuki announces that Japan will reject ("ignore") the Potsdam Declaration.

July 28–29, 1945: *The Boomerang*'s eighth combat mission was against the Shimotsu oil refinery on the Pacific coast of Honshu.

August 5–6, 1945: *The Boomerang*'s ninth combat mission was a return strike on the Ube Coal Liquefaction Company. On the return to Northwest Field, Guam, the aircraft passed the six B-29s of the first atomic bomb mission, flying northbound on a reciprocal course.

August 6, 1945: The American B-29 *Enola Gay* drops the U-235 uranium Little Boy atomic bomb on Hiroshima.

August 8, 1945: The Soviet Union declares war on Japan and invades Manchuria.

August 9, 1945: In Tokyo, an urgent Supreme Council for the Direction of the War meeting to consider the Potsdam Declaration ends in a 3–3 split between the "peace" and "war" factions.

August 9, 1945: U.S. Air Force B-29 *Bock's Car* drops the plutonium Fat Man atomic bomb on Nagasaki.

August 9–10, 1945: *The Boomerang*'s tenth combat mission was a return strike on the Nippon Oil Company refinery at Amagasaki. Enemy resistance, particularly flak, was fierce.

August 9, 1945: Full Japanese cabinet meets but is unable to reach a unanimous decision on accepting the Potsdam Declaration.

August 9–10, 1945: Imperial conference convened for the Supreme Council for the Direction of the War at Gobunko air raid shelter. The Emperor decides to accept the Potsdam Declaration.

August 10, 1945: Japanese cabinet accepts the Emperor's request and transmits to the Allies a diplomatic message accepting the Potsdam Declaration, with the condition that the Emperor's rights and prerogatives as sovereign will not be prejudiced.

August 10, 1945 (Pacific time): Strategic Air Forces Commander General Carl Spaatz advocates dropping an atomic bomb on Tokyo.

August 10, 1945: Allied offensive ground, air, and naval operations against Japan continue during surrender negotiations.

August 10, 1945: Tokyo: War Minister Korechika Anami tells his senior staff officers that they must accept the will of the Emperor to end the war. But there is widespread discontent, because Japan has prepared and hidden 10,000 kamikaze aircraft and has almost three million men ready to fight the Ketsu-go battle.

August 10, 1945: Field-grade and junior staff officers from the War Ministry plot to stage a coup d'état. These conspirators are led by Colonel Okitsugu Arao, Lt. Colonel Masahiko Takeshita, Lt. Colonel Jiro Shiizaki, and Major Kenji Hatanaka.

August 10, 1945: Dissident War Ministry officers issue an inflammatory "Instructions to the Troops" message in defiance of the Emperor's wishes. Rebellious mood grows within the Imperial armed forces.

August 11, 1945 (U.S. time): Secretary of State James F. Byrnes cables the Japanese that, after surrender, the Emperor will be subject to the authority of the Supreme Allied Commander.

August 11, 1945: General Carl Spaatz announces stand-down for B-29 operations (due to bad weather), but the press interprets this bombing pause as a tactic to help the peace negotiations.

August 11, 1945: Japanese military conspirators plan to seize the Imperial Palace and hold the Emperor captive to prevent surrender. They plan to make War Minister Anami the head of a military government that will continue the war through the Ketsu-go in order to wrest better surrender conditions from the Allies.

August 11, 1945: Preparing for surrender, the Emperor decides to broadcast to the Empire once the cabinet has ratified an Imperial Rescript announcing the acceptance of the Potsdam Declaration.

August 12, 1945: The Japanese government receives the Allies' reply to Japan's August 10 message. The Allies' note makes it clear the Emperor will be subject to Allied authority and that the nation will be occupied by Allied forces.

August 12, 1945: War Ministry conspirators urge General Anami to reject this Allied response. He seems sympathetic to their rebellious mood.

August 12, 1945: The Japanese cabinet is deadlocked on whether to accept the latest Allied note.

August 12, 1945: War Ministry conspirators and their colleagues elsewhere in the Army form a practical operational plan to seize the Palace.

August 12, 1945: A delegation of conspirators led by Colonel Arao, Lt. Colonel Takeshita, and Major Hatanaka visits General Anami at his home, seeking his support for the planned coup. He seems to be on their side.

August 13, 1945: The Supreme Council for the Direction of the War is deadlocked 3–3 over the Potsdam Declaration, as amended by the latest Allied note.

August 13, 1945: The full cabinet is also deadlocked on this issue. Prime Minister Suzuki decides to call for another Imperial conference for the Emperor to decide on acceptance of the Potsdam Declaration.

August 13, 1945: Washington has grown impatient over having heard no response from the Japanese. Army Chief of Staff General George C. Marshall cables Generals Douglas MacArthur and Carl Spaatz, relaying President Truman's orders to resume full B-29 operations: "Go ahead with everything we've got."

August 14, 1945, Morning: The Emperor calls a full cabinet meeting in his presence and delivers his final decision to accept the Potsdam Declaration. He pleads for the cabinet to draft an Imperial Rescript to that effect, a recording of which will be broadcast on the radio to the Empire.

August 14, 1945: In Manila, Allied Air Forces Commander General George C. Kenney, having received Marshall's message, orders his staff to proceed with bombing missions against Japan, "on a 24-hr. basis."

August 14, 1945, Tokyo, 1:00 P.M.: War Minister Anami orders his staff officers to abandon any idea of a coup. But Major Hatanaka and others persist in plans to seize the Imperial Palace and hold the Emperor prisoner. They have an added objective: seize and destroy the record of the Imperial Rescript before it can be broadcast.

August 14, 1945, 2:00 P.M.: Anami is still wondering whether he should defy the Emperor and order an attack on the Allied fleet just off the Home Island of Honshu.

August 14, 1945 (midday in Guam): The 315th Bomb Wing (plus elements of three other B-29 Wings from bases elsewhere in the Marianas) is ordered to attack Japan. The 315th's mission—scheduled to take off first—is against the Nippon Oil Company refinery at Akita in northern Honshu. It will be the longest non-stop mission of the war. This is *The Boomerang*'s eleventh combat mission.

August 14, 1945: At 2:49 P.M. in Tokyo (3:49 P.M. on Guam), the Domei News Agency broadcasts a FLASH! message that an Imperial decision accepting the Potsdam Declaration is imminent.

August 14, 1945: The 315th Bomb Wing's aircraft are ordered to shut down engines and wait fifty-three minutes while their commanders weigh the meaning of this news bulletin. Finally the planes are ordered to proceed on the mission. The first aircraft take off at 1642 hours (4:42 P.M. Guam time), a full hour ahead of the other wings.

August 14, 1945, 8:30 P.M.: The Emperor signs the Imperial Rescript.

August 14, 1945, 9–9:30 P.M.: Hatanaka and other rebels deploy troops at the Imperial Palace.

August 14, 1945, 11:00 P.M.: The last Japanese cabinet member signs the Imperial Rescript, thus ratifying it. The 315th Wing's northbound bombers passing just east of Tokyo are detected by radar and cause an area-wide blackout.

Due to the radar alert and blackout, the Emperor waits in the Gobunko air-raid shelter before being driven to the Imperial Household Ministry to record the rescript. Two copies of double sets of the recording are hidden in the building.

August 14, 1945, 11:10 P.M.: The Japanese Foreign Ministry transmits Japan's official surrender message, accepting the terms of the Potsdam Declaration, to the Allies via Swiss diplomatic channels.

August 14, 1945, 11:30 P.M.: In the confusion of the blackout on the grounds of the Imperial Palace, Major Hatanaka and his fellow rebels cannot properly secure the grounds or perimeter without more troops. They eventually confront and kill Lt. General Takeshi Mori, Commander of the Imperial Guards Division, then issue forged orders to mobilize the Division.

August 14, 1945, 4:00 P.M. Washington time: President Harry Truman learns that the Japanese have transmitted their diplomatic note of surrender via the Swiss.

August 15, 1945: From approximately 1 to 4 A.M., rebel soldiers hunt unsuccessfully for the recordings of the Imperial Rescript hidden in the dark warren of the Imperial Household Ministry. Although they search each of the hundreds of tiny rooms, the recordings remain hidden in a small safe, the door of which is obscured by the unbroken darkness of the blackout.

August 15, 1945, 5:00 A.M.: Stymied by the blackout, Hatanaka goes to the studios of the Japan Broadcasting Corporation, determined to deliver his message of an army-wide revolt to the entire Empire. Such a broadcast would have sparked nests of potential rebellion among the Imperial armed forces. But Hatanaka is denied access to the microphone because of the continuing air-raid alert.

August 15, 1945, 5:30 A.M.: General Shizuichi Tanaka, commander of the Eastern District Army, takes control of the Imperial Palace with troops loyal to the Emperor.

August 15, 1945, approximately 5:30 A.M.: War Minister Anami commits suicide.

August 15, 1945, around 8:00 A.M: Flying south near Iwo Jima, *The Boomerang*'s crew hear the official radio report that Japan has surrendered. The plane's engines begin to backfire because of insufficient fuel.

August 15, 1945, 11:10 A.M.: Hatanaka and fellow conspirator Lt. Colonel Shiizaki kill themselves near the Palace. (Other conspirators will commit suicide over the coming days.)

August 15, 1945, 11:31 A.M. (Guam time): *The Boomerang* lands back at Northwest Field after flying almost seventeen hours and 3,800 miles, the longest continuous mission of the war. The aircraft was so short of fuel that the Number 3 engine was starved of gas during the taxi to the hardstand.

August 15, 1945, 12:00 noon (Tokyo time): Emperor Hirohito's recorded Imperial Rescript is broadcast to the Japanese Empire. The Emperor commands his "good and loyal subjects" to refrain from "rash" acts and accept surrender.

September 2, 1945: The Imperial Japanese armed forces and the government of Japan surrender to the Allies during formal ceremonies on the deck of the battleship USS *Missouri*, anchored in Tokyo Bay.

ENDNOTES

CHAPTER ONE: THE SUPERFORTS

[1]David Bergamini, *Japan's Imperial Conspiracy*, *Vol. II* (New York: William Morrow and Company, 1971), p. 1234.

[2]Dan van der Vat, *The Pacific Campaign* (New York: Simon & Schuster, 1991), pp. 253–55. Also see: Forrest C. Pogue, *George C. Marshall: Statesman, 1945–1959* (New York: Viking Press, 1987), p. 5.

[3]Wesley F. Craven and James Lea Cate, editors, *The Army Air Forces in World War II*, *Vol. Five, The Pacific: Matterhorn to Nagasaki, June 1944 to August 1945* (Chicago: The University of Chicago Press, 1953), pp. v–xv.

[4]George E. Harrington and William Leasure, editors, *A New Chapter in Air Power, the 315th Bomb Wing (VH), Guam WWII*, Second Edition (Mansfield, Ohio: Monarch Systems, 1993), p. 23. Also see: Kenneth P. Werrell, *Blankets of Fire: U.S. Bombers Over Japan During World War II* (Washington: Smithsonian Institution Press, 1996), pp. 196–97.

[5]Larry Davis, *B-29 Superfortress in Action* (Carrollton, Texas: Squadron/Signal Publications, 1997), p. 5.

[6]Harrington and Leasure, op. cit., p. 51.

[7]Ronald H. Spector, *Listening to the Enemy, Key Documents and the Role of Communications Intelligence in the War Against Japan* (Wilmington, Delaware: Scholarly Resources, Inc., 1988), pp. 227–30. For a concise but thorough review of Ultra's role in the Pacific war, see: Douglas J. MacEachin, *The Final Months of the War with Japan: Signals Intelligence, U.S. Invasion Planning, and the A-Bomb Decision* (An Intelligence Monograph, Center for the Study of Intelligence, Central Intelligence Agency, Washington, D.C., 1998).

[8]Harrington and Leasure, op. cit., p. 34.

[9]United States Strategic Bombing Survey, Chairman's Office [Report, Pacific War No. 27], *Japan's Struggle to End the War* (Washington, D.C.: U.S. Government Printing Office, 1 July 1946), p. 21.

[10]Letter from Major General Haywood S. Hansell, Jr., USAF (ret.) to Major James M. Boyle, United States Air Force Academy, December 3, 1962. Also see: Jim B. Smith, *The Last Mission, An Eyewitness* Account (Mt. Pleasant, IA, J.B. Smith Enterprises, Ltd., 1995), pp. 50–51. The 315th Wing had been more fortunate with weather on training missions they had flown from Fairmount, Nebraska, to Catalina Island, California, and on 3,000-mile over-water flights from Borinquen Field, Puerto Rico, to Venezuela and back.

[11]Craven and Cate, op. cit., pp. 610–11.

[12]Thomas B. Allen and Norman Polmar, *Code-Name Downfall, The Secret Plan to Invade Japan—And Why Truman Dropped the Bomb* (New York: Simon & Schuster, 1995), p. 89.

[13]Craven and Cate, op. cit., p. 613. Also see: Werrel, op. cit., pp. 154–55.

[14]Werrell, op. cit., p. 159.

[15]Craven and Cate, op. cit., p 614.

[16]Lester Brooks, *Behind Japan's Surrender, The Secret Struggle That Ended an Empire* (New York: McGraw-Hill Book Company, 1968), p. 61 Also see: Richard B. Frank, *Downfall, The End of the Imperial Japanese Empire* (New York: Random House, 1989), p. 4.

[17]Craven and Cate, op. cit., pp. 616–17. Also see: Werrell, op. cit., pp. 160–63.

[18]United States Strategic Bombing Survey [Report of the Pacific War No. 53], *The Effects of Strategic Bombing on Japan's War Economy, Appendix A B C*, Appendix Table C-164: Japanese aircraft production by functional types, by quarters, 1941–1945 (Washington, D.C., U.S. Government Printing Office, 1946), p. 223. Also see p. 23 concerning *zaibatsu*.

[19]Samuel Eliot Morison, *The Two-Ocean War, A Short History of the United States Navy in the Second World War* (Boston: Atlantic Monthly Press, 1963), pp. 520–24.

[20]Allen and Polmar, op. cit., pp. 96–97.

[21]United States Strategic Bombing Survey [Pacific] Naval Analysis Division, *Interrogations of Japanese Officials*, Volume I (Washington, D.C.: U.S. Government Printing Office, 1946), p. 60: Interrogation of Captain Inoguchi, Rikibei, Imperial Japanese Navy.

[22]Edwin P. Hoyt, *The Last Kamikaze, the Story of Admiral Matome Ugaki* (Westport, CT: Praeger, 1993), p. 163.

[23]Allen and Polmar, op. cit., pp. 104–5.

[24]van der Vat, op. cit., pp. 383–84; also see: Craig, op. cit. pp. 9–10.

[25]Interview, Malcolm McConnell and Lt. General James Day, USMC (ret.), April 4, 1998. The late General Day was awarded the Medal of Honor for his exceptional valor on Okinawa more than fifty years after the battle (as a nineteen-year-old corporal in the 5th Marine Division).

[26]Allen and Polmar, op. cit., pp. 170, 221–22.

[27]Headquarters, USAFFE and U.S. Army (Rear), *Japanese Monograph No. 23, Air Defense of the Homeland, 1944–1945*, Distributed by Office of the Chief of Military History, Department of the Army, op. cit. pp. 40–43.

[28]Assistant Chief of Staff—Intelligence, Headquarters Army Air Forces, *Mission Accomplished, Interrogations of Japanese Industrial, Military, and Civil Leaders of World War II* (Washington, D.C.: U.S. Government Printing Office, 1946); interrogation of Lt. General Noburu Tazoe, Chief of Air Staff, Imperial Japanese Army; also see: United States Strategic Bombing Survey [Pacific], Naval Analysis Division, *Interrogations of Japanese Officials, Volume I*, (Washington, D.C.: U.S. Government Printing Office, 1946), p. 23, Interrogation of Captain Fuchida, Mitsuo, Imperial Japanese Navy; and Allen and Polmar, op. cit., p. 110; and Hoyt, op. cit., pp. 181–85, 201; and V Amphibious Corps, *Appendix 3 to Annex C, Operation Plan, Occupation of Japan*, 30 November 1945, p. 10.; also see: United States Strategic Bombing Survey [Pacific] Naval Analysis Division, Vol. II. op. cit., Annex B to USSB 414.

[29]Thomas M. Coffey, *Imperial Tragedy, Japan in World War II, the First Days and the Last* (New York: The World Publishing Company, 1970), p. 264.

[30]*Fifteen Missions, Oil*, unpublished monograph manuscript, p. 3 (Collection of Jim Smith).

[31]United States Strategic Bombing Survey [Pacific], *Interrogations of Japanese Officials, Volume I* (Washington, D.C.: U.S. Government Printing Office, 1946), p. 284. Also see: Japanese Monograph No. 170, *Homeland Antiaircraft Defense Operations Record, Kanto Sector, June 1944–Aug. 1945*, Doc. No. 4260, Center of Military History, Washington, D.C.

[32]Craven and Cate, op. cit., pp. 595–96. The B-29 runway at Iwo Jima's Central Field was not paved and graded to a safe length of 8,500 feet until July 7, 1945, because the asphalt continued to collapse in the island's loose volcanic sand substrate.

CHAPTER TWO: *KOKUTAI* AND KETSU-GO

[1]Herbert P. Bix, *Hirohito and the Making of Modern Japan* (New York: HarperCollins Publishers, 2000), pp. 39, 119–20. This book, based extensively on Japanese primary sources, is the most exhaustive recent study of the wartime emperor. Also see: William Craig, *The Fall of Japan* (New York: The Dial Press, 1967), p. 112; and Gar Alperovitz, *The Decision to Use the Atomic Bomb and the Architecture of an American Myth* (New York: Alfred A. Knopf, 1995), pp. 35–36.

[2]United States Strategic Bombing Survey [Pacific Region], Naval Analysis

Division, *Interrogations of Japanese Officials, Vol. II*, USSB No. 378, Interrogation of Chief of Naval General Staff, Admiral Toyoda, Soemu, p. 313. Also see: General Headquarters, Far East Command, Military Intelligence Section, Historical Division, *Statements of Japanese Officials on World War II (English Translations), Vol. 4.* Statement of ex–Minister of Foreign Affairs Togo, Shigenori, Concerning the Historical Facts Surrounding the Ending of the Pacific War (1), pp. 3–6, Sugamo Prison, Tokyo, 17 May 49, Center of Military History.

[3]This most notorious single incident during the Japanese conquest of China occurred during the three-month "rampage of arson, pillage, murder, and rape" in Nanking, which resulted in the death of more than 300,000 Chinese civilians and prisoners of war. See: Iris Chang, *The Rape of Nanking: The Forgotten Holocaust of World War II* (New York: Basic Books, 1997).

[4]Bergamini, op. cit., pp. 954–55. Also see, Bix, op. cit., pp. 12; 407–14.

[5]Bix, op. cit., pp.119–20.

[6]Brooks, op. cit., p. 91.

[7]Bix, op. cit., pp. 10, 305–6. Also see: Marius B. Jansen, *The Making of Modern Japan* (Cambridge, MA: The Belknap Press of Harvard University Press, 2000), pp. 600–601.

[8]Bix, op. cit., p. 11.

[9]United States Strategic Bombing Survey, *Interrogations of Japanese Officials, Vol. II*, op. cit., Interrogation of Admiral Mitsumasa Yonai, p. 327.

[10]United States Strategic Bombing Survey, *Japan's Struggle to End the War*, op. cit., p. 34.

[11]U.S. Navy, Pacific Fleet, *Hypothetical Defense of Kyushu, Translation of Japanese Staff Exercise (Jan. 1944)*, CINPAC [Commander-in-Chief, Pacific] Bulletin, July 1945, declassified, archives of Jim B. Smith.

[12]United States Strategic Bombing Survey, *Japan's Struggle to End the War*, op. cit., p. 32.

[13]Brooks, op. cit., pp. 137, 140–41,142–43.

[14]Bix, op. cit., pp. 177–78, 370, 601-2.

[15]Bergamini, Vol. II, op. cit., p. 1408.

[16]General Headquarters, Far East Command, Military Intelligence Section, Historical Division, *Statements of Japanese Officials on World War II (English Translations), Vol. 4.*, op. cit., Full Translation of Statement by Former Foreign Minister Togo, p. 44.

[17]General Headquarters, Far East Command, Military Intelligence Section, Historical Division, *Interrogations of Japanese Officials on World War II, Vol. I*, No. 55127, Interrogation of President of Privy Council President Kiichiro Hiranuma, p. 2. (cumulative p. 140).

[18]General Headquarters, Far East Command, Military Intelligence Section, Historical Division, *Statements of Japanese Officials on World War II (English Translations), Vol. 4.*, op. cit., Togo Statement, p. 46.

[19]The Pacific War Research Society, *Japan's Longest Day* (Tokyo: Kodansha International, 1968) p. 84.

[20]Allen and Polmar, op. cit., pp. 219–20.

[21]Assistant Chief of Staff—Intelligence, Headquarters Army Air Forces, *Mission Accomplished, Interrogations of Japanese Industrial, Military, and Civil Leaders of World War II*, op. cit., Interrogation of General Ija Kawabe, former Deputy Chief of Staff, Imperial Japanese Army, p. 35.

[22]General Headquarters, Far East Command, Military Intelligence Section, Historical Division, op. cit., Vol. 3, "Statement Concerning Defense Preparation for Southern Kyushu," op. cit., p. 2.

[23]Fleet Admiral William D. Leahy, *I Was There, The Personal Story of the Chief of Staff to Presidents Roosevelt and Truman Based on His Notes and Diaries Made at the Time* (New York: Whittlesey House, 1950), p. 385. Also see: Allen and Polmar, op. cit., p. 221.

[24]MacEachin, op. cit., p. 6. Also see: General Headquarters, Far East Command, Military Intelligence Section, Historical Division, Vol. 3, "Statement Concerning Defense Preparation for Southern Kyushu," op. cit., pp. 4–5.

[25]MacEachin, op. cit., pp. 17–19.

[26]Headquarters, USAFFE and U.S. Army (Rear), *Japanese Monograph No. 23, Air Defense of the Homeland, 1944–1945*, op. cit., p. 46.

[27]Allen and Polmar, op. cit., p. 225.

[28]Ibid., pp. 224–26.

[29]General Headquarters, Far East Command, Military Intelligence Section, Historical Division, *Statements of Japanese Officials on World War II (English Translations), Vol. 3*, p. 8.

[30]Jansen, op. cit, p. 354; also see: Bergamini, op. cit., p. 1298.

[31]Headquarters, USAFFE and U.S. Army (Rear), *Japanese Monograph No. 23, Air Defense of the Homeland, 1944–1945*, op. cit., pp. 43–46.

[32]General Headquarters, Far East Command, Military Intelligence Section, General Staff, Allied Translator and Interpreter Section, Full Translation of Statement by ex-Capt. Ohmae, Toshikazu, op. cit., p. 51.

[33]Special Staff U.S. Army Historical Division (Historical Manuscript File), *Naval Plans for the Defense of Japan*, pp. 19–20.

[34]Assistant Chief of Staff—Intelligence, Headquarters Army Air Forces, *Mission Accomplished, Interrogations of Japanese Industrial, Military, and Civil Leaders of World War II*, op. cit., Statement of Lieutenant General Noburu Tazoe, p. 35.

[35]Allen and Polmar, op. cit., p. 231.

[36]Frank, op. cit., pp. 187.

[37]Captain Rikihei Inoguchi and Commander Tadashi Nakajima with Roger Pineau, *The Divine Wind, Japan's Kamikaze Force in World War II* (Westport, CT: Greenwood Press, 1959), p. 186.

[38]Frank, op. cit., p. 179.

[39]Allen and Polmar, op. cit., pp. 226–27, 237.

[40]Ibid.

[41]Frank, op. cit., p. 184.

[42]United States Strategic Bombing Survey, *Interrogations of Japanese Officials, Vol. I*, op. cit., Interrogation of Captain Fuchida, Mitsuo, p. 24.

[43]General Headquarters, Far East Command, Military Intelligence Section, Historical Division, *Statements of Japanese Officials on World War II (English Translations)*, op. cit., Vol. 3, p. 5.

[44]Allen and Polmar, op. cit., pp. 173–74; 256–57.

[45]Robert Aron, *Histoire de la Liberation de la France, Juin 1944–Mai 1945* (Paris, Librairie Arthème Fayard, 1959), pp. 15–20; 33; also see: Interview, Malcolm McConnell with staff of La Musée National de la Bataille de Normandie, Bayeux, France, November 19, 2001.

[46]Special Staff U.S. Army Historical Division (Historical Manuscript File), *Naval Plans for the Defense of Japan* (Japanese Monograph No. 85), op. cit., p. 21. Also see: Frank, op. cit., pp. 183, 206.

[47]MacEachin, op. cit. pp. 21–22.

[48]Brooks, op. cit., p. 148.

[49]General Headquarters, Far East Command, Military Intelligence Section, Historical Division, *Statements of Japanese Officials on World War II (English Translations), Vol. 4.*, op. cit., Statement of Foreign Minister Shigenori Togo, p. 21. Also see: United States Strategic Bombing Survey, *Japan's Struggle to End the War*, op. cit., p. 7.

[50]Pogue, *George C. Marshall: Statesman*, op. cit., p. 524.

[51]Harry S. Truman, *Memoirs, Harry S. Truman, Volume One, Year of Decisions* (Garden City, N.Y.: Doubleday & Company, Inc., 1955), pp. 264–66.

CHAPTER THREE: POTSDAM AND TRINITY

[1]Pogue, *George C. Marshall: Statesman*, op. cit., p. 24. Also see: Ed Cray, *General of the Army, George C. Marshall, Soldier and Statesman* (New York: W.W. Norton & Company, 1990), p. 546.

[2]Forrest C. Pogue, *George C. Marshall: Organizer of Victory, 1943–1945* (New York: Viking Press, 1973), pp. 528–29; and Leahy, op. cit., pp. 384–85.

[3]Truman, op. cit., p. 207.

[4]Alperovitz, op. cit., pp. 36–37.

[5]Frank, op. cit., p. 215.

[6]MacEachin, op. cit., pp. 12–13.

[7]Joint War Plans Committee 369/1, 15 June 1945, "Details of the Campaign Against Japan," Record Group 165, National Archives and Records Administration.

[8]MacEachin, op. cit., p. 13.

[9]Truman, op. cit., p. 416.

[10]MacEachin, op. cit., pp. 14–15.

[11]Leahy, op. cit., p. 384.

[12]Gordon Thomas and Max Morgan Witts, *Enola Gay* (New York: Stein and Day, 1977), p. 7.

[13]Craven and Cate, op. cit., p. 704. Also see: Frank, op. cit., p. 253.

[14]Richard Rhodes, *The Making of the Atomic Bomb* (New York: Simon & Schuster, 1986), pp. 305–7.

[15]Werrell, op. cit., pp. 208–9. This estimate was later proven to be incorrect: The German research program was never of the scale necessary to develop a practical bomb.

[16]Peter Wyden, *Day One, Before Hiroshima and After* (New York: Simon & Schuster, 1984), p. 98.

[17]Craven and Cate, op. cit., p. 705.

[18]Wyden, op. cit., pp. 98–99, 104.

[19]Len Giovannitti and Fred Freed, *The Decision to Drop the Bomb* (New York: Coward-McCann, Inc., 1965), p. 63.

[20]Thomas and Witts, op. cit., pp. 11–12.

[21]Rhodes, *The Making of the Atomic Bomb*, op. cit., p. 656.

[22]Ibid., pp. 667–73.

[23]Thomas and Witts, op. cit., p. 175.

[24]Rhodes, *The Making of the Atomic Bomb*, op. cit., p. 685.

[25]Truman, op. cit., p. 415.

[26]Frank, op. cit., pp. 217, 219.

[27]Foreign Relations of the United States: *The Conference of Berlin*, 2 Vols. (Washington, D.C.: Government Printing Office, 1960, II), pp. 147 passim.

[28]Frank, op. cit., p. 258.

[29]Pogue, *George C. Marshall: Statesman*, op. cit., pp. 24, 220.

[30]Pogue, *George C. Marshall: Organizer of Victory*, op. cit., p. 524.

[31]Cray, op. cit., p. 546.

[32]Truman, op. cit., p. 416.

[33]Charles E. Bohlen, *Witness to History, 1929–1969* (New York: W.W. Norton, 1973), pp. 247–48.

[34]David McCullough, *Truman* (New York: Simon & Schuster, 1992), p. 433.

[35]Georgii K. Zhukov, *The Memoirs of Marshal Zhukov* (New York: Delacorte Press, 1971), pp. 674–75.

[36]Truman, op. cit., p. 420.

[37]Frank, op. cit., p. 262.

[38]Letter, 25 July 1945, War Department, Office of the Chief of Staff, Thomas T. Handy, General, Acting Chief of Staff to General Carl Spaatz, Center of Military History, Washington, D.C. Also see: MacEachin, op. cit., Document 18B.

[39]Giovannitti and Freed, op. cit., p. 281; also see: Craven and Cate, op. cit., p. 718.

[40]McCullough, op. cit., p. 437.

[41]Foreign Relations of the United States, op. cit., pp. 147 passim.

CHAPTER FOUR: *THE BOOMERANG AND ENOLA GAY*

[1]Wyden, op. cit., p. 237.

[2]Bix, op. cit., p. 495.

[3]United States Strategic Bombing Survey, *Japan's Struggle to End the War*, op. cit., p. 8.

[4]Frank, op. cit., p. 234. Also see: Bix, op. cit., p. 501.

⁵General Headquarters, Far East Command, Military Intelligence Section, Historical Division, *Statements of Japanese Officials on World War II (English Translations), Vol. 4,* Togo Statement, op. cit., p. 21.

⁶Frank, op. cit., p. 234.

⁷Thomas and Witts, op. cit., pp. 170–71, 228, 243–44.

⁸Henry Sakaida, *Pacific Air Combat, WWII, Voices from the Past* (St. Paul, Minn.: Phalanx Publishing Co., Ltd.,1993), pp. 67–73. The Ki.45 was one of the most effective Japanese fighters employed against B-29s flying both day and night missions, relying both on the destructive power of their 37mm cannon and, in the final months of the war, on kamikaze tactics against the American bombers.

⁹Tactical Mission Report, Mission No. 315, Ube; Headquarters, Twentieth Air Force, APO 234, dated 25 Sept. 45, classified Secret; declassified 1997, Air Force Historical Research Agency, Maxwell Air Force Base, Alabama, pp. 31–32.

¹⁰The authors obtained the information on moon phases, moonrises and -sets, and sunrises and sunsets for the dates and locations described from the U.S. Naval Observatory, Astronomical Applications Department, online.

¹¹Thomas and Witts, op. cit., p. 250.

¹²Richard Rhodes, *Dark Sun, The Making of the Hydrogen Bomb* (New York: Simon & Schuster, 1995), pp. 17, 226–27.

¹³Frank, op. cit., p. 263.

CHAPTER FIVE: "A RAIN OF RUIN"

¹Thomas and Witts, op. cit., p. 256.

²Ibid., p. 261.

³Rhodes, The *Making of the Atomic Bomb*, op. cit., pp. 714–15.

⁴Thomas and Witts, op. cit., p. 262.

⁵Rhodes, *The Making of the Atomic Bomb*, op. cit., p. 733; also see: Frank, op. cit., p. 334.

⁶Frank, op. cit., p. 334.

⁷Thomas and Witts., op. cit., 261.

⁸Frank, op. cit., pp. 262–63.

⁹Truman diary entry quoted in Robert H. Ferrell, *Off the Record: The Private Papers of Harry S. Truman* (New York: Harper & Row, 1990) pp. 55–56.

¹⁰United States Strategic Bombing Survey, Chairman's Office, *The Effects of Atomic Bombs on Hiroshima and Nagasaki* (Washington, D.C.: U.S. Government Printing Office, 1946), pp. 22–23.

¹¹Thomas and Witts, op. cit., pp. 262–65.

¹²Cray, op. cit., pp. 547–48.

¹³Truman, op. cit., pp. 421–22.

¹⁴Presidential Announcement of August 6, 1945, Truman Library, Miscellaneous Historical Document No. 253; also see: Giovannitti and Freed, op. cit., p. 264. The original draft presidential statement began: "Sixteen hours ago an American airplane dropped one bomb on . . ." with the name of the city left blank, to be filled in after the successful strike on the selected target. The statement continued,

"... and destroyed its usefulness to the enemy." The actual statement released read: "Sixteen hours ago an American airplane dropped one bomb on Hiroshima, an important Japanese Army base . . ." See Harry S. Truman Library online: www.trumanlibrary.org.

[15]Letter, Charles H. Miller to Jim B. Smith, April 27, 2001. Miller was the aircraft commander of the 315th Bomb Wing B-29B *For the Luva Mike.*

[16]The Pacific War Research Society, *Japan's Longest Day*, op. cit., p. 20.

[17]Harry S. Truman Library, Miscellaneous Historical Document File No. 258.

[18]United States Strategic Bombing Survey, Chairman's Office, *The Effects of Atomic Bombs on Hiroshima and Nagasaki,* op. cit., p. 21.

[19]General Headquarters, Far East Command, Military Intelligence Section, Historical Division, *Statements of Japanese Officials on World War II (English Translations),* Vol. 4, Togo Statement, op. cit., p. 30.

[20]Giovannitti and Freed, op. cit., p. 265.

[21]Frank, op. cit., pp. 253, 269, 270.

[22]Statement of Koichi Kido, 17 May 49, Doc. No. 61541, p. 5, Center of Military History, Washington, D.C., as cited in Frank, op. cit., pp. 271–72.

[23]The Pacific War Research Society, *Japan's Longest Day*, op. cit., p. 84. Also see: Brooks, op. cit., p. 144; and Craven and Cate, op. cit., p. 638.

[24]General Headquarters, Far East Command, Military Intelligence Section, Historical Division, *Statements of Japanese Officials on World War II (English Translations), Vol. 4,* Doc. No. 54562, Statement by Togo, Shigenori, (cumulative), p. 286; also see: General Headquarters, Far East Command, Military Intelligence Section, Historical Division, *Statements of Japanese Officials on World War II (English Translations), Vol. 4.* Togo Statement, op. cit., p. 31.

[25]Frank, op. cit., p. 272.

[26]General Headquarters, Far East Command, Military Intelligence Section, Historical Division, *Statements of Japanese Officials on World War II (English Translations), Vol. 4,* Togo Statement, op. cit., pp. 31–32.

[27]Craig, op. cit., p. 73; David Bergamini, *Japan's Imperial Conspiracy, Vol. I* (New York: William Morrow and Company, Inc., 1971), p. 107; also see: John Toland, *The Rising Sun, The Decline and Fall of the Japanese Empire, 1936–1945* (New York: Random House, 1970), p. 795.

[28]Craig, op. cit., p. 74.

[29]Frank, op. cit., p. 270.

[30]Ibid., pp. 277–78.

[31]General Headquarters, Far East Command, Military Intelligence Section, Historical Division, "Statements Regarding the Attitude of War Minister Anami and Others Toward Peace Just Prior to Surrender," by ex-Col [sic] Hayashi, Saburo, p. 3.

[32]Craig, op. cit., p. 134.

[33]General Headquarters, Far East Command, Military Intelligence Section, Historical Division, *Statements of Japanese Officials on World War II (English Translations), Vol. 4,* Togo Statement, op. cit., p. 33.

[34]General Headquarters, Far East Command, Military Intelligence Section, General Staff, Historical Division, Doc. No. 55127, Hiranuma Statement, op. cit., p. 12 (cumulative p. 150); also see: United States Strategic Bombing Survey [Pacific Region], Naval Analysis Division, *Interrogations of Japanese Officials, Vol. II*, USSB No. 378, Interrogation of Chief of Naval General Staff, Admiral Toyoda, Soemu, op. cit., p. 322; and General Headquarters, Far East Command, Military Intelligence Section, Historical Division, *Statements of Japanese Officials on World War II (English Translations), Vol. 4*, Togo Statement, op. cit., p. 33.

[35]General Headquarters, Far East Command, Military Intelligence Section, Historical Division, *Statements of Japanese Officials on World War II (English Translations), Vol. 4*, Togo Statement, op. cit., p. 33.

[36]Werrell, op. cit., p. 216.

[37]Bergamini, *Vol. I*, op. cit., p. 69.

[38]Ibid., p. 71.

[39]General Headquarters, Far East Command, Military Intelligence Section, Historical Division, *Statements of Japanese Officials on World War II (English Translations), Vol. 4*, Togo Statement, op. cit., p. 33.

[40]Bergamini, *Vol. I*, op. cit., p. 109.

[41]The Pacific War Research Society, *Japan's Longest Day*, op. cit., p. 27.

[42]General Headquarters, Far East Command, Military Intelligence Section, Historical Division, *Statements of Japanese Officials on World War II (English Translations), Vol. 4*, Togo Statement, op. cit., pp. 33–34.

[43]Craig, op. cit., p. 118.

[44]The Pacific War Research Society, *Japan's Longest Day*, op. cit., p. 29.

[45]Smith, op. cit., pp. 139–41.

[46]Sergeant Jim B. Smith, personal combat mission flight log: "Combat Mission No. 10."

[47]The Pacific War Research Society, *Japan's Longest Day*, op. cit., p. 31.

[48]Craig, op. cit., p. 112.

[49]General Headquarters, Far East Command, Military Intelligence Section, Historical Division, *Statements of Japanese Officials on World War II (English Translations), Vol. 4*, Togo Statement, op. cit., p. 34.

[50]General Headquarters, Far East Command, Military Intelligence Section, General Staff, Allied Translator and Interpreter Section, *Interrogations of Japanese Officials on World War II*, Doc. No. 55127, Hiranuma Statement, op. cit., pp. 151–152.

[51]Craig, op. cit., p. 116.

[52]United States Strategic Bombing Survey, *Japan's Struggle to End the War*, op. cit., p. 8. Note: There is no verbatim transcript of this historic meeting, but Chief Cabinet Secretary Sakomizu later provided the most authoritative version of the words spoken.

[53]General Headquarters, Far East Command, Military Intelligence Section, Historical Division, *Statements of Japanese Officials on World War II (English Translations), Vol. 4*, op. cit., Togo Statement, p. 34.

[54]United States Strategic Bombing Survey, Chairman's Office [Report, Pacific War No. 27], *Japan's Struggle to End the War*, op. cit., pp. 8–9.

[55]Ibid., p. 9. A slightly different wording of Suzuki's statement ("His Majesty's decision should now be made the unanimous decision of this conference.") appears in Toland, op. cit., p. 813.

[56]Craig, op. cit., p. 120; also see: Toland, op. cit., p. 814.

[57]The Pacific War Research Society, *Japan's Longest Day*, op. cit., pp. 35–36; also see: Frank, op. cit., p. 296.

[58]General Headquarters, Far East Command, Military Intelligence Section, Historical Division, *Statements of Japanese Officials on World War II (English Translations), Vol. 4*, Doc. No.5927, Statement by ex-Lt. General Masao Yoshizumi, (cumulative p. 609); also see: Toland, op. cit., p. 823.

[59]Truman, op. cit., p. 427.

CHAPTER SIX: RUMORS OF PEACE

[1]Frank, op. cit., p. 300. Exact numbers of Allied prisoners of war who survived capture by the Japanese were difficult to ascertain in 1945 because missing-in-action totals were high among Allied personnel throughout the Asia-Pacific Theater. One expert estimated the total number of prisoners at 320,000, including 180,000 Asian members of the Allied forces; another study places the number at 193,000, of whom 60,600 were killed or died in captivity. This POW total includes 36,260 Americans, 13,851 of whom (38.2%) were later found to have died or been killed in captivity. In August 1945, the Pentagon estimated that 15,000 remained alive: Frank, op. cit., pp.160–63; 395–96.

[2]Craig, op. cit., p. 126.

[3]James J. Fahey, *Pacific War Diary* (Thorndike, Maine: Thorndike Press, 1963), pp. 602–3, 607–11; also see: Rhodes, *The Making of the Atomic Bomb*, op. cit., p. 699.

[4]Leahy, op. cit., p. 434.

[5]Rhodes, *The Making of the Atomic Bomb*, op. cit., p. 742.

[6]Truman, op. cit., p. 429.

[7]McCullough, op. cit., p. 460.

[8]Frank, op. cit., p. 302; also see: McCullough, op. cit., p. 460.

[9]Frank, op. cit, pp. 255, 302.

[10]Rhodes, *The Making of the Atomic Bomb*, op. cit., p. 744.

[11]Barton J. Bernstein, "The Perils and Politics of Surrender: Ending the War with Japan and Avoiding the Third Atomic Bomb," *Pacific Historical Review*, Vol. XLVI, February 1977, No. 1., p. 17.

[12]Frank, op. cit., p. 327.

[13]Truman, op. cit., p. 43.

[14]Ibid., pp. 303, 327, 430–31.

[15]McCullough, op. cit., p. 460.

[16]Truman, op. cit., p. 432; also see: Fahey, op. cit., pp. 658–59.

[17]Cray, op. cit., p. 550.

[18]General Headquarters, Far East Command, Military Intelligence Section,

General Staff, Allied Translator and Interpreter Section, *Statements of Japanese Officials on World War II*, Vol. 4, Doc. No. 50025A, Statement by Masahiko Takeshita, 18th August, 1949, p. 3.; also see: Toland, op. cit., p. 815. Various versions of Anami's remarks of August 10, 1945 have appeared in published accounts, but all seem to have been based on the Takeshita Statement.

[19]The Pacific War Research Society, *Japan's Longest Day*, op. cit., p. 37. Historian William Craig (*The Fall of Japan*, op. cit, p. 131) has rendered Anami's words as "Those among you who are dissatisfied and wish to stave it [surrender, acceptance of the Potsdam Declaration] off, will have to do it over Anami's body."

[20]Toland, op. cit., p. 815.

[21]The Pacific War Research Society, *Japan's Longest Day*, op. cit., pp. 41–42.

[22]Craig, op. cit., pp. 135–36; also see: The Pacific War Research Society, *Japan's Longest Day*, op. cit., p. 55.

[23]The Pacific War Research Society, *Japan's Longest Day*, op. cit., p. 42.

[24]General Headquarters, Far East Command, Military Intelligence Section, General Staff, Historical Division, Doc. No. 50025A, op. cit, Takeshita Statement, p. 4.

[25]General Headquarters, Far East Command, Military Intelligence Section, General Staff, Historical Division, *Interrogations of Japanese Officials on World War II*, Doc. No. 55127, Hiranuma Statement, op. cit., p. 152.

[26]Interview of Richard B. Frank by Malcolm McConnell, September 8, 2001; also see: The Pacific War Research Society, *Japan's Longest Day*, op. cit., pp. 116–17; and Bix, op. cit., p. 528.

[27]Fahey, op. cit., p. 659.

[28]Letter, Seaman Richard Pryor, "M" Division, USS *Pennsylvania*, August 19, 1945, reprinted on the ship's Web page, www.usspennsylvania.com/richardpryor.htm.

[29]Interview: Malcolm McConnell and Walter Woodward, Centreville, MD, Jan. 1, 2002. Mr. Woodward was a member of the U.S. Army engineer battalion working on the Okinawa coral quarry.

[30]Memorandum for the President, G. C. Marshall, Chief of Staff, 11 August 1945, originally classified Top Secret, declassified 1973, G. C. Marshall Papers, Pentagon Offices, Selected 84/51, Box/File POS-84/51; also see: COMGEN USASTAF from COMGENAIR, 11 August 1945 (WAR 47880), Top Secret, declassified 1984, Air Force Historical Research Agency.

[31]Craig, op. cit., p. 136.

[32]General Headquarters, Far East Command, Military Intelligence Section, General Staff, Allied Translator and Interpreter Section, Doc. No. 56367, 28 Feb. 50, Subject: Coup d'Etat Plan to Prevent the Termination of the War, Statement of ex–Lt. Colonel Masahiko Takeshita, p. 2.

[33]Ibid., pp. 2–3.

[34]Bix, op. cit., p. 10.

[35]Brooks, op. cit., p. 205.; also see: General Headquarters, Far East Command, Military Intelligence Section, General Staff, Allied Translator and Interpreter Section, Doc. No. 50025A, Takeshita, op. cit., p. 3.

[36]Brooks, op. cit., p. 184.

[37]Ibid., p. 209.

[38]United States Strategic Bombing Survey [Pacific] Naval Analysis Division, *Interrogations of Japanese Officials*, "Japanese War Plans and Peace Moves," Interrogation of Admiral Soemu Toyoda, 13–14 November 1945, p. 322; also see: The Pacific War Research Society, *Japan's Longest Day*, op. cit., p. 46.

[39]Brooks, op. cit., p. 217.

[40]United States Strategic Bombing Survey, Toyoda Interrogation, op. cit., p. 322.

[41]Brooks, op. cit., p. 216.

[42]Frank, op. cit., p. 308.

[43]The Pacific War Research Society, *Japan's Longest Day*, op. cit., p. 47.

[44]As noted, many of the detailed descriptions of events in Japan in August 1945 were provided by Japanese officials to Allied interrogators who were often conducting war crimes investigations, which covered several years. It was both human nature and the particular Japanese trait of not breaking ranks to reveal secrets to foreigners that led many of those interrogated to obfuscate. So it is often necessary to sift through the transcripts of these interrogations and compare the statements of one individual given on different dates both with his own testimony and statements covering the same events provided by others. In this regard, the General Headquarters, Far East Command, Military Intelligence Section, General Staff, Allied Translator and Interpreter Section, *Statements of Japanese Officials on World War II*, available at the Center of Military History in Washington, are invaluable.

[45]Toland, op. cit., p. 821.

[46]Brooks, op. cit., p. 221.

[47]Ibid.

[48]General Headquarters, Far East Command, Military Intelligence Section, General Staff, Allied Translator and Interpreter Section, Doc. No. 56367, Takeshita Statement, op. cit., p. 4.

[49]Brooks, op. cit., p. 225.

[50]General Headquarters, Far East Command, Military Intelligence Section, General Staff, Allied Translator and Interpreter Section, Togo Statement, op. cit., p. 36.

[51]Brooks, op. cit., p. 227.

[52]General Headquarters, Far East Command, Military Intelligence Section, General Staff, Allied Translator and Interpreter Section, Doc. No. 56367, Takeshita Statement, op. cit., p. 4.

[53]Toland, op. cit., p. 824.

[54]The Pacific War Research Society, *Japan's Longest Day*, op. cit., p. 50; also see: Brooks, op. cit., p. 229.

[55]Craig, op. cit., p. 157.

[56]Frank, op. cit., p. 310.

[57]Brooks, op. cit., pp. 235–36.

[58]General Headquarters, Far East Command, Military Intelligence Section, General Staff, Allied Translator and Interpreter Section, Togo Statement, op. cit., pp. 37–38.

[59]Coffey, op. cit., p. 462.

[60]Brooks, op. cit., p. 238.

[61]Craig, op. cit., pp. 140–41.

[62]Brooks, op. cit., p. 250.

[63]Toland, op. cit., p. 825; also see: Brooks, op. cit., p. 239.

[64]Brooks, op. cit., p. 240.

[65]Ibid., pp. 241, 247.

[66]General Headquarters, Far East Command, Military Intelligence Section, General Staff, Allied Translator and Interpreter Section, Togo Statement, op. cit., p. 38.

[67]The Pacific War Research Society, *Japan's Longest Day*, op. cit., p. 73.

[68]Coffey, op. cit., p. 427.

[69]Toland, op. cit., p. 826.

[70]The Pacific War Research Society, *Japan's Longest Day*, op. cit., p. 73.

[71]Brooks, op. cit., p. 252.

[72]General Headquarters, Far East Command, Military Intelligence Section, General Staff, Allied Translator and Interpreter Section, Doc. No. 56367, Takeshita Statement, op. cit., pp. 4–5.

[73]Frank, op. cit., p. 318.

[74]General Headquarters, Far East Command, Military Intelligence Section, General Staff, Allied Translator and Interpreter Section, Doc. No., 56367, Takeshita Statement, op. cit., p. 5.

[75]Craig, op. cit., p. 8.

[76]General Headquarters, Far East Command, Military Intelligence Section, General Staff, Allied Translator and Interpreter Section, Doc. No. 56367, Takeshita Statement, op. cit., p. 5; also see: Craig, op. cit., p. 8.

[77]General Headquarters, Far East Command, Military Intelligence Section, General Staff, Allied Translator and Interpreter Section, Doc. No. 56367, Takeshita Statement, op. cit., p. 5.

[78]General Headquarters, Far East Command, Military Intelligence Section, General Staff, Allied Translator and Interpreter Section, Togo Statement, op. cit., pp. 40–41.

[79]Frank, op. cit., p. 513.

[80]Headquarters, Twentieth Air Force, APO 234, Tactical Mission Report, Field Order No. 20., Missions No. 325, 326, 327, 328, 329, 330, 14/15 August 1945, Air Force Historical Research Agency.

[81]WARX 48689, 13 August 1945, 1313 Zulu, Archives of General George C. Kenney: 168.7103-71 V.11 01129430, Air Force Historical Research Agency.

CHAPTER SEVEN: DECISION AND INDECISION

[1]Toland, op. cit., 829.

[2]The Pacific War Research Society, *Japan's Longest Day*, op. cit., p. 77.

[3]Frank, op. cit., p. 314.

[4]General Headquarters, Far East Command, Military Intelligence Section, General Staff, Allied Translator and Interpreter Section, Doc. No. 56367, Takeshita Statement, op. cit., p. 6.

[5]The Pacific War Research Society, *Japan's Longest Day*, op. cit., p. 77.

[6]Frank, op. cit., p. 314.

[7]Craig, op. cit., p. 170.

[8]Brooks, op. cit., p. 264.; also see: Coffey, op. cit., pp. 441–42; Craig, op. cit., p. 171.

[9]United States Strategic Bombing Survey, *Japan's Struggle to End the War*, op. cit., p. 9. Although no one took verbatim notes at this Imperial conference, several participants wrote detailed summaries immediately after the meeting. For example, Foreign Minister Togo dictated an account of the Imperial conference within minutes of the Emperor's departure, and Chief Cabinet Secretary Sakomizu wrote his own contemporaneous account. Other participants referred to their records while undergoing interrogation by Allied authorities after the war, see: United States Strategic Bombing Survey [Pacific] *Interrogations of Japanese Officials*, Vol. 2, OPNAV-P-03-100, No. 378 "Japanese War Plans and Peace Moves," 13–14 November 1945, Interrogation of Admiral Toyoda, Soemu, pp. 322–23.

[10]Craig, op. cit., p. 172.; also see: Toland, op. cit., p. 831.

[11]Brooks, op. cit., pp. 266–67.;also see: Toland, op. cit., p. 831.

[12]Craig, op. cit., p. 172.

[13]The Pacific War Research Society, *Japan's Longest Day*, op. cit., p. 87.

[14]Brooks, op. cit., pp. 268–69.

[15]Military History Section, Headquarters, Army Forces Far East, *Outline of Operations Prior to Termination of War and Activities Connected with the Cessation of Hostilities*, Japanese Monograph No. 119., Office of Military History, Washington, D.C., pp. 9–10.

[16]General Headquarters, Far East Command, Military Intelligence Section, General Staff, Allied Translator and Interpreter Section, Doc. No. 56367, Takeshita Statement, op. cit., p. 7.

[17]The Pacific War Research Society, *Japan's Longest Day*, op. cit., p. 98; and Note 14, p. 330.

[18]Radio Teletype Conference, Aug. 14, 1945, Box 21, Spaatz Papers, Library of Congress, as cited in Frank, op. cit., pp. 313, 430.

[19]WARX 48689, 13 August 1945, 1313 Zulu, Archives of General George C. Kenney: 168.7103-71 V.11 01129430, Air Force Historical Research Agency.

[20]Thomas E. Griffith, Jr., *MacArthur's Airman, General George C. Kenney and the War in the Southwest Pacific* (Lawrence, KS: University Press of Kansas, 1998), p. 228.

[21]*Fifteen Missions, Oil*, op. cit., Track Chart, XXI Bomber Command, 14–15 August 1945 (unpaginated).

[22]Chester Marshall, *Final Assault on the Rising Sun* (North Beach, MN: Specialty Press, 1995), p. 205.

[23]Brooks, op. cit., p. 276. Some accounts of that confused afternoon describe the young officers bursting directly into Anami's office, not into the conference room. See: The Pacific War Research Society, *Japan's Longest Day*, op. cit., p. 90.

[24]General Headquarters, Far East Command, Military Intelligence Section, General Staff, Allied Translator and Interpreter Section, Doc. No. 56367, Takeshita

Statement, op. cit., p. 7; also see: General Headquarters, Far East Command, Military Intelligence Section, General Staff, Allied Translator and Interpreter Section, Full Translation of a Statement by ex–Lt. Gen Yoshizumi, Masao (Director of Military Affairs Bureau), 25 May 1950 and 2 June 1950, Doc. No. 59277, p. 2. (p. 605 of bound cumulative volume).

[25]The Pacific War Research Society, *Japan's Longest Day*, op. cit., pp. 90–91.

[26]General Headquarters, Far East Command, Military Intelligence Section, Historical Division, "A Statement on the Decision Reached by Three Top Army Commanders, Two Field Marshals, and the Commander of the General Air Army at the End of the War," Statement of ex–Lt. General Kawabe, Torashiro, 3 Dec. 48, p. 3.

[27]The Pacific War Research Society, *Japan's Longest Day*, op. cit., p. 105.

[28]Brooks, op. cit., p. 275; also see: Frank, op. cit., p. 315.

[29]Toland, op. cit., p. 834; also see: The Pacific War Research Society, *Japan's Longest Day*, op. cit., pp. 56, 73.

[30]Toland, op. cit., p. 834.

[31]Washington *Evening Star*, August 14, 1945, p. A8.

[32]Interviews, Jim B. Smith and historians at the Air Force Historical Research Agency. December 11–15, 2000.

[33]Frank, op. cit., p. 323.

[34]Cray, op. cit., p. 550.

[35]Washington *Evening Star*, August 14, 1945, p. A8.

[36]Headquarters, Twentieth Air Force, APO 234, Tactical Mission Report, Field Order No. 20., Missions No. 325, 326, 327, 328, 329, 330, 14/15 August 1945, op. cit.

CHAPTER EIGHT: REBELLION

[1]United States Strategic Bombing Survey [Pacific], *Interrogations of Japanese Officials*, Yonai Interrogation 17 November 1945, op. cit., p. 332.

[2]The Pacific War Research Society, *Japan's Longest Day*, op. cit., p. 101.

[3]Military History Section, Headquarters, Army Forces Far East, *Outline of Operations Prior to Termination of War and Activities Connected with the Cessation of Hostilities*, Japanese Monograph No. 119, op. cit., p. 11.

[4]General Headquarters, Far East Command, Military Intelligence Section, General Staff, Allied Translator and Interpreter Section, Doc. No. 56367, Takeshita Statement, op. cit., p. 4.

[5]What follows is Ida's account of this meeting, which he provided after the war to the Japanese historians who wrote *Japan's Longest Day*.

[6]The Pacific War Research Society, *Japan's Longest Day*, op. cit., pp. 137–39; also see: Toland, op. cit., p. 835, and Brooks, op. cit., p. 304.

[7]The Pacific War Research Society, *Japan's Longest Day*, op. cit., 143.

[8]Diary of General George C. Kenney, Entry for August 14, 1945. Archives of General George C. Kenney: 168.7103-71 V.11 01129430, Air Force Historical

Research Agency; also see: Griffith, op. cit., p. 229; and Craven and Cate., op. cit., pp. 733–34.

⁹ Twentieth Air Force, APO 234, San Francisco, 20th AF Mission Reports ". . . Missions Number 325–30 against the Japanese Empire, flown on 14/15 August 1945." (Navigation Track Chart); also see: Craven and Cate, op. cit., p. 732.

¹⁰Coffey, op. cit., p. 461.

¹¹The Pacific War Research Society, *Japan's Longest Day*, op. cit., p. 145.

¹²This official English translation of the Imperial Rescript was prepared by the Military History Section, Headquarters Army Forces Far East, and appears in Japanese Monograph No. 119, op. cit., pp. 19–21.

¹³The Pacific War Research Society, *Japan's Longest Day*, op. cit., p. 160.

¹⁴Brooks, op. cit., p. 291.

¹⁵The Pacific War Research Society, *Japan's Longest Day*, op. cit., p. 149.

¹⁶Coffey, op. cit., pp. 468–69; also see: The Pacific War Research Society, *Japan's Longest Day*, op. cit., pp. 161–62.

¹⁷The Pacific War Research Society, *Japan's Longest Day*, op. cit., pp. 163–64.

¹⁸Truman, op. cit., pp. 435–36.

¹⁹The Pacific War Research Society, *Japan's Longest Day*, op. cit., p. 184.

²⁰The crucial question that Lt. Colonel Ida confronted is phrased succinctly by the Japanese historians of the Pacific War Research Society who wrote *Japan's Longest Day* (op. cit., p. 201): "The fact that Hatanaka's superiors—although they knew, by now, all of them, of his frenzied efforts to foment an Army rebellion—refrained from taking any one of the many possible measures for stopping him was proof, perhaps, that they really did not want to stop him. In theory they disapproved, and they would disapprove in practice if the projected *coup* failed, but if it succeeded . . . ?"

²¹Craig, op. cit., p. 184.

²²Coffey, op. cit., p. 475.

²³Ibid., p. 476.

²⁴Craig, op. cit., p. 190.

²⁵Again, contrary to certain published accounts, the waxing crescent moon set in Tokyo on the night of August 14, 1945 at 10:03 P.M. Some authors have written that there was bright moonlight all that night. One has even stated that the nights of August 14–15 were the "traditional" time for Japanese to view the full moon, thus suggesting that the moon's phases somehow invariably followed the solar calendar. But, as stated above, the authors have verified all data on sunrise and sunset, moonrise and moonset, as well as moon phases, with the U.S. Navy Observatory's Astronomical Applications Department.

²⁶The Pacific War Research Society, *Japan's Longest Day*, op. cit., p. 206.

²⁷Ibid., p. 209.

²⁸Military History Section, Headquarters, Army Forces Far East, *Outline of Operations Prior to Termination of War and Activities Connected with the Cessation of Hostilities*, Japanese Monograph No. 119, op. cit., pp. 19–21.

²⁹Ibid., p. 21.

³⁰Brooks, op. cit., p. 282.

³¹Coffey, op. cit., p. 480.
³²Ibid., p. 208.

CHAPTER NINE: BLACKOUT
¹The Pacific War Research Society, *Japan's Longest Day*, op. cit., p. 219.
²Coffey, op. cit., p. 484.
³General Headquarters, Far East Command, Military Intelligence Section, Historical Division, Statements of Japanese Officials on World War II, op. cit., "Statement Made by: Masahiko Takeshita (brother-in-law of War Minister Anami)," p. 1.
⁴The Pacific War Research Society, *Japan's Longest Day*, op. cit., pp. 213–14.
⁵Ibid., p. 223.
⁶Toland, op. cit., p. 840.
⁷Ibid., p. 841.
⁸Brooks, op. cit., p. 312.
⁹Frank, op. cit., p. 318.
¹⁰Ibid., p. 319.
¹¹Takeshita's detailed description of the events in General Anami's residence are drawn from General Headquarters, Far East Command, Military Intelligence Section, Historical Division, Statements of Japanese Officials on World War II, op. cit., "Statement Made by: Masahiko Takeshita (brother-in-law of War Minister Anami)," pp. 1–3. Unless otherwise indicated, this single-spaced, legal-sized type-script contains all of Takeshita's quoted statements and the actions that he took related to the Allied interrogators. Other Western historians have also obviously used this transcript as a major source.
¹²General Headquarters, Far East Command, Military Intelligence Section, General Staff, Allied Translator and Interpreter Service, 18 Aug 49, Doc. No. 50025A, op. cit., p. 5.
¹³General Headquarters, Far East Command, Military Intelligence Section, Historical Division, Statements of Japanese Officials on World War II, op. cit., "Statement Made by: Masahiko Takeshita (brother-in-law of War Minister Anami)," op. cit., p. 2.
¹⁴The Pacific War Research Society, *Japan's Longest Day*, op. cit., p. 245.
¹⁵General Headquarters, Far East Command, Military Intelligence Section, General Staff, Allied Translator and Interpreter Section, Doc. No. 61338, 5 Aug 50, Full Translation of Statement by Yoshizumi, Masao, pp. 5–6.
¹⁶Brooks, op. cit., p. 321.
¹⁷The Pacific War Research Society, *Japan's Longest Day*, op. cit., p. 237.
¹⁸Coffey, op. cit., p. 496. An almost identical passage appears in the Pacific War Research Society, *Japan's Longest Day*, op. cit., pp. 271–72.
¹⁹The Pacific War Research Society, *Japan's Longest Day*, op. cit., p. 230.
²⁰Accounts of Kenjiro Yabe's courageous, stubborn rearguard action to protect the recordings of the Imperial Rescript are found in several sources: Brooks, op. cit., pp. 319–20; Craig, op. cit., pp. 190–91; Toland, op. cit., p. 843; and the Pacific War Research Society, *Japan's Longest Day*, op. cit., p. 269.

²¹The Pacific War Research Society, *Japan's Longest Day*, op. cit., p. 238.

²²Ibid., p. 239.

²³According to the knowledgeable Japanese sources that coauthor Jim Smith has interviewed—who, for personal reasons, wish to remain unnamed—the deeply ingrained cultural trait of *haji* will probably make it impossible to unravel Major General Takashima's motives during this tense episode.

CHAPTER TEN: THE LAST MISSION

¹Coffey, op. cit., p. 500.

²Frank, op. cit., 319; also see: The Pacific War Research Society, *Japan's Longest Day*, op. cit., pp. 273–74.

³Toland, op. cit., p. 844. This passage is very similar to the Pacific War Research Society, *Japan's Longest Day*, op. cit., p. 246 (published two years earlier than Toland's *The Rising Sun*). Also see: Brooks, op. cit., p. 323.

⁴The Pacific War Research Society, *Japan's Longest Day*, op. cit., p. 247.

⁵Ibid., p. 247.

⁶Brooks, op. cit., pp. 324–25.

⁷This exchange appears in historian Lester Brooks's *Behind Japan's Surrender*, and the cited passage does not indicate the exact time it took place. First dawn ["civil twilight"] in Tokyo on August 15, 1945, was at 4:32 A.M.: Brooks, op. cit., p. 342.

⁸General Headquarters, Far East Command, Military Intelligence Section, Historical Division, Statements of Japanese Officials on World War II, "Statement Made by: Masahiko Takeshita (brother-in-law of War Minister Anami)," op. cit., p. 2.

⁹Brooks, op. cit., pp. 334–35; also see, The Pacific War Research Society, *Japan's Longest Day*, op. cit., p. 294.

¹⁰The Pacific War Research Society, *Japan's Longest Day*, op. cit., pp. 270–71.

¹¹Ibid., p. 277. Although the historians who wrote this work say that Takeshita was "not surprised at the outburst," Takeshita himself told Allied Intelligence interrogators after the war that he "was surprised to hear the Minister" utter this command; see: General Headquarters, Far East Command, Military Intelligence Section, Historical Division, Statements of Japanese Officials on World War II, "Statement Made by: Masahiko Takeshita (brother-in-law of War Minister Anami)," op. cit., p. 2.

¹²The Pacific War Research Society, *Japan's Longest Day*, op. cit., pp. 282–83.

¹³Ibid., p. 284; also see: Craig, op. cit., pp. 197–98.

¹⁴Some accounts—e.g., Brooks, op. cit., p. 344—have Tanaka arriving at the Palace in the dim hint of civil twilight (around 4:25 A.M.), but the Pacific War Research Society, *Japan's Longest Day*, op. cit., p. 289, states unequivocally that Tanaka arrived in full daylight at 5:10 A.M.

¹⁵Brooks, op cit., p. 344.

¹⁶Ibid., p. 346.

¹⁷General Headquarters, Far East Command, Military Intelligence Section, Historical Division, Statements of Japanese Officials on World War II, Doc. No.

63041, Statement by Tsukamoto, Kiyoshi, Former Major, Adjutant to the Eastern Army District Command, 6 Oct 50, Subject: "General Tanaka, Shizuichi in the August 15 Incident," pp. 1–2; also see: Brooks, op. cit., p. 346.

[18]The Pacific War Research Society, *Japan's Longest Day*, op. cit., p. 233.

[19]Ibid., p. 292.

[20]Ibid., p. 294.

[21]Toland, op. cit., p. 847; Bergamini, Vol. 1, op. cit., p. 143, states that Okido arrived "at 5:30 A.M."

[22]General Headquarters, Far East Command, Military Intelligence Section, Historical Division, Statements of Japanese Officials on World War II, Statement of Takeshita, Masahiko, Doc. No. 500025A, op. cit., p. 6.

[23]General Headquarters, Far East Command, Military Intelligence Section, Historical Division, Statements of Japanese Officials on World War II, "Statement Made by: Masahiko Takeshita (brother-in-law of War Minister Anami)," op. cit., p. 3.

[24]Brooks, op. cit., pp. 346–48.

[25]The Pacific War Research Society, *Japan's Longest Day*, op. cit., pp. 288–89, p. 303.

[26]Ibid., p. 303. Also see: Craig, op. cit., p. 198; and Toland, op. cit., pp. 848–49.

[27]Pacific War Research Society, *Japan's Longest Day*, op. cit., p. 276.

[28]Ibid., p. 285.

[29]Frank, op. cit., pp. 321–22; also see: Brooks, op. cit., p. 353.

[30]Truman, op. cit., pp. 436–37.

[31]The Pacific War Research Society, *Japan's Longest Day*, op. cit., p. 324.

[32]Coffey, op. cit., pp. 523–24; also see: The Pacific War Research Society, *Japan's Longest Day*, op. cit., p. 325.

[33]Bix, op. cit., pp. 536–37.

[34]The Pacific War Research Society, *Japan's Longest Day*, op. cit., p. 328.

[35]Hoyt, op. cit., pp. 207–08.

CHAPTER ELEVEN: THE MIGHT-HAVE-BEENS

[1]General Headquarters, Far East Command, Military Intelligence Section, Historical Division, Togo Statement of 17 May 49, op. cit., p. 38.

[2]Hugh Trevor-Roper, valedictory address as Regius Professor of Modern History, Oxford University, May 20, 1980; and as quoted in *History Today*, Vol. 32, Issue 7, July 1982, p. 88.

[3]Morison, op. cit., pp. 571–72.

[4]Robert Cowley, ed. *What If?: The World's Foremost Military Historians Imagine What Might Have Been* (New York: Putnam, 1999). The Library of Congress Catalog list scores of similar speculative histories entitled *What If?*

[5]United States Strategic Bombing Survey [Pacific], Interrogations of Japanese Officials, Yonai Interrogation 17 November 1945, op. cit., p. 332.

[6]Craig, op. cit., p. 232; also see: Toland, op. cit., p. 856.

[7]Craig, op. cit., p. 232.

[8]Gordon W. Prange, with Donald M. Goldstein & Katherine V. Dillon, *God's Samurai* (Washington, D.C.: Brassey's, 1990), p. 170.

[9]Toland, op. cit., pp. 853–54.

[10]"Japanese Suicide Planes Jab at Third Fleet," *The New York Times*, August 14, 1945, p. 1.

[11]Hoyt, op. cit., p. 201; also see: United States Strategic Bombing Survey, Interrogations of Japanese Officials, Vol. I, Interrogation of Captain Fuchida, Mitsuo, re the Kamikaze Corps in Philippines and Okinawa, p. 24.

[12]Defense Printing Service, Microfilm Section, The Pentagon, Washington, D.C., Japanese Monograph No. 65, Southeast Area Air Operations Record, Phase III, Jul. 1944–Aug. 1945.

[13]Spector, op. cit., p. 284; also see: Craven and Cate, op. cit., p. 480, and United States Strategic Bombing Survey, Interrogations of Japanese Officials, Interrogation of Lt. Jg. Okuno, Y., NAV-56. (Okuno was a pilot in the Fifth Air Fleet on Formosa.) His transcript includes this item: "In May 1945 all air crews of his squadron were incorporated into the Fifth Air Fleet and their aircraft prepared for kamikaze tactics."

[14]Japanese Monograph No. 76, Air Operations in the China Area, July 1937–August 1945, p. 195.

[15]Griffith, op. cit., p. 229.

[16]Military History Section, Headquarters, Army Forces Far East, "Outline of Operations Prior to Termination of War," Japanese Monograph No. 199, p. 12.

[17]Ibid., pp. 14, 23; also see: United States Strategic Bombing Survey, Interrogations of Japanese, Naval Analysis Division, Vol. II, op. cit., p. 320.

[18]Frank, op. cit., p. 378.

[19]For a discussion of Anami's unclear role in the surrender, see Frank, op. cit., pp. 315–18.

[20]Spector, op. cit., p. 282.

[21]Craig, op. cit., p. 206; also see: Fleet Admiral Ernest J. King, *U.S. Navy At War, 1941–1945* (Washington, D.C.: United States Navy Department, 1946), p. 189.

[22]Frank, op. cit., p. 327.

[23]Giovannitti and Freed, op. cit., p. 281.

[24]Bernstein, op. cit., pp. 2–3.

[25]General Headquarters, Far East Command, Military Intelligence Section, General Staff, Allied Translator and Interpreter Section, Doc. No. 56367, 28 Feb 50, Subject: Coup d'Etat Plan to Prevent the Termination of the War, Statement of ex–Lt. Colonel Masahiko Takeshita, op. cit., pp. 2–3.

[26]Alperovitz, op. cit., p. 653; also see: Thomas and Witts, op. cit., p. 213; and Werrell, op. cit., p. 687.

[27]Letter from President Harry S. Truman to Professor James L. Cate, January 12, 1953.

[28]Toland, op. cit., p. 852; also see: Coffey, op. cit., p. 523; and, Craig, op. cit., p. 297.

[29]Master Sgt. Gary Pomeroy, "A POW Remembers," Air Force News Service, August 30, 1995, p. 1.

[30]Allen and Polmar, op. cit., p. 162; also see: Chester Marshall with Ray "Hap"

Halloran, *Hap's War, The Incredible Survival Story of a WWII Prisoner of War Slated for Execution* (Collierville, TN: Global Press, 1998), pp. 49–50; and Frank, op. cit., p. 328.

[31]Major General John K. Singlaub, USA (Ret.), with Malcolm McConnell, *Hazardous Duty, An American Soldier in the Twentieth Century* (New York: Summit Books, 1991), pp. 83–100.

[32]Allen and Polmar, op. cit., Appendix D, p. 304.

[33]John Ray Skates, *The Invasion of Japan, Alternative to the Bomb* (Columbia: University of South Carolina Press, 1994), pp. 68–69, 71.

[34]Cecil B. Currey, *Victory at Any Cost* (Washington, D.C.: Brassey's, 1997), pp. 41–42; also see: Lucien Bodard, *The Quicksand War: Prelude to Vietnam* (Boston, MA: Little, Brown, and Company, 1963), p. 9.

[35]"Red Army Deepens Manchurian Bulge," *The New York Times*, August 14, 1945, p. 14.

[36]Pogue, Vol. III, op. cit., p. 528.

[37]Frank, op. cit., pp. 322–23.

[38]For a succinct but authoritative account of these widely overlooked events, see Frank, op. cit., pp. 322–24.

[39]Skates, op. cit., p. 71.

[40]Singlaub with McConnell, op. cit., p. 69; also see David E. Murphy, Sergei A. Kondrashev, and George Bailey, *Battleground Berlin* (New Haven, CN: Yale University Press, 1997), pp. 69, 75.

BIBLIOGRAPHY

Allen, Thomas B., and Norman Polmar, *Code-Name Downfall, The Secret Plan to Invade Japan—And Why Truman Dropped the Bomb,* New York: Simon & Schuster, 1995.

Alperovitz, Gar, *The Decision to Use the Atomic Bomb and the Architecture of an American Myth,* New York: Alfred A. Knopf, 1995.

Aron, Robert, *Histoire de la Liberation de la France, Juin 1944–Mai 1945,* Paris: Librairie Arthème Fayard, 1959.

Assistant Chief of Staff–Intelligence, Headquarters Army Air Forces, *Mission Accomplished, Interrogations of Japanese Industrial, Military, and Civil Leaders of World War II,* Washington, D.C.: U.S. Government Printing Office, 1946; interrogation of Lt. General Noburu Tazoe, Chief of Air Staff, Imperial Japanese Army.

Bergamini, David, *Japan's Imperial Conspiracy,* Vol. I, Vol. II. New York: William Morrow and Company, 1971.

Bernstein, Barton J., "The Perils and Politics of Surrender: Ending the War with Japan and Avoiding the Third Atomic Bomb," *Pacific Historical Review,* Vol. XLVI, February 1977, No. 1.

Bix, Herbert P., *Hirohito and the Making of Modern Japan*. New York: Harper-Collins Publishers, 2000.

Bodard, Lucien, *The Quicksand War: Prelude to Vietnam*. Boston: Little, Brown, and Company, 1963.

Bohlen, Charles E., *Witness to History, 1929–1969*. New York: W.W. Norton, 1973.

Brooks, Lester, *Behind Japan's Surrender, The Secret Struggle That Ended an Empire*. New York: McGraw-Hill Book Company, 1968.

Chang, Iris, *The Rape of Nanking: The Forgotten Holocaust of World War II*. New York: Basic Books, 1997.

Coffey, Thomas M., *Imperial Tragedy, Japan in World War II, the First Days and the Last*, New York: The World Publishing Company, 1970.

COMGEN USASTAF from COMGENAIR, 11 August 1945 (WAR 47880), Top Secret, declassified 1984, Air Force Historical Research Agency.

Craig, William, *The Fall of Japan*. New York: The Dial Press, 1967.

Craven, Wesley F., and James Lea Cate, editors, *The Army Air Forces in World War II, Vol. Five, The Pacific: Matterhorn to Nagasaki, June 1944 to August 1945*, Chicago: The University of Chicago Press, 1953.

Cray, Ed, *General of the Army, George C. Marshall, Soldier and Statesman*, New York: W.W. Norton & Company, 1990.

Currey, Cecil B., *Victory at Any Cost*. Washington, D.C.: Brassey's, 1997.

Davis, Larry, *B-29 Superfortress in Action*, Carrollton, TX: Squadron/Signal Publications, 1997.

Defense Printing Service, Microfilm Section, The Pentagon, Washington, D.C., Japanese Monograph No. 65, Southeast Area Air Operations Record, Phase III, July 1944–Aug. 1945.

Fahey, James J., *Pacific War Diary*. Thorndike, ME: Thorndike Press, 1963.

Ferrell, Robert H., *Off the Record: The Private Papers of Harry S. Truman*. New York: Harper & Row, 1980.

"Fifteen Missions, Oil," unpublished monograph manuscript.

Foreign Relations of the United States, *The Conference of Berlin*, 2 Vols. Washington, D.C.: Government Printing Office, 1960, II.

Frank, Richard B., *Downfall, the End of Imperial Japanese Empire*. New York: Random House, 1989.

General Headquarters, Far East Command, Military Intelligence section, Historical Division, *Interrogations of Japanese Officials on World War II*, Vol. I, Doc. No. 55127, Interrogation of President of Privy Council President Kiichiro Hiranuma.

General Headquarters, Far East Command, Military Intelligence Section, Historical Division, Vol. 3, "Statement Concerning Defense Preparation for Southern Kyushu."

General Headquarters, Far East Command, Military Intelligence Section, General Staff, Allied Translator and Interpreter Section, Full Translation of Statement by ex–Capt. Toshikazu Ohmae.

General Headquarters, Far East Command, Military Intelligence Section, Historical Division, "Statements Regarding the Attitude of War Minister Anami and Others Toward Peace Just Prior to Surrender," by ex-Col. Saburo Hayashi.

General Headquarters, Far East Command, Military Intelligence Section, General Staff, Allied Translator and Interpreter Section, *Statements of Japanese Officials on World War II*, Vol. 4, Doc. No. 50025A, Statement by Masahiko Takeshita, 18 August 1949.

General Headquarters, Far East Command, Military Intelligence Section, General Staff, Allied Translator and Interpreter Section, Doc. No. 56367, 28 Feb. 50, Subject: Coup d'Etat Plan to Prevent the Termination of the War, Statement of ex-Lt. Colonel Masahiko Takeshita.

General Headquarters, Far East Command, Military Intelligence Section, General Staff, Allied Translator and Interpreter Section, Full Translation of a Statement by ex-Lt. Gen. Masao Yoshizumi (Director of Military Affairs Bureau), 25 May 1950 and 2 June 1950, Doc. No. 59277.

General Headquarters, Far East Command, Military Intelligence Section, Historical Division, "A Statement on the Decision Reached by Three Top Army Commanders, Two Field Marshals, and the Commander of the General Air Army at the End of the War," Statement of ex-Lt. General Torashiro Kawabe, 3 Dec. 1945.

General Headquarters, Far East Command, Military Intelligence Section, Historical Division, Statements of Japanese Officials on World War II, Doc. No. 63041, Statement by Kiyoshi Tsukamoto, Former Major, Adjutant to the Eastern Army District Command, 6 Oct. 1950, Subject: "General Tanaka, Shizuichi in the August 15 Incident."

General Headquarters, Far East Command, Military Intelligence Section, Historical Division, *Statements of Japanese Officials on World War II* (English Translations), Vol. 4. Statement of ex-Minister of Foreign Affairs Shigenori Togo, Concerning the Historical Facts Surrounding the Ending of the Pacific War (1), Center of Military History.

General Headquarters, Far East Command, Military Intelligence Section, Historical Division, *Statements of Japanese Officials on World War II* (English Translations), Vol. 4., Full Translation of Statement by Former Foreign Minister Togo.

General Headquarters, Far East Command, Military Intelligence Section, Historical Division, *Statements of Japanese Officials on World War II* (English Translations), Vol. 3.

General Headquarters, Far East Command, Military Intelligence Section, Historical Division, *Statements of Japanese Officials on World War II* (English Translations), Vol. 4. Doc. No.5927, Statement by ex-Lt. General Masao Yoshizumi.

Giovannitti, Len, and Fred Freed, *The Decision to Drop the Bomb*. New York: Coward-McCann, Inc., 1965.

Griffith, Jr., Thomas E., *MacArthur's Airman, General George C. Kenney and the War in the Southwest Pacific*. Lawrence, KS: University Press of Kansas, 1998.

Hansell, Jr., Major General Haywood S., USAF (Ret.), Letter to Major James M. Boyle, United States Air Force Academy, December 3, 1962.

Harrington, George E., and William Leasure, editors, *A New Chapter in Air Power*, *the 315th Bomb Wing (VH), Guam WWII*, Second Edition, Mansfield, OH: Monarch Systems, 1993.

Headquarters, Twentieth Air Force, APO 234, Tactical Mission Report, Field Order No. 20., Missions No. 325, 326, 327, 328, 329, 330, 14/15 August 1945, Air Force Historical Research Agency, Maxwell Air Force Base, AL.

Headquarters, USAFFE and U.S. Army (Rear), Japanese Monograph No. 23, *Air Defense of the Homeland, 1944–1945*, Distributed by Office of the Chief of Military History, Department of the Army.

Hoyt, Edwin P., *The Last Kamikaze: The Story of Admiral Matome Ugaki*. Westport, CT: Praeger, 1993.

Inoguchi, Captain Rikihei and Commander Tadashi Nakajima with Roger Pineau, *The Divine Wind, Japan's Kamikaze Force in World War II*. Westport, CT: Greenwood Press, 1959.

Jansen, Marius B., *The Making of Modern Japan*. Cambridge, MA: The Belknap Press of Harvard University Press, 2000.

Japanese Monograph No. 170, *Homeland Antiaircraft Defense Operations Record, Kanto Sector, June 1944–Aug. 1945*, Doc. No. 4260, Center of Military History, Washington, D.C.

Japanese Monograph No. 76, *Air Operations in the China Area*, July 1937–August 1945.

Joint War Plans Committee 369/1, 15 June 1945, "Details of the Campaign Against Japan," Record Group 165, National Archives and Records Administration.

Kenney, General George C., diary entry for August 14, 1945. Archives of General George C. Kenney: 168.7103-71 V.11 01129430, Air Force Historical Research Agency.

Kido, Koichi, statement of 17 May 49, Doc. No. 61541, Center of Military History, Washington, D.C.

King, Fleet Admiral Ernest J., *U.S. Navy At War, 1941–1945*. Washington, D.C.: United States Navy Department, 1946.

Leahy, Fleet Admiral William D., *I Was There, The Personal Story of the Chief of Staff to Presidents Roosevelt and Truman Based on His Notes and Diaries Made at the Time*. New York: Whittlesey House, 1950.

MacEachin, Douglas J., *The Final Months of the War with Japan: Signals Intelligence, U.S. Invasion Planning, and the A-Bomb Decision*, An Intelligence Monograph, Center for the Study of Intelligence, Central Intelligence Agency, Washington, D.C., 1998.

Marshall, Chester, with Ray "Hap" Halloran, *Hap's War, The Incredible Survival Story of a WWII Prisoner of War Slated for Execution*. Collierville, TN: Global Press, 1998.

Marshall, Chester, *Final Assault on the Rising Sun*. North Beach, MN: Specialty Press, 1995.

McCullough, David, *Truman*. New York: Simon & Schuster, 1992.

Memorandum for the President, G. C. Marshall, Chief of Staff, 11 August 1945, originally classified Top Secret, declassified, 1973, G. C. Marshall Papers, Pentagon Offices, Selected 84/31, Box/File POS-84/31.

Military History Section, Headquarters, Army Forces Far East, *Outline of Operations Prior to Termination of War and Activities Connected with the Cessation of Hostilities*, Japanese Monograph No. 119., Office of Military History, Washington, D.C.

Miller, Charles H., letter to Jim B. Smith, April 27, 2001.

Morison, Samuel Eliot, *The Two-Ocean War, A Short History of the United States Navy in the Second World War*, Boston: Atlantic Monthly Press, 1963.

Murphy, David E., Sergei A. Kondrashev, and George Bailey, *Battleground Berlin*, New Haven, CT: Yale University Press, 1997.

Pogue, Forrest C., *George C. Marshall: Organizer of Victory, 1943–1945*, New York: Viking Press, 1973.

Pogue, Forrest C., *George C. Marshall: Statesman, 1945–1959*. New York: Viking Press, 1987.

Pomeroy, Master Sgt. Gary, "A POW Remembers," Air Force News Service, August 30, 1995.

Prange, Gordon W., with Donald M. Goldstein and Katherine V. Dillon, *God's Samurai*. Washington, D.C.: Brassey's, 1990.

Presidential Announcement of August 6, 1945, Truman Library, Miscellaneous Historical Document No. 253.

"Red Army Deepens Manchurian Bulge," *The New York Times*, August 14, 1945.

Rhodes, Richard, *Dark Sun, The Making of the Hydrogen Bomb*. New York: Simon & Schuster, 1995.

Rhodes, Richard, *The Making of the Atomic Bomb*. New York: Simon & Schuster, 1986.

Sakaida, Henry, *Pacific Air Combat, WWII, Voices from the Past*. St. Paul, MN: Phalanx Publishing Co., 1993.

Singlaub, Major General John K., USA (Ret.), with Malcolm McConnell, *Hazardous Duty, An American Soldier in the Twentieth Century*. New York: Summit Books, 1991.

Skates, John Ray, *The Invasion of Japan, Alternative to the Bomb*. Columbia: University of South Carolina Press, 1994.

Smith, Jim B., *The Last Mission, An Eyewitness Account*, Mt. Pleasant, IA: J. B. Smith Enterprises, Ltd., 1995.

Smith, Sergeant Jim B., Personal Combat Mission Flight Log.

Special Staff U.S. Army Historical Division (Historical Manuscript File), *Naval Plans for the Defense of Japan*.

Spector, Ronald H., *Listening to the Enemy, Key Documents and the Role of Communications Intelligence in the War Against Japan*. Wilmington, DE: Scholarly Resources, Inc., 1988.

Tactical Mission Report, Mission No. 315, Ube; Headquarters, Twentieth Air Force, APO 234, dated 25 Sept. 45, classified Secret; declassified 1997, Air Force Historical Research Agency, Maxwell Air Force Base, AL.

The Pacific War Research Society, *Japan's Longest Day*. Tokyo: Kodansha International, 1968.

Thomas, Gordon and Max Morgan Witts, *Enola Gay*, New York: Stein and Day, 1977.

Toland, John, *The Rising Sun, The Decline and Fall of the Japanese Empire, 1936–1945*. New York: Random House, 1970.

Trevor-Roper, Hugh, valedictory address as Regius Professor of Modern History, Oxford University, May 20, 1980; and as quoted in *History Today*, Vol. 32, Issue 7, July 1982.

Truman, Harry S., *Memoirs, Harry S. Truman, Volume One, Year of Decisions*. Garden City, NY: Doubleday & Company, Inc., 1955.

Twentieth Air Force, APO 234, San Francisco, 20th AF Mission Reports ". . . Missions Number 325–330 against the Japanese Empire, flown on 14/15 August 1945."

U.S. Navy, Pacific Fleet, *Hypothetical Defense of Kyushu, Translation of Japanese Staff Exercise (Jan. 1944)*. CINPAC Bulletin, July 1945, declassified.

United States Strategic Bombing Survey [Pacific Region], Naval Analysis Division, *Interrogations of Japanese Officials*, Vol. II. USSB No. 378, Interrogation of Chief of Naval General Staff, Admiral Toyoda, Soemu.

United States Strategic Bombing Survey [Pacific] Naval Analysis Division, *Interrogations of Japanese Officials*, Volume I. Interrogation of Captain Inoguchi, Rikibei, Imperial Japanese Navy, 1946.

United States Strategic Bombing Survey [Pacific] Naval Analysis Division, *Interrogations of Japanese Officials*, "Japanese War Plans and Peace Moves." Interrogation of Admiral Soemu Toyoda, 13–14 November 1945.

United States Strategic Bombing Survey [Pacific], Naval Analysis Division, *Interrogations of Japanese Officials*, Vol. I. Interrogation of Captain Fuchida, Mitsuo, Imperial Japanese Navy, 1946.

United States Strategic Bombing Survey [Report of the Pacific War No. 53], *The Effects of Strategic Bombing on Japan's War Economy*, Appendix A B C, Appendix Table C-164: Japanese aircraft production by functional types, by quarters, 1941-1945, Washington, D.C.: U.S. Government Printing Office, 1946.

United States Strategic Bombing Survey, Chairman's Office, [Report, Pacific War No. 27], *Japan's Struggle to End the War*. Washington, D.C.: U.S. Government Printing Office, 1 July 1946.

United States Strategic Bombing Survey, Chairman's Office, *The Effects of Atomic Bombs on Hiroshima and Nagasaki*. Washington, D.C.: U.S. Government Printing Office, 1946.

United States Strategic Bombing Survey, *Interrogations of Japanese Officials*, Vol. II. Interrogation of Admiral Mitsumasa Yonai.

United States Strategic Bombing Survey, *Interrogations of Japanese Officials*, Vol. I. Interrogation of Captain Fuchida, Mitsuo, re the Kamikaze Corps in Philippines and Okinawa.

United States Strategic Bombing Survey, *Interrogations of Japanese Officials*. NAV-56, Interrogation of Lt. Jg. Okuno, Y.

V Amphibious Corps, Appendix 3 to Annex C, *Operation Plan, Occupation of Japan*. 30 November 1945.

van der Vat, Dan, *The Pacific Campaign*. New York: Simon & Schuster, 1991.

War Department, Letter 25 July 1945, Office of the Chief of Staff, Thomas T. Handy, General, Acting Chief of Staff to General Carl Spaatz, Center of Military History.

WARX 48689, 13 August 1945, 1313 Zulu, Archives of General George C. Kenney: 168.7103-71 V.11 01129430, Air Force Historical Research Agency, Maxwell Air Force Base, AL.

Washington *Evening Star*, August 14, 1945.

Werrell, Kenneth P., *Blankets of Fire, U.S. Bombers Over Japan During World War II.* Washington, D.C.: Smithsonian Institution Press, 1996.

Wyden, Peter, *Day One, Before Hiroshima and After*. New York: Simon & Schuster, 1984.

Zhukov, Georgii K., *The Memoirs of Marshal Zhukov*. New York: Delacorte Press, 1971.

ACKNOWLEDGMENTS

The authors wish to gratefully acknowledge the assistance of the researchers, librarians, and archivists at the Los Angeles County Library, the Queen Anne County (Maryland) Free Library, the Nimitz Library at the U.S. Naval Academy, the Library of Congress, the National Archives and Records Administration, the Center of Military History, the U.S. Naval Historical Center, and the Air Force Historical Research Agency. The Late Lt. General James Day, USMC, Medal of Honor, provided invaluable insights into the battle of Okinawa. Historian Richard B. Frank also generously shared the insights he has gained over years of research into the final months of World War II. The contributions of former 1st Lt. Stanley W. Nightingale and other B-29 veterans too numerous to name were also vital to this book.

Finally, the authors wish to thank their agent, Mel Berger, of the William Morris Agency for recognizing the historical significance of this story and for sharing his enthusiasm with Gerald Howard, Editorial Director of Broadway Books.

As cited in the Bibliography, much of the source material on which this book is based is original: Jim B. Smith and other 315th Bomb Wing air crew's eyewitness accounts; official wartime mission reports and charts; and other contemporaneous XXI Bomber Command and U.S. Strategic Air Forces and War Department documents.

The authors also worked closely with the librarians and archivists noted in the Acknowledgments to obtain original postwar intelligence documents such as the General Headquarters, Far East Command, Military Intelligence Section General Staffs Allied Translators and Interpreter Sections' translations of statements by Japanese officers and officials, as well as the multivolume United States Strategic Bombing Survey Interrogations of Japanese Officials, and documents from the Truman Presidential Museum and Library.

Further, as acknowledged in the text and Endnotes, the authors followed the pioneering lead of many academic, popular, and specialized military historians who have focused on the closing years and months of World War II, most notably: Thomas B. Allen and Norman Polmar; Gar Alperovitz; David Bergamini; Barton J. Bernstein; Herbert P. Bix; Lester Brooks; Iris Chang; Thomas M. Coffey; William Craig; Wesley F. Craven and James Lea Cate; Ed Cray; Richard B. Frank; Len Giovannitti and Fred Freed; Thomas E. Griffith; George E. Harrington and William Leasure; Edwin P. Hoyt; Captain Rikihei Inoguchi and Commander Tadishi Nakajima (with Roger Pineau); Marius B. Jansen; Douglas J. MacEachin; Chester Marshall; Samuel Eliot Morison; Forrest C. Pogue; Gordon W. Prange (with Donald M. Goldstein and Kathryn V. Dillon); Richard Rhodes; Henry Sakaida; Major General John K. Singlaub, USA (Ret.) (with Malcolm McConnell); John Ray Skates; Ronald H. Spector; The Pacific War Research Society; Gordon Thomas and Max Morgan Witts; John Toland; Hugh Trevor-Roper; Harry S. Truman; Kenneth P. Werrell; Peter Wyden; and Georgii Zhukov.

Many of these historians also explored the original-source intelligence documents cited above and drew extensively on each other's published works. Therefore, the final days of World War II have been well documented. But the unique role the 315th Bomb Wing played in disrupting the Japanese Imperial Army coup d'état on the night of August 14–15, 1945, has remained largely unknown until now.